PDX H

Matt Reeder

ISBN: 978-0-9889125-2-6
First edition, 2018

All photos by Matt Reeder.

Maps in this book were created using CalTopo. For more information about CalTopo, see http://www.caltopo.com

For more information about Matt Reeder, his books and his adventures, see: http://www. offthebeatentrailpdx.com

Cover photo: hikers on the northeast side of Mount Adams (Hike 71)
Bottom cover photos: Wahclella Falls (Hike 25), Council Lake (Hike 86) and fall foliage at Coldwater Lake (Hike 92)
Frontispiece photo: a rare Mountain Lady Slipper orchid
Back photo: flowers at the Dalles Mountain Ranch (Hike 39)

Public land belongs to everyone. Do what you can to keep it that way.

Disclaimer: Countless hours were spent hiking, researching and writing the information found here. The author personally checked and verified all of the information here to the fullest extent of his abilities, and hiked every trail at least once- but in some cases as many as ten times. That being said, errors are always possible with a project as large as this. The author and the Ruddy Hill Press are not responsible for any mishaps that may occur while using this book. Furthermore, the landscape is constantly changing. Trail closures, road washouts, fire damage and land ownership changes can close hikes and alter the accuracy of the information found in this book. Last but not least, hiking is an inherently dangerous activity. Please prepare yourself before you head outside, make sure you check local conditions and know your limitations and those of everyone with whom you are hiking. Know before you go!

Acknowledgments and thank yous:

This book is dedicated to everyone who ever asked me for advice on where to go on rainy winter weekends, during wildflower season, where to see the best fall colors and so on- I took it to heart, and this book is the result.

First thanks, of course, go to my wonderful wife Wendy. Thank you for understanding my obsession, and allowing me to nurture it. Much love, as always!

Thanks to my mother Susan and my stepfather Ted, who took me hiking as a young child and let me explore almost to my heart's desire. I owe you everything!

Thanks to Gene Blick for always being available on weekdays, and for visiting some places so frequently it was easy to figure out the best time to visit.

Thanks to Keith Dechant for giving me pointed suggestions, always on target, and for finding hair metal as hilarious as I do.

Thanks to Ria Kotzé for being my biggest fan, for supplying me with chocolate and whisky, and for always being on point with suggestions and ideas. It means the world to me!

Thanks to the cromulent Karl Langenwalter, for always understanding and for always being willing to explore, even when you'd rather sleep in. This morning person thanks you!

Thanks to Cabe Nicksic for having crazier and more ambitious ideas than me, and for helping me see mine to fruition on the rare occasion our plans align.

Thanks to the Mazamas, and especially the Adventurous Young Mazamas, for allowing me to lead hikes for all these years. You've helped me explore the Pacific Northwest, and I'm proud to be a Mazama.

I'd like to also thank the following friends and allies who helped me get the word out into the world, and who helped me with the occasional suggestion, kind word or spare GPS track when one was needed: Caralee Angell, Joy Autumn, Marcum Bell, Hélène Bergeron, Tim Burke, Toby Creelan, Heather Cristia, Kyle Coleman, Krista Collins, April Ann Fong, Alex Hagiepetros, Charlotte Fritz, Joseph Gardiner, Rachel Goad, Doug Hecker, Chris Hickman, Cheryl Hill, Lisa D. Holmes, Phil Huckelberry, Jessica Jahns, Laura James-Blunk, Jeremiah Jenkins, Mike Kacmar, Ashley Karitis, Chelsea Kline, Tom Kloster, Regis Krug, Jaime Kulbel, Jessica Lackey, Greg Lief, Sarah Miller, Selena Niles, Cristin O'Brien, Rebecca Olsen, Geoff Ower, Stephanie Purtle, Brad and Dawn Rasmussen, Kate Ristau, Erika Robert, Craig Romano, Adam Sawyer, Reed Scott-Schwalbach, Kyle Smith, John Sparks, Shelley Stearns, Marie and Andy Streenz, Sean Thomas, Zach Urness, Verena Winter, Kevin Wright.

Finally, I wish to extend my endless love and gratitude to the following musicians, artists, and performers for giving me inspiration and helping me get through seven years of long nights and endless road trips while researching this and my other two books: The Beatles, Built to Spill, Buzzcocks, Courtney Barnett, The Cure, David Bowie, Brian Eno, Explosions In The Sky, Grateful Dead, Interpol, Led Zeppelin, Local H, Mudhoney, Nirvana, Paul Simon, Pavement, Pearl Jam, Priests, Prince, R.E.M., Radiohead, Ramones, Run the Jewels, Sigur Rós, Sleater-Kinney, Smashing Pumpkins, Sonic Youth, Soundgarden (RIP Chris), Spoon, St. Vincent, Sunny Day Real Estate, The Thermals, Titus Andronicus, Yo La Tengo, Neil Young.

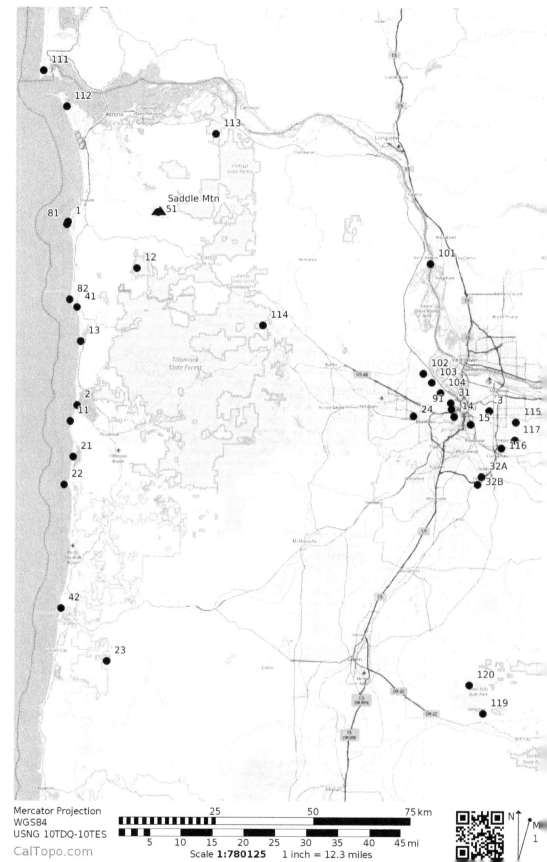

111

112

Astoria

113

Clatsop
State Forest

Saddle Mtn
51

81 1
Seaside

12

82
41

13

114

Tillamook
State Forest

Banks

US-26

Forest Grove Hillsboro

2

11

Beaverton

21

102
103
104
31
91
24 14J
15
3

Vancouver

101

St Helens

115
117
116

32A
32B

22

Tillamook

Lake Oswego

Tigard

Tualatin

Sherwood

Newberg

Wilsonville

42

McMinnville

Woodburn

23

Lincoln City

Dallas

Salem

120

119

OR 22

OR 22

Newport

OR 99E

OR 99E

Mill City

Mercator Projection
WGS84
USNG 10TDQ-10TES
CalTopo.com

25   50   75 km

N
M
1

5   10   15   20   25   30   35   40   45 mi

Scale 1:780125   1 inch = 12.3 miles

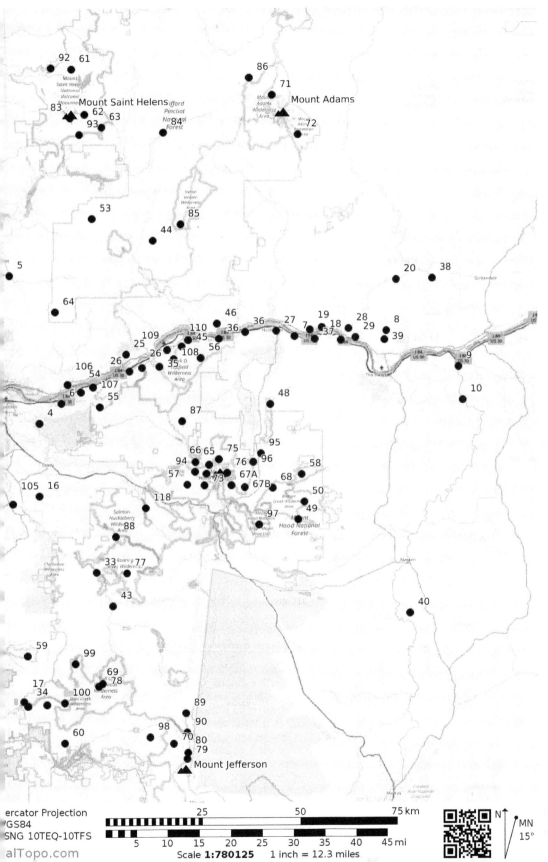

Mount Saint Helens

Mount Adams

Mount Jefferson

ercator Projection
'GS84
SNG 10TEQ-10TFS
alTopo.com

Scale **1:780125**   1 inch = 12.3 miles

25   50   75 km

5   10   15   20   25   30   35   40   45 mi

N
MN
15°

closer to Portland is lovely in the winter but subject to ice storms and trail washouts. Even though these hikes are accessible, they are typically not at their best until March or April.

One factor to consider before you go anywhere in the winter is not the weather at the destination, but what you can expect getting there. It doesn't matter if it's lovely at the beach if you have to travel over snowy, icy passes to get there. It is for this reason that you should always check the weather for the drive there as well as the destination.

In other seasons the weather is less of an issue but should still be considered. In the spring, expect rain and sunshine, often in the same day. Before you venture out of the lowlands, make sure you understand where to expect snow. Most hikes in the Cascades are not reliably snow-free until June or July at the earliest! It is for this reason that the spring hikes in this book are mostly in the lowlands and the Columbia River Gorge. In any case, you should always prepare for spring hikes as though it were still winter - sunny days in May can feel like March if the wind picks up.

We all wait for summer, and most hikers cherish the endless sunny days from July to September more than any other season. The high peaks of the Cascades are at long last snow-free, the days long, the skies blue and the possibilities seemingly limitless. The primary weather concerns in summer are heat and thunderstorms. Hot days are common, and can make for some miserable hiking (go to the Coast instead), even at the high elevations. Thunderstorms are common on hot days in the Cascades; avoid exposed ridges (such as Cooper Spur and Park Ridge) when there is any threat of storms - getting caught up there in a lightning storm would be a serious problem!

Fall is like spring - expect the unexpected. Warm, sunny days and cold, rainy days are equally common. As the calendar turns towards October, you should begin checking snow levels before any trip to the Cascades. Snow is a regular occurrence above 5,000 feet in October, and above 3,000 feet in November. Autumn storms are among the most dangerous, as they are often unexpected and just as intense as winter storms. I tend to check the weather more during these months than at any other time of year.

Regardless of the time of year and where you plan on going, you should always plan for bad weather. All hikers should pack a good rain jacket, rain pants, extra clothing (no cotton) as well as a spare set of socks whenever possible. This might seem like overkill for much of the year but bad weather can stop you in your tracks at any time. Do not assume you will be fine because the forecast looks good - it can change quickly, leaving you in bad shape far from home. The best strategy is preparation.

Accessibility:
Beyond the weather, there is also the question of whether or not you can actually get there and complete the hike. This is primarily an issue with snowpack. You should assume that all trails on Mount Adams, Mount Saint Helens, Mount Hood and Mount Jefferson are under snow from November to June. There are times when you can sneak up into the mountains during this period, but they are few and far between. Do not try to drive into the mountains during the winter months - not only are the hikes buried under snow, but so are the roads. Only federal, state and county highways are maintained in the winter. Consider this is as another reason to stay close to civilization.

For the record, here is a handy guide to when trails are reliably snow-free:
- Under 2,000 feet: open year-round except during winter cold snaps
- 2,500 feet: April - November (but often open during warmer periods in winter)
- 3,500 feet: mid May - November
- 4,500 feet: June 15 - November 10
- 5,500 feet: July 15 - October 15
- 6,500 feet: August 1 - October 1

Mount Saint Helens from Ape Canyon (Hike 62).

Speaking of accessibility, you should look online before you go and see if there are any road closures, trail closures, active wildfires or other possible impediments to the hike - sometimes it's impossible to know before you get there, but most of the time this is information you can check before you even leave the house. Resources for this information is listed on page 19 under "Resources". Do this before you go anywhere - once you get into the mountains, most places lack cell service, leaving you in the dark if you didn't do your homework first.

Difficulty:
Some people like easy hikes and some people like difficult hikes; most people like both. But asking hikers what constitutes an easy hike and a difficult hike can give you many different answers. This is because the concept of difficulty is a construct - everybody's fitness level is different, and difficulty can vary based on weather, conditions and other factors not considered when rating the relative difficulty of a hike. This is why you will notice that I don't rate them based on difficulty.

If you simply must have difficulty ratings, here is a good guide:

- Easy – less than 7 miles and 1,000 feet of elevation gain
- Moderate – 6 – 10 miles with less than 2,000 feet of elevation gain
- Difficult – 8 or more miles with more than 2,000 feet of elevation gain
- Very Difficult – 12 or more miles with more than 3,000 feet of elevation gain
- Hiking Legend – 15 or more miles with more than 4,000 feet of elevation gain

From a more practical standpoint, I have made a concerted effort in this book to feature many hikes of all difficulty levels. My favorite hikes are often the long, extremely difficult hikes classified under "Hiking Legend" - but I enjoy any type of hike, and the longer and more difficult hikes are usually buried under snow all winter.

Drivetime from Portland:
Some people only want to hike close to Portland, and this explains why trails in the Gorge are so crowded in the summer. For me, the amount I'm willing to drive corresponds to the payoff I'm expecting from the hike. This is the case at any time of year. Most hikers prefer to stay close to home (for this book I am assuming this is in the Portland metro area), and so many of the hikes listed for the winter months (November through February) are an hour or less from downtown Portland. Conversely, I am willing to drive longer distances in the summer to see something truly spectacular; you will find that the drive distances are further away in the summer months in this book - I have tried to offer a wide variety of hikes in some of the most beautiful terrain in the entire region.

All drive times in this book are listed from Pioneer Courthouse Square, at the very center of Portland. These are average times. I live in east Portland and it takes me 15-20 minutes less to drive to the Gorge and Mount Hood than listed here, but 15-20 more minutes to drive to the Coast. Hikers in Beaverton and Hillsboro will find this to be the opposite. Hikers in Vancouver are closer to Mount Saint Helens but further from Opal Creek and Mount Jefferson, while hikers in Oregon City and West Linn will find the opposite. In the several years spent researching, writing, arranging and organizing this book (as well as my other two books), I went on more than 300 unique hikes ranging from in-town rambles to serious backpacking expeditions. What you find here is 120 or so of my favorite adventures, some in the city of Portland and some further away - but none further than a 3 hour drive from Portland. To return to my original rule of thumb, if the hike is far away, it needs to make the long drive worth it. I think these do.

The WOW factor:
You go hiking because you want to see something beautiful, something that boosts your soul, something that enchants and amazes. You'll find plenty of that here. But with all of this in mind, how do you pick the best time to visit a place? I've tried to do that here. There are some things to consider. First of all: is there a particular aspect of the hike that is seasonal in nature? You've likely seen photos of Dog Mountain's famed wildflower meadows (Hike 46); in most years the flower display there peaks in May or early June, and this is the best time to do this hike. Hikers who do the hike in summer are faced with a hot, dusty and steep trail and few highlights other than view at the summit - which will almost certainly be hazy. Oh, and the snakes are out in force. You should absolutely go on a sunny day in May.

While this is the most obvious example, there are many other such examples out there. What this book seeks to do is identify the best possible moment to do every hike. This is not always obvious, and no doubt many hikers, experienced or not, will disagree with some of my assessments. This is part of the fun. For example: I love wildflowers and waterfalls, and hikes that feature one or both are placed in the specific month each is at its peak. For example, virtually every hike presented in April and May features fantastic displays of wildflowers. Wildflowers are also a major factor in the summer months too, along with big big views. Every hike presented in October features excellent displays of fall color, from the Valley to the high Cascades. Even the hikes in December and January are chosen for a specific reason, from the basis thesis of this book: what is the best hike you can do right now?

An explanation is given for each hike as to why I have chosen that particular month to present the hike, along with the highlights you can expect to see. In some cases I have also noted other times of the year when that particular hike is a good choice. You can also see the note about "Other seasons" in the details of each hike. On rare occasions I also explain particular times to avoid certain hikes, such as Dog Mountain in the summer, or Bagby Hot Springs during the winter months. This is only necessary when it isn't obvious.

The Sandy River flows through Oxbow Park east of Portland (Hike 4).

Preparation:
So now that we've established when and where to go, let's talk about preparation. Hiking is a joyous activity, but also a potentially dangerous one. Over the years, I've faced many a problem on the trail, or on the drive to the trailhead; in the past ten years or so, I've encountered belligerent tree poachers far up in Clackamas country, dealt with a swarm of very angry and very aggressive yellowjackets (also in Clackamas country), got cliffed out on the shaly side of a waterfall north of Mount Jefferson, dealt with a frightening case of hypothermia in the Old Cascades, braved heat exhaustion (also in the Old Cascades) and I've nearly gotten lost more times than I can possibly count.

Being as prepared as I could possibly be helped me deal with these situations. While you cannot prepare for every possible situation, there are many things you can do to get ready and ensure you'll be able to handle the worst that fate, the hiking gods and Mother Nature can throw your way.

The first order of preparation for a hike is knowing what to pack. First of all, don't wear cotton if you can possibly avoid it. Once it gets wet it stays wet, and slowly (or quickly) contributes to your core temperature dropping once you're wet. You will be miserable, too. The best choice is synthetic clothing specifically designed for outdoor activities, such as capilene in winter and nylon / polyester blends for hot summer days. A good raincoat and a good pair of boots are both worth their weight in gold. Always pack extra clothes when possible - you will appreciate a change of clothes either during the hike or after, and in a bad situation, they might save your life.

When you pack your bag, remember the Ten Essentials. These items, most of them lightweight and easy to pack, might save your life in an emergency. Make a small kit with as many of these items as possible and keep it in your pack **at all times**.

The Ten Essentials:
1. A map of the area (preferably topographic and highly-detailed)
2. Compass and/or GPS (bring extra batteries)
3. Extra food
4. Extra water (especially in the summer)
5. Extra clothing (no cotton!)
6. A headlamp or flashlight
7. First Aid Kit
8. Waterproof matches or a reliable lighter (or both)
9. Sunglasses and sunscreen
10. Knife and/or multitool with knife

There are six more items I highly recommend bringing to supplement the ten essentials:
11. A Water filter or water purification tablets
12. An extra pair of warm socks wrapped in a waterproof plastic bag
13. Gloves, preferably waterproof
14. Duct tape (useful for repairing tears and emergency waterproofing)
15. A whistle
16. An emergency space blanket

Perhaps the most important thing you can do to prepare aside from the Ten Essentials is very simple: **before you go anywhere, let somebody know where you are going and when you plan on returning**. Your loved ones will appreciate this simple act of preparation before you leave town, and upon your return they will appreciate your call or text, knowing that you're safe. And if you don't come back, it is enormously helpful for search and rescue teams to know where you are. People get lost and die every year in the woods and mountains near Portland because they didn't think to tell anyone where they were going, and when they were planning on returning. Don't be one of those people.

An understanding of basic first aid is equally important. I strongly recommend taking a Wilderness First Aid (WFA) or Mountaineering First Aid (MFA) class to help you understand how to navigate medical emergencies in the backcountry. Better still is the Wilderness First Responder (WFR) course, which is designed to teach as much as you can possibly learn about medical emergencies in the backcountry. **DO NOT** rely on your phone to save you! Many of the hikes in this book are located in places where cell service is not available. For more information about these classes, go online and find one near you.

Maps and legends:
Maps in this book were created using CalTopo. All trails are marked with a thick black line, which represents my GPS track of the hike. These are the most accurate locations of each trail. Sometimes the Forest Service marked the trail in the wrong location; you will see a thin dashed line that diverges from my thick black line in these cases. Additional hiking options not part of the main hike are marked by thin dashed lines on each map.

Road Access: All of the hikes in this book are accessible with a standard 2-wheel drive low-clearance vehicle. Naturally, some roads are better than others. While many trailheads in this book are found on 2-lane paved roads that receive regular maintenance, others are at the far end of gravel forest roads that do not receive regular maintenance. Some of these roads are rocky and rough; these roads are duly noted, with recommendations for the level of ground clearance you might need. Be prepared for absolutely anything on the roads. I have made every effort to ensure the accuracy of my driving directions and clearly explain the road conditions where there might be a cause for concern. US and state highways are labeled as US or OR (for example: US 26, OR 22 and WA 503) while forest roads (which are maintained by the Forest Service), are labeled as FR (for example, FR 44 or FR 4421). As a general rule, federal and state highways are well-maintained, plowed in the winter and well-signed. Forest roads vary, but two-number forest roads (such as FR 44) tend to be paved or good gravel, and are well-maintained. Four-number forest roads vary wildly in both quality and frequency of maintenance. Furthermore, the condition of gravel roads tends to change with each year and in some cases every season. Roads that do not receive regular maintenance and steep, winding roads are the ones most likely to be in rough shape. If you are still not sure about road conditions after reading this book, check with your local ranger station or ask online (see links below) - somebody out there will probably know.

Public Transit: When I first moved to Portland I didn't know how to drive. I was reliant on public transportation (as well as the benevolence of others) to get my hike on. Eventually I learned to drive, but the experience of being carless stayed with me. I have tried to offer as many hikes accessible via public transit as I possibly can. In this case public transit directions to these hikes are listed under the driving directions.

Resources: Knowing current conditions is also a vital part of preparation. Before you venture out into the woods, you should familiarize yourself with the following resources:

- **Off the Beaten Trail** (http://www.offthebeatentrailpdx.com) - This is my website and I update it whenever I have time. Here you'll find high-resolution maps, current conditions, photos, the occasional essay and extra hikes that did not make this book. You'll also find information about my other books, both past and future.
- **Oregon Hikers** (http://www.oregonhikers.org) – An online forum and field guide dedicated to hiking, snowshoeing and backpacking throughout Oregon, with a focus on the Portland area (the website was formerly known as Portland Hikers). In the forums you can view trip reports for up-to-date information on hikes all across the region. Stop here before you leave the house for current information and browse the forums for more great ideas!
- **Oregon Wildflowers** (http://oregonwildflowers.org) – Similar to Oregon Hikers but with a focus on wildflowers. You can view trip reports and see some of the webmaster Greg Lief's excellent wildflower photos. This is an indispensable resource for planning trips to the area's wildflower meadows.
- **National Weather Service** (http://www.weather.gov/) – The National Weather Service does an excellent job with forecasting weather anywhere you want to go. In the winter it's helpful to check the region you're planning on visiting to get an idea about the snow levels on that particular day. Regardless of season, any time you see an active watch or warning it is best to heed their advice and pick a different destination (or just stay home).
- **Oregon Tripcheck** (https://tripcheck.com/Pages/RCMap.asp) – Tripcheck is a vital resource for learning about road conditions. If you're curious about construction projects, landslides, traffic jams and snowstorms, this is the place to go. Best of all, there are also a great number of road cameras, enough to give you an idea of what driving conditions are like in a particular place. This is especially useful during the winter when are trying to decide whether you want to drive over the Coast Range or through the Gorge to go hiking.

For questions about specific places, current conditions and specific information, it is best to call the local ranger station or visitors center for each destination. There are too many to list here, but a quick Internet search should lead you to the particular state park, national monument, Forest Service ranger district or local park jurisdiction in question to help you gather all the information you need.

Should you not want to set out into the wilderness on your own, consider hiking with an area hiking club! The Mazamas, based out of Portland, lead hikes and backpacking trips to many of these destinations when possible (full disclosure: I lead hikes and outings for the Mazamas). You do not need to be a member of the Mazamas to participate in Mazamas activities. Visit www.mazamas.org for more information.

With all that said, let's go hiking!

JANUARY

		Distance	EV Gain	Drive
1.	Ecola State Park	5.7 mi	1,200 ft	90 min
2.	Bayocean Spit	7.8 mi	100 ft	90 min
3.	Mount Tabor	2.5 mi	350 ft	15 min
4.	Oxbow Regional Park	4 mi	300 ft	40 min
5.	Moulton Falls	6.6 mi	500 ft	55 min
6.	Latourell, Shepperds Dell and Bridal Veil Falls	3.4 mi	800 ft	30 min
7.	Mosier Twin Tunnels	8.0 mi	1,000 ft	65 min
8.	Stacker Butte	13.2 mi	2,900 ft	90 min
9.	Heritage Landing and Ferry Springs	7.9 mi	700 ft	90 min
10.	Deschutes River Trail	11.8 mi	300 ft	90 min

It's January. The days are short, the nights are long, and it's rainy and cold most days. After the holidays you just want to get out and hike, and start working yourself back into shape for spring. You'll even deal with rain just to get a good hike in. Fear not- these ten hikes are excellent ways to spend a January day! With short days and low snow levels, these hikes are the best of what is out there this time of year.

There are a few things you need to know about hiking in January. As always, you need to be prepared for conditions wherever you end up going. This means the ten essentials, a full tank of gas and a charged phone. If it's been very cold recently, stay out of the Gorge- the roads and trails will be dangerously icy. This of course is an excellent time to go to the Coast. I'm going to tell you a secret: in the winter, it is often warmer on the Coast than it is in the Valley. Watch weather forecasts closely, as every now and then you can catch a random 65 degree day on the Coast. Such days are the sustenance that will help get you through another Oregon winter. It is worth driving home in the dark after a glorious day at Ecola State Park or Bayocean Spit (or other nearby destinations, which you can find in other chapters).

Last but not least, the eastern end of the Gorge is an excellent escape in January. While most of the hikes in this area can be found in other chapters (primarily March and April, during peak wildflower season), the mouth of the Deschutes River makes for an excellent winter escape. The first time I visited the area, it was 48 degrees and rainy in Portland, but 65 degrees and sunny along the Deschutes River. Located in what is essentially desert, the weather is cold but often sunny in winter. Plan on a trip out there at some point in January, where you'll find hikes from 4 to 40 miles.

Wherever you go, you'll be sure to have an excellent time provided you took the time to prepare for whatever you might encounter in January. You should always be prepared!

Photo on opposite page: Boxcar above the Deschutes River Trail (Hike 10)

2.   Bayocean Spit

Distance: 7.8 mile loop
Elevation Gain: 100 feet
Trailhead elevation: 21 feet
Trail high point: 40 feet
Other seasons: all year
Map: none needed
Pass: none needed
Drivetime from Portland: 100 minutes

Directions:
- Drive west from Portland on US 26 to the junction with OR 6 west of Hillsboro.
- Turn left at the junction onto OR 6 towards Tillamook.
- Drive 51 miles on OR 6 through the Coast Range to Tillamook.
- At a junction with US 101 in downtown Tillamook, continue straight.
- After just 0.4 mile, the street curves left and reaches a junction with 3rd Street. Turn right here to begin driving the Three Capes Loop.
- Drive 5 miles to a junction with Bayocean Spit's gravel access road. Turn right here.
- Follow the lower road (the upper is the return road of this one-way loop) for 0.9 mile of very potholed gravel to the trailhead parking lot.
- Pay very close attention to forecasts for the Coast Range when visiting in winter. During snowy and icy periods OR 6 is very dangerous as it passes through the Wilson River's narrow, rugged canyon. Plan this hike for a warmer week in January and check road conditions before you go.

Hiking north on Bayocean Spit's beach. Rainy, blustery days are the norm here in the winter, and visiting the coast on such stormy days provides a memorable, even surreal experience. Just bring a good raincoat and the sense to turn around when needed.

Why January: Once upon a time Bayocean Spit was the site of the town of Bayocean. Over time the ocean slowly consumed the town, and by 1960 the town was abandoned. Today it is difficult to find a trace of what was once a town of 2,000 residents. But the hike here is better than ever, and excellent on winter days when everything else is snowed under. As with all coastal hikes, Bayocean Spit is also an excellent destination on summer days when the Valley bakes in summer heat.

Hike: From the trailhead follow a trail west through the dunes 0.4 mile to the beach. Turn right here and begin your walk along the beach. As always, this is easier at lower tides- check tide tables before you leave the house. Walk along the beach 3 miles to the tip of Bayocean Spit, where a jetty marks the end of the spit. Make your way around the piles of driftwood at the end of the spit to locate the road that follows the Tillamook Bay side of the spit. Turn right here.

The walk back along the road is more interesting than you would think. There are views across Tillamook Bay to the town of Garibaldi and out to the Coast Range. Eventually the road enters the forest and climbs a bit, passing what were once forested islands before the spit grew and became a peninsula as sand accumulated behind the jetty. At 7 miles a trail leads right to part of the townsite. Once the site of a town of 2,000 people, the lack

of a road into the town made visiting difficult; most people arrived via a steam ship. The town asked the Army Corps of engineers to construct two jetties to make passage over water easier; instead, the Army Corps built just one jetty, and this caused sand to accumulate, and storms and erosion eventually led to the destruction of the town. Construction of a second jetty caused sand to accumulate, creating the spit that exists now. Today nothing remains of the town worth seeing. Continue walking down the road 0.8 mile to the trailhead and the end of your hike.

3. Mount Tabor

Distance: 2.5 mile loop
Elevation Gain: 350 feet
Trailhead elevation: 300 feet
Trail high point: 643 feet
Other seasons: all year
Map: none needed
Pass: none needed
Drivetime from Portland: 10 minutes

Directions:
- Drive east from downtown to the corner of SE Belmont Street and SE 60th Avenue.
- Turn left on SE 60th Ave and drive south three blocks south to the corner of SE 60th Ave and SE Salmon Street.
- I like to start the loop here but the only parking available is street parking. If you're looking for a dedicated parking lot, turn left onto SE Salmon Street and drive up into the park. Intercept the hike described below from wherever you ended up parking.
- This is one of the easiest hikes to reach in the city on Trimet. The #15 Bus stops at the corner of SE 60th and SE Belmont (Stop ID 450), while the #73 bus stops at the corner of SE 60th and SE Salmon Street (Stop IDs 7380 and 7381) if you're coming from elsewhere in the city.

Why January: Mount Tabor is Portland's back yard, and if you live anywhere on the east side of Portland, you've probably been there at least a few times. When I first moved to Portland I visited regularly, in all seasons. I've been to picnics, meetings and even a wedding there. But what first drew me to the park was its extensive trail network and convenient location. Mount Tabor, like so many of the large hills that dot the east side of the Portland metro area, is an extinct volcano. You can come here at any time, but sometimes in the winter you just need to get outside, rain or shine. A rainy or snowy day in January is an excellent time to hike at Tabor.

Hike: As with any hike that features so many choices, this description is merely a suggestion. Mount Tabor Park has more trails than you could ever imagine, and you could easily do many small variations on this loop. Use the map here to help you navigate this park.

1. Start your loop at the corner of SE 60th Avenue and SE Salmon Street. Walk down the street to a corner outside Reservoir 6 and turn left. Follow this trail to a junction at the far left corner of the reservoir. Walk up the short trail left of the reservoir and arrive at a junction with the Green Trail (marked by a green post). Turn left here and commence following the Green Trail around the northwest side of Mount Tabor Park. As you walk along, you will meet a great many trails through here. If you are unsure of what to do at any point, simply follow the green posts and arrows used to mark this trail. You will follow the Green Trail to the Mount Tabor Visitors Center at a little over 0.8 mile, where you will find a signboard, bathrooms and more. Across the street is a picnic shelter, as well an intersection with the blue and red trails.
2. The only part of this hike that is difficult to navigate is the area around the Visitors Center. The plethora of options can overwhelm hikers. Cross the street and follow the blue and red trails over to the picnic shelter. Continue walking uphill, passing a children's play area. Keep left here and you will locate the continuation of the trail in the area. Continue hiking around the north side of Mount Tabor until you reach the Mount Tabor Stairs at 1.1 miles. Turn left here.
3. Walking up the stairs is one of my favorite things about coming to Mount Tabor. This long staircase stretches from the park's northeast boundary all the way to the summit. You may be tempted to live out your *Rocky* fantasies and run all the way to the top but it's a long way up, more than most people can run without getting winded.

4. The stairs reach the summit loop at 1.2 miles. How long you spend at the summit is up to you. If the weather is nice enough to let you stop, there are picnic shelters and benches all over. In summer this is one of the busiest parks in the city but in January you should easily be able to find a bench or table all your own. Follow the paved loop around the summit to the south end, where you will locate the Harvey Scott statue. Scott was a pioneer born in Illinois who emigrated to Oregon as a child and ended up editor-in-chief of *The Oregonian*, among other noteworthy accomplishments.
5. From the south end of Mount Tabor's summit loop (just opposite the Harvey Scott statue), locate a trail heading steeply downhill. Follow this trail to a 4-way junction at a lamppost at 1.6 miles. Turn right here.
6. Hike downhill to a junction at a crossing of Reservoir Loop Road. If you're pressed for time, simply continue downhill.
7. If you've got a spare five minutes, follow the trail you see darting off to your upper left towards a side summit. This short trail leads to Mount Tabor's southwest summit, where you'll find a park bench under a grove of large Douglas-firs. Then return to the previous junction.
8. From the junction on Reservoir Loop Road, continue downhill following a trail above the left (south) side of the upper Mount Tabor Reservoir. You will have views out to downtown here, as well as much of inner southeast Portland. When you reach the road at the west side of the reservoir, turn right and walk until you locate the large staircase leading downhill to the larger reservoir, Reservoir 6. Once you reach the bottom of the stairs, turn right and follow the trail to the northeast corner of the reservoir, where you'll locate the junction from the beginning of this hike. Turn left and return to SE 60th Avenue. Once on SE 60th, turn right and walk three blocks back to the corner of SE 60th Avenue and SE Salmon Street, and the end of this hike.

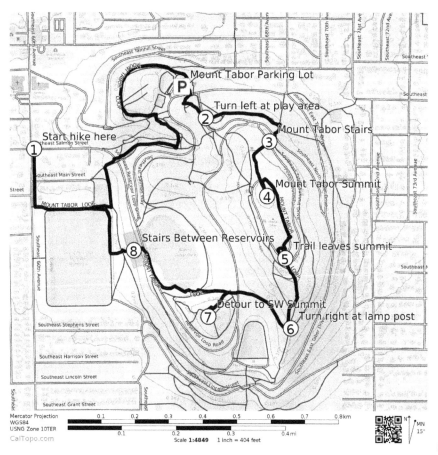

4. Oxbow Regional Park

	Lower Loop	Lower Loop and Alder Ridge
Distance:	4 mile loop	6 mile loop
Elevation Gain:	300 feet	600 feet
Trailhead Elevation:	86 feet	86 feet
Trail High Point:	229 feet	408 feet
Other Seasons:	all year	all year
Map:	Map available in park	Map available in park
Pass:	$5 park entrance fee	$5 park entrance fee
Drivetime from PDX:	40 minutes	40 minutes

Directions:
- From Portland, drive Interstate 84 east to Troutdale.
- At Exit 16, leave the freeway and turn right on SE 238th Avenue.
- Drive 2.6 miles south on SE 238th Avenue (which becomes NE Hogan Drive) to a junction with NE Division St.
- Turn left on NE Division Street and drive 3.4 miles to a fork. Keep right, following a sign for Oxbow Park.
- Continue 2.2 miles to a junction with SE Hosner Road, also known as Oxbow Parkway.
- Turn left and drive downhill 1.5 miles to Oxbow's entrance. Pay the $5 parking fee and continue on the road into the park.
- Drive just under a mile to the Happy Creek Parking Area, on the left. Park by the bathroom. The hike begins on the gravel trail leaving from the bathroom.

Why January: Oxbow Regional Park is the best of the many parks managed by Metro, a local government agency that provides services to the Portland metro area. Situated on a long bend along the Sandy River, the park provides miles of hiking and equestrian trails as well as some of the nicest group picnic sites in western Oregon. As the park is not all that far from Portland, it is very popular - but far less so in winter. This is an outstanding hike all of the time, but never more so than when everything else is snowed under.

Hike: Begin at the Happy Creek Parking Area. Walk up the road 100 feet or so to the trailhead on the left side of the road, marked by signpost C. This trail follows the Sandy River closely from the bluffs above, passing group picnic sites and the occasional trail down to the river. There is a proliferation of trails but in general you should stay on the trail that closely follows the river. Fences keep the trail from getting too close to river level, as the bluffs above the river are in a continual state of erosion. At 1.4 miles, the trail seems to abruptly end at a boat launch in the river. Turn right and walk up the launch access road for about 100 yards until you reach a parking lot with bathroom. At the parking lot, look for the trail sign paralleling the campground access road, which is also signed for the amphitheater. Follow this trail along the edge of the campground and then downhill until you reach a side trail for a small beach, which you reach at 1.9 miles from the trailhead. This is an excellent spot for a break. While at the beach you will get your first good look at a curious feature- trees sticking out of the Sandy's sandy bluffs above the river. These trees are actually hundreds of years old, having been buried during a lahar triggered by an eruption of Mount Hood late in the 18th Century.

From the beach, continue hiking along the bend in the river another 0.4 mile until you reach a picnic shelter at Group Site 2. This cozy shelter is a welcome rest stop on a rainy

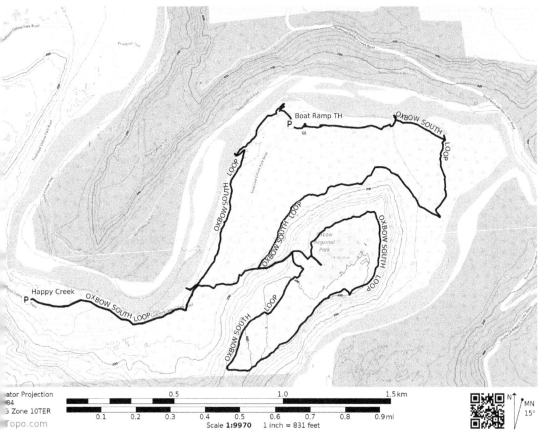

ator Projection
84
Zone 10TER
Topo.com

Scale **1:9970**   1 inch = 831 feet

day, as it's not often you get to take a break and still stay dry in the winter. Turn right here on a wide trail that looks like an access road. This trail passes through some lovely moss-draped forest, passing a junction on your left in just 0.1 mile as it angles back towards the campground. You will arrive at another fork just a little ways down the trail; right is marked only by a sign forbidding horses; instead you should keep left. The trail then passes through one of the nicer ancient forests close to Portland, a forest that seems to radiate an electric shade of the green on sunny days. At 3.2 miles, reach another junction with a wide gravel trail cutting sharply uphill. For an easier and shorter hike, turn right and hike downhill to Group Picnic Site A, on the far end of which you will locate the trail that follows the river. But if you've got more time and energy I suggest heading uphill to the top of Alder Ridge for a longer, more strenuous loop.

Turn left on the Alder Ridge Trail and hike steeply uphill to a junction with a loop trail. Before you hike the loop around the ridge, take a moment to check out the meadow straight ahead. Then hike the loop trail through the forest along the sharp edge of Alder Ridge. This trail passes some larger cedar trees and offers occasional views down to the river. When you reach the end of the loop, turn left on the gravel trail and hike steeply downhill 0.4 mile to Group Picnic Site A. Locate the river trail on the far end of the site, and turn left to hike 0.7 mile back to the trailhead.

5. Moulton Falls

Distance: 6.6 miles out and back
Elevation Gain: 500 feet
Trailhead elevation: 531 feet
Trail high point: 701 feet
Other seasons: all year except in winter storms; very crowded in summer
Map: none needed
Pass: none needed
Drivetime from Portland: 60 minutes

Directions:
- Drive north on Interstate 205 across the Columbia River into Washington.
- Leave the freeway at Exit 30A/B/C. Keep left for Exit 30B, then follow signs for WA 500, which travels north towards Battle Ground.
- Along the way, WA 500 becomes WA 503 as it travels north on NE 117th Avenue.
- Continue north, now on WA 503 for approximately 7 miles to a junction with Main Street (WA 502) at the edge of Battle Ground.
- Keep straight on WA 503 and drive 5.6 miles to a junction on your right with NE Rock Creek Road, signed for Lucia and Moulton Falls.
- Turn right and drive 2.7 miles to a junction with 172nd Avenue next to a bridge.
- Keep straight and drive 2.5 miles to a junction with NE Hantwick Road.
- Turn right and drive this narrow road 0.6 mile to the trailhead on your left.

Why January: In January, hiking is often limited to the lowest elevations, nearest the Portland metro area. Many of the most scenic hikes follow rampaging rivers to waterfalls, swollen by winter rain. This popular and easy trail, converted from a rail line many years ago, passes through the scenic canyon of the East Fork Lewis River en route to Moulton Falls and a high bridge over the river. From there you can continue to Yacolt Falls and a small train station, making for a lovely winter hike.

Hike: From the trailhead, locate the paved trail heading east towards the East Fork of the Lewis River. You will descend slightly to a junction, where you turn right. The trail curves around a bend and commences following a rail line through the swampy bottoms along the river. Pass a spur trail on your left leading to a bench just above a pond. From here, the trail begins following the river, offering excellent views down to the river's scenic gorge. This is not exactly a wilderness experience; in addition to the railroad that passes through this canyon, there are numerous houses on the opposite side of the river, and road noise occasionally intrudes on the tranquility of the area. It is nevertheless beautiful,

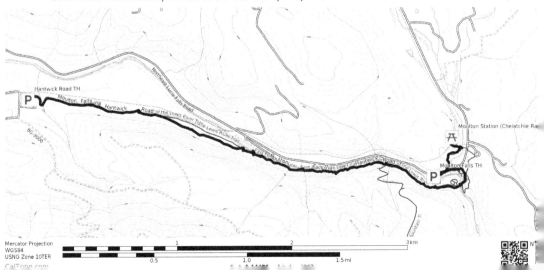

Mercator Projection
WGS84
USNG Zone 10TER
CalTopo.com

The East Fork of the Lewis River near Moulton Falls.

and the river is a particularly lovely shade between blue and green here. Large, mossy cedars and firs tower over the road, adding to the scene.

At 2.4 miles from the trailhead, reach a junction with the Bells Mountain Trail. Stay on the main trail here as it begins to drop towards the river. You will first pass Moulton Falls, which is more or less a series or rapids in the winter; not far from here you will pass a picnic area on your left before reaching the concrete bridge over the river. Here the East Fork is deep, green and entrancing. At 2.8 miles from the trailhead, the bridge is a worthy goal in its own right. If you've got the time you should continue across the river and up to Yacolt Falls.

To find the falls, cross the bridge and keep left. You will quickly arrive at a picnic area above Moulton Falls, where you will get a view of the bridge from below. Cross a concrete bridge beside the road over Big Tree Creek and immediately locate the pedestrian crosswalk. The trail crosses the road and continues up the creek 0.2 mile to Yacolt Falls. This 34-foot falls is a rampaging torrent in winter. A trail descends to a platform above the falls, where the spray from the falls is immense. The bridge over the falls is removed every winter. Beyond the falls, the trail continues uphill 0.1 mile to a train station, part of the Chelatchie Prairie Railroad. In December a Christmas train runs to this station, where passengers can purchase Christmas trees as part of the experience. The station provides cover on rainy days, so common in January.

Return the way you came.

6. Latourell Falls and Bridal Veil Falls

	Latourell Falls	Shepperd's Dell Falls	Bridal Veil Falls
Distance:	2.2 mile loop	0.2 mile out/back	0.8 mile out / back
Elevation Gain:	600 feet	50 feet	200 feet
Trailhead Elevation:	161 feet	170 feet	180 feet
Trail High Point:	650 feet	170 feet	180 feet
Other Seasons:	all year	all year	all year
Map:	none needed	none needed	none needed
Pass:	none needed	none needed	none needed
Drivetime from PDX:	35 minutes	35 minutes	35 minutes

Directions:
- From Portland, drive east on Interstate 84 to Exit 28, signed for Bridal Veil and the Historic Highway.
- Drive to the end of the exit and turn right onto the Historic Highway.
- Drive 2.8 miles, passing the Bridal Veil and Shepperd's Dell Trailheads along the way, to the Latourell Falls Trailhead.
- You can do these three hikes in any order, but I always start with Latourell and work my way back to Bridal Veil.

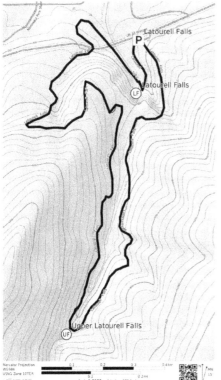

Why January: On spring and summer weekends, the western end of the Gorge is a veritable tourist trap. I am often overwhelmed by the crowds in this part of the Gorge- except in the winter. With short days and plentiful rain, you'll see far fewer people here in January. Bring a friend, a camera and a good raincoat and you'll find a peace that isn't possible here at other times during the year. Avoid periods of ice at all costs. These times often make for fantastic photos, but are extremely dangerous without the proper equipment for both your vehicle and your feet.

Hike: Begin at Latourell Falls. The closest to Portland of the Gorge waterfalls, this is also one of the most photogenic. Begin at the small parking lot and immediately reach a trail junction: left to hike above the falls; or right to descend to the base of the falls. Keep left and begin hiking uphill, eventually switchbacking to the top of the falls. After 0.7 mile of hiking uphill on the banks above Latourell Creek, reach Upper Latourell Falls. The trail reaches the base of this 120 foot falls and crosses the creek on a bridge. This falls is not as photogenic as its sibling downstream but is a neat spot to stop just the same.

Latourell Falls on a cold, wet day in January.

Beyond the upper falls, the trail climbs a bit and then begins to traverse out of Latourell Creek's canyon. The trail descends gradually through open forest, eventually reaching a tunnel that passes under the Historic Highway. Cross under the road and switchback down into Latourell Creek's canyon. You are almost instantly greeted with Latourell Falls, staring you in the face. This 224 foot falls is highly photogenic! Most impressive is the display of columnar basalt on both sides of the falls; photographers will wish to spend a lot of time in this spot. When you are done, walk uphill 2 minutes to the trailhead.

Get back in your car and drive a little over a mile east to Shepperd's Dell Falls. There is room to park only a few cars on the left side of the road; if there are no spots available, you might want to consider heading east to Bridal Veil Falls and then returning to Shepperd's Dell later. Regardless, visiting the falls only takes a few minutes. Once you've parked, follow the short trail leading to a precarious spot between two tiers of the 220-foot falls. There is a concrete fence protecting hikers, but it's still a good idea to avoid coming here on cold, icy days. This is a cool spot, but a frustrating one- you cannot see either tier of the falls all that well. Do not leave the trail to get a better view of the falls- there are no better views, and it would be very easy to get swept downstream to your death.

For a final, even more satisfying waterfall experience, head east to nearby Bridal Veil Falls. Drive 1 mile east on the Historic Highway to the Bridal Veil Falls Trailhead. Find the trail down to the falls by the bathroom, and hike downhill 0.4 mile to the falls. Unlike most Gorge waterfalls, this one is located at the very bottom of the Gorge, tumbling below the Scenic Highway. This is an exceptionally scenic spot, and you will want to spend time taking it all in. After taking the time to appreciate the falls, return the way you came.

If you've got more time after visiting these three waterfalls, consider driving east along the Scenic Highway to Wahkeena Falls and then Multnomah Falls. The trails that leave from these falls are described in Hike 107. These trails are frequently open even in January but not always. If it's been cold recently expect ice along the trails.

7. Mosier Twin Tunnels

	via Hood River	via Mosier
Distance:	9.8 miles out and back	2.6 miles out and back
Elevation Gain:	500 feet	200 feet
Trailhead Elevation:	348 feet	215 feet
Trail High Point:	546 feet	400 feet
Other Seasons:	all year	all year
Map:	none needed	none needed
Pass:	$5 day use fee (or SP pass)	$5 day use fee (or SP pass)
Drivetime from PDX:	65 minutes	70 minutes

Directions to Hatfield West (Hood River) Trailhead:
- From Portland, drive Interstate 84 east to Hood River and leave the highway at Exit 64, signed for OR 35. At the bottom of the exit ramp, turn right onto OR 35.
- Drive uphill to a four-way junction at the eastern end of Hood River.
- Turn left here and drive 1.2 miles uphill to road's end at the Hatfield West TH.
- Be sure to pay the $5 fee at the machine if you don't already have a State Parks pass.

Directions to Hatfield East (Mosier) Trailhead:
- From Portland, drive Interstate 84 east past Hood River to Mosier.
- Leave the freeway at Exit 69, signed for Mosier.
- At the end of the exit ramp, turn right to drive towards Mosier.
- Immediately after crossing a bridge, turn left on Rock Creek Road.
- Drive this road 1 mile to the trailhead on the left side of the road.
- Be sure to pay the $5 fee at the machine if you don't already have a State Parks pass.

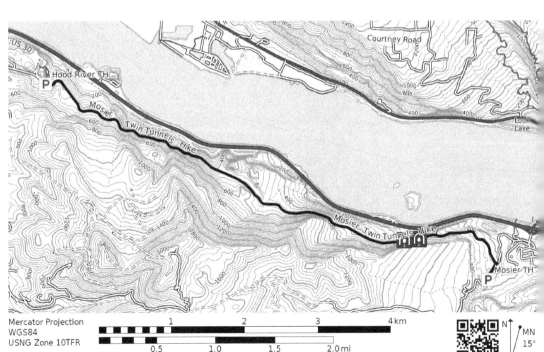

Why January: This fascinating stretch of the Historic Columbia River Highway features great views, interesting geology, and best of all, two large tunnels carved into the cliffs of the Gorge. This stretch of highway was faithfully restored in the Nineties to its former glory, and is quite popular with cyclists. But its convenient access makes it ideal for a January hike, and the tunnels make for a good rest spot on days when the weather wears you down. Though not quite in the rain shadow, it is often drier out here in the winter than in Portland. You should nevertheless avoid this hike during icy periods, as it is quite slippery.

Hike: You can do this hike one of three ways: out and back from Hood River, out and back from Mosier, or as a car shuttle from one trailhead to the other. As I did the hike from Hood River to Mosier and back, I will describe it from west to east. Begin at the Hatfield West Trailhead, heading east on the paved trailhead from the parking lot. The trail climbs slightly before leveling out well above Interstate 84. A right-of-way conflict forced the builders of the Historic Highway high up onto the cliffs, and this is where the road stays for the entire hike. Though highway noise is always present on this hike, it rarely intrudes on the experience. In fact, it presents an interesting contrast: imagine cars driving down this narrow road and then look down at the freeway below and marvel at how far automobile travel has changed over the past one hundred years.

As you hike along the road, you will begin to notice the transition between the west Gorge and east Gorge; in the five miles on this trail, the terrain changes from darker Douglas fir woods to drier and more open terrain with scattered Ponderosa pines. There is an excellent viewpoint at about the halfway mark that offers panoramic views of the Gorge from Hood River to The Dalles. Beyond here the way is increasingly open, with good views. Reach the tunnels at 3.6 miles from the western trailhead. The tunnels were build to accommodate two-way traffic but were still narrow, and seemed more so as cars got larger and larger. The tunnels were abandoned and filled after the construction of a route along the river in the 1950s. They were later restored to their original state with help from Senator Mark Hatfield, and officially reopened in 2000. Hiking through them is a revelation; two windows reveal excellent views of The Gorge. Beyond the tunnels the trail descends through increasingly open terrain 1.3 miles to its eastern trailhead near Mosier.

8. Stacker Butte

	From Upper TH	From Lower TH
Distance:	5.8 miles out and back	13.2 miles out and back
Elevation Gain:	1,300 feet	2,900 feet
Trailhead Elevation:	1,920 feet	376 feet
Trail High Point:	3,218 feet	3,218 feet
Other Seasons:	October- April	October- April
Map:	none needed	none needed
Pass:	Washington Discover Pass	Washington Discover Pass
Drivetime from PDX:	105 minutes	90 minutes

Directions to Lower TH:
- From Portland drive east on Interstate 84 for 80 miles to The Dalles.
- At a sign for US 197 at Exit 87, leave the freeway. Turn left and cross the Columbia River on US 197, also known as Dallesport Road.
- Continue on this highway for 2 more miles to a junction with WA 14.
- Drive 3.6 miles to the trailhead on your left, just before the road crosses a creek.

Directions to Upper TH:
- From the junction of US 197 and WA 14, turn right.
- In just 1 mile, turn left on the Dalles Mountain Road at a sign for Marshal's Winery.
- Continue straight on this road past a junction for the winery and continue 3.3 miles of gravel road to a junction at a barn.
- Turn a sharp left here and drive up the steep and rutted gravel road another 1.4 miles to a small parking lot at a locked gate. The hike description begins at the locked gate.

Why January: The wildflower meadows of The Dalles Mountain Ranch are one of the most beautiful destinations in the Gorge in the spring. Visitors come from far away to bask in the fields of balsamroot and lupine found here, and it is not uncommon to arrive at the trailhead and find over 100 cars. The construction of a new and large trail network has alleviated some of the congestion but not all. Here is one thing that most people don't know: this is also a fantastic place to go hiking in the winter, and is in many ways as good as it is in the spring. Sure, the flowers are gone, but so are the people. The views are better on clear days, and you stand a pretty good chance of seeing wildlife. Just make sure you plan for very cold weather- the summit of Stacker Butte on a windy day in January might be the coldest place in this entire book.

Hike: There are three trailheads here, but the easier hike starts at the uppermost trailhead in Columbia Hills State Park. From the gate on Stacker Butte Road, set out uphill on the road. Views open up immediately of Mount Hood and points further south right from the trailhead- you can see all of The Dalles, which is why the area is often referred to as The Dalles Mountain Ranch. The road winds up the treeless slopes of Stacker Butte. As you ascend, take some time to appreciate the beauty of winter here- the open skies, the muted yellow and gold of the winter grass, the shape of your shadow and the silence of winter solitude. Keen eyes may spot deer or coyotes on the slopes above and across from you while birds serenade you. About 1.6 miles from the road gate, the road passes a radio tower and maintenance building on your right and begins climbing steeply towards the summit of Stacker Butte. Past this point the winds can be intense (on some days this is putting it lightly) and snow is often found the road. Continue another 1.3 miles to the summit, where you will find a collection of radio towers managed by the Federal Aviation Administration. The view up here is incredible, stretching from Mount Adams to the Three Sisters and 50 miles of the Columbia River Gorge. There is no shelter from the brutal winds up here- on colder days the wind chill will drop below 0° F, making your stay at the top mercifully brief. You can follow the road to the western end of the summit, but regardless of where you decide to turn around, return the way you came.

If you opted for the longer hike, good for you! This is one of the rare conditioning hikes that is open in January. The trail departs from the base of Eightmile Creek Falls and wraps around the top of this lovely cascade. Even from here the views of Mount Hood, looming over The Dalles, are excellent. Beyond the falls, this brand-new trail climbs gradually along Eightmile Creek's canyon, eventually crossing the creek at 1 mile from the lower TH. At a junction with a loop trail not far past the creek crossing, keep left (the loop offers another excellent winter option if you don't feel like hiking to the sum-

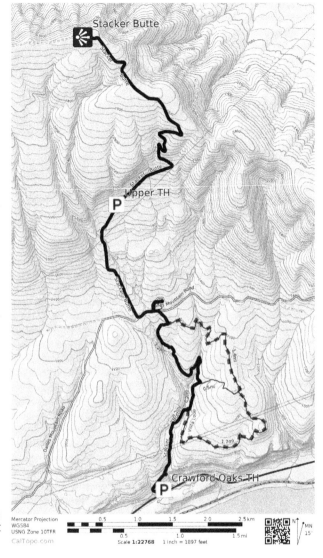

mit of Stacker Butte). The trail continues uphill, dipping into and out of gullies, until at last the barns and farm implements of the middle trailhead come into view. Reach the barn at 2.6 miles and turn left for a short ways until you reach a road junction just past the barn. This spot is quite chaotic during the height of wildflower season, as hundreds of hikers and photographers crowd the area, all looking for their slice of spring wildflower glory. It won't be like this in January, and that's totally fine. From here, turn right on the Stacker Butte Road and walk 1.4 miles to the locked gate that signals the upper trailhead, and from there, continue 2.9 miles to the summit of Stacker Butte. Return the way you came.

On your way back you can make a loop by following recently-constructed trails across the Dalles Mountain Ranch property. These trails add over a mile to your day's total but are worth your time and energy if you've got any left. You'll have excellent views out across the Gorge to The Dalles and Mount Hood. For more information, see Hike 39.

9.   Heritage Landing and Ferry Springs

	Heritage Landing	Ferry Springs Loop
Distance:	3.2 miles out and back	4.7 mile semi-loop
Elevation Gain:	100 feet	600 feet
Trailhead Elevation:	198 feet	181 feet
Trail High Point:	241 feet	750 feet
Other Seasons:	all year except summer	all year except summer
Map:	none needed	none needed
Pass:	None	None
Drivetime from PDX:	90 minutes	90 minutes

Directions to Heritage Landing:
- From Portland, drive 75 miles to The Dalles on Interstate 84 and continue another 13 miles to Exit 97.
- Following signs for the Deschutes Recreation Area, leave the freeway at Exit 97 and arrive at a junction.
- Turn left and drive 3 miles to a bridge over the Deschutes River.
- Just before the bridge, turn right and drive 0.4 mile to the Heritage Landing Trailhead, right as the road begins to curve to the right, away from the river.

Directions to Ferry Springs Trailhead:
- Follow the above directions to the bridge over the Deschutes.
- Cross the river and turn right into the campground.
- Drive through the campground and park at the south end of the B campground loop, near the camp host and bathrooms.
- The trail is straight ahead at the end of a grassy field.

Why January: When winter hits the hardest, and the rainy days and grey skies get you down, it's time to head east until you find sunshine. I love to drive out to the Deschutes River's desert canyon east of The Dalles, where the odds are good for sunny days even in January. These two hikes, both short and fairly easy, highlight the scenic beauty of this canyon without asking too much in return. For a longer and more demanding experience here, turn the page and check out the longer trail following the Deschutes River.

Heritage Landing: The shortest and easiest trail in the Deschutes Canyon, the Heritage Landing Trail is also the only trail on the river's west bank. The Heritage Landing Trail drops a bit to river level and proceeds to follow the Deschutes River upstream. You will often approach the river as you head upstream, but never all that closely. As you hike upriver, look out to the raging Deschutes: the river is seen here at its widest, an oasis in the desert. You will almost certainly see birds of all kinds, and with

some luck you may even spot one of the herons that winter here. The trail passes a lone juniper tree, and becomes faint as it approaches Rattlesnake Bend. Follow the trail until it peters out near a knoll. You can scramble up the knoll for a nice view of the Deschutes canyon. Just above you is a railroad line, on which trains pass through a few times a day. Please resist the temptation to create a loop using the train tracks, and instead return the way you came.

Ferry Springs Loop: To locate this trail, drive across the river to the east bank of the Deschutes, turn right into the campground at Deschutes State Park and drive to the parking lot where the road is gated. This short loop on the opposite side of the river is the only way to see the Deschutes Canyon from the top. Although this hike could also be paired with the Deschutes River Trail Hike (see the following two pages), it is also ideal when paired with the Heritage Landing Hike.

Begin by locating the Deschutes River Trail at the far southern end of the campground. Walk to the end of the field at the southern end of the campground and locate the trail here. You will almost immediately reach a trail junction. Turn left and climb steeply up to a junction with the Deschutes River Trail, a former rail line. Turn right to follow this wide trail. At a little over a mile, reach a junction on your left with the Ferry Springs Trail. Turn left.

This trail climbs steadily but never steeply to the top of the canyon. Along the way you will have excellent views across the canyon and out to the Columbia River. The trail reaches tiny Ferry Springs at 1.7 miles, at the top of Deschutes River's wide canyon. Continue along the trail as it drops back to the Deschutes River Trail at 2.7 miles. You can turn right and follow the main trail, but it is more scenic to cross the main trail and continue on a trail that parallels the wide bench above the river. Stay on this trail until you meet the connector trail just above the grassy field. Turn right and hike a quarter-mile back to the trailhead.

If you're interested in a longer hike than either of the hikes described here, the Deschutes River Trail follows its namesake more than 20 miles up the river to a remote trailhead north of Sherars Bridge. For more information on this long but worthwhile trek, see the following two pages.

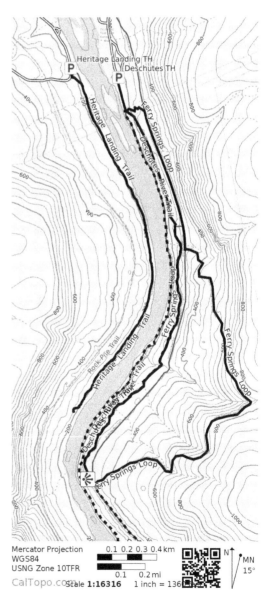

Mercator Projection
WGS84
USNG Zone 10TFR

0.1 0.2 0.3 0.4 km

0.1   0.2 mi

CalTopo.com   Scale **1:16316**   1 inch = 1360

N

MN
15°

10. Deschutes River Trail

Distance: 11.8 miles out and back
Elevation Gain: 200 feet
Trailhead elevation: 217 feet
Trail high point: 331 feet
Other seasons: October- May
Map: Columbia River Gorge (Geo-graphics)
Pass: none needed if staying only for the day ($5 overnight)
Drivetime from Portland: 90 minutes

Directions:
* From Portland, drive 75 miles to The Dalles on Interstate 84 and continue another 13 miles to Exit 97.
* Following signs for the Deschutes Recreation Area, leave the freeway at Exit 97 and arrive at a junction.
* Turn left and drive 3 miles to Deschutes State Park. Cross the river and turn right into the campground.
* Drive through the campground and park at the south end of the B campground loop, near the camp host and bathrooms.
* The trail is straight ahead at the end of a grassy field.

Why January: The Deschutes River canyon east of The Dalles is my winter sanctuary. Out here in the desert the days are sunny and cold in January, allowing me to soak in the sunshine I need to make it through the cold, rainy Portland winter. Upon arrival it become obvious that you've really, truly gone somewhere different- it's dry, open, barren and breathtakingly beautiful. If you're chasing sunshine, you would be hard-pressed to find a better destination than here, deep in the rain shadow east of the Cascades. Even in winter you will also encounter lots of wildlife, among them deer, rabbits, a wide variety of birds and if you are lucky, bighorn sheep. Best of all: there are over 30 miles of trails in this canyon, allowing hikers to spend days exploring this beautiful canyon. What are you waiting for?

Hike: Begin at the grassy field at the far end of the campground. Walk through the field and locate a trail that follows the Deschutes River. You will soon arrive at a trail junction: left takes you uphill to the official Deschutes River Trail, a former rail line that has been converted to a wide and vir-tually level trail. This is your return trail; instead continue straight to follow the river more closely. The riverside trail remains level for the most part, occasionally even offering benches for weary hikers. At a little under 2 miles, pass under a talus slope of huge boulders where you reach a trail junction: left leads you uphill steeply to the main trail while right allows you to continue at river level. Keep right and carefully pick your way around the boulders, after which the trail opens up a lot more. You will soon reach an open field, site of a former homestead. Keep straight around what still resembles a farm and reach a junction with the main trail at 3.2 miles. A quick downhill jaunt to your right takes you to a bathroom at a huge campsite. Hikers desiring an easy hike can turn around here, following either the

riverside or main trails back to the trailhead.

If you're looking for a longer trek, follow the main trail as it begins climbing above the Deschutes. The next 2.7 miles are a delight, as the trail follows a wide bench above the raging river. Rising above the trail to your left is a fantastic display of columnar basalt, a volcanic rock formation. Below you to the right is the river; I never tire of this stretch of trail. At 5.9 miles, the trail passes a gate and reaches an old wooden boxcar. This is your destination, and you would be hard pressed to find a cooler place to have lunch anywhere in January! The boxcar is a remnant of a race between competing railroads to punch a line into the Deschutes canyon in the early 20th Century. The Oregon Trunk Railroad laid down tracks on the western bank of the river, while the Deschutes Railroad laid down tracks on the eastern side of the canyon in an attempt to build a line from The Dalles to Bend. The rivalry reached a fever pitch around 1910, escalating into sabotage and feuding. Eventually the line on the western side of the canyon won out, and trains continue to run along the other side of the canyon to this day; you will likely see at least one train over the course of your hike.

Unless you desire a much longer day you should return the way you came. The old rail line allows energetic hikers and intrepid winter backpackers the chance to hike more than 15 miles further upriver to a remote upper trailhead at Mack's Canyon, but I'm not recommending it here. Along the way you'll pass the remains of an old homestead along with many excellent campsites. Backpacking in winter here is an excellent adventure- if you have the gear and the intestinal fortitude to do it. Trail runners and mountain bikers will love this longer trek, but you're just out for the day, there's not much point in hiking past the boxcar.

On your return trip, you can follow the riverside trail again but I recommend sticking to the official trail. You will have excellent views out to the river. Once you reach a junction with the Ferry Springs Trail (see Hike 9), turn left and follow a trail following the canyon rim. This trail will eventually take you to a junction with the short connector trail just above the grassy field at the trailhead. Turn left, hike to the bottom of the canyon and turn right to return to the trailhead.

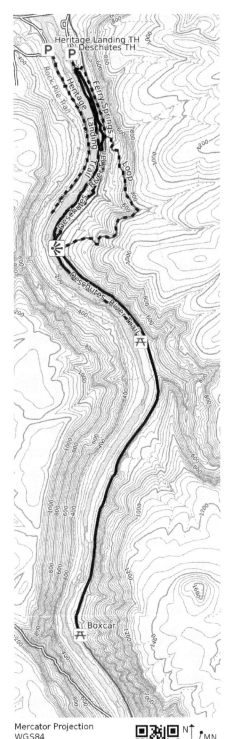

Mercator Projection
WGS84
USNG Zone 10TFR
CalTopo.com

MN
15°

FEBRUARY

		Distance	EV Gain	Drive
11.	Oceanside Beaches and Cape Meares	3.4 mi	310 ft	110 min
12.	Soapstone Lake	2.7 mi	400 ft	85 min
13.	Nehalem Spit	4.9 mi	100 ft	110 min
14.	Council Crest	3.6 mi	800 ft	10 min
15.	Oaks Bottom Park	2.8 mi	100 ft	10 min
16.	Eagle-Fern Park	1.7 mi	400 ft	50 min
17.	Henline Falls	1.8 mi	200 ft	100 min
17B.	Cedar Creek Road	3.6 mi	400 ft	110 min
18.	Catherine Creek and Tracy Hill	5.7 mi	1,300 ft	75 min
19.	Coyote Wall and the Labyrinth	5.7 mi	1,400 ft	70 min
20.	Klickitat Mineral Springs	5.2 mi	100 ft	90 min

The long road out of winter begins in February, when the days warm ever so slightly and grow longer, and snow becomes less of a threat in the lower elevations. Slowly it becomes easier to journey out of the lowlands, and there are often a few more sunny days to bask in the views. The first flowers of spring begin appearing in the eastern end of the Columbia River Gorge, signaling the eventual arrival of spring. On the sunny days that sometimes come it seems like spring is at last here. But it isn't, at least not yet. February is a difficult month to plan for, as the mountain snows are at their apex and the weather is predictably unpredictable. It is as maddening as it is beautiful.

While all of the hikes presented here are of easy to moderate difficulty, many of them can be extended to further explore the trail networks in their respective areas. These hikes are open for hiking the entire year, but are never better than in late winter, when waterfalls flow at peak strength, when the first flowers of spring poke through the ground and when everything is lush and green. Just make sure you plan ahead!

You should prepare for hikes in February as you would prepare in November, December and January. Always monitor the weather forecast and snow levels before you leave the house, particularly when traveling over the Coast Range or through the Gorge, places where ice and snow can cause dangerous travel conditions. And as always, be sure to pack the Ten Essentials and let somebody know your plans, whether you're hiking to the summit of Council Crest or driving to the eastern end of the Gorge.

Photo on opposite page: Coyote Wall (Hike 19)

11. Oceanside Beaches and Cape Meares

	Oceanside Beach	Short Beach	Cape Meares
Distance:	1 mile out / back	1.2 miles out / back	1.2 miles out / back
Elevation Gain:	10 feet	100 feet	200 feet
Trailhead Elevation:	27 feet	111 feet	335 feet
Trail High Point:	27 feet	111 feet	563 feet
Other Seasons:	all year	all year	all year
Map:	none needed	none needed	none needed
Pass:	none needed	none needed	none needed
Drivetime:	100 minutes	105 minutes	110 minutes

Directions:
- Drive west from Portland on US 26 to the junction with OR 6 west of Hillsboro.
- Turn left at the junction onto OR 6 towards Tillamook.
- Drive 51 miles on OR 6 through the Coast Range to Tillamook.
- At a junction with US 101 in downtown Tillamook, continue straight.
- After just 0.4 mile, the street curves left and reaches a junction with 3rd Street. Turn right here to begin driving the Three Capes Loop.
- Drive 4.7 miles to a junction at a sign for Cape Lookout State Park. Keep right here.
- Continue 4 more miles to a junction signed for Oceanside Beach.
- Turn left here and drive 0.2 mile to a lot at Oceanside Beach.
- For Short Beach, continue on the main road past Oceanside for 1.2 miles to the Short Beach Trailhead on the left side of the road. There is minimal parking- do not park where you see a No Parking sign!
- To drive to Cape Meares from Short Beach, continue north 1.3 miles to a junction at a pass- as of 2017 the road is barricaded here. Turn left and drive 0.7 miles to the end of the spur road at a large lot for Cape Meares.

Why February: Three of the best destinations on the entire Oregon Coast are located close together on the rugged coastline southwest of Tillamook. Oceanside Beach, Short Beach and Cape Meares offer a total of 3.4 miles of beach and trail- and yet there's enough intrigue and scenic beauty here to keep you occupied for days: there's a tunnel to a seemingly secret beach, a wooden staircase to a beach full of seastacks and waterfalls, and one of Oregon's great lighthouses. Plan on a full day, bring a raincoat and pack some soup or some coffee to make the most of a fantastic exploration on the Tillamook coast. Check your tide tables first- both beach hikes are only good at lower tide, as the beaches are mostly impassible at high tide.

Oceanside Beach: Start by hiking down to the beach. Locate the tunnel here on the rocky headland on the north side of the beach. The tunnel is a bit sketchy, but offers passage to the beach on the other side of the headland. Once you are through the tunnel, you will walk north on the beach. This beach is narrow and is better navigated at low tide. You can continue almost half a mile to Agate Beach, where you may see rockhounds at low tide. At higher tides you'll be greeted by rough waves as soon as you exit the tunnel, an intimidating and even frightening sight. Return the way you come.

Short Beach: A local built the elaborate staircase down to the beach, a feature that is in itself reason to come here. But theres so much more- sea stacks,waterfalls and views up to Cape Meares. From the trailhead, locate the trail and walk down the meticulously constructed staircase towards the beach. A local named Roy Wilson built this staircase on his own, where previously there was a steep and dangerously slick footpath. Once you reach the beach, you'll be near its south end. Turn right to walk up the beach. Just as with Oceanside Beach, this is a much easier proposition when the tide is low. At low tides it is easy to pass between the rocks of the beach and the large sea stack; at higher tides you'll have to walk up on the rocks above high-tide line, which is much less easy. Seabirds are everywhere. Keep walking up the beach, passing Larsen Creek's waterfall, until you're forced to turn around. At low tide you can walk all the way to the base of Cape Meares, but as with all other beach hikes: make sure you know the tide table for this area, and understand how much time you have to spend at the beach. Stay away from the incoming tide, whose waves can surprise unsuspecting hikers. Return the way you came.

Cape Meares: The rugged cliffs of Cape Meares are far more popular than Oceanside and Short Beach, and you should expect to encounter many more people out here. From the parking lot, follow the paved trail downhill and to the right towards Cape Meares' lighthouse. Reach the lighthouse after about 0.3 mile. The lighthouse has a unique style: it is smaller and shorter than most other lighthouses along the Oregon Coast. The lighthouse features a distinctive Fresnel lens manufactured in Paris in the late 1880s. Tours of the lighthouse are available during the summer months, but usually not in February.

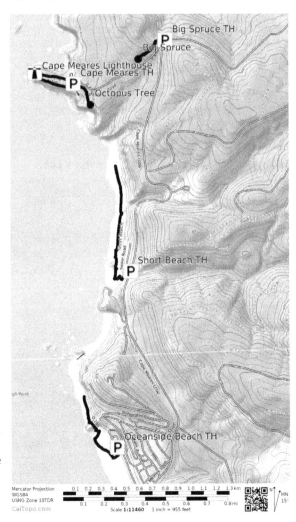

From the lighthouse, follow either path back to the parking lot and locate the Octopus Tree path behind the bathrooms. Continue to this enormous tree. There are views down to Short Beach as well. Return the way you came. Before you leave the area, be sure to check out the Big Spruce Trail that departs from the barricade at the turnoff for Cape Meares. This short trail leads to an enormous coastal Sitka Spruce located here. It's worth the 10 minute walk.

12. Soapstone Lake

Distance: 2.7 miles out and back
Elevation Gain: 400 feet
Trailhead elevation: 459 feet
Trail high point: 588 feet
Other seasons: all year
Map: none needed
Pass: None needed
Drivetime from Portland: 85 minutes

Directions:
- Follow US 26 west of Portland for approximately 65 miles to a junction with OR 53.
- Turn left and drive this serpentine highway 4.6 miles to a junction at a sign for the Soapstone Lake Trailhead.
- Turn left here and drive 0.3 mile to the trailhead on the left side of the road.

Why February: Lovely in any season, this little-known path passes through verdant woods and an intriguing meadow en route to a secluded lake in the western foothills of the Coast Range. This is perfect hike for a rainy day in February when you just want a short hike in the woods, or better yet, as a leg stretcher on the way to Nehalem Bay (see the next two pages). As with all trails in the Coast Range, expect mud in February.

Hike: From the trailhead, follow the wide trail slightly downhill through lush, verdant woods. The trail passes through what seems to almost be a tunnel of ferns and trees until it opens up at the edge of a meadow. The meadow is a fascinating place- here a man from Finland named Erik Lindgren built a house by Soapstone Creek in 1922. No trace remains of the house today, but the meadow is a lovely and peaceful place. Just beyond

Walking up the stairs just below Soapstone Lake.

the meadow, the trail crosses Soapstone Creek on a new bridge at about 2/3 of a mile from the trailhead. The trail then climbs back out of Soapstone Creek's valley on a set of stairs made from railroad ties (see the photo on the opposite page). This stretch of trail is especially lovely, as it passes a few larger cedars and Douglas-firs. Note the enormous stump on the right side of the trail here, a relic of an earlier, far more impressive forest. Everything is green and lush here, just as it should be. At just under a mile the trail reaches a junction just above Soapstone Lake. Take a right turn and loop around the lake in a counterclockwise direction. Pass an enormous spruce and then traverse a boardwalk at the far end of the lake. The trail skirts the lakeshore on the other side, before reaching the lake's outlet, where you can see the beaver dams that created the lake. When you reach the junction again, turn right to hike back to the trailhead.

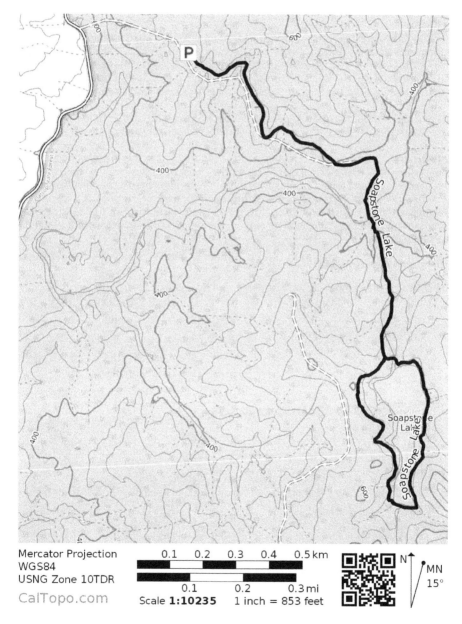

Mercator Projection
WGS84
USNG Zone 10TDR

CalTopo.com

0.1   0.2   0.3   0.4   0.5 km

0.1   0.2   0.3 mi
Scale **1:10235**   1 inch = 853 feet

N

MN
15°

13. Nehalem Spit

Distance: 4.9 mile loop
Elevation Gain: 100 feet
Trailhead elevation: 20 feet
Trail high point: 47 feet
Other seasons: all year
Map: None needed.
Pass: State Park Day-use fee ($5) or year pass
Drivetime from Portland: 110 minutes

Directions:
- Follow US 26 west of Portland for approximately 65 miles to a junction with OR 53.
- Turn left and drive 18.6 curvy miles to a junction with US 101.
- Drive north on US 101 for 2.5 miles to a junction at a sign for Nehalem Bay State Park.
- Turn left and follow this road into the park. Keep straight at all junctions until you reach road's end at the day use area, 2.9 miles from the junction on US 101. This is the trailhead.
- If you need to purchase a day pass, drive back to the fee booth on the right side of the road (this will be on the left side if you're driving back) and purchase a pass here.

Why February: There is a time and a place for everything, and this includes hikes along the beach in winter. There are better hikes on the Coast than this mellow ramble along Nehalem Bay's spit and jetty, but on sunny days in February when it feels like spring or even summer could be just around the corner, this loop will hit the spot. If 5 miles of exceedingly easy hiking just isn't enough, consider adding on the hike to Soapstone Lake featured on the previous 2 pages. The two combined make for an excellent and full day of late winter hiking.

Equestrians on Nehalem Spit.

Hike: The hike begins at the day use area. While this is a loop and you can hike it in either direction, you came here to go to the beach- so take the trail departing from near the bathroom and follow it through the sand dunes to the beach. This will undoubtedly be the most difficult part of your hike. Once at the beach, turn left and proceed to walk down the beach. Before you get too far down the beach, remember to look back to the north- you'll have an excellent view of Neahkahnie Mountain (Hike 41), as well as the jumbled, rocky peaks a friend of mine has dubbed the "Clatsop Alps". From here it's an easy walk down the beach, just out of reach of the waves crashing ashore. As with all beach hikes, keep a very close eye on the waves and tide- straying too close to the incoming tide can get you wet, or worse yet, sucked out to sea by a sneaker wave. Be sure to check the tide tables for this area before visiting- while you can complete the hike at higher tides, it is certainly easier at low tide.

Reach the end of the beach at Nehalem Bay's north jetty at 2.4 miles from the trailhead. Around the jetty is an enormous collection of driftwood, blown here during winter's many storms. This spot, near high tide line, makes a good place to stop for a break. The collection of driftwood offers hikers with many convenient logs on which to sit. Though the surf is usually quite choppy here, you may see fishing boats braving the rough waters. If you've come here on a rainy, blustery February day, this spot is exposed and bleak, and it will be difficult to stay for more than a few minutes. On sunny days, it may be difficult to leave. But leave you must!

From here you have two very different options for completing your loop. The easiest option is to find the post just north of the jetty that marks the end of the jeep road cutting through the middle of the spit. This is the recommended option, just for the ease of travel. Locate the post, and follow this old jeep road through the spit for 2.5 miles back to the trailhead. A harder option is to follow the bay side of the beach back to the day use area- but this is really only possible at low tide, and offers little of interest other than slightly different views.

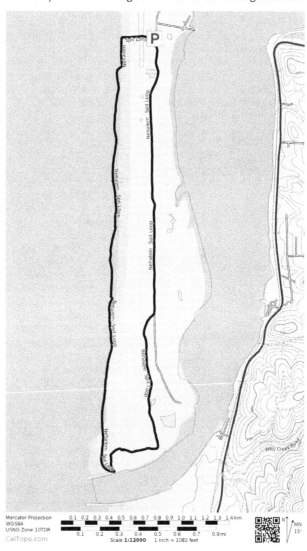

14. Council Crest

Distance via Marquam Shelter TH: 3.6 miles out and back
Elevation Gain: 800 feet
Trailhead Elevation: 279 feet
Trail High Point: 1,075 feet
Other seasons: all year
Map: Marquam Nature Park Trail Map (Friends of Marquam Nature Park)
Pass: none needed
Drivetime from Portland: 10 minutes

Directions:
- Drive out of downtown Portland to the junction of SW Broadway and SW 6th Avenue, just south of Interstate 405.
- Veer right on SW 6th Avenue and follow it for several blocks south until it becomes SW Terwilliger Blvd.
- After just 0.3 mile, continue right onto SW Sam Jackson Park Road.
- Drive 0.2 mile to the trailhead on your right. There is a 2-hour time limit in this small lot, so you'll either need to hike quickly or just take your chances.
- This trailhead is easily accessible by public transportation. From downtown, take Bus #8 (Jackson Park/NE 15th to Marquam Hill) south to the intersection of SW Terwilliger Blvd. and SW Sam Jackson Park Road (stop ID 5804). Get off the bus here, opposite the gas station, and carefully walk along the shoulder of SW Sam Jackson Park Road 0.2 mile to the trailhead on the right.

Why February: This easy hike up to Council Crest, the highest point in the hills of southwest Portland, is always handy for a nice bit of exercise. Just ten minutes by car or public transportation from downtown Portland, it is a welcome refuge from city life that amazingly, rarely feels crowded. Consider coming here on a weekday for easy access and quiet hiking. From the summit, you can see from Mount Rainier to Mount Hood as well as much of the city of Portland. Before you start the hike, download the map of Marquam Nature Park's trails – this will help you navigate the trails and streets you will meet on your hike.

Hike: Begin at the Marquam Shelter. Look for a paved trail heading uphill, signed for Council Crest. Ignore junctions on your left with the Shelter Trail (which heads south towards Terwilliger Blvd.) and on your right with the Sunnyside Trail (a possible loop option on your way down) over the first few minutes of your hike and commence hiking uphill through a shaded canyon on what will become the Marquam Trail. Follow signs for Council Crest on your way up. The trail climbs at a steady grade through a dark, forested canyon, passing the occasional house just outside park property. At 0.7 mile, reach a reunion with the Sunnyside Trail on your right. Keep left (uphill) and reach a crossing of SW Sherwood Drive at 0.8 mile. Cross the street and continue uphill on the Marquam Trail. The trail continues its ascent of Council Crest, passing a few large trees along the way, until you reach a crossing of SW Fairmount Blvd. at 1.3 miles. Cross the street and continue following the Marquam Trail uphill to a crossing of SW Greenway Avenue, which you cross and continue uphill. The trail seems to end

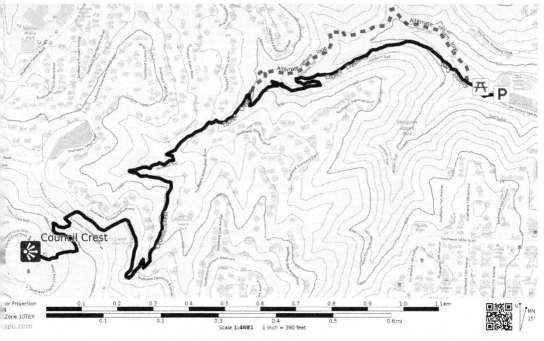

Scale 1:4681   1 inch = 390 feet

at a grassy field on the south side of Council Crest's open summit prairie. Veer right and continue to the open summit of Council Crest at 1.8 miles, where you will find benches and a round viewing area with signs pointing to each of the volcanic peaks on the horizon. Mount Hood is closest, looming to the southeast over metropolitan Portland.

The highest point in southwest Portland (it is not the highest point in the city; there are in fact higher points in Forest Park), Council Crest has a long and interesting history. A streetcar line to the summit was constructed in 1906, followed by an amusement park on the summit that opened in 1907. The amusement park only lasted until 1929, while the streetcar operated until 1949. Today, the summit features only a water tower and large radio tower, but the view is intact. Plan your hike for a sunny day to best experience the views here.

Return the way you came. On your way down you can make a short loop by turning left on the Sunnyside Trail just after you cross SW Sherwood Drive; this lovely trail follows the north side of Marquam Shelter's canyon, depositing you at the shelter right at the trailhead.

If you have the time and energy and are willing to spend the time establishing either a car or bus shuttle, you can continue north from the summit of Council Crest towards Washington Park, Pittock Mansion and Lower Macleay Park. This one-way traverse of three of Portland's best parks is one of my favorite winter hikes but is best attempted on a weekday when bus service is more frequent. If you'd like to give this traverse a shot, consult Trimet's website (www.trimet.org) and see Hikes 91 (Hoyt Arboretum) and 32 (Lower Macleay Park) for more information about the trails further north from Council Crest.

15. Oaks Bottom Park

Distance: 2.8 mile loop
Elevation Gain: 100 feet
Trailhead elevation: 96 feet
Trail high point: 96 feet
Other seasons: all year
Map: None needed
Pass: none needed
Drivetime from Portland: 10 minutes

Directions:
- In Portland, drive to the corner of SE Milwaukie Avenue and SE Powell Boulevard, just across the Ross Island Bridge.
- Drive south on SE Milwaukie Avenue 1.1 miles to the Oaks Bottom Parking Lot on the right side of the street.
- You can also get here by taking the #19 bus. Get off at the corner of SE Milwaukie and SE Mitchell St (Stop ID 3935).

Why February: Portland has some of the best parks of any city in the country, but few of them are like Oaks Bottom. Here you can walk through a park that is a veritable wildlife sanctuary along the Willamette River, passing views of the city and the river. This hike is great when you need a couple of hours away from the hustle and bustle of city life, on sunny days and rainy days alike.

Hike: Begin at the small trailhead and walk downhill on the paved access trail until you reach a junction at the bottom of the bluff. This is the beginning of the loop through Oaks Bottom. Here you should keep left on the Bluff Trail (right is your return route). The Bluff

The Willamette River and the south end of Ross Island from a trail at Oaks Bottom.

Trail skirts under SE Milwaukie Avenue's aforementioned bluff, following the wetlands to your right via a long series of boardwalks. The trail passes under a large building- a mortuary in fact- which features a large and very cool mural that does not fully reveal itself until you are far enough away to see it in its entirety (the mural is visible from the far side of Oaks Bottom Lake later in the hike, not to mention from I-5 on the opposite side of the river). Soon the Bluff Trail curves to the left, passing around Oaks Bottom Lake. Keep your eyes peeled here, as herons are frequently seen hanging out on and around the lake in the winter months. When you reach the far end of the lake, there is an unsigned junction. The more obvious trail continues straight towards the Sellwood neighborhood, but your should turn right to continue the loop.

This short trail cuts across the meadow south of Oaks Bottom Lake, passing a junction and quickly arriving at an underpass below a set of train tracks. Just beyond the underpass, reach a junction with the paved Springwater Corridor Bike Path (this is another way to visit Oaks Bottom, but bikes are not permitted on many of the trails here), opposite Oaks Park. If you've got the time, this small amusement park is a fun side trip, but who goes to amusement parks in Feb-

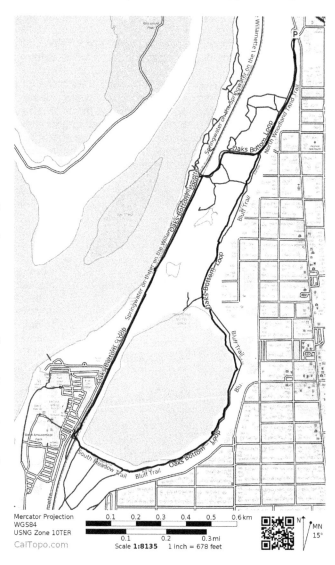

ruary? Instead turn right and walk along the paved Springwater Corridor as it follows Oaks Bottom Lake for 0.7 mile. While on the Springwater, make sure to keep your eyes out for cyclists behind you, who zoom down this trail with great frequency. Views open up across Oaks Bottom Lake to the great mortuary mural under which you passed earlier. When visiting here my attention is always drawn to the various reds, yellows and greens of the trees and plants here in the winter- in a way, this winter foliage is as lovely as the fall foliage in many other places. At 2.2 miles, reach another underpass, this time leading back into Oaks Bottom Park. Before you turn right to hike back to the trailhead, turn left and walk a short trail out to a viewpoint of the Willamette River and Ross Island. Then return to the last junction and walk under the underpass. This path leads you 0.2 mile to the first junction of your hike. Turn left here and hike 0.3 of gradual uphill to the trailhead.

Mercator Projection
WGS84
USNG Zone 10TER
CalTopo.com

0.1   0.2   0.3   0.4   0.5   0.6 km
0.1   0.2   0.3 mi
Scale **1:8135**   1 inch = 678 feet

MN
15°

16. Eagle-Fern Park

Distance: 1.7 mile loop
Elevation Gain: 400 feet
Trailhead elevation: 525 feet
Trail high point: 818 feet
Other seasons: all year
Map: Pick up a map at the park entrance or download a trail map online
Pass: Pay $5 at the park entrance booth
Drivetime from Portland: 50 minutes

Directions:
- Starting at Interstate 205, exit 13, drive 14.3 miles towards Estacada on OR 224.
- Approximately 1 mile past the junction with OR 211, turn left at a sign for Eagle Fern Park onto Wildcat Mountain Dr.
- Keep straight at a junction in just 0.2 mile. Continue another 1.8 miles to a junction with SE Eagle-Fern Road.
- Turn right and drive 2.3 miles to Eagle-Fern Park on your right.
- Turn right into the park and pay the $5 park access fee as soon as you park.

Why February: By February, winter doldrums have set in for many hikers. It's sometimes hard to get out of bed and get out on the trail when it seems like it's been raining for three straight months. I know, I've been there pretty much every winter of my life in the Pacific Northwest. Sometimes you just need to get outside, no matter the weather. This easy and wildly scenic loop in Eagle Fern Park not far from Estacada will ease what ails you. It's easy enough to complete in a couple hours, but beautiful enough to satiate you until the next time you get outside. Expect muddy trails and the occasional downed tree in winter, but also a lot more solitude than you'll find here on summer weekends.

Hike: From the parking lot, locate the signboard showing the trail network in the park. As of early 2017, this signboard did not accurately depict the trail network- so look for a paper map available in the park (or download it online ahead of time) to help you navigate the trails here. Follow the trail towards Eagle Creek (not the same one in the Gorge) and cross it on a huge and very cool suspension bridge. For much of winter the creek will be running very high, appearing more like a river than many rivers in western Oregon. On the other side of the bridge, the trail enters a cathedral forest of huge cedars and Douglas firs. This is a truly impressive place - in my opinion, this is the finest grove of ancient forest in the entire Willamette Valley. The wide gravel trail, intended to be all-access, passes marked posts meant to educate

The suspension bridge at Eagle-Fern Park.

younger hikers (see the trail map available in the park). After a little under 0.4 mile, reach a junction with the longer loop trail. Turn right here.

The longer loop trail is not maintained to the same standard as the all-access trail, and you should expect some mud and the occasional downed tree in the winter. The trail is indeed maintained all year, but as with anywhere during the winter months, expect the unexpected. The trail climbs steadily uphill away from Eagle Creek into a classic cathedral forest on the ridge above. You will have occasional glimpses back down to the river but for the most part the trail remains deep in the forest. Along the way you will also pass some truly enormous trees, some of them more than six feet thick. At about a mile the trail begins to switchback downhill to return to creek level. This part of the trail can be a little muddy in February. When you reach the bottom of the canyon, the trail does a sort of fake-out, passing very close to Eagle Creek before climbing a bit to bypass a bluff above the creek. A short side trail leads to the edge of the bluff, which offers excellent views of Eagle Creek's wide canyon. Then switchback down to a reunion with the all-access trail at 1.5 miles. Turn right and quickly reach the suspension bridge over Eagle Creek. Cross the bridge and walk back to your car in the parking lot.

Hikers who want a little more time on the trail can follow, Loop D, a more obscure loop trail on the opposite side of Eagle Fern Park. To locate the trail, drive out of the park entrance and turn left. After just a few hundred feet, turn right on Southeast Kitzmiller Road. Look for a trail sign in just 0.1 mile. There is room to park about three cars on the left side of the road. The Loop D Trail climbs through another impressive grove of ancient forest, but is almost entirely within view of Kitzmiller Road. Unfortunately, this trail doesn't really go anywhere. Hopefully in the future the park will add more miles to the trail system here, but for the time being this, along with the loop described above, is all there is.

17. Henline Falls

Distance: 1.8 miles out and back
Elevation Gain: 200 feet
Trailhead Elevation: 1,590 feet
Trail high point: 1,790 feet
Other seasons: all year
Map: None needed
Pass: None needed.
Drivetime from Portland: 100 minutes

Directions:
*   From Portland, drive south approximately 47 miles to Salem.
*   Once you reach Salem, leave the freeway at Exit 253, signed for OR 22.
*   Drive OR 22 east for 23 miles to the second of two flashing lights in the small town of Mehama.
*   Opposite the North Fork Crossing restaurant, turn left at a sign for the Little North Fork Santiam River.
*   Follow this winding road upstream for 15 miles of pavement.
*   At the National Forest boundary the road changes to gravel, becomes FR 2209 and continues 1.3 miles to a junction with FR 2207.
*   For Henline Falls, continue straight 100 yards to the parking area on the left side of the road.

Why February: Snow blankets the Cascade foothills in most years, leaving most hikes impossible to reach, let alone hike. Even Opal Creek, tucked away in a lowland valley, is often snowed in for long stretches of the winter. Luckily enough, Henline Falls is a nearby alternative to Opal Creek that offers similar thrills in a much smaller package. There's no old-growth here but the falls is among the most impressive and photogenic in the foothills of the Cascades. While you're in the area, take the time to visit nearby Three Pools, one of the most beautiful spots in the Opal Creek region. If you've got even more time, consider hiking up the nearby Cedar Creek Road (see the following two pages).

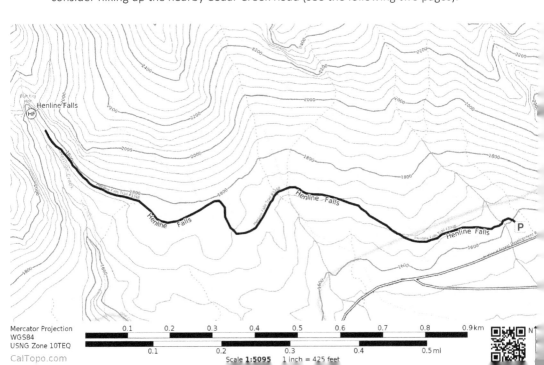

Mercator Projection
WGS84
USNG Zone 10TEQ
CalTopo.com
Scale **1:5095**   1 inch = 425 feet

Henline Falls

Hike: From the trailhead, the trail follows an old roadbed 0.5 mile to a trail junction with the obscure and rough Ogle Mountain Trail on your right. While you could hike this rough and obscure trail steeply uphill into Henline Creek's dark and narrow canyon, the trail does not go anywhere interesting and will likely be snowed in not far from the junction. So instead keep left to continue hiking towards Henline Falls. From here the trail passes through a forest of tall, thin trees that burned in a 2015 fire before depositing hikers at the base of Henline Falls at just under 1 mile from the trailhead. Henline Falls plunges 126 roaring feet into a narrow cleft of rock. In winter it is difficult to get close to the falls without getting soaked by the spray. Remnants of the mine that was located here are everywhere, and it is fun to investigate these ruins; just be careful! You might also notice the abandoned mine shaft in the rocks to the right of the falls. Once upon a time you could hike into the shaft for a ways but it is now boarded up- a reminder that it is too dangerous to enter. Though less than 2 miles round trip, you could easily spend two hours here – between the photographic opportunities, the mine shaft and mining relics, there is a great deal to see. When you are done, return the way you came.

So you drove all this way to go on a 2 mile hike; thankfully there are other things you can do here to fill out your day. Start with Three Pools, an impossibly beautiful narrows on the Little North Santiam River. To find Three Pools, drive back 100 yards to the junction of FR 2209 and 2207. At a signboard, turn left and drive downhill 1 mile to the well-marked day use area. Turn right into an enormous parking lot (NW Forest Pass required) and find a place to park. From the parking lot, walk the short trail down to a beach where the Little North Santiam River flows through a series of rock pinnacles and deep, emerald-green pools. As you may have guessed by the size of the parking lot, this area is extremely popular on hot summer weekends. In the winter, however, it is virtually deserted and provides the easy access to an incredibly beautiful stretch of the Little North Fork. On cloudy and rainy days the river seems to glow green. You have to see this place for yourself. There is no hiking here, but you can explore upstream and downstream on this side of the river a few hundred yards for additional photographic vantage points.

Bonus Hike: Cedar Creek Road

Distance: 3.6 miles out and back to Sullivan Creek Falls
Elevation Gain: 400 feet
Trailhead Elevation: 1,502 feet
Trail high point: 1,931 feet
Other seasons: December- March
Map: None needed
Pass: None needed.
Drivetime from Portland: 110 minutes

Directions:
- From Portland, drive south approximately 47 miles to Salem.
- Once you reach Salem, leave the freeway at Exit 253, signed for OR 22.
- Drive OR 22 east for 23 miles to the second of two flashing lights in the small town of Mehama.
- Opposite the North Fork Crossing restaurant, turn left at a sign for the Little North Fork Santiam River.
- Follow this winding road upstream for 15 miles of pavement.
- At the National Forest boundary the road changes to gravel, becomes FR 2209 and continues 1.3 miles to a junction with FR 2207.
- Turn right and drive 3 miles downhill to Shady Cove Campground.
- Park on the left side of the road here, just before the bridge.

Why February: Once upon a time this entire region of the Cascades was undeveloped wilderness, and ancient forest covered every canyon. As settlers moved into the valley and Cascade foothills, roads were built into the mountains to log and mine whatever could be extracted from the mountains. Over time, only small fragments remained of the original wilderness that once covered this region. Opal Creek, east of Salem, is perhaps the most impressive fragment of wilderness remaining in this part of the Cascades. That famed canyon (described in Hike 100) was nearly logged, and required a citizen campaign spanning decades to save it from development. For a look at the flipside of this development, consider nearby Cedar Creek. Just one canyon over from Opal Creek, a road was punched into Cedar Creek and many of its side canyons were logged. In spite of this, the

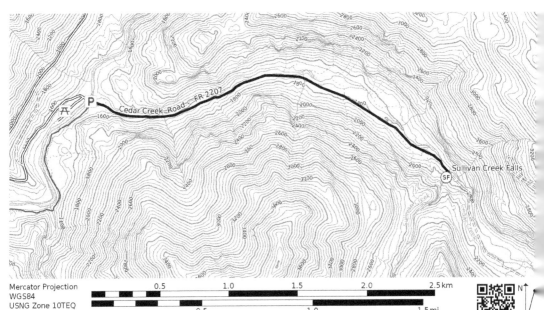

Mercator Projection
WGS84
USNG Zone 10TEQ
CalTopo.com

Scale **1:17331**   1 inch = 1444 feet

Cedar Creek canyon is extremely rugged and imposing country. It is never more so than in winter. Many will blanch at the thought of hiking on a road but consider this-the canyon's low elevation ensures it is open in the winter, and because the road is snowed in above the canyon, nobody drives it in the winter. When I was growing up in Salem, this was my favorite winter hike, and in many ways it remains so. The weather in February is less snowy than in December or January. Prepare for this like you would for a standard hike, even if the trail is in fact a forest road.

Hike: Begin at Shady Cove Campground. Cross the bridge over the Little North Santiam River and pass the upper trailhead for the Little North Santiam River Trail (see Hike 34). From here, you will follow roaring, tumbling, uncompromising Cedar Creek upstream through its narrow, rocky canyon. The road stays above the creek at first, but scramble trails lead downhill to campsites beside the creek. In February mist often hangs above the canyon walls, on days when it isn't outright pouring rain. Water seems to be falling from every canyon wall, pouring through cracks, and running across the road on its way to the creek. In spite of this, the road is well-maintained most of the time, aside from some large potholes that seem to form every winter. Of course you could just drive the road- but walking has a way of making you notice things you wouldn't from behind the wheel of your vehicle.

After about a mile, the road enters a remnant grove of ancient forest. While not as impressive as the giants found at nearby Opal Creek, there are still some large specimens of Douglas fir to be found here. The canyon narrows as you near Sullivan Creek Falls at 1.8 miles from Shady Cove. Below the road, Cedar Creek passes through an impressively rocky canyon, thundering over cascades and smashing through narrow cracks. Above you, Sullivan Creek Falls tumbles down 160 feet from the rocky canyon above the road into a sparkling green splash pool. Water is everywhere. This is the recommended turnaround spot, so return the way you came. If you want to continue beyond Sullivan Creek Falls, the canyon flattens out considerably. The road crosses a bridge over Cedar Creek a little more than a mile from Sullivan Creek Falls before switchbacking up and out of the narrow canyon. If you're continuing beyond the bridge, you'll likely need snowshoes and a lot more time, energy and patience.

18. Catherine Creek and Tracy Hill

	Catherine Creek Short Loop	Tracy Hill Loop
Distance:	2.2 mile loop	5.7 miles
Elevation Gain:	400 feet	1,300 feet
Trailhead Elevation:	269 feet	269 feet
Trail High Point:	613 feet	1,515 feet
Other Seasons:	all year except summer	all year except summer
Map:	none needed	none needed
Pass:	NW Forest Pass	NW Forest Pass
Drivetime from PDX:	75 minutes	75 minutes

Directions:
- From Portland drive east on Interstate 84 to Hood River.
- Following signs for OR 35, leave the freeway at Exit 64 and turn left at the end of the off ramp.
- Immediately arrive at the bridge over the Columbia River.
- Pay the $1 toll and cross the narrow bridge.
- On the other side of the river at a junction turn right onto WA 14.
- Drive 5.7 miles to a junction with Old Highway 8 on your left. Turn left here.
- Drive 1.4 miles to the well-signed Catherine Creek Trailhead on the left.

Why February: The Catherine Creek-Coyote Wall area east of White Salmon and Bingen is at the precipice of the Gorge's transition zone. Out here the terrain is more open, drier, and more reminiscent of the interior northwest than of the rainy, verdant terrain found closer to Portland. Due to its sunnier climate and open terrain, this is one of the first places to find wildflowers in the spring, and yes, that means as early as February. The two loops featured here offer much to the hiker, from a natural rock arch to spectacular views to a better chance of a dry day in February- and so much more. This area is beautiful in other seasons too, such as in April for fantastic spring wildflowers and in November for nice displays of fall color, but I like it best in February when it's less crowded.

Hike: Whether you're just planning on hiking the short loop or the longer loop up and over Tracy Hill, you'll start at the Catherine Creek Trailhead. The grassy field at the trailhead is a good place to see grass widows, a pink flower that is among the first to bloom after the winter. Locate the trail, actually an old road, as it angles to the right towards Catherine Creek. Follow this road down into Catherine Creek's small canyon, passing under ponderosa pines and white oak, crossing the creek on a makeshift wooden bridge. Soon you will pass under a rock arch on the ridge above. If you're hiking the short loop, you'll pass above the arch later on. For now, continue until you reach a junction at 0.9 mile. This grassy road angling away to the left is the start of the longer Tracy Hill Loop.

The Tracy Hill Loop begins by following an old, grassy road up to a powerline corridor. Follow the road as it passes under powerlines and becomes a trail. Though unmarked, the trail is obvious for its entirety. The trail curves north and proceeds to follow Catherine Creek from a bench well above the creek. Stay on the trail here, as poison oak grows profusely here. You won't see the trademark leaves of three in February, but the plant's stems are still toxic to the touch. The Tracy Hill trail continues climbing the open slopes above Catherine Creek, eventually turning abruptly away from the creek at 2.5 miles from the trailhead. You will pass over a plateau along wide Tracy Hill, reaching the trail's high point at a series of posts at about 2.75 miles from the trailhead. The views up here are fantastic, and welcome a rest stop. Ticks are active even in February, so make sure you check yourself and especially any dogs with you before continuing.

From here, the Tracy Hill trail enters an oak forest before turning south, back towards the Columbia River. The trail braids a couple times but you should keep left at each junction. You'll romp down the open slopes above Major Creek, eventually arriving at a junction with an old road at 4.4 miles. Continuing straight will take you to a different trailhead along Old Hwy 8, necessitating a road walk of almost a half-mile. Instead, turn a sharp right at this junction and follow an old road until it intersects with the main Catherine Creek Trail not far from the arch. Keep straight here and continue downhill into Catherine Creek's canyon, and beyond to the trailhead.

If you just came for the shorter hike to the arch and down, hike up Catherine Creek's canyon beyond the Tracy Hill Junction until you top under the same powerlines. Keep right here at junctions as the trail follows the ridge above the creek. Pass along the top of the arch, now cordoned off to keep people away from its fragile slopes. You'll continue downhill until you reach Old Hwy 8. Turn right here and walk the road back to the trailhead.

If you've got some extra time, the paved loop below Old Hwy 8 is a nice addition to your day. This 0.7 mile loop takes you through meadows, passing oak trees and views of the Columbia before passing above a small waterfall on Catherine Creek. The loop is a good place to see grass widows too. If you come here in May, the rocky spots on this lower loop are one of the few places in our region where you can spot bitterroot, a beautiful pink flower that blooms later than most other flowers.

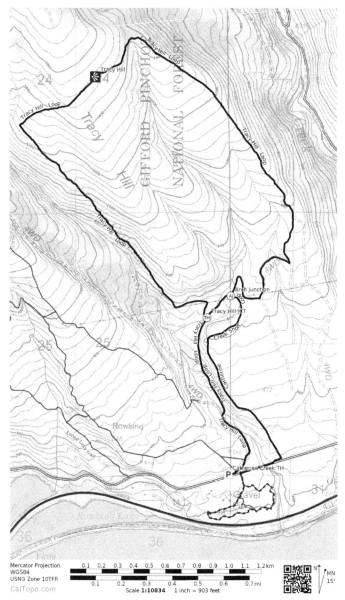

19. Coyote Wall and the Labyrinth

Distance: 5.7 mile loop
Elevation Gain: 1,400 feet
Trailhead elevation: 85 feet
Trail high point: 1,237 feet
Other seasons: all year
Map: None needed.
Pass: NW Forest Pass
Drivetime from Portland: 70 minutes

Directions:
- From Portland drive east on Interstate 84 to Hood River.
- Following signs for OR 35, leave the freeway at Exit 64 and turn left at the end of the off ramp.
- Immediately arrive at the bridge over the Columbia River.
- Pay the $1 toll and cross the narrow bridge.
- On the other side of the river at a junction turn right onto WA 14.
- Drive 4.6 miles east on this road to a junction with Courtney Road on your left.
- Turn left and immediately arrive at the trailhead. Come early as the lot fills very fast, especially on the sunny and warm days you sometimes get in February.

Why February: By the time February rolls around, most hikers are weary of winter and waiting for spring to begin. A cherished rite of passage for many hikers at this time of year is to look for the first grass widows of the year in the Gorge. This magenta flower is the first to bloom every year in the Gorge, and Coyote Wall in February is perhaps the best place to see these beautiful flowers. Even better, a visit to Coyote Wall and the Labyrinth reveals hidden waterfalls, sweeping views and occasional wildlife sightings. Come here on a sunny day to experience the true beginning of spring!

Oak trees inside the Labyrinth.

Hike: Begin at Coyote Wall's recently-constructed trailhead. Follow the old road around a lake and under Coyote Wall's cliffs. You'll meet the wide trail heading up the syncline of Coyote Wall at 0.5 mile; this is the start of your loop. Continue straight another 0.3 mile to a junction with the Labyrinth Trail, just before a road cut. Turn left here.

The Labyrinth Trail wastes no time in climbing up and out of the bottomlands. You'll climb up a few switchbacks and cut through a gap into an oak forest before reaching Labyrinth Falls at 1.2 miles from the trailhead. This falls, while no taller than 30 feet, is quite scenic as it tumbles into an oak forest tucked away in a small glen typical of this part of the Gorge. From here, you'll climb up into the Labyrinth, a fascinating area of oak forest, smallish rock pinnacles and in February, sun and shadow. Look behind you on sunny days for views out to Mount Hood. As you continue your hike, you may notice trails cutting off to your left and right here and there; the Washington Trails Association has spent years reconstructing the complex and confusing trail network here. You should stick to the main trail every time you meet a trail that does not fit the description here. After leaving the Labyrinth, the trail climbs the open slopes on the backside of Coyote Wall, gaining about 600 feet in elevation from the Labyrinth. Reach a junction with an old dirt road at trail's end at 2.7 miles. Turn left and hike this wide, muddy road as it drops into a small canyon, the same creek that tumbles into the Labyrinth. Cross the creek as best you can. Not far from the crossing, you'll meet the wide dirt trail that follows the rim of Coyote Wall's syncline. Turn left.

As with everywhere else on Coyote Wall, mountain bikers are very common on this trail. Keep your eyes and ears peeled and step out of the way as needed. Some bikers will be traveling quite fast, so some vigilance is needed. You'll follow this wide trail down the wall for 2 miles, getting thrillingly close to the edge of the wall at times. As you descend, keep an eye out for grass widows, the magenta flower that signals the arrival of spring. Depending on how cold winter was, you might see them higher up on the trail, or only close to the bottom of the wall- or in very cold winters, not at all. Most years there are at least a few flowers in bloom along the bottom of this trail by the beginning of February. At 5.2 miles from the start of the hike and 2 miles from the last junction, the Coyote Wall Trail dead ends at the old road that marked the start of your hike. Turn right and walk 0.5 mile back to the trailhead.

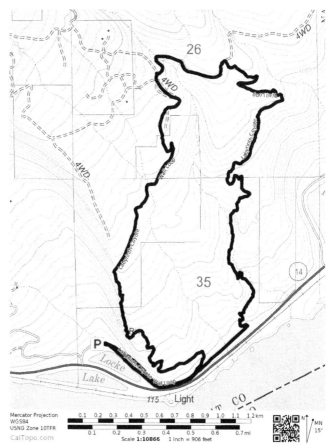

20. Klickitat Mineral Springs

Distance: 5.2 miles out and back
Elevation Gain: 100 feet
Trailhead elevation: 527 feet
Trail high point: 539 feet
Other seasons: February – May; October – November
Map: None needed
Pass: none needed
Drivetime from Portland: 110 minutes

Directions:
- Drive east from Portland on Interstate 84 to Hood River.
- At the far end of Hood River, leave the freeway at exit 64 and turn left at the bottom of the ramp, following signs for White Salmon.
- Pay the $1 toll and drive across the bridge over the Columbia to a junction with WA 14 on the far side.
- Turn right and drive WA 14 for 10.7 miles to Lyle.
- Turn left at a junction with WA 142 and drive north along the river 16.2 miles, passing through the town of Klickitat along the way, to a junction with Horseshoe Bend Road on your right.
- Cross the bridge over the river and reach a junction with Schilling Road on your right after just 0.1 mile.
- Turn right onto Schilling Road and drive 0.1 mile to a small parking area on your right. This is the trailhead.

Why February: A hike with a fascinating history, this easy ramble along the raging Klickitat River is ideal for those cold days in February when you need something to get you out of

The old bottling plant on the west bank of the Klickitat River.

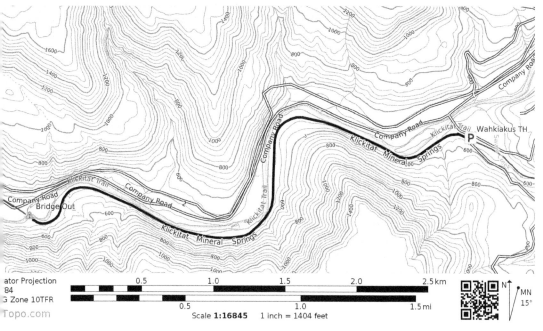

ator Projection
84
3 Zone 10TFR
Topo.com

Scale **1:16845**   1 inch = 1404 feet

the house. Although the drive is a bit long for February and the hike isn't as wild as you might prefer, there's a lot to love here. You'll pass the remains of a mineral water plant, get up close and personal with the great Klickitat and maybe even see some of the many bald eagles who spend the winter here. It makes the long drive worth your while!

Hike: The hike is about as straightforward as hikes go – you follow the Klickitat Trail along the river. This former railroad line was converted into a hiking and biking trail in the 1990s, and is exactly as you would expect: a wide and level trail that follows the river closely. The trail starts a bit away from the river but soon begins to follow the river closely. In the winter brush might overhang the trail in some spots but in general the trail is very well-maintained, as it is all along the Klickitat River.

After a mile, the way opens up at a wide flat next to the river – an excellent destination in its own right. This is the site of the former mineral springs. Area tribes had long used the warm, carbonated water that bubbled up along the Klickitat River in their sweat houses. The site was developed by a series of investors in the late 19th and early 20th Century, but the water did not keep well and it was eventually decided that the business could not turn a profit. In the 1930s, a dry ice plant was built here using the CO2 that bubbled up naturally from the ground, the source of the carbonation. While this business was profitable, the remoteness of the site eventually resulted in the plant's closure in 1968. Today water still bubbles from a pipe by the river, not far from the trail. The water has a sulfurous odor and is not too pleasant, but this small geyser-like spring will likely amuse you nevertheless. One building from this facility remains, on other side of the river, and its chimney is a sanctuary for Vaux's Swifts. Beyond the mineral springs, the trail passes a knoll with an excellent view of a wide bend in the river and enters a thicket next to the river. This section may be swampy in winter. The trail then opens up once more, but now you are directly across from the highway; expect some noise from passing cars and trucks.

At 2.6 miles, you will abruptly arrive at trail's end, at the ruins of a railroad trestle across the river. The lack of a river crossing ensures you won't find the kind of crowds here you might find along other portions of the Klickitat River Trail, but the trestle site has grown in quite a bit and is thus a rather lackluster destination on its own. If you're looking for a place to rest, consider backtracking a bit the nearest clearing to bask in the sun beside the river. After this, return the way you came.

MARCH

		Distance	EV Gain	Drive
21.	Netarts Spit	10 miles	0 feet	100 min
22.	Cape Lookout	8.6 miles	1,550 ft	105 min
23.	Drift Creek Falls	3.6 miles	500 feet	130 min
24.	Tualatin Hills Nature Park	4.4 miles	100 feet	20 min
25.	Elowah and Wahclella Falls	5.4 miles	800 feet	45 min
26.	Hamilton Mountain	7.8 miles	2,100 ft	55 min
27.	Hood River Pipeline Trail	2.8 mi	130 ft	60 min
28.	Lower Klickitat River Trail	10.4 mi	250 ft	80 min
29.	Lyle Cherry Orchard	4.8 mi	1,000 ft	85 min
30.	Cottonwood Canyon	9.8 mi	400 ft	140 min

Ahhh, March! The month of the year in which winter turns to spring, the weather is merely lousy rather than appalling. With the longer days and warmer temperatures, you can at last start to explore some of the area's summits without needing snowshoes. The warmer days and the longer days finally allow you to explore some of the area's canyons without fear of ice (most of the time). And last but not least, flower season kicks off in earnest in March, especially in the Columbia River Gorge.

Of all the months of the year, only October can rival the unpredictability of March weather. You should be prepared for almost anything. Over the years I've lived in the Portland area, I've experienced everything from ice storms and snow to sunny and 75, and almost everything imaginable in between. Always be sure to bring the Ten Essentials even if you've managed to catch one of those glorious sunny days. Make sure you have a full tank of gas when you leave civilization behind. And above all else, make sure you tell somebody else where you are going. Even on those sunny days, one mistake, one missed step or one bad break can very easily become a life-threatening situation.

Most of the hikes here are fine in any weather, but some are much nicer when the weather is nice. The hikes on the east side of the Gorge are all much better in sunny weather; given that these hikes are located in the rain shadow east of the Cascades, you are much more likely to encounter nice weather. As always at this time of the year, you should check the weather forecast for the nearest town before you leave the house. Last but not least, March also marks the beginning of tick season in the Gorge; make sure you check your clothing during and after hikes in the Gorge, particularly those in the eastern Gorge. The best strategy for dealing with ticks is vigilance.

Photo on opposite page: Wahclella Falls (Hike 25)

21. Netarts Spit

Distance: 10.0 miles out and back
Elevation Gain: zero
Trailhead elevation: 28 feet
Trail high point: 39 feet
Other seasons: all year
Map: None needed
Pass: Pay $5 to enter Cape Lookout State Park.
Drivetime from Portland: 100 minutes

Directions:
- Drive west from Portland on US 26 to the junction with OR 6 west of Hillsboro.
- Turn left at the junction onto OR 6 towards Tillamook.
- Drive 51 miles on OR 6 through the Coast Range to Tillamook.
- At a junction with US 101 in downtown Tillamook, continue straight.
- After just 0.4 mile, the street curves left and reaches a junction with 3rd Street. Turn right here to begin driving the Three Capes Loop.
- After 5 miles, ignore signs for Netarts and turn left on Whiskey Creek Road.
- Continue south another 5.2 miles to the south entrance of Cape Lookout State Park.
- Turn right into the park and find a parking spot in the lower parking lot (not the campground), which provides beach access.

Why March: There are very few secluded beaches on the northern Oregon coast; perhaps the most secluded is Netarts Spit, part of Cape Lookout State Park west of Tillamook. The hike out to the tip of the spit is excellent any time of the year but is especially recommended on a stormy day in late winter, when this lonely strip of beach can feel like the edge of the world. Plan for such a stormy day and hope to be pleasantly surprised. Just as you always should, make sure you check the weather forecast before you leave home.

Hike: Before you leave home, be sure to check the tide tables for Netarts; you may be forced to hike up and over dunes during high tides. For now, set out from the parking lot and immediately head towards the beach. Turn right to start your trek north along the beach. Windblown trees frame the dunes to your right, offering different views of the spit. It is fun to clamber up to the top of the dunes (you may be forced to do so during high tide) and explore the interior of the spit, but the way is far less easy than just walking along the beach.

As you head north, you'll have views toward Three Arch Rocks and the towns of Netarts and Oceanside. Keep your eyes on the ground too, as sand dollars, shells and agates are all commonly found along the beach. In any case, you'll find copious amounts of drift-wood here, and on windy days, this might be the only refuge available. The spit can be absolutely inhospitable during bad weather.

At a little over 5 miles, you'll reach the end of the spit at a rounded beach. Sea lions are a common sight and sound here, as is a variety of seabirds. Look for a place to rest amidst the driftwood. While it may seem like a good idea to make a loop along the backside of Netarts Spit, the way is in fact blocked by impassible mud flats. You'll need to return the way you came. On the way back, keep an eye out for waterfalls, tumbling off the cliffs of Cape Lookout. Look inland for the trailhead when you reach the end of the beach, below Cape Lookout's cliffs.

If you're still looking for more hiking, you can follow the Oregon Coast Trail a little under 2 miles to the Cape Lookout Trailhead, at which point you can continue further south towards Cape Lookout's lovely South Beach, or out to Cape Lookout itself (see the next two pages). While adding on miles is not something most hikers will want to do in a single day, this connector trail does feature views out to Netarts Spit and the forest is quite peaceful.

If you're looking for a place to stay in the area, I strongly recommend Cape Lookout State Park. Most hikers won't feel like camping in March but the yurts and cabins here are well worth the trouble it takes to book them. Plan ahead for reservations!

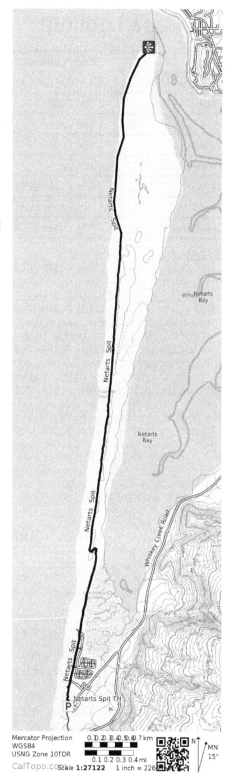

Mercator Projection
WGS84
USNG Zone 10TDR
CalTopo.com   Scale 1:27122   1 inch = 2260

22. Cape Lookout

	Cape Lookout	South Beach
Distance:	4.8 miles out and back	3.8 miles out and back
Elevation Gain:	700 feet	850 feet (on return)
Trailhead Elevation:	866 feet	866 feet
Trail High Point:	866 feet	866 feet
Other Seasons:	all year	all year
Map:	None needed	None needed
Pass:	None required	None required
Drivetime from PDX:	105 minutes	105 minutes

Directions:
- Drive west from Portland on US 26 to the junction with OR 6 west of Hillsboro.
- Turn left at the junction onto OR 6 towards Tillamook.
- Drive 51 miles on OR 6 through the Coast Range to Tillamook.
- At a junction with US 101 in downtown Tillamook, continue straight.
- After just 0.4 mile, the street curves left and reaches a junction with 3rd Street. Turn right here to begin driving the Three Capes Loop.
- After 5 miles, ignore signs for Netarts and turn left on Whiskey Creek Road.
- Continue south another 5.2 miles to the south entrance of Cape Lookout State Park.
- Ignore the turnoff into the campground and continue south another 2.7 miles to the Cape Lookout Trailhead on your right.

Why March: Cape Lookout juts 2 miles out into the Pacific Ocean, looking formidable and imposing from all sides- and yet, amazingly, there is an easy trail through the cape's old-growth forest out to a phenomenal viewpoint at the tip of the cape. It goes without saying that this is a great hike in any season, but never more in March, when it is the best place on the Oregon Coast to see migrating whales. Bring binoculars and hope for the best! Hikers with more energy should hike the beautiful trail downhill to Cape Lookout's south beach, where 2 miles of secluded beach stretch out below Cape Lookout's cliffs.

Hike: Begin by locating the signboard at the Cape Lookout Trail. Continue straight to hike to Cape Lookout. After just 0.1 mile, reach a junction with the trail to Cape Lookout's south beach. It's your choice as to which to hike first, but I'm going to assume you're hiking to the tip of Cape Lookout first. Continue west towards the edge of Cape Lookout. The occasionally muddy trail passes by some huge trees, gradually descending towards a saddle at a little over a mile. Occasional views open up to the long expanse of Netarts Spit (Hike 21) to the north. It might be hard to believe, but the cape is actually the remains of a huge lava flow that surged down the Columbia River and out to the coast some 15 million years ago. This is an interesting thing to contemplate as you continue out towards the tip of the cape. From the saddle in the middle of the cape, the trail climbs again and opens up into hanging meadows on the sunny south side of the cape. Hikers afraid of heights may have some issues here as there are a few exposed spots near the end of the trail. At 2.4 miles, the trail abruptly arrives at the tip of the cape, where a metal fence announces the end of the trail. There is a bench here that will likely be occupied, given the hike's popularity. The viewpoint here can feel kind of crowded, especially during whale-watching season. You might need to spend some time up here if you are also whale-watching, but it's worth the wait. When you're ready to turn around, return the way you came.

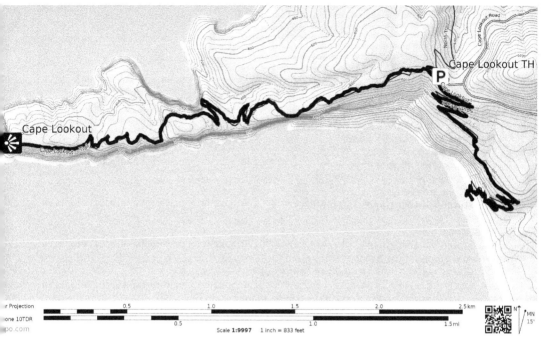

r Projection
one 10TDR
po.com

0.5   1.0   1.5   2.0   2.5 km

0.5   1.0   1.5 mi

Scale **1:9997**   1 inch = 833 feet

N
MN
15°

To hike down to south beach, return to the junction near the trailhead and head downhill. The first mile descends gradually though open woods, offering few views. As you begin to approach the beach, however, the way opens up somewhat, featuring views north to Cape Lookout's huge cliffs. The forest down here is gorgeous too, as scattered sitka spruce trees tower over electric-green sword ferns. The trail passes a bench and skirts cliffs above the beach before beginning a series of switch-backs down towards the beach. You'll pass above a Boy Scout Camp (stay on the trail) and drop a few more switchbacks before arriving at last at south beach. The beach is a quiet oasis below Cape Lookout's cliffs, and because you need to lose 850 feet to get here, not many make the trip down. There will be people, of course- but compared to the Cape Lookout Trail, you should be able to find a secluded spot to hang out. On sunny days this is a wonderful place to bring out the beach blanket and have a picnic. Walking down the beach for a couple miles is also recommended. As lovely as it is, camping is strictly prohibited as it is elsewhere on the Coast, so you'll have to pack up the beach gear and return to the trailhead before nightfall.

23. Drift Creek Falls

Distance: 3.6 miles out and back
Elevation Gain: 500 feet
Trailhead elevation: 956 feet
Trail high point: 956 feet
Other Seasons: all year
Map: None needed
Pass: None needed
Drivetime from Portland: 130 minutes

Directions:
- From Portland, drive southwest on OR 99W towards McMinnville.
- At a junction just before 99W enters McMinnville, follow signs for OR 18 and Lincoln City as OR 18 skirts around the south side of McMinnville.
- Continue on OR 18 towards Lincoln City. Stay on OR 18 as it merges with OR 22 and then splits off again to continue driving towards Lincoln City.
- Approximately 48 miles from McMinnville, turn left onto FR 17 at a sign for Drift Creek Falls.
- Drive FR 17, known as the Bear Creek Road, for 9 winding, narrow miles to the Drift Creek Falls Trailhead on the left side of the road. Watch out for blind curves on your way in and out.

Why March: The hike to Drift Creek Falls is known primarily for the huge suspension bridge over Drift Creek's canyon (see the photo on the opposite page). And what a bridge it is! But this hike has many other charms as well, from March flowers such as trillium

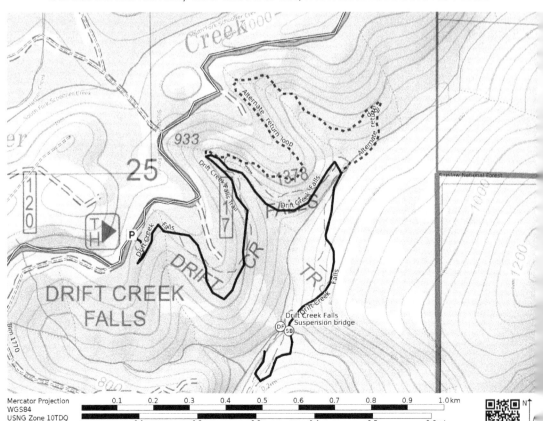

Mercator Projection
WGS84
USNG Zone 10TDQ
CalTopo.com

Scale 1:5949   1 inch = 496 feet

Crossing the suspension bridge just above Drift Creek Falls.

and yellow violet, to huge old-growth forest in the canyon, to the waterfall itself. Put it all together and you've got an ideal March hike that works on rainy days when you want a short hike just to get out and go somewhere, or on sunny days when you're on your way to the beach and want to stretch your legs first.

Hike: From the trailhead, you'll immediately begin hiking downhill on a wide trail that meanders through second-growth forest above Drift Creek. As you descend into the canyon, you will eventually enter a pocket old-growth forest, so rare in this part of the Coast Range. Along the way you will pass a pair of trail junctions; keep right both times to continue your trek towards the falls. The trail crosses a side creek and follows the canyon through dense forest until you emerge quickly at the largest, longest and most impressive suspension bridge you'll ever see on a trail in Oregon. Many people come just to see the bridge, which is 240 feet long and which teeters some 100 feet over Drift Creek, just next to the falls. The view is impressive! Be polite and don't try to sway the bridge as some folks do; many will not appreciate this. The falls is almost an afterthought; to see it better, continue downhill past the bridge on a steep trail to the canyon bottom, where you will have a better view of this 66-foot plunge.

Plan on some time at the base of the falls. This is the end of your hike, and this is a neat spot. It is quite fun to look up at the people on the bridge. You will notice a lot of boulders and debris here in the canyon bottom; these are remnants of a landslide in August 2010 that dramatically altered the appearance of the falls and the look of the canyon. Many insist it was prettier before the slide, but it's still beautiful. The trail ends at the canyon bottom next to the falls, so you will need to return the way you came.

On the way back, you can turn right at the first junction and make a short loop using an older alignment of the Drift Creek Falls Trail. This adds a short distance to your hike, but this older trail is pretty and less-used than the main trail. This short detour brings you back to a junction near the first long switchback on the hike, at which point you continue a little over 0.6 mile to the trailhead and your vehicle.

24. Tualatin Hills Nature Park

Distance: 4.4 mile loop
Elevation Gain: 100 feet
Trailhead elevation: 201 feet
Trail high point: 201 feet
Other seasons: all year
Map: None needed (follow maps in the park)
Pass: None needed
Drivetime from Portland: 30 minutes

Directions:
- Drive west from downtown on US 26.
- Continue past the OR 217 to Exit 67, signed for NW Murray Blvd. Exit here.
- At the bottom of the exit ramp turn left onto NW Murray Blvd and drive south 2.1 miles to a junction with NW Millikan Way. Turn right.
- Drive NW Millikan Way 0.6 miles to Tualatin Hills Nature Park. Turn right and drive into the park's visitor center parking lot, your trailhead.
- If you'd rather take public transit, instead take the MAX Blue Line west towards Beaverton. Get off at the Merlo Road / SW 158th Avenue MAX Stop. Once the train has moved on, walk across the tracks and locate a paved trail on the opposite side of the tracks heading away from SW Merlo Road. This is the beginning of your hike.

Why March: Sometimes all you have is a few hours to get outside, and you want to go for a nice hike not too far away. These are the times when it's good to find a hike in the metro area and get in as many miles as you can in the short time you have. Tualatin Hills Nature Park is a great destination for days like this. The labyrinthine trail network here passes wetlands, creeks and a varied and intriguing forest, allowing hikers a diversity of flora and fauna not found elsewhere in the metro area. Later in March this is one of the best places in the area to observe early-blooming flowers such as trillium and yellow violet, and you are certain to see more wildlife than you would expect for a location this urban. Best of all, the trailhead is along the MAX, allowing hikers without a vehicle easy access to one of the best hikes in the metro area.

Hike: Before we continue, a note about the trails here: as this is a public park with a comprehensive trail network, where you go is entirely up to you. It is impossible to get lost here. That being said, following the directions here will give you the longest and most diverse hike possible. Departing from the visitor center, walk west on the Vine Maple Trail to a junction with the Oak Trail. Keep straight here and soon arrive at a junction with the Big Fir Trail on your left and the start of your loop.

Turn left and walk for a couple minutes to a junction with the Ponderosa Loop Trail, again on your left. Turn left here. Soon you will enter a forest dominated by, amazingly, ponderosa pines. These trees are more commonly found on the eastern side of the Cascade Range. Park managers believe the ponderosa pines here are of a different species better adapted to the Willamette Valley's damp, cool climate. After a half-mile, the Ponderosa Loop ends at another junction with the Big Fir Trail. Turn left here, ignore a junction with the Owl Trail and soon arrive at a junction with the Trillium Trail. Turn left to hike this short side loop, which passes some impressive displays of white trilliums in late March. You will quickly arrive at a reunion with the Big Fir Trail. Turn left here and pass a junction with the Eliot Path on your right – you will use this trail to continue your loop, but ignore this junction for the time being. After just a few steps you will arrive at yet another trail junction, this time a spur on your left. Turn left and hike down to a bench beside a pond, where you are likely to see birds – possibly even a lot of birds. This is a good rest spot. Return to the Big Fir Trail. Turn left on the Big Fir Trail, cross Beaverton Creek and arrive at a junction on the other side. Turn left and hike the Ash Loop as it follows wetlands for 0.3 mile. Meet the Big Fir Trail again; take a moment to turn left to go inspect the cedars in the forest here, then return to the last junction. Turn left onto the Chickadee Trail and follow its boardwalks along the wetlands of Beaverton Creek until you meet the Big Fir Trail. Turn left here, cross Beaverton Creek again and arrive at the junction with the Eliot Path. Turn left and hike to the junction with the Vine Maple Trail. From here, the Vine Maple Trail continues west for about 0.4 mile to a junction with the Old Wagon Trail on your right. Turn right and hike this quiet trail through the woods, and then below a Trimet garage for 0.7 mile to a junction with the Oak Trail. Left leads to the SW Merlo Road MAX stop, but to continue your loop, keep right to stay on the Oak Trail. You will follow this wide trail over boardwalks, along marshes and through the woods a little over a half-mile to a major junction with the Vine Maple Trail. Turn left here and walk the short distance back to the trailhead.

If you took the MAX, you will get off at the SW Merlo Road MAX stop. To access the trails in the park, walk across the tracks from the station and locate the paved trail on the opposite side heading away from Merlo Road. Follow this paved trail a short distance to a junction on your right with the Oak Trail. Turn right here and almost immediately reach a junction with the Old Wagon Trail on your right, the beginning of your loop. Keep left to begin your loop, and follow the directions above through the park.

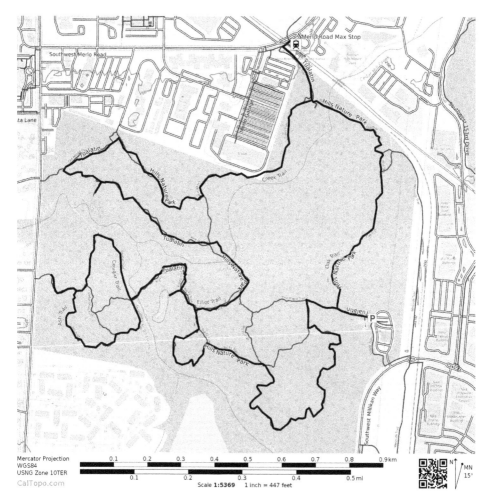

Mercator Projection
WGS84
USNG Zone 10TER
CalTopo.com

Scale 1:5369   1 inch = 447 feet

25. Elowah and Wahclella Falls

	Elowah and Upper McCord Falls	Wahclella Falls
Distance:	3 miles out and back	2.4 mile semi-loop
Elevation Gain:	600 feet	200 feet
Trailhead Elevation:	139 feet	59 feet
Trail High Point:	600 feet	300 feet
Other Seasons:	all year	all year
Map:	None needed	None needed
Pass:	None needed.	NW Forest Pass
Drivetime from PDX:	40 minutes	45 minutes

Directions:
- From Portland, drive east on Interstate 84 to exit 35, signed for Ainsworth State Park and the Historic Highway.
- Leave the freeway and arrive at a junction with NE Frontage Road.
- Turn left and drive 2.2 miles to the Elowah Falls Trailhead, just before Frontage Road merges back onto Interstate 84.
- To continue to Wahclella Falls, get back on Interstate 84 and drive 3 miles to Exit 40, signed for Bonneville Dam.
- Exit the freeway here and immediately reach a junction. Left is the Tooth Rock lot while straight leads you directly to the Wahclella Falls lot.
- Continue straight to the Wahclella Falls lot. If it is full, go back and park at Tooth Rock.

Why March: Two of the most spectacular short trails in the Columbia River Gorge are found near Bonneville Dam, just off Interstate 84. Both lead to some of the Gorge's best waterfalls, and both make for great short hikes. While these two short trails are great at any time of year, March is my favorite time to visit; the falls are still running strong, early season flowers are numerous and the weather dramatic. As the two hikes are only a few miles apart, you should combine both for a great day in the Gorge!

Note: This area is believed to have burned badly during the Eagle Creek Fire in September 2017. The extent of the damage is unknown as of press time; expect these trails to be closed until at least Spring 2018. The trail to Upper McCord Falls may be closed longer than that, but hopefully it will be reopened sooner rather than later. It's worth the wait.

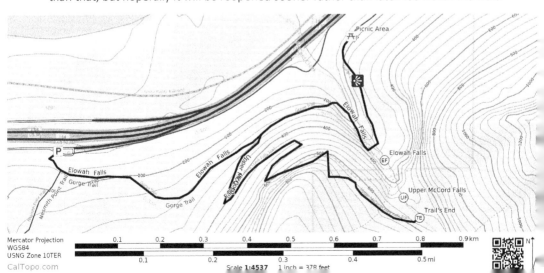

Elowah Falls Hike: I recommend beginning at Elowah Falls. Begin by hiking a short distance to a junction with the Gorge Trail. Right leads all the way up to Nesmith Point but you turn left. The trail passes through a second-growth forest to another trail junction, this time with the spur trail to Upper McCord Creek Falls. It's your choice which way to go, but I recommend continuing on towards Elowah Falls first. Reach McCord Creek's narrow canyon and switchback sharply down to a bridge below wispy Elowah Falls, a 213-foot plunge whose spray will thoroughly soak you if you get too close. Continue up the Gorge Trail to a junction just above the interstate, where a short side trail leads to an abandoned picnic area complete with a decaying picnic table. When finished, return to the junction with the Upper McCord Creek Trail and turn left. You will soon begin climbing up the

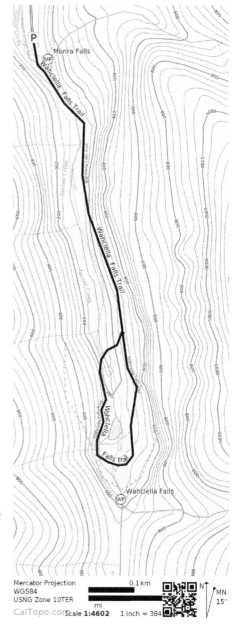

canyon wall via a series of switchbacks until you top out at a cliff edge above Elowah Falls. The trail clings to the edge of a cliff as it traverses above Elowah Falls; guardrails comfort those afraid of heights. Look down to Bonneville Dam and out to Mount Adams, rising above Table Mountain to the north. Leave the cliff face and enter the forest again, where you will soon arrive at a viewpoint above beautiful Upper McCord Falls, a twin plunge for much of the year. The trail continues around the top of the falls before it ends on the banks of McCord Creek. If you are curious, there are no more waterfalls upstream. Return the way you came.

Wahclella Falls Hike: To visit Wahclella Falls, return to Interstate 84 and drive 2.5 miles east to the trailhead near Bonneville Dam. The trail to the falls passes a small dam used by the Bonneville Fish hatchery and passes immediately next to gushing Munra Falls, which is close enough to touch! Continue upstream and climb a bit along a muddy trail to a junction and the beginning of your loop. The fastest way to the falls is left, but the most scenic route heads downhill to the right. Turn right and switchback down to a bridge over raging Tanner Creek. Cross the bridge and trade forest for a massive talus slope littered with enormous boulders, remnants of a huge landslide in 1973. Soon Wahclella Falls comes into view at the head of the canyon. Continue on the trail to another bridge, this one just below the falls. A small picnic area directly above the splash pool reveals Wahclella Falls' upper tier, tucked away in a narrow gorge visible only from this vantage point. While you can walk right up to the pool, the spray is intense and extremely cold. When you finish taking pictures and exploring, keep left to return to junction described above, and continue the way you came to the trailhead.

26. Hamilton Mountain

Distance: 7.8 miles semi-loop
Elevation Gain: 2,100 feet
Trailhead elevation: 393 feet
Trail high point: 2,412 feet
Other seasons: all year (beware of winter snow and ice)
Map: download a map of the trail system online
Pass: Washington Discovery Pass ($10 day / $30 year)
Drivetime from Portland: 50 minutes

Directions:
- From Portland, drive across the river on Interstate 205 to Vancouver.
- Immediately after you cross the river, take exit 27 signed for Camas and WA 14.
- Drive WA 14 through Camas and into the Gorge.
- Approximately 28 miles east of I-205, reach Beacon State Park.
- Turn left into Hamilton Mountain's trailhead.

Why March: Like many other hikes in the Gorge, Hamilton Mountain is accessible year-round. I love coming here in early spring, particularly on one of those sunny days where it seems like summer isn't far off. This is the best time to visit: the waterfalls are raging, the flowers are welcome after winter's long chill and the skies are crisp, offering views up and down the Gorge. This is an extremely popular hike and you should expect crowds and long lines in the parking lot. Try to visit on a weekday if you can. Later in March is better, as snow sometimes blocks the upper reaches of Hamilton Mountain early in the month.

Hike: From the traillhead, climb uphill on the wide trail through second-growth forest. The trail climbs gradually, passing occasional openings with views east to the Columbia River and the Oregon side of the Gorge. Soon you will enter Hardy Creek's narrow canyon as the trail passes by the top of Hardy Falls. A short side trail leads to a view of the top of the falls, offering limited views of the cataract. Continue on the main trail a short distance to a trail junction at a bridge over Hardy Creek near the base of Rodney Falls. Turn left on the short side trail leading up to Pool of the Winds, a viewpoint that is almost inside Rodney Falls - although the spray will likely get you very wet, this side trip is mandatory! Return to the main trail, cross the bridge over Rodney Creek and soon reach a junction at the beginning of your loop at 1.5 miles. Keep right.

The trail begins climbing steadily through the forest until it emerges below Hamilton Mountain's cliffs. Switchback uphill, passing lovely displays of early spring flowers, as you make your way up a long series of switchbacks that offer excellent views south towards the Oregon side of the Gorge, with Mount Hood peeking out behind the lip of the Gorge. The trail reaches Hamilton Mountain's false summit at 2.9 miles. Continue another 0.1 mile to a junction, where a short trail leads to the mountain's true summit. From here, follow the trail down from the summit, taking in views east to Table Mountain and snowy Mount Adams, until you reach a junction with a closed road at 3.9 miles. Turn left and follow the road downhill for 1.2 miles to a junction with your return trail beside Hardy Creek. Turn left to leave the road and follow this trail through the forest on the west side of Hamilton Mountain 1.4 miles to a reunion with the main trail just above Rodney Falls. Turn right here and hike the 1.5 miles back to the trailhead.

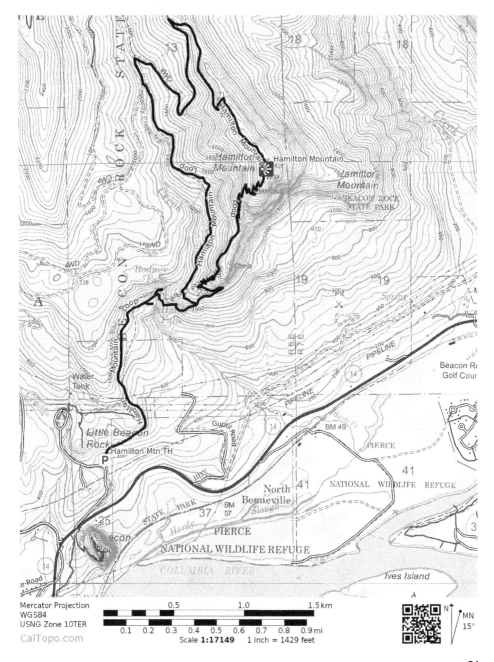

Mercator Projection
WGS84
USNG Zone 10TER
CalTopo.com

Scale **1:17149**   1 inch = 1429 feet

27. Hood River Pipeline Trail

Distance: 2.8 miles out and back
Elevation Gain: 130 feet
Trailhead Elevation: 100 feet
Trail High Point: 229 feet
Other Seasons: all year
Map: None needed
Pass: None needed
Drivetime from Portland: 60 minutes

Directions:
- From Portland, drive east on Interstate 84 to approximately 64 miles to Exit 64, signed for OR 35 and Hood River.
- Exit the freeway here and turn right to follow OR 35.
- Almost immediately reach a four-way stop, and continue straight.
- Just 0.2 mile after the four-way stop, turn right on Powerdale Road (which may be unsigned) drive downhill to a parking lot by an abandoned power station.
- The trail follows the railroad tracks that run through here.

Why March: The Pipeline Trail was for a very long time a local secret. Who wouldn't love the chance to walk on top of a giant pipe, across and then following a raging river through a scenic canyon? This is a spectacularly fun walk, a mandatory stop if you are in the Hood River area. The hike is fantastic year-round, but I like to come here in early spring, often in mid to late March. There are wildflowers here early in the season, the river is running high and, if you're lucky, you might even get to watch some folks rafting down the Hood River. This is as much fun as you can possibly have in the Gorge in a short amount of time.

Walking the Hood River Pipeline Trail.

Hike: Begin at the small park near the power station. Locate the train tracks and parallel them, following the path of the pipeline (this section was removed several years ago). The route follows the tracks for a little while , but you rarely need to walk on the tracks themselves. Not far past the trailhead you will need to follow the tracks for a short ways as the route cuts through a narrow spot in the canyon, but otherwise there is a wide trail on the riverside, well away from the tracks. The rail line is the property of the Hood River Railroad, and trains do still run on this line; please be respectful of their property rights along the line.

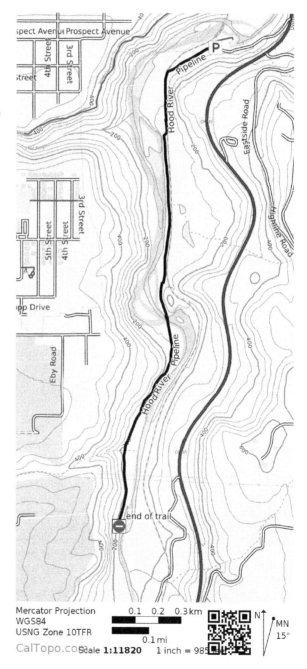

At 0.7 mile, look for a trail off to your right as the tracks bend off to the left. Follow this trail and arrive in short order at a huge metal bridge over the Hood River, which is so wide it momentarily splits into three channels. The bridge is where the pipeline begins, and is a lot of fun. Cross the bridge and on the far side, take a moment to walk down the ladder to a small beach on the river. What a cool spot!

Climb back up the ladder, and follow the pipeline trail for 0.7 mile along a narrow bench above the river. Most of the railing and fencing is still intact, although there are spots where trees have fallen and now present an obstacle. The pipeline was once used to bring water downriver to a dam – and in the process, water would spray out from various spots along the pipeline. When floods in November 2006 tore out several sections of the pipeline, it ended the flow of water. Without a dam, the pipeline's fate is cloudy. For now, keep going until you reach the end of the pipe at 1.4 miles from the trailhead. You can see here how the floodwaters tore out a large part of the bank, making it impossible to replace the pipe. This is a cool spot to hang out – you may even see people in rafts or kayaks, floating down the raging Hood River. Bring a book and some beer and hang out, if you please! Return the way you came.

Mercator Projection
WGS84
USNG Zone 10TFR

CalTopo.com Scale **1:11820**   1 inch = 985

0.1 0.2 0.3 km

0.1 mi

N

MN
15°

28. Lower Klickitat River Trail

Distance: 10.4 miles one-way with car shuttle
Elevation Gain: 250 feet elevation loss
Trailhead elevation: 389 feet
Trail high point: 389 feet
Other seasons: January- April; November- December
Map: None needed.
Pass: None needed.
Drivetime from Portland: 80 minutes (lower TH); 100 minutes (Pitt TH)

Directions to the lower TH:
* From Portland drive east on Interstate 84 to Hood River.
* Following signs for OR 35, leave the freeway at Exit 64 and turn left at the end of the off ramp.
* Immediately arrive at the bridge over the Columbia River.
* Pay the $1 toll and cross the narrow bridge.
* Once across the river, turn right at a junction with WA 14 and drive 10.7 miles to Lyle.
* The lower trailhead is at the intersection of WA 14 and WA 142 – if you cannot arrange a car shuttle, begin your hike here and hike upstream on the bike trail.
* The bike trail continues to a bridge over the Klickitat River. Cross the river and turn right on the Klickitat River Trail on the far side of the river.

Directions to the upper TH:
* From the lower TH in Lyle, turn left on WA 142 and drive 10.2 miles to the small community of Pitt, just after the highway crosses the Klickitat River.
* There is a small parking lot on the right side of the road with room for a few cars.
* The trail leaves from a gate on the other (south) side of the bridge.

Why March: Many times in the winter I drive east until I find the sunshine. Often this leads me to the Klickitat River Trail, which begins in the town of Lyle. The lower section of the trail is the most convenient, and is at its best in March; the flower display here in March, particularly later in the month, is fantastic and the slopes are green and lush. The Klickitat River canyon is also the winter home to a large number of bald eagles, and sightings are common here in March. If you can, arrange a car shuttle and hike this convenient segment of trail downriver, all one way- it's best this way.

Hike: Begin at the Pitt Trailhead. The trail parallels the river, never straying from a consistent grade. There is a reason for this – as you may have suspected, you are indeed hiking down an abandoned railroad grade. The canyon walls above you teem with life! Keep an eye out for bald eagles, who winter in the Klickitat River Canyon. March reveals countless masses of wildflowers, among them grass widows, yellow bells, pink and yellow desert parsley as well as the occasional patch of shooting stars and yellow fawn lilies. Later in the month keep an eye out for early displays of balsamroot and lupine on the slopes above the trail. As you pass through the occasional grove of ponderosa pines, you will be sucked in by this hike's charm. Along the way downstream you will pass the occasional house, and you will also see a number of houses on the opposite side of the river; if you were hoping for a wilderness experience, you chose the wrong place. Follow private property signs whenever posted. At about 5 miles downriver, you will pass a campsite on your right with a small wooden bench – this makes for an ideal lunch spot, as it is almost exactly halfway. Furthermore, if you cannot arrange a car shuttle for this hike, this is a good spot to turnaround from either trailhead.

Further downriver, the trail approaches a gorge above the river, and at 1 mile, finally crosses the Klickitat on a long bridge. This spot is absolutely spectacular – here the river squeezes through a narrow gorge while a side creek tumbles through its own canyon before emptying into the Klickitat. You have two bridges from which to choose – paralleling the trail bridge is a road bridge. Both offer outstanding views of the river. From here, follow the east bank of the river on a paved bicycle trail for a little over a mile to Lyle.

If you've got a bit of time after you finish your hike, consider walking the Klickitat-Balfour Loop on the other (west) side of the Klickitat River. This short loop drops down from Old Hwy 8 and passes the slopes above the Klickitat to a small picnic area under a grove of tall ponderosa pines. This makes a nice picnic spot. The short loop is 0.8 mile round-trip.

Mercator Projection
WGS84
USNG Zone 10TFR
CalTopo.com

Scale **1:49063**   1 inch = 4089 feet

29. Lyle Cherry Orchard

Distance: 4.8 miles out and back
Elevation Gain: 1,000 feet
Trailhead elevation: 111 feet
Trail high point: 1,117 feet
Other seasons: January – May
Map: None available
Pass: none needed – sign a waiver near the trailhead
Drivetime from Portland: 85 minutes

Directions:
* Drive east from Portland on Interstate 84 to Hood River.
* At the far end of Hood River, leave the freeway at exit 64 and turn left at the bottom of the ramp, following signs for White Salmon.
* Pay the $1 toll and drive across the bridge over the Columbia to a junction with WA 14 on the far side.
* Turn right and drive WA 14 for 10.7 miles to Lyle.
* Continue on WA 14 beyond the far end of town, through a pair of tunnels for a little over a mile to the trailhead on the left side of the road. There is room for about 20 cars.

Why March: Lyle Cherry Orchard offers one of the finest early-season wildflower hikes in the Columbia River Gorge. The hike supports one of the nicest displays of grass widows you'll find anywhere in the Gorge, and late in March you may even spot some balsamroot and other flowers more associated with April and May. Of course, you'll have to deal with poison oak and ticks, the twin menaces of the eastern side of the Gorge. It is worth it. Plan on visiting on one of those beautiful March days when spring finally makes its presence known; plan on a sunny day out here, and go elsewhere on rainy, windy days.

Hiking the trail up to Lyle Cherry Orchard.

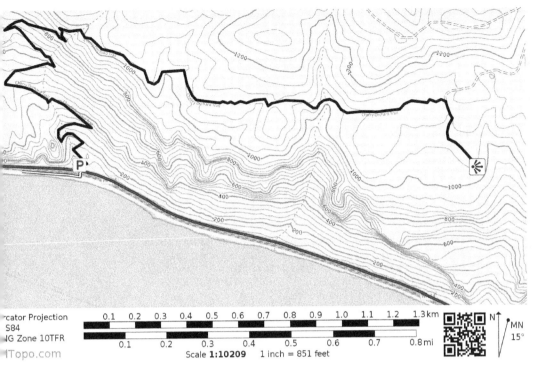

cator Projection
S84
IG Zone 10TFR

ITopo.com

Scale **1:10209**   1 inch = 851 feet

Hike: Begin by climbing through an oak forest to a signbox a short ways up the trail. Be sure to sign the waiver here, as you are hiking on private property owned by the Friends of the Columbia Gorge Land Trust. From here, you'll continue climbing uphill through oak forest until you reach a plateau at about a half-mile from the trailhead. In March you'll no doubt notice the grass widows at your feet. This magenta flower is among the first flowers to appear in the Gorge in the spring, and this hike features perhaps the finest displays of this beautiful flower. From here, you'll climb up the open slopes of the canyon wall to a second plateau at about 0.8 mile from the trailhead. You can follow user trails out to the edge of the cliffs here for more wildflowers and increasingly great views. You could spend an hour or more just wandering out here.

Continue uphill on the Lyle Cherry Orchard Trail until you crest the lip of the canyon at 1.2 miles. Once you top out, the trail enters an oak forest whose dominant understory is poison oak; while the leaves of this poisonous plant will likely not have leafed out in March, you should stick the trail just the same. You'll pass a pair of ponds with large frog populations before reaching trail's end at a dirt road 2.2 miles from the trailhead. Turn right and follow the road to a large field. Turn right on an obvious path and hike to the eastern (left) end of the field to find the cherry orchard, now just a small collection of three 100-year old cherry trees. Settlers planted the trees at the turn of the last century, and only a few survive today. The cherry trees bloom towards the end of March, and with good timing you'll be able to see them at the height of their glory. While the trees that remain are scraggly, the overall scene is beautiful and lends itself to contemplation. Bring a picnic or a book and plan on spending some time here.

On the way back be sure to turn left on the unmarked trail just 0.2 mile from Lyle Cherry Orchard. From here return the way you came.

30. Cottonwood Canyon

Distance: 9.8 miles out and back
Elevation Gain: 200 feet
Trailhead elevation: 559 feet
Trail high point: 592 feet
Other seasons: all year (avoid summer heat)
Map: Grab a map of the area at the park entrance or download it online.
Pass: None needed if you're just day hiking
Drivetime from Portland: 140 minutes

Directions:
- From Portland, drive east on Interstate 84 approximately 100 miles to Biggs Junction, where US 97 crosses both I-84 and then the Columbia River.
- At Exit 104, leave the freeway and drive south on US 97.
- Drive south on US 97 for 8.5 miles to an exit for OR 206.
- Take the exit for OR 206, and turn left at the top of the exit ramp onto OR 206, in the direction of Wasco.
- After almost 1 mile, arrive in Wasco. Follow signs for OR 206 through this small town.
- Drive 14.8 miles beyond Wasco on OR 206 to the bottom of the John Day River's deep canyon.
- Turn right at the sign for Cottonwood Canyon State Park, loop under the highway and drive to a large day-use lot on the north side of the highway.
- Do not drive into the campground unless you plan on camping there.

Why March: It's a long drive from Portland but Cottonwood Canyon is worth the time it takes to get there. This is one of Oregon's newest state parks, and the trails opened only in late 2013. As a result, nobody has heard of this place. The rewards are many: a deep, impressive desert canyon with few people and fantastic scenery; copious sunshine, early

wildflowers and if you are very lucky, a sighting of the herd of bighorn sheep that live in the canyon. March is a great time to visit, as the skies are often blue, the days not so cold and the flower show has begun in earnest. While there are several trails here, the best of them is the Pinnacles Trail, a pleasant path that follows the John Day River for nearly 5 miles. The later you come in March, the better.

Hike: Begin at the day-use lot. Look for a sign for the Sage Steppe Trail, which climbs up above the campground (climb being a relative term – there is almost no elevation gain on this hike) until it meets the Pinnacles Trail. When you reach this latter trail, continue straight on what is obviously an old jeep road. The name of the Pinnacles Trail no doubt comes from the impressive rock walls above you on the trail, which you can regard as you hike through this beautiful canyon. As you are hiking an old jeep road at the bottom of a canyon, there is almost no elevation gain. The trail is wide, allowing you to hike beside your companions. If you've ever hiked

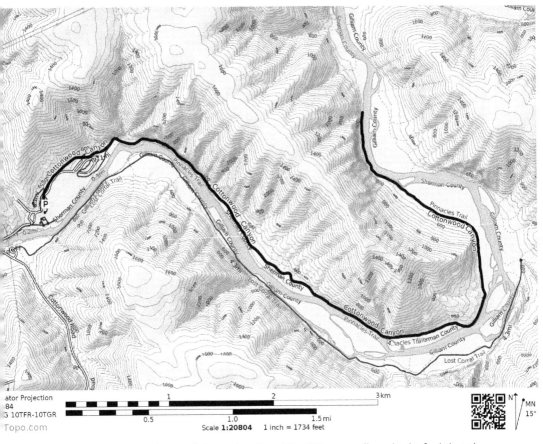

ator Projection
.84
3 10TFR-10TGR
Topo.com
Scale 1:20804   1 inch = 1734 feet

0.5   1.0   1.5 mi

1   2   3 km

N
MN
15°

the Deschutes River Trail east of The Dalles (see Hike 10), you will no doubt feel that the Cottonwood Canyon area is eerily similar.

As you make your way downstream on the Pinnacles Trail, pay attention to the little things – the miniature sand dunes on the left side of the trail at one point; the overwhelming aroma of sage, which grows everywhere here; and in the muted blues, oranges and reds of the canyon's vegetation, yet to leaf out in March. Keep your eyes peeled to the canyon walls, and if you are lucky you may even spot a few of the bighorn sheep who call this area home. What you will not see are, strangely, cottonwoods, as they were felled by the early settlers in the canyon. Hopefully they will be replanted as Cottonwood Canyon State Park grows and becomes more well-known.

The trail begins to deteriorate at about 4.5 miles, and ends at a rockpile at 4.9 miles. You have nowhere to go but back, so take the time to have a picnic in the sun before turning around. Return the way you came.

If you've got the energy to hike more, there are lots more trails- but all of them also follow the John Day River, providing you with a strikingly similar experience. The planned trail network here will expand over the next several years, so keep an eye out for future trails that climb to the top of this scenic canyon, and explore lush side canyons in this desert oasis. As of now you can explore off-trail in almost total solitude- but the terrain is rugged, and future trails will be much appreciated.

APRIL

	Hike	Distance	EV Gain	Drive
31.	Lower Macleay Park	5.2 miles	900 ft	10 min
32A.	Camassia Natural Area	1.2 miles	100 ft	30 min
32B.	Canemah Bluff Natural Area	1.7 miles	200 ft	30 min
33.	Clackamas River Trail	9.4 miles	1,500 ft	75 min
34.	Little North Santiam River Trail	9 miles	1,800 ft	110 min
35.	Eagle Creek	13 miles	1,300 ft	40 min
36.	Starvation Loop and Mitchell Point	5.1 miles	2,100 ft	60 min
37.	Mosier Plateau	2 miles	400 ft	75 min
38.	Swale Canyon	10.2 mi`	450 ft	100 min
39.	Crawford Oaks Loop	6.6 mi	1,000 ft	100 min
40.	Criterion Ranch	10.8 mi	700 ft	135 min
BONUS	Smith Rock	4 miles	800 ft	170 min

Ahhhhh, April. Spring is finally here, the flowers are blooming and the sunshine so, so, so welcoming. It is in April that the hiking gets really, really good. I mean no offense to the winter hikes of course, but in April the bar is a lot higher. This is the cream of the crop for the Portland area, and some of the best hikes in the entire region. And unlike some of the other entires in this book, these hikes are all good, rain or shine.

The old saying goes that April showers bring May flowers. But April is the best month of the year in the Portland area for wildflowers in most years, and for me, April is all about the flowers. The hikes presented here offer some of the best displays of wildflowers in the region. The woodland hikes such as Eagle Creek and the Little North Santiam River feature a mix of wildflowers and impressive displays of verdant, green forest. The hikes on the eastern side of the Gorge and in southwest Washington are some of the finest wildflower hikes anywhere in our region.

April is also the month when many fairweather hikers put on their boots for the first time all winter and this of course brings crowds. Expect many more folks on the trails than you would in the winter. Some of these hikes are among the most crowded in the region. It is still possible to find solitude in April, however; plan on early starts, or better yet, come on a weekday. If you're focused on photography, early morning and later in the afternoon are the best times to photograph wildflowers, while cloudy days are best for photographing waterfalls.

Regardless of when you visit, you should always be prepared as you would for winter hikes. While snow is unlikely at most of these destinations, thunderstorms and cold, driving rain showers are frequent occurrences in April. It could be 45 and raining, or it could be 75 and sunny- April weather is predictably unpredictable. It is best to prepare for any weather and hope for the best.

Photo on opposite page: Pup Creek Falls just above the Clackamas River (Hike 33)

31. Lower Macleay Park

Distance: 5.2 mile out and back
Elevation Gain: 900 feet
Trailhead elevation: 101 feet
Trail high point: 955 feet
Other seasons: all year
Map: Forest Park [Green Trails]
Pass: None needed
Drive time from Portland: 10 minutes

Directions:
- In Portland, drive up into northwest Portland to the corner of NW 25th & NW Thurman Street.
- Turn left on NW Thurman Street and drive two blocks to NW 27th Street. Turn right, drive one block to Upshur Street and turn left.
- The trailhead, Lower Macleay Park, is at the end of Upshur Street. There is a small parking lot there but you'll likely need to find parking in the neighborhood.
- Better yet, you can take either the #15 or the #77 bus to within a few blocks of the park. Consult http://www.trimet.org for more information.

Why April: This extremely popular hike combines two of Portland's most beautiful parks into one convenient semi-loop. Though you'll see lots of people no matter when you come, the best time to do this hike is easily April, when the forest floor comes alive with profuse displays of trillium, when Balch Creek is still running strong and when views stretch out from Pittock Mansion to five Cascade snowpeaks on clear days. What could possibly be better in such an urban setting?

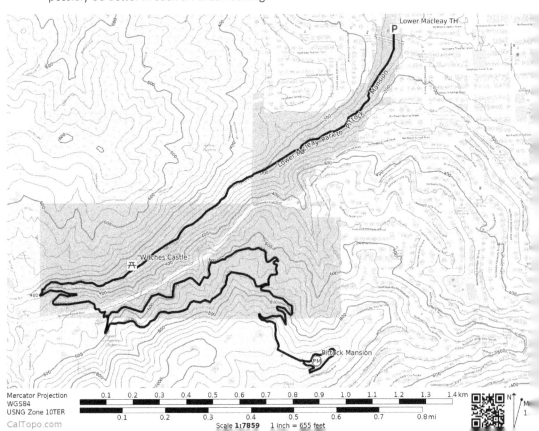

Hike: Begin by hiking the Lower Macleay Park under Thurman Street's trestle bridge and into the canyon of Balch Creek. Notice how the creek is diverted into a wooden tunnel next to the trail; it resurfaces about a mile downstream near the Willamette River. You'll cross this beautiful creek on a wide trail that transitions from pavement to gravel to dirt and parallel this surprisingly wild stream. After about a half mile, cross the creek again next to a small waterfall, complete with splash pool. This is a great place to stop, and keen eyes may spot native trout and crawfish in the pool below if it isn't too muddy. From here the trail parallels the creek on the right as it cuts through a tunnel of huge Douglas firs. Though you may be able to spot houses above you, this stretch of trail feels quite wild. Keep your dogs on leash here, as Balch Creek and its small population of trout are fragile.

After almost a mile, reach a junction with the Wildwood Trail at a huge stone shelter that was once a bathroom (despite any number of urban legends you may have heard about the place). From here, keep straight on the Wildwood Trail and continue another 0.3 mile up a beautiful stretch of Balch Creek to a bridge. Cross the bridge and hike three well-graded switchbacks up to a parking lot and trailhead on NW Cornell Road. Look both ways and cross this busy street. Almost immediately, you are greeted with a trail junction with the Upper Macleay Trail. Keep left on the Wildwood Trail and begin a gradual uphill climb through impressive forest. Ferns dominate the understory but also look for white trilliums, so numerous in April. Also keep an eye out for trail runners, who often outnumber hikers on this stretch of trail.

Pass a junction with the Cumberland Trail on your left, switchback uphill and arrive at a four-way junction with the Upper Macleay Trail at 2.1 miles. Continue straight on the Wildwood and climb another 0.4 mile of well-graded switchbacks up to Pittock Mansion's huge parking lot. Turn left and walk out to the mansion. Turn left and walk around the mansion to its front lawn, a park with a picture-perfect view of Portland, backed by Mount Hood. With keen eyes and a good knowledge of the city, you should be able to spot many of the Portland's famous landmarks. Look around and you'll also be able to see the three Washington volcanoes from various spots on the mansion's grounds. Very keen eyes can spot the top of Mount Jefferson looming over ridges to the south of Portland. On a sunny day, this is a perfect place for a picnic! Though others were able to drive here, you actually earned your lunch. You can also mark the occasion by taking a tour of the mansion, provided you have the time and the desire.

Inside the "Witches Castle".

On your return, hike down to the four-way junction with the Upper Macleay Trail and this time turn left. You will soon leave behind most of the trail runners as you descend through side canyons on this quiet path. After a little more than a half-mile you return to the junction with the Wildwood Trail just above Cornell Road. Turn left on the Wildwood, cross Cornell Road and return the way you came.

32A. Camassia Natural Area

Distance: 1.2 mile loop
Elevation Gain: 100 feet
Trailhead elevation: 270 feet
Trail high point: 370 feet
Other seasons: March- May
Map: pick up a map of the trail system at the trailhead
Pass: None needed
Drivetime from Portland: 25 minutes

Directions:
- From Portland, drive south towards West Linn on Interstate 205.
- Leave the freeway at Exit 8 and turn left on OR 43, which becomes Willamette Drive.
- Immediately get in the right lane after you turn and then veer right on Willamette Falls Drive.
- Drive 0.3 mile to a junction with Sunset Avenue. Fork to the right.
- Drive uphill on Sunset Avenue, cross over the freeway and immediately turn right onto Walnut Street.
- Drive to the end of the street and find a place to park.

Why April: Camassia Natural Area is an amazing natural refuge in the metro area, but never more so than in April, when the display of wildflowers found here rivals anything you will find in the Gorge or elsewhere. The short distance ensures that almost anybody can hike this trail, even those who hung up their hiking boots many moons ago. Please be careful to stay on the trail, as boots can crush the flowers nearby; not only this, but poison oak grows profusely in the woods here, ensuring a miserable few days after your visit if you were bad enough to step off the trail.

Boardwalks lead the way through Camassia Natural Area.

Hike: The hike begins at a fence, where a signboard marks the start of the trail. Hike a short distance to a junction, the start of your loop. The official recommendation of the park is to hike the loop in a clockwise direction (starting on your left) but realistically speaking the choice is yours. Let's start by turning left. The trail soon leaves the forest, arriving at the first of many meadows you will encounter. Here you will encounter a trail junction. The recommended loop continues to the right (and is signed) but it is worth your time to instead turn left. This trail leads uphill to an alternate trailhead on Windsor Terrace, but along the way passes though some lovely forest full of April flowers. Keep an eye out for poison oak along the trail, too. Then return to the previous junction and turn left to continue the loop.

The next part of the loop passes through some of the finest wildflower meadows in the area, and certainly the nicest wildflower meadow in the Portland metro area. In late April this meadow comes alive with countless wildflowers, most prominently poofy pink rosy plectritis and blue-purple camas, a lily commonly found in this type of environment. You will not doubt find yourself snapping photos by the dozen. After a short distance you will reach yet another trail junction. This trail leads to West Linn High School and is only worth hiking if you've got a bit of extra time and a desire to hike every side trail here. Beyond this junction, the loop passes through more meadows before returning to the woods at a little under 1 mile. Continue straight over boardwalks through the woods to the closure of the loop. Turn left and walk the short distance to the trailhead.

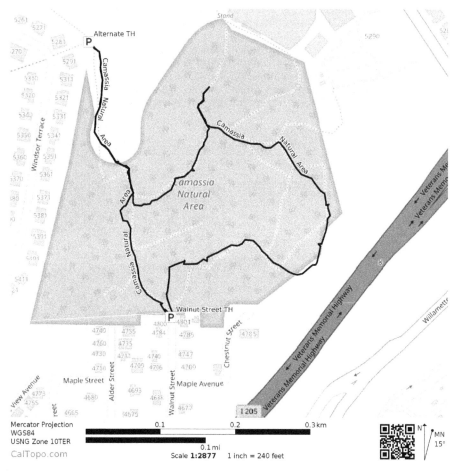

32B. Canemah Bluff Natural Area

Distance: 1.7 mile loop
Elevation Gain: 200 feet
Trailhead elevation: 195 feet
Trail high point: 353 feet
Other seasons: March- May
Map: pick up a map of the trail system at the trailhead
Pass: None needed
Drivetime from Portland: 30 minutes

Directions:
- From Portland, drive south towards Oregon City on Interstate 205.
- Leave the freeway at Exit 9, signed for Oregon City.
- At the bottom of the off ramp, turn left onto SE McLoughlin Blvd (OR 99E).
- Drive through downtown Oregon City and stay on OR 99E.
- Follow OR 99E as it climbs out of downtown Oregon City and passes above Willamette Falls (a worthwhile stop if you have time).
- At 1.8 miles from the 205 exit, turn left onto Hedges St.
- Drive a short distance and turn left onto 3rd Street.
- Drive a short distance on 3rd Street and turn right on Ganong Street.
- Ganong Street rounds a corner and becomes 4th Street. Continue straight on 4th Street to its end at Canemah Childrens Park. This is the trailhead.

Why April: Like nearby Camassia Natural Area, Canemah Bluff features fantastic displays of April flowers. But unlike Camassia, Canemah also features views north to Willamette Falls, a pioneer cemetery (which, alas, cannot be visited) and lovely woods full of tall trees. It is a complete hike in less than 2 miles, and is located just south of Oregon City. If you've only got a few hours, take the time to visit this lovely preserve.

Hike: Begin at the playground. Before you depart for the hike, walk down to the right side of the playground to a fence, where you will have a view downriver to Willamette Falls and downtown Oregon City. Follow then the paved trail that leaves from the playground as it becomes the Camas Springs Trail. The trail follows the bluffs above the Willamette, passing meadows of April wildflowers. Most prominent of these flowers is blue camas, after which the trail is named. The trail soon leaves the meadows and enters the forest, reaching a junction with the pioneer cemetery's access road. Across the road is the Licorice Fern Trail, a trail you will hike later in the day. For the moment, turn right on the road. Stay on the road until you reach the cemetery, which is usually gated and fenced off. Pay your respects for a moment, and then turn left on a short spur trail that brings you to another junction with the Licorice Fern Trail. For a shorter hike, you can turn left and follow the trail back to the cemetery access road. Instead, turn right and very soon arrive at a junction with the Old Slide Trail. Turn right.

The Old Slide Trail is an old road that cuts steeply through the woods, so this is where you get your only elevation gain of the hike. Follow this trail uphill until it begins to descend again, once again reaching the Licorice Fern Trail at about 1 mile from the trailhead. Turning right will eventually lead you back into the neighborhood while turning left will take you back to the cemetery road access. For the time being, turn left and return to the cemetery road, and continue until you reach the Frog Pond Trail. Turn left and hike this short trail back to the parking lot.

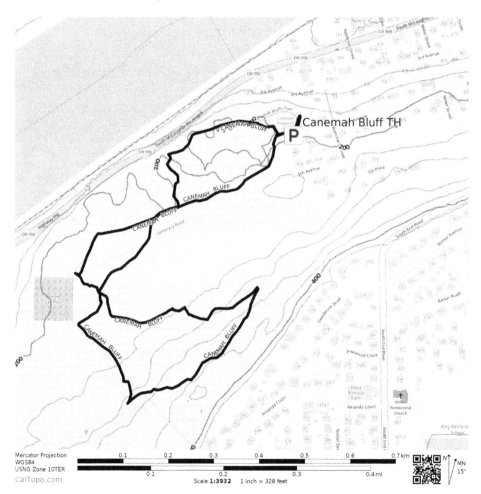

33. Clackamas River Trail

	From lower TH	From upper TH
Distance:	8 miles out & back	9.4 miles out & back
Elevation Gain:	800 feet	1,500 feet
Trailhead Elevation:	911 feet	1,372 feet
Trail High Point:	1,505 feet	1,505 feet
Other Seasons:	all year (avoid icy periods)	all year (avoid icy periods)
Map:	None needed	None needed
Pass:	Pay at TH- requires special fee	None needed
Drivetime from PDX:	65 minutes	75 minutes

Directions to lower trailhead:
- From Portland, drive southeast on OR 224 to Estacada.
- Continue on OR 224 past Estacada 14.7 miles to a junction with Fish Creek Road, just after you cross the Clackamas River.
- Turn right and drive 0.3 mile to the trailhead parking lot on your right.

Directions to upper trailhead:
- From the junction of OR 224 and the Fish Creek Road (see above), drive 6.5 miles southeast on OR 224.
- At a junction with Sandstone Road (FR 4620), turn right.
- Drive 0.6 mile south on this road to the Indian Henry Trailhead on your right.

Why April: Consistently beautiful throughout the year, the Clackamas River Trail is a wild getaway cherished by area hikers. I often come here in the fall and winter when the mountains get snowed in, and every time I marvel at the scenic beauty of the Clackamas River Canyon. But the canyon is never more beautiful than in April, when everything turns green, both the river and Pup Creek Falls are flowing high and the forest speckled with a wide variety of eye-catching wildflowers. For the best experience, plan on a car shuttle and bring your friends so you can hike the whole trail. Otherwise, hike both ends of the trail when you have the chance.

Hike: Begin at the lower trailhead, along Fish Creek. The trail rises a bit and climbs to a prominence above the Clackamas River. This first part of the trail passes through forest burned in a 2002 fire. This stretch of trail washes out frequently and can be quite muddy even in April, so make sure you bring good boots; poles are a good idea too. If the trail has washed out and you reach a point that is unsafe to cross, turn around and drive to the upper trailhead described later in this entry. The trail stays high on this bench above the river for most of its first 2 miles. Once you pass this segment of the Clackamas River trail, you will descend a little bit into a tranquil forest of ancient cedars beside the Clackamas River at 3 miles from the trailhead. Here a side tumbles over the slopes above the trail, offering a chance for exploration. The ways continues through green, verdant forest to a junction with the Pup Creek Falls spur trail at 3.8 miles. Turn right here and hike this short trail to a viewpoint of Pup Creek Falls at 4 miles. This beauty plunges 249 feet off the basalt walls of the Clackamas River's canyon, offering the perfect destination for this hike from either direction. Unless you've established a car shuttle, return the way you came.

If you're starting at the upper trailhead instead, you'll find this upper section of the Clackamas River Trail even more scenic, but it is also longer and features more elevation gain. The trail begins at a roadside trailhead near Indian Henry Campground and gradually climbs and descends along the Clackamas River's lush canyon walls. These gentle ascents and descents are why this segment of trail has much more elevation gain than the lower stretch. As you hike, keep your eyes on the forest floor, where you may see pink calypso orchids. These small but gorgeous flowers have a delightful scent for only a day or two, so you may need to sniff a few before you find one with a scent. The trail passes under the canyon's huge overhanging walls before settling into the lush forest, where it mellows out somewhat. The trail crosses Cat Creek at 2.6 miles, and soon you will reach the Narrows, a dramatic gorge in the river at 3 miles. A short side trail leads you to the brink of this precipice, directly above the raging waters of the Clackamas. In recent years daring souls would cross the river here on a downed tree, but thankfully the tree is gone, removing all temptation. Back on the trail, you will pass through a powerline corridor at around 4 miles from the trailhead. Watch out for poison oak here. Once through the corridor, the trail reaches a difficult crossing of Pup Creek. There is no bridge, so look for a log upstream on which to cross. Once across, turn left on the Pup Creek Falls spur trail to locate the falls. Return the way you came, unless you established a car shuttle at the lower trailhead.

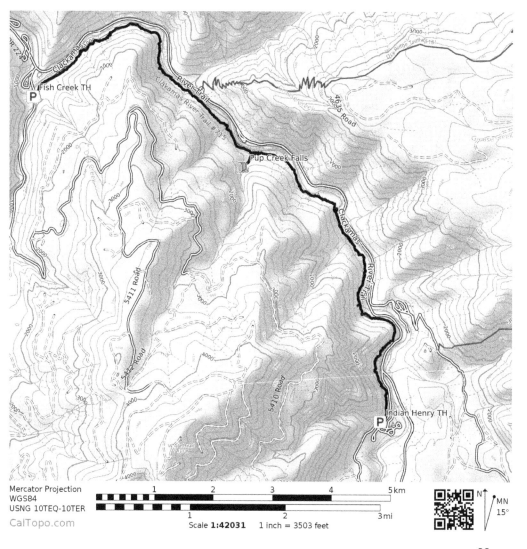

34. Little North Santiam River Trail

Distance: 9 miles out and back
Elevation Gain: 1,800 feet
Trailhead elevation: 1,294 feet
Trail high point: 1,791 feet
Others seasons: all year
Map: Opal Creek Wilderness (Imus)
Pass: none needed
Drivetime from Portland: 110 minutes

Directions:
- From Portland, drive south on Interstate 5 to Salem.
- At Exit 253 in Salem, leave the freeway and reach a junction with OR 22, signed for Detroit Lake and Bend. Turn left here.
- Drive OR 22 east for 23 miles to the second flashing light in Mehama.
- At a sign for the Little North Fork Recreation Area (and directly across from the North
- Fork Crossing restaurant), turn left.
- Follow the paved two-lane road up the Little North Fork for 14.5 miles to a junction
- with Elkhorn Drive SE in the small community of Elkhorn.
- Turn right and drive across the bridge over the river.
- Drive 0.5 mile to the trailhead, a parking lot on your left with a signboard.

Why April: There's never a bad time to hike this trail, but it's best in the spring. The wild-flowers are blooming, the river is roaring and the crowds diminished. This is also the rare trail that is great in any weather, and in many ways is better on rainy days as the forest and river both glow surreal shades of green. Sunny days are nevertheless magnificent, and well worth the trip down. Plan for anything here and prepare to be delighted.

Hike: The trail begins at the edge of the small community of Elkhorn. You will skirt through a recovering forest with houses in sight for the first 0.2 mile before crossing a small side stream and descending into glorious woods beside the even more glorious Little North Santiam. Everything is green, moist and radiant! At 0.6 mile follow a short side trail to a bench beside a roaring cascade in the river. This is a great place to relax

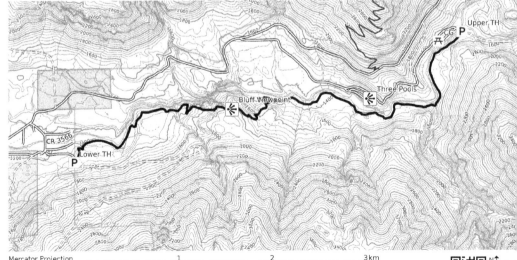

Mercator Projection
WGS84
USNG Zone 10TEQ
CalTopo.com

Scale **1:24171**   1 inch = 2014 feet

One of many creeks that flow into the Little North Santiam River.

but don't turn back yet as the best is yet to come! The next mile is a joy as you wind through deep forest just above the Little North Santiam, crossing roaring side creeks on scenic wooden bridges beneath towering Douglas firs. Notice how the river seems to be an electric shade of green; this is not the water but the green rock below magnified by the incredible clarity of the water. This feature is common throughout the Little North Santiam drainage and is found on all of the creeks upstream.

Soon the canyon begins to contract and the trail climbs to avoid a very narrow gorge. Along the way up, listen for the roar of Triple Falls on Henline Creek, tumbling directly into the river just across the gorge. The falls is visible but tree branches make it difficult to get an unobstructed view of the falls. Once past the falls, the trail continues its climb up the canyon wall, topping out at a rocky bluff high above the river with a view across to Henline Mountain's cliffs. Note the madrone tree on this bluff, a rarity in the Cascades. This makes a nice spot to stop and catch your breath and if it's clear, the views of the Little North Santiam canyon will be outstanding. The trail stays high above the river for a bit before dropping swiftly back to river level at 3.0 miles.

At 3.3 miles, you can look across the river to Three Pools, a popular day-use site. Here the Little North Santiam roars through a series of narrow rock channels, creating three deep, swimmable pools. A single rock pillar stands sentinel above the scene. Downstream the river flows gently through a placid stretch of water that is almost too green to be believed. Three Pools is extremely popular on summer weekends...and is almost deserted in other seasons. Sadly, you cannot cross the river here (consider stopping by after the hike) so continue hiking upstream. Along the way you'll cross Little Cedar Creek on a new bridge before reaching the upper trailhead, at a scenic wooden road bridge over the Little North Santiam River 4.5 miles from your car. Across the river is lovely Shady Cove Campground. You could shuttle this hike but then, you won't have the pleasure of hiking it again, now will you?

35. Eagle Creek

Distance: 13 miles out and back
Elevation Gain: 1,300 feet
Trailhead elevation: 60 feet
Trail high point: 1,357 feet
Others seasons: all year (avoid winter ice and snow)
Map: Columbia River Gorge (Geo-Graphics)
Pass: NW Forest Pass
Drivetime from Portland: 40 minutes

Directions:
- Drive Interstate 84 east of Portland to Eagle Creek Exit 41.
- Almost immediately after exiting the freeway, you park in a lot on the left next to a fish hatchery.
- There is another trailhead down the road about a half-mile, but this lot often fills very early in the day and is the subject of frequent thefts and break-ins. The lower lot is monitored and generally safe.

Why April: One of the most popular hikes in Oregon is also one of the best. Follow a spectacular trail above a narrow gorge featuring waterfall after waterfall, each one better than the last. While you can come here at any time during the year, April is by far the best month of the year to visit; winter is too cold and icy, summer is too crowded, and in fall the creek is too dry. In April, the trees at last have their leaves, the flowers are blooming and the creek raging. It just doesn't get better than this.

Note: The Eagle Creek Canyon was burned during the Eagle Creek Fire, which began near Punchbowl Falls in September 2017. The extent of the damage is unknown as of press time, but expect it to be significant. This trail will likely be closed through 2018. Check online to see if the trail has reopened.

Hike: Begin on the wide trail as it parallels wide Eagle Creek. Begin slowly climbing, as the trail ascends to a narrow ledge above the canyon of Eagle Creek. In some places, the trail was blasted out of the ledge – thankfully, chains are in place to help out those uncomfortable with heights. At 0.6 miles, look across the canyon to Wauna Falls, a 150-foot tiered waterfall – this is your first taste of the many waterfalls here. After another 0.6 mile, pass by an oddity that mostly remains out of sight – a pair of twin waterfalls, Metlako and Sorenson Falls. A spur trail that led to a viewpoint of Metlako Falls slid into the canyon bottom in December 2016. From here, the trail continues another 0.9 mile to a junction with the spur trail down to Punchbowl Falls. For an easy dayhike, take the spur down to a view of scenic Punchbowl Falls, set in a scenic bowl that truly lives up to its name.

From here, the trail returns to the ledge above the creek, and in a little more than a mile later, traverses a cliff edge opposite Loowit Falls. Those afraid of heights may struggle with this stretch of the trail. At 3.3 miles, reach the aptly-named High Bridge, where the trail crosses Eagle Creek high above a narrow gorge. This is an incredible spot and well worth your time. If you're looking for a nice place to eat lunch, continue upstream another 0.3 mile to Tenas Camp, where there are numerous campsites and places to stretch out for a few minutes of rest. For a more difficult hike, continue upstream as the canyon opens up somewhat. You will pass Skoonichuck Falls, which is mostly out of sight in the canyon below (there are user trails down to viewpoints) before crossing the creek again on a bridge at 4.5 miles. Just a short while later, pass Wy'East Camp and its namesake falls, Wy'East Falls. From here, pass a junction with the Eagle-Benson Trail continue upstream. At 6.2 miles from the trailhead, at last reach aptly-named Tunnel Falls. At 165 feet tall, this gorgeous waterfall is an impressive sight indeed. Even more impressive is the tunnel that

Lower TH

P

Eagle Creek TH

P

Metlako Falls
MF

Punchbowl Falls
PF

Eagle Creek

To Twister

Loowit Falls
LF

Skoonichuck Falls
SF

Falls

Benson Ruckle Trail

Ruckel Creek

Pacific Crest Trail

Wy'East Falls
WF

Tunnel Falls
TF

Twister Falls
TW

ator Projection
384
G Zone 10TER

Topo.com

| 1 | 2 | 3 | 4 km |

| 0.5 | 1.0 | 1.5 | 2.0 mi |

Scale **1:37976**   1 inch = 3165 feet

N
MN
15°

was blasted out of the rock behind the falls, allowing safe passage upstream.

Most guidebooks have you stop here, but you must keep going. The trail continues around a bend as it clings to the side of the cliff above Eagle Creek, and becomes downright frightening (or awesome, depending on your perspective) as it passes above 130-foot Twister Falls. The stretch of trail from Tunnel to Twister Falls is one of the most thrilling in the Pacific Northwest. Hikers with a fear of heights will find this stretch of trail terrifying. Most hikers turn around just after Twister Falls. If you've got just a little more energy, you can continue another 0.3 mile to Sevenmile Falls, the final waterfall on Eagle Creek and by far the quietest. Return the way you came.

36. Starvation Loop and Mitchell Point

	Starvation Loop	Mitchell Point
Distance:	3.1 mile loop	2 miles out and back
Elevation Gain:	900 feet	1,200 feet
Trailhead Elevation:	119 feet	100 feet
Trail High Point:	785 feet	1,200 feet
Other Seasons:	all year	all year
Map:	CR Gorge (Geo-Graphics)	CR Gorge (Geo-Graphics)
Pass	none needed	none needed
Drivetime from PDX:	55 minutes	60 minutes

Directions:
- From Portland, drive east on Interstate 84 to Exit 55, signed for Starvation Falls.
- Drive into the circular parking lot. This is the trailhead.
- To continue to Mitchell Point drive 3 miles east on I-84 to Exit 58, signed for the Mitchell Point Overlook.
- Exit the freeway here and drive into the parking lot for Mitchell Point, your trailhead.
- **Note:** The Mitchell Point Trailhead can only be reached from eastbound Interstate 84. If you are coming from Hood River, drive to the Viento Exit 56; turn around here and head east to Exit 58. Start at Starvation Falls if you're doing both hikes.

Why April: Here are two hikes that give you a lot of bang for you buck. Both trailheads are just an hour from Portland; the first offers you a loop that passes four waterfalls, hanging wildflower meadows and great views, while the second delivers you to one of the best views of the Gorge. Both are at their best in April, when the flowers are blooming, the slopes grassy, green and glorious and the weather is delightfully variable. Why not make a day trip and hike them both? While each is great on its own, the two hikes make for a fantastic pairing, especially on a sunny day.

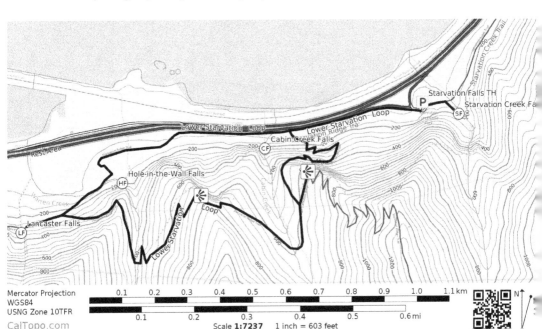

Starvation Creek Loop Hike: Begin at the Starvation Falls Parking Lot. Before you start your hike in earnest, take the time to walk east 100 yards to the base of Starvation Creek Falls. This 227 foot tiered falls got its name when two trains became stuck in a blizzard here in the winter of 1884. Nobody actually starved, but the experience was enough to christen the area with the name Starvation Creek. After visiting the falls, return to the parking lot and follow the trail heading west. You'll follow the exit ramp of the freeway until the trail enters the woods. After a few minutes, reach a junction with the Starvation Cutoff Trail, the start of your loop. Turn left and hike up this amazingly steep trail as it vaults uphill, out of the canyon holding Starvation Creek Falls. You'll gain 400 feet in just 0.4 mile on your way to a junction with the Starvation Ridge Trail, a main access route to Mount Defiance far above you. While you aren't going that far, there is an excellent viewpoint on the Starvation Trail to your left just 100 yards. Follow the trail out to the viewpoint, where you can look out to Dog Mountain, Wind Mountain and other parts of the Gorge. Watch your step here- it's straight down!

Return to the trail junction and continue hiking downhill on the Starvation Trail. You'll cross Cabin Creek and begin another uphill traverse, this time crossing the spine of the ridge that separates Cabin and Warren Creeks. As you descend towards Warren Creek, the trail passes a gorgeous hanging meadow full of April flowers. Cross Warren Creek and follow the trail as it descends to a reunion with the Mount Defiance Trail at a little under 2 miles. While your return trail is to the right, Lancaster Falls is a worthy detour just 0.1 mile to your left. The trail crosses Wonder Creek at a precarious spot just below the base of the falls. Lancaster Falls is a whopping 303 feet tall but you can only really see the bottom 20 feet or so. When you are done, follow the trail east, towards the trailhead. Over the last mile of your hike you'll pass Hole-In-The-Wall Falls (so named because Warren Creek was diverted to prevent flooding over the Historic Highway; the original waterfall is a short bushwhack off the trail- but water rarely flows over this falls) and Cabin Creek Falls before closing the loop at the Starvation Cutoff Junction. Follow the trail along the highway to the trailhead.

Mitchell Point Hike: From the south end of the parking lot, look for a trail heading south towards the cliffs. The trail follows a small creek before turning away and climbing towards Mitchell Point. After some time the trail reaches a talus slope framed dramatically by white oak and great views of the west end of the Gorge. Follow the trail through the talus to some nice older forest. In April the forest floor here is carpeted with the pink calypso orchids, but also poison oak. One mile from the trailhead, reach a set of powerlines at an open saddle. Turn left to follow the steep and exposed trail 0.3 mile through hanging meadows to the exposed summit of Mitchell Point. The views up here are incredible but watch your step!

Return the way you came.

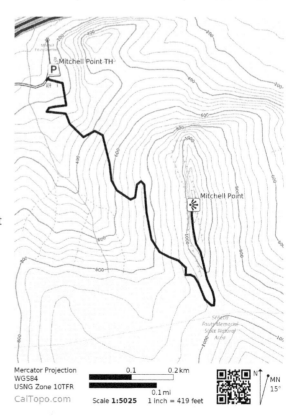

Mercator Projection
WGS84
USNG Zone 10TFR
CalTopo.com

0.1   0.2 km

0.1 mi
Scale **1:5025**   1 inch = 419 feet

N
MN
15°

37. Mosier Plateau

Distance: 2 miles out and back
Elevation Gain: 450 feet
Trailhead elevation: 122 feet
Trail high point: 574 feet
Other seasons: all year (avoid summer heat)
Map: none available
Pass: none needed
Drivetime from Portland: 75 minutes

Directions to Mosier Plateau TH:
* From Portland, drive east on Interstate 84 east to Hood River.
* At Exit 69, signed for Mosier, leave the freeway and turn right to follow old US 30 through the small community of Mosier.
* Drive through town for 0.5 mile to a bridge over Mosier Creek, where you will see a pullout on the left side of the road that provides room for a few cars. This is the trailhead.
* The trail departs up the hill on the south (uphill) side of the road.

Why April: A brand-new trail constructed by Friends of the Gorge and the Nature Conservancy, the Mosier Plateau Trail is a delight that passes many scenic highlights in one excellent mile. You will pass an historic cemetery, a beautiful and unexpected waterfall, and arrive at a view-packed knoll above Mosier. This is a great place to take casual hikers and visitors from out of state in April, as the trail hits on almost everything that makes the Gorge such a wonderful place. This is a fun hike to combine with some of the area's other hikes, but it is equally fun if you only have a couple hours and wish to experience the best of what this part of the Gorge has to offer.

Looking west over the Gorge from Mosier Plateau.

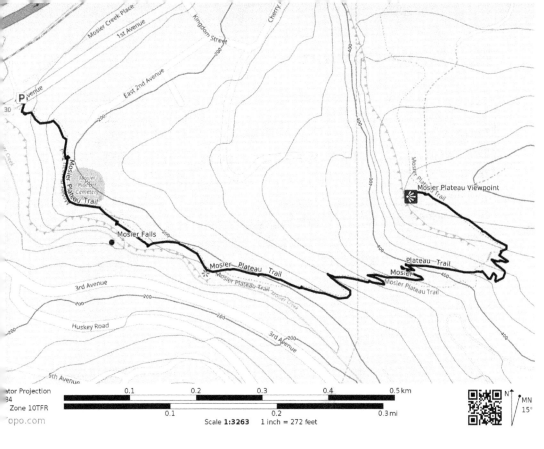

Hike: Begin at the old cemetery trail on the east side of Mosier Creek. Climb uphill, passing a house before arriving at the Mosier Cemetery after a tenth of a mile. Some of the graves are quite old; among them is Benjamin Mosier, the town founder. The trail continues as it straddles a bluff above Mosier Creek's narrow gorge. At 0.3 mile, arrive at a bench above lovely Mosier Falls. It is odd to see a waterfall here, in a dry canyon on the edge of a town with houses on the opposite side of the creek – but it is very welcome! From the falls, the trail continues along the canyon wall for another 0.2 mile until it begins a series of switchbacks out of the canyon. The flowers on this hillside peak in April, with the usual suspects balsamroot and lupine leading the charge. At 1 mile from the trailhead, arrive at a viewpoint atop a knoll, where the view opens up downriver through the Gorge to Hood River and down to Dog Mountain. A bench offers a convenient place to rest. You could make a loop by continuing downhill on the trail below the viewpoint, but this takes you to a different trailhead 1 mile east of Mosier, there by necessitating a road walk. It is instead better to return the way you came.

If you're looking for a longer day, you can combine this hike with the trail out to Rowena Crest (Hike 46), just 7 miles to the east. The only downside is that the Rowena Crest Hike is extraordinarily popular (especially in April) and if you're starting at Mosier Plateau, you'll likely have trouble finding a place to park by the time you get to Rowena Crest. Consider combining this hike with any other number of shorter Gorge hikes, such as the Starvation Falls Loop (Hike 36), Mitchell Point (Hike 36), Lyle Cherry Orchard (Hike 29), The Dalles Mountain Ranch (Hike 39) or other, more obscure hikes not included in this book, such as Weldon Wagon Road and Rattlesnake Falls. There is, after all, no finer place to be than the Gorge in April. Where you go is limited only by your athletic abilities and the time you're willing to spend exploring the area.

38. Swale Canyon

	To Trestle Six	Full trail
Distance:	10.2 miles out and back	13 miles one way
Elevation Gain:	450 feet	1,000 feet of descent
Trailhead Elevation:	1,562 feet	1,562 feet
Trail High Point:	1,562 feet	1,562 feet
Other Seasons:	January- March	January- March
Map:	None needed	None needed
Pass:	None needed.	None needed.
Drivetime from PDX:	100 minutes	100 minutes

Directions:
- From Portland drive east on Interstate 84 to Hood River.
- Leave the freeway at Exit 64 and turn left at the end of the off ramp.
- Immediately arrive at the bridge over the Columbia River.
- Pay the $1 toll and cross the narrow bridge.
- On the other side of the river at a junction turn right and drive 11 miles to Lyle.
- In the center of town turn left on the Centerville Highway and drive this two-lane paved road 14.7 miles through the country to a junction with Harms Road.
- Turn left here and drive this gravel road 0.5 mile to a marked trailhead where the old Klickitat Railway crossed the road.
- There is room for a few cars on the trailhead side of the road.

Why April: In the shadow of Stacker Butte (Hike 8), Swale Canyon is a wonderful escape into a narrow canyon in the eastern Gorge. April is the time to visit as it is very cold here in the winter, and very hot in the summer. Furthermore, this is a fantastic hike for flowers, with a greater variety than you find in many other places due to its riparian setting. If you're lucky, you may even see some of the wildlife that call this canyon home. Alas, you can only stay for the day, as camping is banned along the Klickitat Trail.

Hike: From the remote upper trailhead set off downstream on the converted rail trail through a pastoral setting of farmlands in the shadow of Stacker Butte (Hike 40). The trail rounds a bend and reaches a fenced gate- make sure you close it after you pass through, as the gate is there to protect the canyon from cattle grazing. As you descend into the canyon, keep an eye out for marmots! Though far from their usual terrain, this canyon supports a colony of marmots, who live on the rockslides on each side of the creek. As you descend, the canyon reveals itself to you, step by step. You will cross Swale Creek again and again on trestles, all that remains of the railway that now serves as trail. The canyon walls tower over you now. You may spot the occasional house above, a reminder to stay on the trail (another is the ubiquity of ticks, which are quite common in Swale Canyon). The green canyon walls grow taller above you; the interior of Swale Canyon is a peaceful place. Unfortunately, backpacking is prohibited here.

The scenery in Swale Canyon is uniformly beautiful, making it difficult to turn around. Perhaps the most likely spot is at Trestle Six, where the creek passes through a small gorge with several bedrock pools on the creek. This spot is 5.1 miles from the Harms Road Trailhead, making it ideal for a moderate hike. Return the way you came.

If you choose to continue downstream from here, I recommend setting up a car shuttle to the Wahkiakus Trailhead before beginning your hike. To reach this lower trailhead, drive to Lyle as described above and turn left (north) on WA 142. Drive 16.2 miles to the small town of Wahkiakus and turn right on Horseshoe Bend Road. Cross the Klickitat River and turn into a parking lot signed for the Klickitat River Trail. To find the upper trailhead from here, continue on Horseshoe Bend for 4.9 miles of bumpy gravel to a junction with Harms Road. Continue straight on gravel Harms Road for 3.5 miles to the Harms Road TH. The roads between the two trailheads are mostly gravel and the shuttle will take as much as 45 minutes to set up. The section of trail below Trestle Six is beautiful, but as you near Wahkiakus, forest begins to block views of the canyon above. The trail passes several houses near Wahkiahkus, and over the years hikers have reported the occasional run-in with the residents here; best to mind your business as you hike to the lower trailhead.

If you've got more time after the hike, the Klickitat River Trail does continue upstream along Swale Creek for 2 more miles to its upper terminus at Warwick. This stretch of trail is flat and open, and is neat for folks who love big skies and flat trails. It is nevertheless somewhat redundant, as the scenery is identical to what you passed through just west of the Harms Road Trailhead.

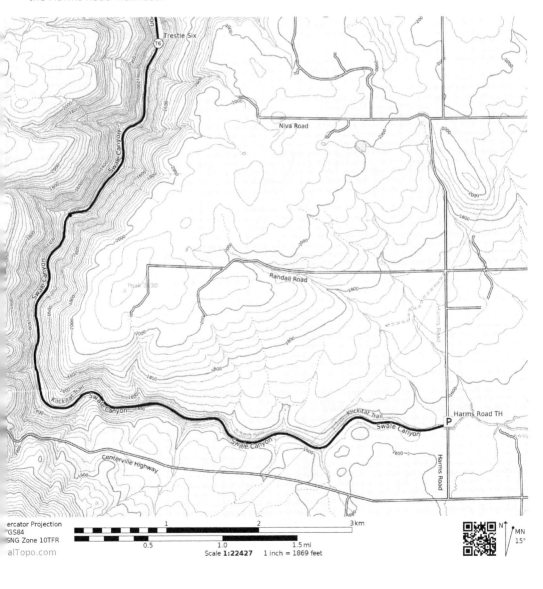

39. Crawford Oaks Loop

Distance: 6.6 mile loop
Elevation Gain: 1,000 feet
Trailhead elevation: 375 feet
Trail high point: 1,189 feet
Other seasons: year-round but very cold in winter and very hot in summer
Map: Pick up one of the free maps at the trailhead
Pass: Washington Discovery Pass ($10 day / $30 year)
Drivetime from Portland: 100 minutes

Directions:
* From Portland drive east on Interstate 84 for 80 miles to The Dalles.
* At a sign for US 197 at Exit 87, leave the freeway. Turn left and cross the Columbia River.
* Continue on this highway for 2 more miles to a junction with WA 14.
* Turn right and drive 2.8 miles to the Crawford Oaks TH on the left side of the road.
* Turn into the parking lot and (hopefully) find a spot. Earlier in the day is better.

Why April: The vast wildflower meadows of Columbia Hills State Park are the place to be in late April. Located just across the Columbia River from The Dalles, the trail network here begs to be explored when the annual wildflower show peaks in April. This new loop explores the most scenic terrain in the park, offering hikers the absolute best of what this area has to offer: fields of balsamroot and lupine, fabulous views south to Mount Hood and even a waterfall to spice things up. It doesn't get better than this.

Hike: Begin at the Crawford Oaks Trailhead. In the relatively recent past this was a gated jeep road with no parking area, but now the trails here are well-maintained and well-manicured. You still get to start on the jeep road, though. Follow the old road left from the parking lot as it switchbacks steeply uphill towards the top of Eightmile Creek's waterfall. Views of Mount Hood tantalize on the way up, but they get much better as you continue along this hike. Once you pass the top of the falls the trail levels out somewhat, following the huge oak trees that grow near the creek. At exactly 1 mile from the trailhead, the trail crosses Eightmile Creek and reaches a junction that marks the start of your loop. Either direction works well, but I look doing this hike in a clockwise direction. So keep left here.

The next 1.4 miles are an absolute joy. The fields of wildflowers are impressive everywhere, but are perhaps most impressive along trickling Eightmile Creek. Keep left at a junction after just 0.2 mile to continue following Eightmile Creek (right leads is a shortcut to a different part of the loop but misses some of the best flower displays). The trail follows the creek uphill, passing outstanding views south to Mount Hood and stunning displays of yellow balsamroot and purple lupine. Wildflower fans will find much to love here beyond the showy flowers – bring a guidebook and plan extra time to see all that you can see. At 2.4 miles, the trail reaches a junction near the buildings of The Dalles Mountain Ranch – which is actually just another name for this part of Columbia Hills State Park. Turning left at this junction will take you to the ranch, and also an upper trailhead near here complete with bathroom; to continue on the loop, keep right.

The loop now heads east, dipping twice into small draws. The second of these is a branch of Eightmile Creek, and is the last bit of shade you'll have on the hike. This makes an excellent place to stop and rest if it's hot or windy out, as there is absolutely no shade the rest of the way. From here, continue east on the loop trail and gain a bit of elevation to a T-junction with an old jeep road at 3.3 miles (or exactly halfway). Turn right. You will now head south, passing a junction with the Military Road Trail (the aforementioned cutoff that leads back to Eightmile Creek). Continue south, passing under powerlines and through fields of flowers. Views open up to the Columbia River and south to Mount Hood. On very clear days Mount Jefferson appears on the far southern horizon. This stretch of trail is often very windy. The loop is completed at 5.6 miles, where you meet the old jeep road near Eightmile Creek. Turn left, cross the creek and follow the trail downhill to the trailhead.

Hikers with more time have lots of options in this area. You could hike to the summit of Stacker Butte, where the view stretches from Mount Adams to the Three Sisters but the wind often proves to be too fierce to enjoy the view. Just follow the road uphill from the ranch 3.5 miles to the summit of the mountain. You could also hike around Horsethief Butte, the trailhead for which is found just 0.4 mile west of the Crawford Oaks Trailhead. Whatever you choose to do, it's bound to be fun!

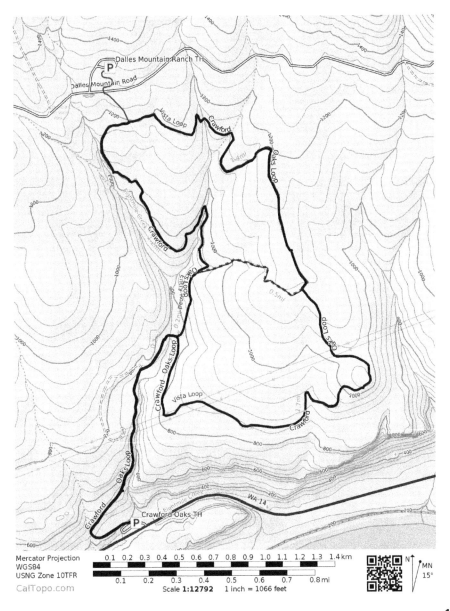

Mercator Projection
WGS84
USNG Zone 10TFR
CalTopo.com

Scale **1:12792**   1 inch = 1066 feet

MN
15°

40. Criterion Ranch

Distance: 10.8 miles out and back
Elevation Gain: 700 feet
Trailhead elevation: 3,177 feet
Trail high point: 3,177 feet
Other seasons: October
Map: Download map on the BLM's website
Pass: None needed
Drivetime from Portland: 130 minutes

Directions:

- Drive east from Portland on Interstate 84 to The Dalles.
- Take exit 87, and continue straight to drive south on US 197.
- Continue south on US 197 for 38 miles to Maupin.
- Drive south of Maupin on US 197 for 10.9 miles to the Criterion Ranch Trailhead on your right, next to a collection of radio towers. There is room for about 10 cars.
- It is equally easy to drive here over Mount Hood via Government Camp, although snow sometimes makes this a tricky proposition even in April. Drive southeast of Portland on US 26 to Government Camp. Continue driving southeast on US 26 another 16 miles to a junction with OR 216 on your left, signed for Maupin. Turn left on OR 216 and drive 25 miles to road's end at a junction with US 197, just north of Maupin. From there, follow the directions above to continue to the Criterion Ranch Trailhead.

Why April: Criterion Ranch is one of the most beautiful hikes in the state of Oregon in late April and early May, when wildflowers line the trail and the view stretches all the way from Mount Adams to the Three Sisters. It's a long drive from Portland but it's worth the trek at least once in your life. Just be sure to tread lightly, prepare for almost any kind of weather and bring as much water as you think you might need. You aren't likely to encounter crowds here, far away from the Willamette Valley. You are likely, however, to find sunny weather and bracing winds. You may even see a herd of deer, and who knows what else!

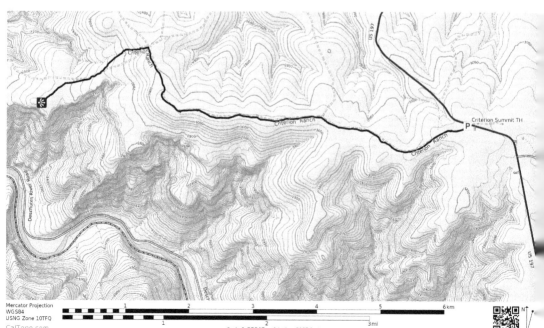

Follow an old jeep road through Criterion Ranch, under puffy clouds and among sagebrush.

Hike: Begin at the trailhead, which is also the high point of the hike. The going is easy, as you walk along an old jeep road. Although grass sometimes encroaches on the road, the way is never in doubt. Along the way, views open up in all directions – southwest to the Three Sisters, north to Mount Hood and Mount Adams and west across the canyon to the northeast corner of the Warm Springs Reservation. As you hike you may see a few cows grazing in this open rangeland; other than that, the only sounds are the wind and chirping of birds. Wildflowers line the trail in April and May; look for excellent displays of lupine as you make your way along the road. In some places the scent of lupine is almost intoxicating!

At just under 4 miles, reach an unsigned junction at a gate. Turn left and begin following a jeep road as it begins a modest descent towards the canyon wall. As you descend, your attention will be drawn to the view of Mount Hood to the north, towering above Maupin, and to the fields of balsamroot that stretch out at your feet. Keep descending, and soon you'll notice a high point on your left with a post. Make your way cross-country to the point, where you will be greeted with one of Oregon's great views: the serpentine curves of the Deschutes River lie at your feet, at the bottom of a green, flower-spangled canyon; to your north is Mount Hood, towering above the eastern foothills of the Cascades; and all around you are flowers, rugged hills and cerulean blue skies. Make this your turnaround spot.

From here you can return the way you came, or you can go off-trail to seek out new and different views, meadows and hidden canyons. You can also follow the jeep road all the way down to the Deschutes River, but much of the canyon bottom is private property – so in other words, you won't be able to backpack. Instead return to the junction at the gate, and turn right to hike 4 miles back to the trailhead.

Bonus Hike: Smith Rock

Distance: 4 mile loop (with longer options)
Elevation Gain: 800 feet
Trailhead elevation: 2,845 feet
Trail high point: 3,299 feet
Other seasons: year-round but very cold in winter and very hot in summer
Map: Pick up one of the free maps at the trailhead
Pass: State Park Pass (purchase at the trailhead)
Drivetime from Portland: 170 minutes

Directions:
* From Portland, drive US 26 east over Mount Hood and into the desert approximately 110 miles to a junction with US 97 near Madras.
* Fork right here and drive south here and drive 19 miles to Terrebonne.
* At a signed junction in the middle of Terrebonne, turn left onto Smith Rock Way.
* From here, follow signs to Smith Rock State Park.

Why April: In the Pacific Northwest, winter seems endless. By the time April rolls around, many Oregonians are ready to head to the hills, only to be thwarted by rainy days and deep snowdrifts. What they really need to do is to head east until they find the sun. Sometimes this requires driving all the way across the mountains, to Smith Rock and the Crooked River near Terrebonne. It's a long drive, but the destination is so worthy that you won't mind. Imagine a small piece of Utah's desert majesty transplanted into Central Oregon. Were this elsewhere it would likely be a national park, and for rock climbers, it's better than most national parks. It takes a full weekend to really explore what makes this area so wonderful, but it's a fantastic day trip too if you don't mind some driving. As it is, it's only two and a half hours from my home in outer southeast Portland- perfect for a day trip.

Hike: Begin at the parking lot, where you are greeted immediately with the orange massif of Smith Rock's cliffs. This is rock climbing nirvana – expect the vast majority of people here to wear helmets and carry ropes. People come from all over to climb here, and they are seldom disappointed. You can experience the best of Smith Rock without ever setting hands and feet on the rock here. Hike downhill on either trail to the bridge over the Crooked River. Cross the river and reach a junction with the trail that follows the Crooked River. Here you are faced with a choice: up the ridge, or along the river? I like to follow the river first, so turn left.

The wide, dusty trail follows the Crooked River as it bends around Smith Rock's cliffs. The crowds thin out as you follow the river, as most tourists don't come this way and most climbers head to the cliffs near Asterisk Pass not long past the Crooked River Bridge. As you hike, your attention will be drawn up towards the cliffs in all their creative angles and psychedelic colors that appear different every time you look at them. It isn't easy to explore them, so you should stick to the main trail. You will meet a junction for the Mesa Verde Trail- keep left for the River Trail. Soon you will arrive on the far side of Smith Rock, where you are faced with a junction near a large boulder. You need to turn right here to continue the loop, but with a map you can explore the brand-new trail network that traverses the less-visited northern side of the park. This area is less scenic, but also far less crowded. But to follow the suggested loop, turn right.

The trail starts out fairly level but soon launches steeply uphill, climbing furiously to make the top of the ridge. As you climb, wide-ranging views begin to open up; look out a lineup of Cascade peaks from the Three Sisters to Mount Jefferson. The perfectly conical peak on the horizon is Black Butte. Closer at hand, the view at last opens up to Monkey Face, a 400-foot tall rock pinnacle with the most apt name in Oregon geography. The trail passes closely under Monkey Face as you ascend, and soon you will reach the top of the ridge. Shortly after you crest the top of this narrow ridge, turn right and follow a trail to a cliff edge directly opposite the head of Monkey Face. You will likely see climbers resting inside the Monkey's mouth – good for them! Here, as elsewhere in the park, one of the joys of coming here is watching climbers do their thing. From here, follow the main trail across the narrow plateau to locate the wide and well-graded Misery Ridge Trail. Switchback down this wildly scenic promenade of a path to the canyon bottom, where you will soon locate the Crooked River Bridge. If you have some more time, you can turn left to hike north along the Crooked River at the foot of more beautiful cliffs; otherwise, cross the bridge and hike uphill to return to the trailhead.

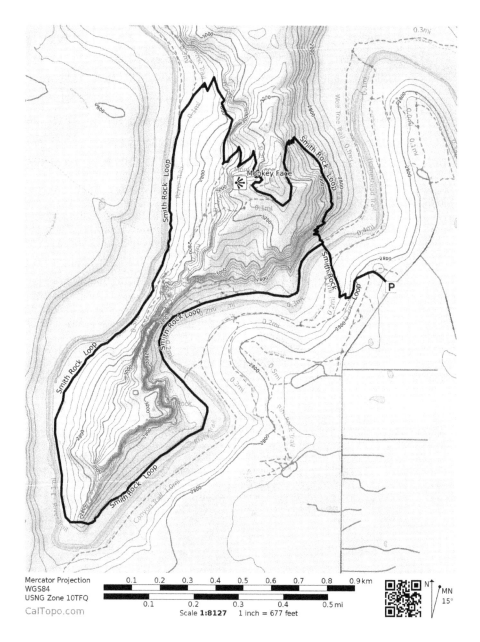

MAY

		Distance	EV Gain	Drivetime
41.	Neahkahnie Mountain	8 miles	2,200 ft	100 min
42.	Cascade Head	4.8 miles	1,200 ft	120 min
43.	Upper Clackamas River	7 miles	900 ft	85 min
44.	Falls Creek Falls	4 miles	700 ft	80 min
45.	Indian Point	8.6 miles	3,000 ft	50 min
46.	Dog Mountain	7.3 miles	2,900 ft	55 min
47.	Rowena Crest and Tom McCall Point	4.8 miles	1,300 ft	70 min
48.	Bald Butte	8.6 miles	2,400 ft	80 min
49.	Badger Creek	12 miles	1,200 ft	120 min
50.	School Canyon	8 miles	1,800 ft	125 min
BONUS	White River Falls	1 mile	200 ft	125 min

May is where it's at in the Pacific Northwest. The weather begins to turn warm, the flowers are out and the days long. While much of the Cascades are still snowed under, many hiking destinations are in their prime. This is especially so for hikes in the Gorge and east of the Cascades, where flowers are at their peak and the heat is not so oppressive. The options presented here are a mix of lowland hikes and treks to scenic viewpoints and wildflower meadows.

As the weather heats up and the days get longer it gets easier to figure out where to go. You will notice that many of the hikes above feature large elevation gains. This is the month to start getting in shape for summer hiking (if you haven't already). Many of these hikes start low and climb high, to mountaintops and ridgecrests. May is the month these hikes are at last reliably snow-free. But rain is still a likelihood on many May days. Make sure you save many of these hikes, especially Indian Point (Hike 45), Dog Mountain (Hike 46), Bald Butte (Hike 48) and School Canyon (Hike 50) for sunny days. On the other hand, the Upper Clackamas River (Hike 43), Falls Creek Falls (Hike 44) and Badger Creek (Hike 49) are ideal hikes for those cool, rainy days we often get throughout May.

Some of these hikes are extremely popular, and you should expect crowds whenever you go. Dog Mountain in particular is one of the most popular hikes in entire Pacific Northwest., so popular that a shuttle bus system has been instituted to reduce crowds in the parking lot. If you're looking to avoid crowds, consider some of the other hikes offered here. If you're really looking to avoid crowds, remember a simple rule of thumb: the further you travel away from the metro area, the less crowded it will be. May is one of the best months of the year for hiking; wherever you go, it's sure to be a great time.

Right: The Columbia River and Dog Mountain from just above Indian Point (Hike 45)

41. Neahkahnie Mountain

Distance: 8 miles out and back
Elevation Gain: 2,200 feet
Trailhead elevation: 100 feet
Trail high point: 1,600 feet
Other seasons: all year
Map: pick up a map of the trail system at the trailhead
Pass: None needed
Drivetime from Portland: 100 minutes

Directions:
* From Portland, drive US 26 approximately 74 miles northwest to its end at a junction with US 101 just north of Cannon Beach.
* Merge onto US 101 and drive south past Cannon Beach for 14 miles to Oswald West State Park.
* Pull into the day use parking lot on your left for Short Sand Beach, where US 101 crosses Short Sand Creek. There is no day use fee as of this writing.

Why May: There are few hikes like Neahkahnie Mountain. The view from the summit stretches out to the vast panorama of the Pacific Ocean, spreading out from the rugged coastline south of Manzanita. You can come here at any time, but the weather is often inhospitable in winter and the crowds too overwhelming in summer. April and May are my favorite months to do this hike, when the days are long, sunshine is more frequent and the flowers are blooming. This is a very popular hike- expect crowds. You can shorten this hike by starting at two trailheads closer to the Neahkahnie Mountain's summit, but why? The longest hike here is by far the best.

Hike: Begin by ducking under US 101 on a wide trail signed for Short Sands Beach. This beautiful trail parallels scenic Short Sands Creek as it passes by and under enormous coastal Sitka spruce trees. Driving to the coast is always discouraging as you pass many a clearcut on the way – it is refreshing to find a place where the big trees still stand. This

will be the case for the rest of your hike. Reach a junction with the Oregon Coast Trail after a little more than a half-mile. Depending on the tide, you may want to continue out to gorgeous Short Sand Beach; if the tide is low, head out to the beach now and soak in the beautiful scenery. If the tide is high, turn left on the Oregon Coast Trail and begin hiking up to Neahkahnie Mountain.

The Oregon Coast Trail passes another trail on the left from the now-closed campground here and reaches a suspension bridge over Necarney Creek. Falling trees closed the campground in 2009, and it will likely remain closed permanently. Cross the bridge and begin hiking uphill on a well-graded trail in a forest of huge trees. You'll even hike through the roots of a particularly large Sitka spruce on your way uphill. At about 1.5 miles from the trailhead, the trail levels out atop the unnamed cape. Soon you will exit the forest and enter a huge meadow below US 101. At a trail junction, turn right and hike 200 yards out to a windswept viewpoint above Devil's Cauldron, where the Pacific has cut a cove into huge sandstone cliffs. Then return to the main trail and hike up to US 101, where you will find a small parking area. This is where most people park to climb up Neahkahnie Mountain, but you got to hang out on the beach and hike through a huge old-growth forest. It's a fair trade for hiking 3 more miles. Carefully cross the highway and begin hiking uphill.

You'll have great views of the Pacific in the first few switchbacks before you enter an impressive old-growth forest. The trail climbs at a moderate pace for a mile before leveling out as it wraps around Neahkahnie Mountain's wide summit. Continue until you reach the open meadows just below the summit of Neahkahnie. Do not scramble up the steep, fragile meadows; continue back into the forest below the summit meadows to locate a trail that heads up towards the summit on your left. A short uphill traverse takes you to the summit, where the expansive view is well worth a long rest. In spring, look for pink fawn lilies, red paintbrush and many other flowers.

Unless you managed to set up a car shuttle to the crowded southern trailhead, return the way you came. To find the southern trailhead, drive south of the Short Sand Beach TH on US 101 for 2.4 miles to a junction on your left, marked by a hiker symbol. Turn left here and drive 0.4 miles of bumpy gravel road to the trailhead. It is 1.5 miles of steep uphill from this trailhead to the summit of Neahkahnie Mountain. A lot of people appreciate this access for its brevity but I much prefer the longer approach.

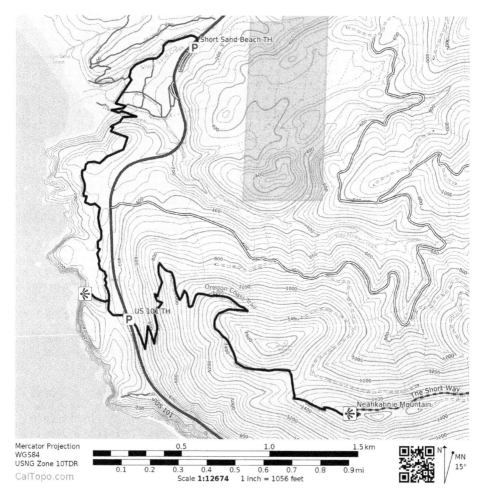

42. Cascade Head

Distance: 4.8 miles out and back
Elevation Gain: 1,200 feet
Trailhead elevation: 14 feet
Trail high point: 1,217 feet
Other seasons: all year
Map: None needed.
Pass: None needed.
Drivetime from Portland: 120 minutes

Directions:
* From Portland drive southwest first on OR 99W out of the metro area.
* About 15 miles south of downtown, reach a junction with OR 18, signed for Lincoln City and the Oregon Coast. Turn right here to drive towards the Coast.
* Drive OR 18 through McMinnville and through the Van Duzer Corridor, passing two junctions with OR 22 along the way. Stay on OR 18.
* About 52 miles from the junction with OR 99W, OR 18 ends at a junction with US 101 north of Lincoln City.
* Turn right and drive north on US 101 for 1 mile to a junction with NE Three Rocks Road on the left.
* Turn left and drive 2.3 miles to the trailhead on the left side of the road.

Why May: There are good coastal hikes and there are GREAT coastal hikes. Featuring great views and good wildflower displays, Cascade Head definitely falls into the latter category. Unlike most hikes on the Coast, this one is great year-round, in winter as well as in summer. The trail is at its best, however, in May. The trail is less muddy, the days longer and the wildflowers blooming. Start early, though; this is among the most popular hikes on the Oregon Coast. If you'd rather come earlier in the year, the hike is open year-round. February and March are quite nice, but the trail is very muddy in the winter. Summer is nice, too, but the famed wildflower meadows are mostly dried up by summer, and the trail very, very crowded.

Hike: From the trailhead, follow signs back along the road for a short distance and then continue as the trail dips into a side canyon. The trail then follows a side road some more, finally crossing it at 0.4 mile. As the trail follows a right-of-way along a road and through private property, it is important that you obey all signs where posted, and stay off the road. After a brief downhill on a gravel road, you will finally reach the old trailhead at a little over 0.5 mile. As there is little to no parking here, it is not difficult to understand why the trailhead was moved given the popularity of the hike. Turn right to start hiking up the trail towards Cascade Head.

The trail, now fully away from the road, climbs into a magical forest of huge Sitka spruce trees, which only grow to this size close to the ocean. Everything appears green and verdant. The trail continues to climb uphill and begins to angle west towards the hanging meadows of Cascade Head. The trail crosses a few side creeks and eventually trades forest for meadows at about 1.3 miles from the trailhead. Every step from this point on brings you better and better views as you ascend the open slopes of Cascade Head. Be sure to stay on the main trail here, as volunteers have diligently closed all user-built side trails. Besides, the side trails don't go anywhere- and in fact, there are cliffs everywhere here, so there's no point in putting yourself in a bad situation just for curiosity's sake. As you hike uphill, your eyes will no doubt be drawn back to the south, towards the beaches and cliffs of Three Rocks. On a sunny day this is one of the Oregon Coast's most iconic views. The trail reaches the summit at 2.4 miles, where a post marks the spot. If you've brought a picnic, this is the place to spread out. In truth the view is a little better further down the trail, but you've got lots of flat ground here on which to relax, something that isn't possible down the trail. The trail does continue beyond the summit but this area is closed from January 1 to July 15 for habitat protection. Please respect any and all closure signs and turn around before you reach the woods. Return the way you came.

If you visit later in the year you can connect this hike to the Harts Cove Trail, on the north side of Cascade Head. Harts Cove is a beautiful destination but is only open from July 16 to December 31 to protect fragile habitat. This closure, combined with the wealth of other fantastic coastal destinations closer to Portland, is why Harts Cove is not featured in this book. For more information on Harts Cove, see my website or elsewhere online.

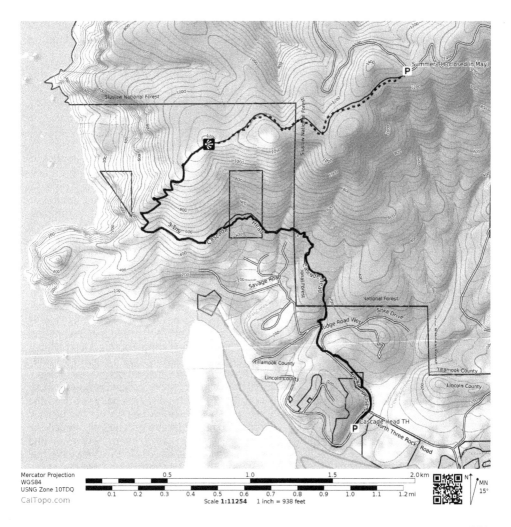

43. Upper Clackamas River

	Alder Flats Trail	Riverside Trail
Distance:	1.8 miles out and back	5.2 miles out and back
Elevation Gain:	400 feet	500 feet
Trailhead Elevation:	1,536 feet	1,503 feet
Trail High Point:	1,655 feet	1,576 feet
Other Seasons:	all year	all year (avoid icy periods)
Map:	none available	none available
Pass:	NW Forest Pass	none needed
Drivetime from PDX:	75 minutes	85 minutes

Directions to Alder Flat TH:
- From Portland, drive southeast on OR 224 to Estacada.
- Continue on OR 224 past Estacada 24.4 miles to the Alder Flat Trailhead on your right, just past milepost 49. If you reach Ripplebrook Info Station, just a few minutes down the road, you've gone too far.

Directions to Riverside TH:
- From the Ripplebrook Info Station, continue on OR 224 to a bridge over the Oak Grove Fork of the Clackamas River. Beyond the bridge, keep straight at a junction on what is now FR 46.
- Drive 1.8 miles to the Riverside Trailhead on your right.

Why May: The Clackamas River is a wonderful escape any time of the year. Here hikers can experience a wild and scenic beauty worthy of calendars and postcards without even a fraction of the crowds you find in the Gorge. May is an especially great time to visit the Clackmas, when the mountains are still snowed in, the river is raging and the area still deserted after the long winter. This hike is equally great on rainy, cold days and on warm, sunny days. When visiting in May, keep an eye on the forest floor, where you'll see a variety of colorful woodland flowers.

Clackamas white iris

Alder Flats Hike: This short and easy trail to a large camping area beside the Clackamas River is a favorite of area hikers, and is an ideal destination for short backpacking trips. The Alder Flat Trail begins by cutting a straight path between some huge trees. You'll skirt a pond before beginning a gentle descent into the Clackamas River's wide canyon. The forest here is especially scenic in the spring, and in May you will be enchanted by its wildflowers, tall trees and green glory. Reach the river at 1 mile from the trailhead. Here you'll find several large campsites beside the river. Take the time to take in this beautiful scene but please respect the privacy of campers here. Return the way you came.

Riverside Trail Hike: Once upon a time trails followed the Clackamas River from Estacada to its source near Olallie Lake. Most of this route was paved over, and the present-day routes of OR 224 and FR 46 follow these old routes. The Clackamas River Trail (Hike 33) and the Riverside Trail are the remnants of this old route, and both are favorite spring hikes that I return to, year after year (they are also great in every other season, as well).

The trail begins at the Riverside Trailhead. You could begin elsewhere, but this is the only trailhead along this trail that does not require a special use fee. After only a couple of minutes, reach a junction with the Riverside Trail. Left takes you upstream towards a campground, but the nicest scenery is found downstream. The Riverside Trail sets out on a roller coaster ride of small ups and downs as it weaves in and out of side canyons amongst ancient forest. The forest is a mossy, electric green and the many and varied flowers that dot the forest floor

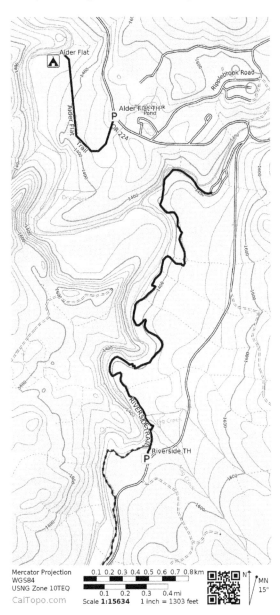

add color to the scene. Particularly noteworthy are pink calypso orchids, commonly seen here in May. As you hike along, you may also notice the Clackamas white iris, found only in this part of the Cascades. The flower grows profusely in the forest here throughout May.

The trail passes a pair of viewpoints out to a rock pinnacle above the raging river, one of the most photogenic spots on the Clackamas River. At 1.5 miles the trail passes a series of rocky beaches, where at last you can access the river. From here, the Riverside Trail continues downstream, ducking into side canyons amidst huge and ancient Douglas firs. At 2.1 miles, the trail rounds a bend and begins following the Oak Grove Fork of the Clackamas River. You can continue another 0.5 mile along the Oak Grove Fork to the trail's end at Rainbow Campground. Return the way you came.

Hikers desiring more time on the trail can continue upriver 1.5 miles beyond the Riverside Trailhead towards Riverside Campground. This stretch of trail is less scenic than what is described above, but if you've got the time and energy it is a worthy addition to your day's hike. The trail terminates in Riverside Campground, which is subject to its own, wholly separate day-use fee. If you're just hiking through it is free, of course- but if you want to park here, you'd be better served making a reservation at the campground. From there, of course, you can hike straight from your campsite.

Mercator Projection
WGS84
USNG Zone 10TEQ
CalTopo.com

Scale **1:15634**   1 inch = 1303 feet

0.1 0.2 0.3 0.4 0.5 0.6 0.7 0.8km
0.1   0.2   0.3   0.4 mi

44. Falls Creek Falls

Distance: 4 miles out and back
Elevation Gain: 700 feet
Trailhead elevation: 1,409 feet
Trail High Point: 2,097 feet
Other seasons: April- November
Map: Wind River (Green Trails #397)
Pass: NW Forest Pass
Drivetime from Portland: 80 minutes

Directions:
- From Portland drive Interstate 84 east to Cascade Locks.
- At Exit 44, leave the freeway and drive downhill into Cascade Locks.
- Turn right and drive to the Bridge of the Gods; pay the $2 toll and cross the river.
- On the far end of the bridge, turn right onto WA 14.
- Drive 5.9 miles, passing through Stevenson along the way, to a junction on your left signed for the Wind River and Carson.
- Turn left and drive 14.3 miles up the Wind River Road to a junction not far past the Carson Fish Hatchery. Turn left here to stay on the Wind River Road.
- Drive just 0.8 mile to a junction with FR 3062, signed for Falls Creek Falls.
- Turn right and drive 2 miles of potholed gravel to a junction with FR 057.
- Keep right and drive 0.4 mile to the trailhead.

Why May: The Gifford Pinchot is a waterfall wonderland. Few places in the US can rival the magnificent collection of cataracts found in Southwest Washington. Unfortunately, most of the best waterfalls found here are accessible only by those with the stamina and ability to bushwhack through inhospitable terrain. Falls Creek Falls, located north of Carson, is the best waterfall in Southwest Washington accessible by trail. While it is great at all times of the year, it is never better than in May, when the falls flows at peak volume, the flowers bloom in the woodland surroundings, and the trail not yet as crowded as it will be on hot summer weekends.

Hike: Begin at the Falls Creek Trailhead. You will follow a wide trail, once a road, to a bridge over Falls Creek. Here the creek rages through a slot canyon, and the bridge crosses the creek in a particularly photogenic spot. Cross the creek and enter a pocket of ancient forest above Falls Creek. In May hikers will be enchanted and overwhelmed by the lushness of the woodland environs here. Before long the trail begins to pull away from the

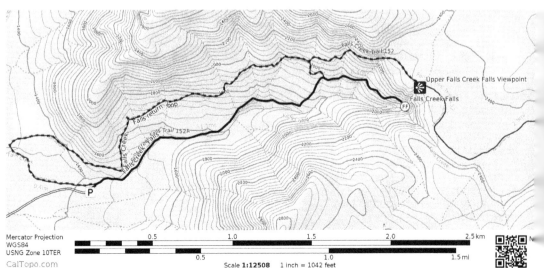

The Upper Tiers of Falls Creek Falls

creek a bit, your sign that you are nearing the falls. Reach a junction with a connector trail to the Falls Creek Trail (primarily used by horses and mountain bikers) at 1.4 miles. Keep straight and follow the trail under rock faces and beneath huge Douglas firs towards the overpowering sound of the falls. The upper tier of Falls Creek Falls soon comes into view, thundering from the cliffs above. The trail then drops a bit to a flats at the base of the lower two tiers of the falls. What a magnificent, awe-inspiring sight it is! Here Falls Creek Falls thunders 335 feet into a huge splash pool, surrounded by mossy cliffs. On rainy days the area takes on a primeval feeling in spite of the ever-present hand of man; on sunny days, everything seems impossibly green and impossibly bright. The falls is very difficult to photograph in its entirety (and at the viewpoint, you can only see the lower two tiers). You will want to spend a long time here, basking in the falls and the majesty of this setting. When finished, return the way you came.

Hikers wishing for a longer hike can turn this hike into a loop, with a side trip to a viewpoint of the uppermost tier of Falls Creek Falls. Return to the connector trail and turn right. You will hike uphill for 0.2 mile to the junction with the Falls Creek Horse Trail. Your loop takes you to the left, but for the upper viewpoint, turn right. You will continue hiking uphill and then level out. After 0.6 mile on the Falls Creek Trail, you will reach a junction with a trail on your right. Turn right and follow this short trail to a campsite near the rim of Falls Creek's canyon. There is a view down to the upper tier of Falls Creek Falls here, though the rest of the falls, alas, remains out of sight. Return then to the connector trail junction, and this time, continue straight on the Falls Creek Trail.

The remainder of the hike is somewhat monotonous, though still interesting enough to keep you from getting too bored. The Falls Creek Trail descends gradually through second-growth woods 1.8 miles to a crossing of Falls Creek at a bridge. Keep left at a junction here (right leads to a lesser-used trailhead mostly frequented by mountain bikers intent on biking the Falls Creek Trail). After you turn left, continue 0.5 mile to the trailhead and the completion of the loop.

45. Indian Point

Distance: 8.6 mile loop
Elevation Gain: 3,000 feet
Trailhead elevation: 222 feet
Trail high point: 2,950 feet
Other seasons: all year
Map: Bonneville Dam (Green Trails #429)
Pass: NW Forest Pass
Drivetime from Portland: 50 minutes

Directions:
- Drive east from Portland on Interstate 84 to Cascade Locks.
- Take exit 44, and drive into Cascade Locks.
- Drive through town, east, and then pass under the freeway at the far end of town.
- Continue straight and east on Frontage Road.
- After 2 miles you will come to a sign for Herman Creek Campground.
- Turn right and drive the narrow paved road uphill to the trailhead.

Why May: Indian Point has perhaps the best view in the entire Columbia River Gorge. The view comes at a very steep price, both literally and figuratively; to attain the view you must be willing to venture out into one of the most exposed spots in the entire Columbia River Gorge, something that will be frightening to many people. It is absolutely worth it. In May, the trail is lined with wildflowers, the forest overwhelmingly green and the weather is neither too hot nor too cold – an imperative for this hike, especially for the trek out to Indian Point.

Note: Like most other hikes in the western Gorge, this area was burned during the Eagle Creek Fire in September 2017. The extent of the damage is unknown as of press time; expect these trails to be closed until at least Spring 2018.

Hike: Begin at the Herman Creek Trailhead. The trail curls around a slope and climbs to the powerline corridor. Continue straight on the trail as it begins to climb in earnest. At 0.7 mile, reach a junction with the Herman Bridge Trail. Keep left and continue hiking

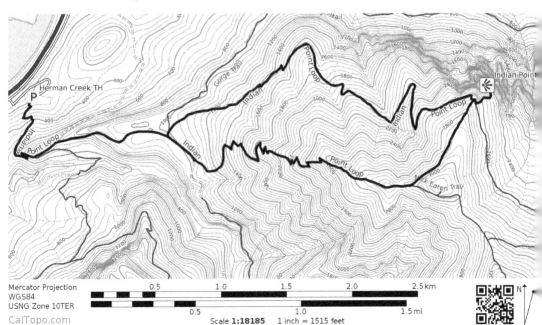

Mercator Projection
WGS84
USNG Zone 10TER

CalTopo.com

Scale **1:18185**   1 inch = 1515 feet

Indian Point

uphill to a four-way junction at 1.4 miles in a spot known as Herman Camp. This is the start of your loop. As usual, I suggest hiking the steeper trail uphill and returning on the less steep trail to save your knees. So keep straight on the Herman Creek Trail another 0.2 mile to a junction on your left with the Nick Eaton Way Trail. This steep trail will leave you huffing and puffing, gaining 2,100 feet in just 1.8 miles. The upper stretches of the trail are home to some fantastic wildflower meadows in May: look for larkspur, paintbrush, lupine, chocolate lilies and many more; the small, poofy pink flower that grows profusely in meadows is rosy plectritus, common in this part of the Gorge. At 3.4 miles, reach a junction with the Nick Eaton Cutoff Trail; turn left here. This short and easy trail crosses over to the east side of the ridge, meeting the Gorton Creek Trail in 0.6 mile. Turn right and hike 0.1 mile to the unsigned but very obvious spur trail on your left. This is the trail out to Indian Point.

The Indian Point Trail drops steeply through the forest and enters a narrow promontory, flanked by steep drop-offs on both sides. After just 0.1 mile, reach the rocky edge of Indian Point. To reach the base of the point, you must continue straight across a narrow peninsula of rock. While this peninsula is maybe twenty feet wide, it is a very, very, very long ways down on both sides. This stretch of trail will be terrifying for some hikers – and exhilarating for others. It is here that you gain the best views, so you will need to decide just how much you want the view. Some extremely foolhardy people climb up to the top of the point. This is a very bad idea, and it is not recommended to anybody not gifted with climbing skills, good luck and no fear of death. There are excellent views from the trail, and you should be content with that. To finish the hike, return to the Gorton Creek Trail and turn right. Pass the Nick Eaton Cutoff Junction and continue straight. This trail descends gradually through cool, soothing woods for 2.7 miles to the four-way junction at Herman Camp. Turn right on the Herman Creek Trail and follow your footsteps downhill the final 1.4 miles to the trailhead and your vehicle.

46. Dog Mountain

Distance: 7.3 mile loop
Elevation Gain: 2,900 feet
Trailhead elevation: 110 feet
Trail high point: 2,949 feet
Other seasons: all year
Map: Columbia River Gorge (National Geographic)
Pass: NW Forest Pass
Drivetime from Portland: 55 minutes

Directions:
- Drive east from Portland on Interstate 84 to Cascade Locks.
- Take exit 44, and drive into Cascade Locks.
- Follow signs for the Bridge of the Gods, pay the $2 toll and cross the bridge.
- On the Washington side of the bridge, turn right on SR 14 and drive 12.9 miles to the obvious trailhead on the left.
- The parking situation here is a mess. Due to the extreme popularity of the hike, Skamania County has reduced the number of parking spots here and created a shuttle bus system. Come early in the morning or late in the afternoon if you want a spot.

Why May: There is no finer place to be in May than Dog Mountain's summit meadows during the height of its famed wildflower bloom. This is one of the most popular hikes in the region, and this popularity has created a zoo-like atmosphere. The best strategy is to arrive as early as possible on a weekend (think 7AM), or better yet, visit on a weekday. This is doubly important as the Forest Service has severely reduced the number of parking spots at the trailhead, creating a messy situation. A shuttle bus runs from Stevenson to the trailhead, but the bus starts at 10AM and runs only until 4PM, depriving hikers of scheduling flexibility.

Before we get to the hike, there are three things you need to know: first of all, rattle-snakes live on Dog Mountain. Watch your step, particularly if you are hiking early in the morning or late at night. Second of all, poison oak lines the trail over the first mile and last mile of this hike. Don't step off the trail for any reason, don't wear shorts and be sure to wash your clothing in cold water when you get home. Finally, don't waste your time on this hike during almost any other season. The flower bloom fades by early June, at which time the hike becomes unbearably hot for the rest of the summer. On clear days the view is excellent, but not more so than many other Gorge hikes that offer more shade and less poison oak. Winter brings cold, windy and wet weather; if you can catch a clear and calm day, this is an excellent winter hike, but those days are few and far between. Come here in the spring for the best experience.

Hike: Start at Dog Mountain's chaotic trailhead. You have two options for the hike, the Dog Mountain Trail and the Augspurger Trail. Start on your right, on the Dog Mountain Trail. You will quickly pass the bathroom and begin hiking uphill on a steep trail that will warm you up whether you like it or not. After just 0.7 mile, reach a fork in the trail. Left is the more difficult trail, while right is less difficult – both go to the same place, but I prefer the less difficult trail as it is far more scenic and less steep. After some more switchbacks the less difficult trail mellows out somewhat and views of the Gorge begin to unfold. At 1.8 miles, reach the lower viewpoint on the trail. This is your first taste of the views and wildflower meadows for which this hike is famed. From here, climb uphill to a reunion with the more difficult trail at 2.3 miles, after which point the good stuff truly begins. The last 0.8 mile to the summit is a feast of the senses: you will hike steeply uphill through some of the finest wildflower meadows in the Gorge, while the views stretch far to the

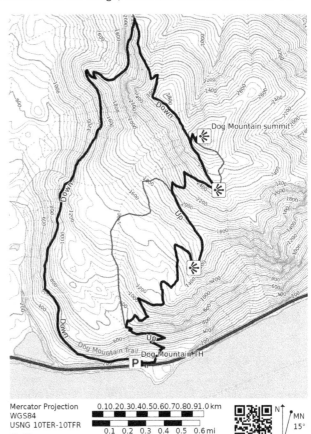

west. This is one of the most photogenic places in the Pacific Northwest. At 3 miles, reach a junction with the Augspurger Trail, your return route. Keep right and switch-back to the summit, where the view sprawls out at your feet. A better lunch spot would be hard to imagine.

To return the trailhead, hike back to the junction with the Augspurger Trail and turn right. This trail follows the west side of Dog Mountain, staying mostly in the forest. It is far quieter than the Dog Mountain Trail, and its gradual grade is pleasing. Your knees will thank you as you descend. Few hikers choose to ascend this way. At 4.3 miles, reach a junc-tion with the Augspurger Mountain Trail; energetic hikers can continue almost 5 miles to the summit of this seldom-visited peak. Most hikers will prefer to continue downhill on the Augspurger Trailhead another 3 miles to the Dog Mountain Trailhead.

Mercator Projection
WGS84
USNG 10TER-10TFR
CalTopo.com

0.1 0.2 0.3 0.4 0.5 0.6 mi
Scale **1:21151**   1 inch = 1763 feet

N
MN
15°

47. Rowena Crest and Tom McCall Point

	Rowena Crest	Tom McCall Point
Distance:	2 miles out and back	2.8 miles out and back
Elevation Gain:	300 feet	1,000 feet
Trailhead Elevation:	715 feet	715 feet
Trail High Point:	715 feet	1,722 feet
Other Seasons:	all year (avoid summer heat)	June- November
Map:	None needed.	None needed.
Pass:	None needed.	None needed.
Drivetime from PDX:	80 minutes	80 minutes

Directions:
- From Portland, drive east on Interstate 84 east to Hood River.
- At Exit 69, signed for Mosier, leave the freeway and turn right to follow old US 30 through the small community of Mosier.
- From Mosier, drive 6.7 miles to the Rowena Crest Viewpoint, where you will find the trailhead for both Rowena Crest and Tom McCall Point. Park wherever you can.

Why May: With two excellent destinations, a plethora of fantastic views and fields of May wildflowers, Rowena Crest and Tom McCall Point are two hikes for the price of one! Both sport some of the best wildflower displays in the Gorge, fantastic views and both are easy enough you'll have enough time to do something else if you so choose.

Balsamroot line the trail at Rowena Crest.

Hike: While it doesn't matter which hike you do first, I like to start by going downhill, towards the lip of Rowena Crest's tongue-shaped plateau. The wide trail zigzags across the tableland, passing stupendous displays of balsamroot and lupine in May (this is also an excellent place to see grass widows, the pink harbinger of spring that sprouts up in late February and early March, as well as shooting stars and pink desert parsley in March and April). At the end of one bend, follow a side trail with a scenic, very old gate over to an outstanding viewpoint east towards The Dalles. This is an excellent spot to take a break, out of sight from the throngs of people you will sometimes see on the Rowena Crest Trail. Once back on the main trail, keep an eye out for poison oak as you continue downhill. Pass two ponds and begin to near the edge of the plateau. The trail threads a bit as it nears the edge, and ends all together at the edge of a cliff 1 mile from the Rowena Crest Trailhead. This is an excellent rest stop – there are plenty of rocks ideal for a rest and the view is excellent. Directly across the river from you is the town of Lyle. You'll be able to

spot the Klickitat River Trail, which departs from the bridge over the Klickitat River in the middle of town. There is nowhere to go but back up, so return the way you came to the trailhead.

Once you return to the trailhead, locate the wide trail heading south from the parking area towards the summit of Tom McCall Point. This trail is officially closed until May 1st to keep the trail from becoming too eroded during the winter and spring rains; please respect the closure and wait until the upper trail officially opens to hike it. You should also keep an eye out for rattlesnakes, which are sometimes seen here on warmer days. The trail passes through a meadow that is overflowing with yellow balsamroot in early May. Enter a forest of young oak and begin climbing on a wide trail. Early in the spring, keep a close eye out here for poison oak, which lines the trail in some spots. Likewise, ticks are a major nuisance here, so be sure to inspect your clothing at least once during the hike.

The trail climbs at a considerable grade, eventually leaving the forest. The views open up to the Gorge, revealing magnificent vistas on all sides. Mount Hood looms over the forests of Surveyor Ridge, while Mount Adams comes into view behind you. Reach the summit of Tom McCall Point at 1.5 miles, where you will have an almost 360-degree view of the Gorge. Great viewpoints rarely come with this little effort (although, I admit the trail up is a bit steep at times). After you catch a breather, return the way you came back to Rowena Crest.

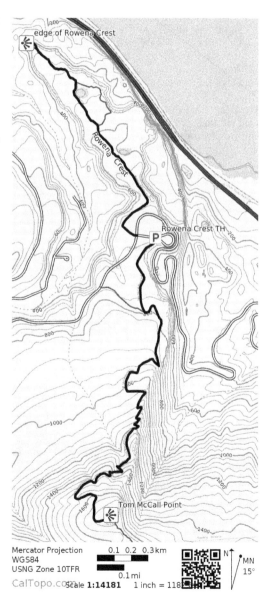

Mercator Projection
WGS84
USNG Zone 10TFR

0.1 0.2 0.3 km

0.1 mi

CalTopo.com   Scale **1:14181**   1 inch = 118...

N
MN
15°

48. Bald Butte

Distance: 8.6 miles out and back
Elevation Gain: 2,400 feet
Trailhead elevation: 1,747 feet
Trail high point: 3,781 feet
Other seasons: April- November
Map: None needed.
Pass: None needed.
Drivetime from Portland: 80 minutes

Directions:
- From Portland, drive Interstate 84 to Hood River and leave the highway at Exit 64, signed for OR 35. At the bottom of the exit ramp, turn right onto OR 35.
- Drive south 14.4 miles towards Mount Hood.
- Just past Tollbridge County Park, turn left on Smullen Road at a sign for the Oak Ridge Trail.
- Drive 0.25 mile to another sign and turn left on a gravel road into the trailhead.

Why May: Bald Butte is an excellent alternative to Dog Mountain if you're looking for a great wildflower hike with views in May. To be perfectly honest, I like this hike a lot more than Dog Mountain. There is a wider variety of wildflowers, the view of Mount Hood is a lot better, and the trail passes some large ponderosa pines, always a plus. Better yet,

this hike is far less crowded than Dog Mountain, and less crowded than most hikes that are this close to population centers. The only downside, if you can call it that, is that you must share part of the trail with mountain bikers. But the mountain bikers are generally a hospitable bunch, and they love this trail as much as you will.

Hike: The trail is fairly level at first, skirting a clearcut with views out to Mount Hood. Here you'll find a variety of woodland flowers such as wild rose and (non-native) bachelor button. Before long, however, the trail enters the woods and begins climbing gradually up an open, grassy slope. As the trail switchbacks up the open hillside, views open up across the upper Hood River valley to Mount Hood, which appears quite close. Even closer at your feet are the wildflowers that grow profusely along the trail in May. Look for yellow balsamroot, blue and purple lupine, bachelor buttons, paintbrush and still others. This stretch of the trail will slow your progress, both due to its relative steepness and to its scenic beauty.

At 1.5 miles, the trail levels out somewhat and reenters the forest. You will pass several large ponderosa pines. The trail soon enters deeper forest, where you are treated to a lovely display of woodland flowers such as pink calypso orchids and blue hounds tongue. There are also occasional views north to the summit of Bald Butte, which appears further away than it actually is. At 2.3 miles, the trail crosses a road. Keep straight and reach a junction with the Surveyor's Ridge Trail. Turn left.

While the Oak Ridge Trail is closed to mountain biking, the Surveyor's Ridge Trail is a popular mountain biking thoroughfare and thus you will need to pay attention to avoid any unexpected accidents. The bikers who use the trail are typically quite courteous and you should be as well to ensure that everybody shares the trail in peace. The Surveyors Ridge Trail climbs a bit, and then begins to lose elevation as it drops to a saddle about 3.6 miles from the trailhead. There is a parking area nearby that marks the end of the Surveyor Ridge Trail. To reach the summit of Bald Butte, follow an old jeep road that heads steeply uphill north under the powerlines. The road climbs steeply to a false summit, drops back into the forest, then climbs at an even steeper grade up a flower-spangled hillside to the true summit of Bald Butte, which you reach at 4.3 miles from the trailhead. The view is tremendous, extending out the entire length of the Hood River Valley. Look to your left (southwest) to Mount Hood, towering over the far end of the valley. To the left of Mount Hood is bulky Lookout Mountain, rising above the rugged ridges of the Badger Creek Wilderness. To the north is Hood River, with Mount Saint Helens and Mount Rainier looming over the Cascades to the northwest. A better picnic spot would be hard to imagine. The wind up here can be ferocious on occasion, and you may need to beat a quick retreat into the forest on the windiest days. Return the way you came.

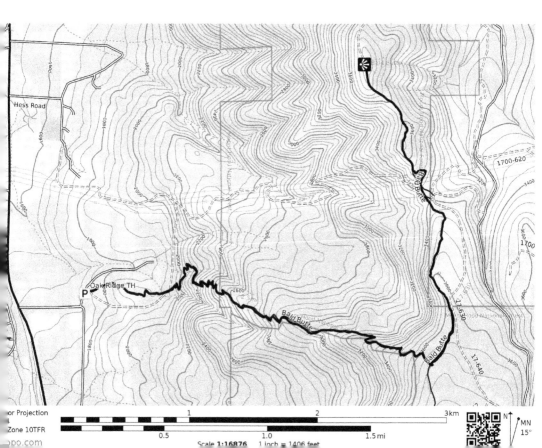

49. Badger Creek

Distance: 12 miles out and back
Elevation Gain: 1,200 feet
Trailhead Elevation: 2,175 feet
Trail High Point: 3,092 feet
Other seasons: April- November
Map: Flag Point (Green Trails #463)
Pass: None needed
Drivetime from Portland: 120 minutes

Directions:

- From Portland drive US 26 east to a junction with OR 35 on the side of Mt. Hood.
- Turn onto OR 35 and continue for 4.6 miles to a junction with FR 48, signed for Wamic and Rock Creek Reservoir, just after you cross the White River.
- Turn right and drive east on FR 48 for exactly 24 miles.
- At a junction with FR 4810, turn left.
- Turn left and drive 0.3 mile to a Y-junction. Fork to the right here to stay on FR 4810.
- Drive 1.9 miles to a junction with FR 4811 just outside Rock Creek Reservoir.
- At a junction signed for Bonney Crossing CG, turn right on FR 4811.
- Drive 1.2 paved but narrow miles to another junction signed for Bonney Crossing CG, this time with FR 2710.
- Turn right and drive 1.8 narrow gravel miles downhill to the Badger Creek TH, just after you cross Badger Creek. Be careful on the last 0.8 mile as it is narrow and bumpy; it would be unpleasant to meet another vehicle heading in the opposite direction here as the road is quite narrow.
- You may need to park in Bonney Crossing CG on the south bank of Badger Creek opposite the trailhead. There is only room for 2-3 cars at the Badger Creek trailhead and the lot fills fast on weekend days.

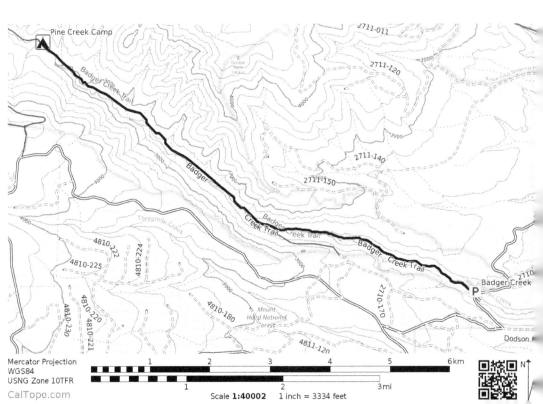

Weather-beaten and shot-up trail signs at the Badger Creek Trailhead.

Why May: There's no finer place to visit in May than the Badger Creek Wilderness. Located well into Mount Hood's vast rain shadow, the area melts out much earlier than destinations west of the Cascade Crest. The Badger Creek Wilderness (particularly the eastern side of the wilderness) has a curious and heartbreaking beauty, with colorful and rare wildflowers, varied and beautiful forests, enchanting rock pinnacles and deep canyons. This is among my favorite places on earth.

Hike: The trail begins at a signboard next to tumbling Badger Creek. The creek will be your companion for the entirety of the hike, as the trail generally stays within shouting distance of this lovely mountain stream. The trail passes under a forest more typical of valleys west of the Cascades, consisting mostly of Douglas firs and Mountain hemlock with only a few scattered ponderosa pines. Keep your eyes on the valley floor, where in May you'll see lots of woodland flowers, including the pink calypso orchid – this beautiful bloom, also known as the lady's slipper orchid, has a wondrous fragrance for a day or two after blooming. The trail follows the creek at a respectable distance, rarely coming close but rarely drifting out of sight.

Backpackers will enjoy the Badger Creek Trail, as there are campsites seemingly every half-mile or so throughout the duration of the hike. Expect many of them to be filled on sunny weekend days, which may necessitate you hiking further than you were planning. Perhaps the best of the campsites is also the end of the recommended hike: at 6 miles from the trailhead, the Badger Creek Trail passes a flat next to Badger Creek, at its confluence with cascading Pine Creek. It doesn't get much better than this, and hikers should turn around here, beside the confluence of two beautiful streams. If you are backpacking and cannot find a site, there are a few past Pine Creek, including an excellent one at the junction with the Pine Creek Trail a half-mile beyond the confluence of Pine and Badger Creeks. From here the trail continues more than 5 miles to Badger Lake, but this upper stretch of trail is often buried under snow in May and is not much fun this time of year.

50. School Canyon

Distance: 8 miles out and back
Elevation Gain: 1,800 feet
Trailhead elevation:
Trail High Point:
Other seasons: April – November
Map: Flag Point (Green Trails #463)
Pass: None needed
Drivetime from Portland: 125 minutes

Directions:
- Drive I-84 east of Portland approximately 80 miles to The Dalles.
- Leave the highway at exit 87 and follow signs to US 197, heading south out of The Dalles towards Tygh Valley.
- Drive US 197 south 27 miles to a junction with Shadybrook Road, just north of Tygh Valley.
- Turn right on Shadybrook Road and drive 1.1 miles to a junction with Fairgrounds Road. Turn left here.
- After just 0.7 mile, turn right on the Badger Creek Road and drive this gravel road 6.6 miles to a junction with Ball Point Road, FR27.
- From the junction of Badger Creek Road and Ball Point Road, turn right onto Ball Point Road (FR 27).
- Drive 2.1 paved miles to the School Canyon Trailhead on your left.

Why May: You could call this hike Ball Point, or you could call it School Canyon – but whatever you call it, this is a beautiful hike that cuts through the heart of the pine oak grassland for which this area is known. In May you'll pass fields of lupine, look out into the far off expanse of central Oregon and hike under some of the nicest groves of ponderosa pine in the area. There's so much to see and do here, and this hike is far enough away from Portland, that it may be difficult to leave. Creative and adventurous hikers can make a loop with the Little Badger Creek Trail by way of either a bushwhack or short car shuttle.

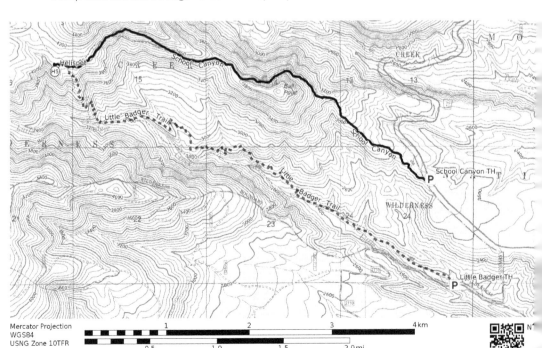

Hike: The trail begins in open woods that are characteristic of the pine-oak grassland ecosystem that the Badger Creek area straddles. Weave in and out of forest as you look towards Ball Point ahead of you. Much of the eastern half of the Badger Creek Wilderness burned in a 2007 fire, and indeed you'll see scorched trees here and there as you climb towards Ball Point. Your goal is not the summit of this colorfully-named peak but a ridge halfway up its flank. Upon leaving forest, climb steeply up an open hillside speckled with balsamroot, lupine and red paintbrush to a saddle with views back to the east towards central Oregon. The panorama extends from the Columbia River and its windfarms all the way to Mount Jefferson and the Three Sisters, far to the south. The lake in the valley below to your right is the Pine Hollow Reservoir near Tygh Valley. On a clear day the views seem to stretch out into the infinite.

Upon leaving the saddle, the trail heads uphill to your right and traverses the northern slopes of Ball Point. Round a bend and enter forest regenerating from the 2007 fire. Note how the larger trees, both Douglas firs and ponderosa pines, though scarred, survived the fire intact, a result of their thick, fire-resistant bark. Below you is the rugged canyon of Tygh Creek; keen eyes may spot the Tygh Creek Trail on the far side of the canyon. The trail eventually passes around Ball Point and enters deep forest, consisting mostly of ponderosa pine. At 3.6 miles the trail reaches a junction with the Little Badger Creek Trail, arriving from your left. Continue straight another 0.1 mile to a junction with a short spur trail on your left, signed for a helispot. Turn left here and walk the short trail out to a rocky promontory: here you will find a fascinating and intriguing collection of fluted rock pinnacles of all shapes and sizes. This is the recommended stopping point; return the way you came.

Energetic hikers can make a loop with the Little Badger Trail. Follow the Little Badger Trail downhill and then back along Little Badger Creek for 4 miles to a trailhead on FR 2710. Even though the two trailheads are approximately 0.5 mile apart as the crow flies, it requires 3.5 miles of driving to make the shuttle. From the School Canyon TH, drive back on FR 27 to FR 2710 and turn right. Continue 1.5 gravel miles to the Little Badger TH. A short bushwhack is another way to make this loop, but this is easier said than done- trust me.

Bonus Hike: White River Falls

Lower Falls distance: 1 mile out and back
Elevation Gain: 200 feet
Trailhead elevation: 1,057 feet
Trail high point: 1,057 feet
Other seasons: all year
Map: None needed.
Pass: None needed.
Drivetime from Portland: 120 minutes

Directions:
- Drive Interstate 84 east of Portland approximately 80 miles to The Dalles.
- Leave the highway at Exit 87 and follow signs to US 197, heading south out of The Dalles.
- Drive US 197 south for 28 miles to a junction with OR 216 in Tygh Valley, signed for White River Falls and Sherars Bridge.
- Turn left here and drive east for 4 miles to the well-marked state park.
- Turn right and drive into the park's small lot.

Why May: White River Falls is a world apart despite being only two hours from Portland. Located in a desert canyon near the town of Tygh Valley, the falls is in the most surprising of locations. Driving to the trailhead, it would be hard to imagine that there's a waterfall anywhere nearby- and yet, upon arrival, all who visit are entranced. There's an argument to be made that this is the best waterfall in Oregon. May is perhaps the best time to visit, as the falls are flowing strong, the flowers along the trail are at their peak and the days not all that hot. Hikers desiring more time on the trail should turn to the previous two hikes, which are located not all that far from here on the other side of Tygh Valley.

Hike: From the parking lot, the falls is audible and quite inviting. Walk down the paved path to a fenced overlook of the falls. While the view of the falls isn't the best, the view down the canyon is stupendous. This is where you are headed. Continue down the paved trail until you reach a small bridge over a side canyon. Keep right and hike downhill on a

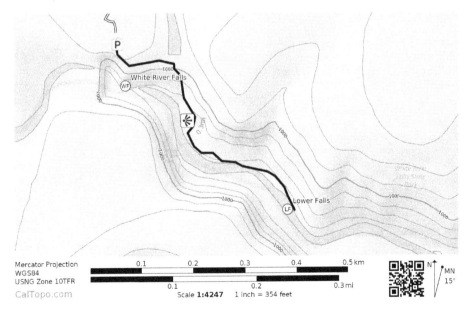

White River Falls.

steep dirt trail until at last the falls comes into sight on your right. About halfway down the canyon, note a side trail on your right. Turn here and walk out to the edge of this rocky promontory for the best view, and best photography angle of White River Falls. The lower tier of the falls, a favorite in the whitewater kayaking community, has been officially renamed Celestial Falls. To me it's the same waterfall- one of the most powerful and beautiful in the state of Oregon. There is usually a rainbow (sunny days are the rule here) to add to the scene.

Below the viewpoint, the trail drops a short distance to the canyon floor. Here you'll find an abandoned building, the remnants of a hydroelectric project from the 1920s. Inside is a fascinating collection of rusting machinery but beware- the building is condemned, and I'm supposed to tell you that it's not a good idea to go inside. Instead, return to the trail and continue hiking downstream. From here, the trail gets fainter as it cuts through the sagebrush deeper into the White River's desert canyon.

While you are here, take the time to think about the White River. The river flows out of a glacier on the east side of Mount Hood and gathers strength as it roars through a deep and remote canyon on the southeast side of the Mount Hood National Forest known only to rafters and kayakers. By the time the river emerges just south of Tygh Valley, it is a powerful stream draining much of the eastern foothills of the Cascades. You'll be hiking along this raging river as you work your way towards Lower White River Falls. Scattered ponderosa pines add color to the scene but your companions are mostly sagebrush and wild rose, which blooms in May. At a half-mile from the parking lot, reach Lower White River Falls. Although the falls is only 15 feet tall, it is a most photogenic scene. The river rages through a basalt amphitheater as good as any you'll find in the area. The large rocky bench above the falls is a great spot to hang out for a while, below the sun and next to one of Oregon's great rivers. When you can bear it, return the way you came.

JUNE

		Distance	EV Gain	Drive
51.	Saddle Mountain	5.6 mi	1,600 ft	90 min
52.	Marys Peak	9.4 mi	2,500 ft	120 min
53.	Siouxon Creek	11.8 mi	1,600 ft	100 min
54.	Angels Rest	4.4 mi	1,500 ft	30 min
55.	Larch Mountain	14.4 mi	4,000 ft	35 min
56.	Green Point Mountain	18.5 mi	4,800 ft	55 min
57.	Burnt Lake	8 mi	1,500 ft	70 min
58.	Fifteenmile Creek	10.3 mi	1,900 ft	110 min
59.	Rooster Rock	10.8 mi	3,800 ft	80 min
60.	Dome Rock	10.2 mi	3,600 ft	110 min

June is one of the most beautiful months of the year but also perhaps the most frustrating. You've waited all year for the gorgeous weather of June, but sometimes all you get is more rain and cool weather (a phenomenon known locally as "Junuary"). At least the days are long, and on sunny days, it feels like the world is your oyster, like you can do anything at all.

The hikes presented here offer a vast array of experiences, terrains and difficulty levels. There are wildflower hikes on the high peaks of the Coast Range, several scenic hikes in the Columbia River Gorge, beautiful streamside hikes in the Cascades and long treks to two of the most interesting summits in the mountains southeast of Portland. Some of these hikes are easy enough that almost any hiker can do them; others are among the most difficult in this book. The hikes to the summit of Larch Mountain, Rooster Rock and Dome Rock are excellent for conditioning but are worthy goals in their own right.

Preparing for hikes in June can be an exercise in frustration. While it might be tempting to switch into your summer clothing, grab your light pack and go out with little on your body, you must still prepare as though it were winter. Snow is still a possibility above 4,000 feet even in June, and you may encounter snow left over from the long winter on several of these hikes if you visit earlier in June. The aforementioned "Junuary" days are particularly deflating, as you wish summer would just hurry up and get here. You should always pack rain gear, an extra pair of socks and extra food and water just in case your day is longer than anticipated. And yes, you should always check the weather forecast before you leave the house- knowledge is power.

Chinook Falls just above Siouxon Creek (Hike 53)

51. Saddle Mountain

Distance: 5 miles out and back
Elevation Gain: 1,603 feet
Trailhead elevation: 1,680 feet
Trail high point: 3,283 feet
Other seasons: March- November
Map: None needed
Pass: None needed
Drivetime from Portland: 100 minutes

Directions:
- From Portland, drive US 26 approximately 64 miles northwest to a sign for Saddle Mountain State Park, near milepost 10.
- Turn right on this road and drive 7 miles of bumpy pavement, ignoring all side roads, to road's end at a large trailhead parking lot.

Why June: If you can only do one hike in the Coast Range of Northwest Oregon, make it this moderate hike up to the summit of Saddle Mountain, south of Astoria. On a clear day, you can see out to the Pacific Ocean and east to Mount Saint Helens and Mount Hood. Astoria looks surprisingly close. In June, the entire hike is lined with wildflowers, from trailhead to summit. Even on rainy days, the flowers and forest make this a fantastic hike. Just don't expect solitude- this is among the most popular hikes in the state.

Hike: The trail begins ascending through a lush forest carpeted with oxalis and neon green moss. The trail passes the small campground located near the trailhead and commences climbing uphill at a steady grade. You will pass a side trail to the Humbug Mountain viewpoint – if you've got extra time, this is a steep but interesting side trail that leads to a view

Looking up to Saddle Mountain's summit cliffs from near the trailhead.

of Saddle Mountain, but is not in any way essential. Stay on the main trail and begin climbing through the woods on a well-graded and very well-maintained trail. As you hike towards the summit, keep your eyes towards the ground, as the wildflowers along the trail are among the most varied and colorful of any hike in Oregon. In the woods, you will see purple irises, red paintbrush, blue larkspur, orange tiger lilies and so many more. Wildflower enthusiasts and photographers will find their progress slow indeed on the way up.

Before too long the trail leaves the forest and enters the huge hanging meadows for which Saddle Mountain is famous. The wildflowers are even more numerous and varied here. Rather than list them all here, I suggest bringing a wildflower guide with you, or downloading an app to identify the many flowers along the trail. At 2 miles from the trailhead, you will top out at the false summit of Saddle Mountain, just above the saddle. The trail rounds a corner and begins a short descent into the saddle, where the true summit appears above.

As you descend, keep an eye out for Mount Rainier on the northeastern horizon, just to the left of the false summit's cliffs. Drop down to the saddle, and then climb the last 0.4 mile steeply uphill to the mountain's true summit at 2.5 miles. The view is far-reaching, panoramic and truly stunning. To the west, the Pacific Ocean stretches to the far horizon. Look for Astoria to the northwest, with Astoria Column visible on a hilltop above Astoria. To the east, look for the high peaks of the Cascades, towering over the Willamette Valley. In addition to the aforementioned Mount Rainier, peaks from Mount Adams to Mount Jefferson line the horizon, although it takes a clear day to actually see them. This is among the finest places in the region for a picnic, on top of the world in the Coast Range. Return the way you came.

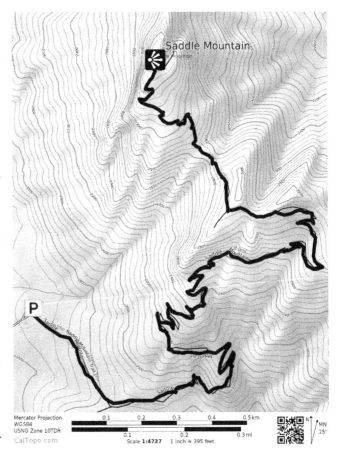

52. Marys Peak

Distance: 9.2 miles out and back
Elevation Gain: 2,300 feet
Trailhead elevation: 1,770 feet
Trail high point: 4,097 feet
Other seasons: May- November
Map: None needed
Pass: None needed
Drivetime from Portland: 120 minutes

Directions:
- From Portland, drive I-5 south 65 miles to exit 234B.
- Following signs for US 20 merge onto the highway and drive 12 miles to Corvallis
- Turn right and stay on US 20 another 7 miles to a junction with OR 34.
- Keep to your right on US 20 another 1.7 miles to a junction with Woods Creek Road.
- Turn right and follow paved road that eventually turns to gravel. The road ends 7.5 miles from the highway at a gate and parking area. The trail is on your left.

Why June: The highest point in the Oregon Coast Range, Marys Peak commands a view from the Pacific to the Cascades. Wildflowers grow in amazing abundance on the summit's enormous, humped meadow. Marys Peak is a place every Oregonian should visit at least once and thanks to a paved road that leads to the summit meadows, every Oregonian can visit. You could drive to the summit meadows, but it's far better and more interesting to hike up on a beautiful, quiet trail amidst rare coastal old-growth and woodland flowers. This is one of the best hikes in the state, crowds and cars be damned.

The North Ridge Trail near the summit parking lot on Marys Peak.

Hike: Begin at a gate and almost immediately fork to the right on the well-marked trail. Hike through a lovely Douglas fir forest with a verdant carpet of moss. In May and June the Oregon iris grows profusely here, rewarding hikers of this lower trail. Keep a look out for other flowers as well, including yellow monkeyflower and red columbine, both of which are almost as abundant here as the iris. After 0.5 mile, reach a junction and turn right. Almost immediately begin climbing via a series of switchbacks. While never steep, the climbing is constant for the next 3 miles as you work up the forested north ridge of Marys Peak. Here you will find some of the larger trees left in this part of the Coast Range – while not in national forest, they are instead protected because they are in Corvallis' municipal watershed.

At 3.5 miles from the trailhead meet a junction with the Tie Trail at a bench. Turn right here and soon level out in a lovely noble fir forest that slowly opens up to offer vistas of the vast summit meadows of Marys Peak. Just 0.5 mile later reach the large parking lot at the upper end of the North Ridge Trail. On summer weekends this is a busy place. Spot the road heading up the vast green meadow before you and follow it as it curls around to the weather station at the summit, some 4,097 feet above sea level. The view is breathtaking – on a clear day you can see from Mount Adams in Washington to Diamond Peak, south of the Three Sisters, and from a thin sliver of the Pacific Ocean to the Cascades and over the entirety of the Willamette Valley. At your feet is a carpet of larkspur, paintbrush, lupine and dozens of other wildflowers.

Despite the summit's weather station equipment this is one of the most inspiring places in the state of Oregon. If the weather is threatening, this is one of Oregon's windiest, most inhospitable places. During my first visit here I was forced to huddle around one of the summit buildings during an intense storm. You should plan your hike for a sunny day towards the end of June and bring a picnic!

Return the way you came.

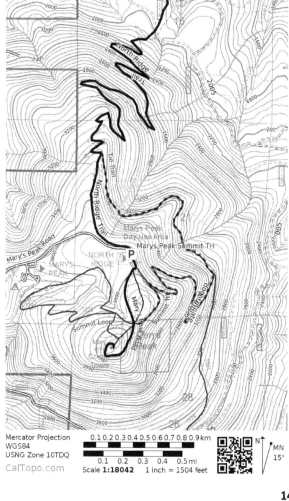

Mercator Projection
WGS84
USNG Zone 10TDQ
CalTopo.com

0.1 0.2 0.3 0.4 0.5 0.6 0.7 0.8 0.9 km
0.1   0.2   0.3   0.4   0.5 mi
Scale **1:18042**   1 inch = 1504 feet

N
MN
15°

53. Siouxon Creek

	Chinook Falls	Wildcat Falls overlook
Distance:	9.4 miles out and back	11.8 miles out and back
Elevation Gain:	1,200 feet	1,600 feet
Trailhead Elevation:	1,349 feet	1,309 feet
Trail High Point:	1,609 feet	1,609 feet
Other Seasons:	April - October	April- October
Map:	Lookout Mtn (GT #396)	Lookout Mtn (GT #396)
Pass:	None needed	None needed
Drivetime from PDX:	100 minutes	100 minutes

Directions:
- Begin by driving to the intersection of WA 503 and Main Street in Battle Ground.
- Drive north on WA 503 for 12.6 miles to Amboy.
- Continue 4.5 miles beyond Amboy on WA 503 to Chelatchie.
- At the general store in Chelatchie, turn right on NE Healy Road, also known as FR 54.
- Drive 5.2 miles to a fork in the road. As you drive, the pavement degrades, and you need to pay attention for sunken and broken sections of pavement, as well as the occasional pothole.
- Keep right here at this junction and again at the next junction, and drive another 4 miles to a junction with FR 57.
- The right fork is signed for Carson, many miles to the east; instead you want to fork to the left (uphill) on FR 57.
- Drive 1.3 miles to a junction with FR 5701. Turn sharply to the left here on FR 5701.
- Drive 3.7 miles of rough pavement to the Siouxon Creek Trailhead at road's end.
- Drive very slowly on this stretch of road as FR 5701 has numerous potholes, fissures, and warped pavement that will take out your oilpan if you aren't paying attention.

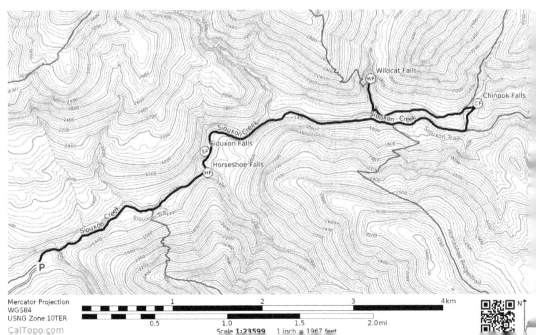

Mercator Projection
WGS84
USNG Zone 10TER
CalTopo.com

Scale **1:23599** 1 inch = 1967 feet

Why June: Siouxon Creek is a fantastic hike in any season, but never more so than in June. The creek and waterfalls are still running high, woodland flowers are numerous and the hike great on those cloudy days in June that make you long for summer to hurry up and get here. This is, of course, also an excellent hike on a sunny day. This is also a fantastic early-season backpacking trip but beware – you'll have company. There are as many back-packers as there are sites.

Hike: Begin at the Siouxon Creek Trailhead and drop quickly to a trail junction with the Siouxon Trail. Turn right and follow a wide trail through the woods, paralleling Siouxon Creek but rarely approaching it. Ignore a fork on your right for the Horseshoe Ridge Trail, which loops up and over a ridge to your right. At 2 miles from the trailhead, cross a bridge over the top of lacy Horseshoe Falls, and then descend to a junction with a user trail to the base of the falls. There is a campsite here at the base of the falls, but camping there also blocks the trail for others who may want to enjoy this lovely spot. Beyond Horseshoe Falls, the trail passes above twisting Siouxon Falls and proceeds to parallel Siouxon Creek for 1.8 miles to a trail junction on your left with the Wildcat Trail. Instead continue 1 more mile to a bridge over Siouxon Creek at a deep and very photogenic spot on the creek. Below you the creek appears to be a deep shade of green. While this is fantastic, don't turn around yet! Continue on the trail another 0.2 mile to the base of Chinook Falls, a 62-foot horsetail set in a mossy grotto. This is where most hikers should turn around, as the way gets much more difficult from here.

To continue the hike, you'll need to cross Chinook Creek on a large log. Once across the creek, you'll begin climbing for the first time as the trail has to gain elevation to pass a narrow spot above Siouxon Creek. Soon the trail drops a bit to the green, mossy flats beside Wildcat Creek. Look around for a log on which to cross Wildcat Creek – at last visit, the crossing was very easy. On the other side of the creek, you reach a junction with the Wildcat Trail. Left leads you directly to a crossing of Siouxon Creek; for now, fork to the right and begin climbing above Wildcat Creek. The trail passes above Lower Wildcat Falls' twisting corkscrew before reaching a narrow vantage point above Wildcat Falls' narrow pool at 5.8 miles from the trailhead. The view of the falls isn't perfect, but the 225' falls is quite impressive. Later in the year it's possible to return to the trailhead by simply crossing Siouxon Creek below Wildcat Falls but this is difficult and potentially dangerous. The creek is far too swift and deep to safely ford even in June.

Instead return the way you came, back via Chinook Falls and along the creek.

Wildcat Falls.

54. Angels Rest

Distance: 4.4 miles out and back
Elevation Gain: 1,500 feet
Trailhead Elevation: 121 feet
Trail High Point: 1,617 feet
Other seasons: all year
Map: Bridal Veil (Green Trails #428)
Pass: None needed.
Drivetime from Portland: 30 minutes

Directions:
- From Portland, drive east on Interstate 84 to exit 28, signed for Bridal Veil.
- Continue onto E Bridal Veil Road for 0.3 mile to a junction with the Historic Columbia River Highway.
- At the junction, turn right into the Angels Rest Trailhead.

Why June: Angels Rest is the first place many Portland-area hikers go when they want to get out for a hike, and it's hard to question their decision. The view from the summit cliffs rivals any in the Gorge, and at only 40 minutes away from downtown, it's the closest really nice hike to the city. Best of all, the hike is easy enough that almost anybody can make it to the summit. This combination brings enormous crowds, especially in June. It is not uncommon to arrive at the trailhead and find well over 100 cars parked. On days like this, you may ask yourself if it's even worth it. Here are three tips avoid the crowds: start early in the day (hit the trail by 8AM), come on a weekday, or come here late for sunset. I like to come here late in the day near the June solstice to watch the sun set over Portland. However you choose to do it, this hike is a cherished rite of passage for Portland-area hikers. Unlike many of our most popular hikes, this one lives up to the hype.

Looking east from just below the summit of Angels Rest.

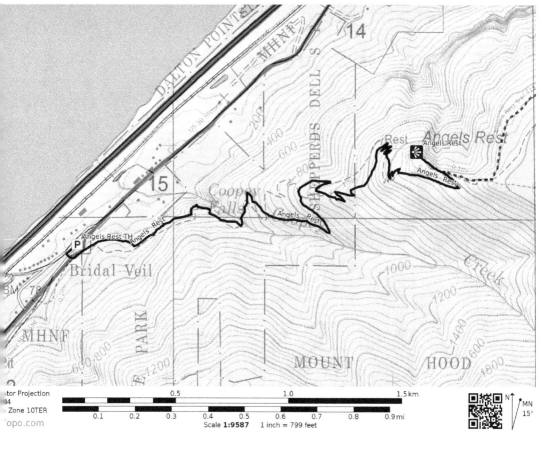

Scale **1:9587** 1 inch = 799 feet

Note: Like most other hikes in the western Gorge, this area was burned during the Eagle Creek Fire in September 2017. The extent of the damage is unknown as of press time; expect these trails to be closed until at least Spring 2018.

Hike: The trail is very straightforward. Climb a wide, well-worn, and muddy trail through second-growth forest up and away from the Gorge floor. In April keep your eyes on the forest floor, where you will see a variety of flowers, among them white trillium, yellow violet and purple anemone. Pass above Coopey Creek's tall lower falls and soon cross the creek. From here the trail continues switchbacking up through the forest. As you ascend, views begin to open up of the west Gorge. At about 1.8 miles, pass a rockslide, a clue that you are almost there. Continue uphill another quarter-mile to an unsigned junction on your left. While the main trail goes uphill to your right, you want to turn on the trail heading downhill to your left.

Follow this short trail downhill as it skirts around rocks to the edge of Angels Rest's wide promontory. Watch where you put your hands, as poison oak grows in a few of the rock cracks along the crest of Angels Rest. The view is exceptional, particularly looking west back towards Portland. Sunset is the best time to photograph Angels Rest, as the day's dying light illuminates the west end of the Gorge and the Portland metro area in shades of orange and purple. This is a fantastic place for an evening picnic; in spite of the crowds, the plateau offers enough space for everyone to have at least a little privacy. When you are ready, return the way you came.

If you'd like a longer hike, you can start at Wahkeena Falls or even Multnomah Falls. This longer hike features several waterfalls and provides a more complete hiking experience. For more information about these trails, see Hike 107.

55. Larch Mountain

Distance: 14.6 miles out and back
Elevation Gain: 4,000 feet
Trailhead elevation: 38 feet
Trail high point: 4,038 feet
Other seasons: June- November
Map: Bridal Veil (Green Trails #428)
Pass: None needed
Drivetime from Portland: 45 minutes

Directions:
- Drive east from Portland on Interstate 84 to Multnomah Falls, exit 31. Beware that this is a left-lane exit. Park in the huge lot by the freeway.
- On Fridays, Saturdays and Sundays a shuttle bus runs from Gateway Transit Center in NE Portland to Multnomah Falls. For more information about the Columbia Gorge Express, see http://columbiagorgeexpress.com/

Why June: The long trek from Multnomah Falls to the summit of Larch Mountain is one of the best hikes near Portland. You will start beside Oregon's tallest waterfall and hike along a gorgeous rushing stream, eventually arriving at the top of perhaps the best view in the western Gorge. June is my favorite time to come do this hike, after the snow melts in the shadow of Larch Mountain, the waterfalls are still flowing strong and the flowers are numerous. Such a trek is too much for some hikers – the less able will appreciate that you can also drive to within a short walk of the summit of Larch Mountain. If you're hiking the whole way up plan on an early start and prepare for any weather from cold rain to hot weather – all of which are possible in June. Later in June is better most years.

Note: Like most other hikes in the western Gorge, this area was burned during the Eagle Creek Fire in September 2017. The extent of the damage is unknown as of press time; expect these trails to be closed until at least Spring 2018.

Hike: Begin at Multnomah Falls. Walk to the lodge and locate the trail heading uphill to the Benson Bridge, which spans the top of the lower tier of Multnomah Falls. From here, you will climb steeply up the east side of Multnomah Falls' huge amphitheater on a paved trail. Ten switchbacks and one mile later you will arrive at a junction near the top of Multnomah Falls. The trail crosses Multnomah Creek and passes first by highly scenic Weisendanger Falls and then Ecola Falls before reaching a junction with the Wahkeena Trail #420 at 1.7 miles. Continue straight and leave the tourists behind – in fact, the stretch from the Wahkeena Junction to the base of Larch Mountain is among the quieter stretches of trail in the Gorge. From this junction the trail continues 1 more mile to a crossing of the Multnomah Basin Road. This is a good spot to take a breather, as you've climbed 1,600 feet in just 2.7 miles so far.

At the junction, walk along the road about twenty feet to locate the Larch Mountain Trail on your right. Turn right to continue the trek towards Larch Mountain. The trail continues along Multnomah Creek 0.3 mile more to a junction with the Franklin Ridge Trail on your left. If you're feeling worn out, consider this alternative, which connects over to the Oneonta Trail and then back, offering you a hike of 12 miles and 2,700 feet of elevation gain; but you came for Larch Mountain, so continue straight. From here you will follow Multnomah Creek, crossing it one last time at 3.7 miles. The trail then switchbacks once and commences a long climb towards Larch Mountain. The grade is easy but the long miles can make this stretch punishing on hot days. You will cross a large talus slope and enter a forest of huge, ancient Douglas-firs as you enter dark forest cradled in Larch Mountain's crater. Keep an eye out for June wildflowers on the cool forest floor, among them violets, bunchberry, coralroot and the occasional tiger lily. Rhododendrons and beargrass also add color to the scene.

At 5 miles from the trailhead you will reach a junction with the Multnomah Spur Trail. Keep straight and continue another 0.4 mile to a wide junction with an abandoned road. Here you will likely begin to see other hikers again, as many use this road to intersect the Larch Mountain Trail for a much easier but less satisfying hike. The way from here gets a little steeper as you near Larch Mountain's huge summit. At long last, the trail reaches a junction near Larch Mountain's summit picnic area. Left leads you to Sherrard Point, the mountain's summit, while right leads you to the parking lot at the mountain's upper trail-head. Keep left here, and keep left again on the paved trail to Sherrard Point, the view-packed summit of Larch Mountain.

The view, as you might expect, is amazing. Volcanoes from Mount Rainier to Mount Jefferson are visible on clear days, with Mount Hood the star of the show less than thirty miles away. Unlike most other hikes in Gorge and Cascades, you can also see Portland from the summit. If you just drove here for the view, this is a great place to visit at sunset, as the Columbia River turns shades of gold and the lights of the Portland metro area come on, seemingly all at once. If you hiked up you'll just have to use your imagination.

Return the way you came, unless you've arranged for a car shuttle to pick you up at the summit. If you're just interested in the view at the top, drive back west on Interstate 84 to Exit 22, signed for Corbett. Drive uphill to Corbett and turn left on the Historic Columbia River Highway. Continue 1.9 miles to a junction with Larch Mountain Road, where you turn right. Drive 14 miles of winding pavement to the summit parking area (NW Forest Pass required). From here it's a short walk to the summit, so short it almost feels like cheating.

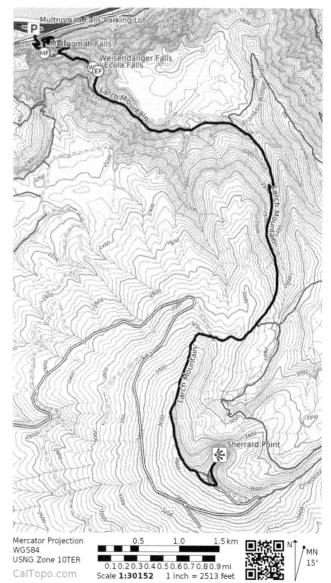

Mercator Projection
WGS84
USNG Zone 10TER
CalTopo.com

Scale **1:30152**   1 inch = 2513 feet

151

56. Green Point Mountain

Distance: 18.5 miles out and back
Elevation Gain: 4,800 feet
Trailhead elevation: 200 feet
Trail high point: 4,736 feet
Other seasons: June- November
Map: Hood River (Green Trails #430)
Pass: None needed
Drivetime from Portland: 60 minutes

Directions:
- Head east on Interstate 84 from Portland to Wyeth exit 51.
- Follow the exit road to a junction with the Herman Creek Road and turn right.
- Almost immediately afterwards turn left into Wyeth Campground and follow the road to its end.
- There is a small parking lot here. If the road is blocked, park at the entrance.

Why June: This hike, so fantastic in June when the wildflowers bloom and the days aren't so hot, presents you with a classic dilemma: do you opt for the easier hike with a long drive on a terrible road? Or do you opt for the easy drive and long hike? Most people prefer the longer drive and shorter hike, but it's more of an adventure to start at the bottom of the Gorge and make this a long, extremely fulfilling hike or overnight backpack. However you do it, this trip makes for an excellent June adventure about which you can brag to your friends when they complain about other Gorge Trails being too crowded. As a long hike this makes for an excellent alternative to the inferior but more famous Mount Defiance Loop (which is not featured in this book).

The old signal hut above Rainy Lake.

Note: Like most other hikes in the western Gorge, this area was burned during the Eagle Creek Fire in September 2017. The extent of the damage is unknown as of press time; expect these trails to be closed until at least Spring 2018.

Hike: Begin by hiking straight on a wide, level trail. In just a couple hundred yards you will arrive at a well-signed junction with the Gorge Trail (#400), which terminates here. Turn left to hike on the Wyeth Trail, which climbs and climbs and climbs some more. You will switch-back slightly up the slope and then down through the powerline corridor. Soon cross Harphan Creek and then launch uphill on the first of many, many switchbacks. The steepest part of the trail is the beginning, and soon you will settle into a rhythm that will eventually catapult you up to the rim of the Gorge. Watch out for poison oak on your way up, as it grows profusely on the lower section of the trail. While the trail mostly stays in the forest, keep your eyes out for June wildflowers such as larkspur, chocolate lilies and paintbrush. At 5.1 miles, after having gained almost 4,000 feet, you'll crest the ridge and quickly arrive at a trail junction with the Green Point Mountain Trail. Fork to the right to continue towards Green Point Mountain.

You'll continue gaining elevation here as the trail wastes no time shooting uphill towards the top of Green Point Mountain's long ridge. Once you crest the hill, you'll settle into a long traverse along the wooded ridge. You may encounter snow here earlier in June, especially after colder winters. If you encounter snow and you are comfortable continuing, all you need to do is simply continue straight along the ridge. After 2 miles of mellow ridgewalking, reach a 4-way junction with the Gorton Cutoff Trail and North Lake Trails.

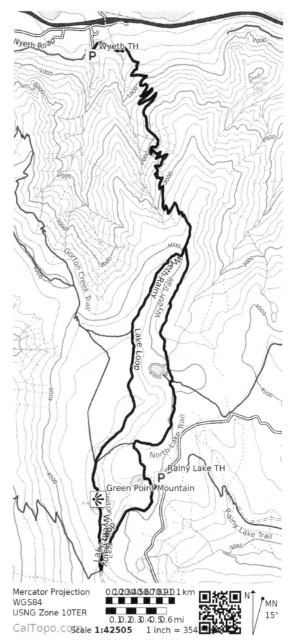

Continue straight and soon you'll arrive at the rocky summit of Green Point Mountain. The view here is impressive, looking south to Mount Hood and north to Mount Adams, and almost everything else in between. Below you is Rainy Lake, backed by Mount Defiance. If you just want the view, you can turn around for a 14 mile hike- but the loop is worth your time. Continuing from here, hike downhill from the summit 1 mile to a curious 4-way junction complete with a cabin that served as a signal hut during World War II. Turn sharply downhill to your left here and hike 1 mile on what is a converted road to descend to Rainy Lake's car campground, the hike's upper trailhead.

From the Rainy Lake car campground, look for the Rainy Lake Trail (No. 423-A). The trail departs from the campground and quickly arrives at Rainy Lake. The trail skirts the edge of this brushy lake, offering few unobstructed views. This is a shame, too, as this pretty lake is backed by the rocky slopes of Green Point Mountain. Continue along the trail as it passes through a peaceful forest, gently dropping and gaining elevation for about 1.5 miles to beautiful North Lake, set in old-growth forest. There are excellent campsites here should you decide to backpack; backpackers should probably opt to do the loop in reverse, stopping here first. From here, continue north from the lake another mile to the 3-way junction with the Green Point Ridge Trail. Continue straight, now on the Wyeth Trail, for 5.1 miles of steep downhill to the Wyeth Trailhead.

57. Burnt Lake

Distance: 8 miles out and back
Elevation Gain: 1,500 feet
Trailhead Elevation: 2,684 feet
Trail High Point: 4,135 feet
Other seasons: July- October
Map: Mount Hood Wilderness (Geo-Graphics)
Pass: NW Forest Pass
Drivetime from Portland: 80 minutes

Directions:
- From Portland drive east on US 26 for 27 miles to Zigzag.
- At a stop light with a sign for East Lolo Pass Road (FR 18), turn left on Lolo Pass Road.
- Drive Lolo Pass Road 4.2 miles to a junction on your right with FR 1825.
- Turn right and drive 0.6 mile to a junction at a bridge.
- Turn right and cross the bridge to stay on FR 1825.
- Drive 0.5 mile to a fork. Keep left here, following signs for Ramona Falls.
- Drive 1.3 miles to a junction. Turn right here for Burnt Lake.
- In just 0.2 mile, the road changes to gravel at Lost Creek Campground.
- Drive 1.3 miles to the trailhead at road's end. When I last visited in the summer of 2016 the road was in excellent shape, but over the years it has been plagued with potholes and ruts such that most passenger cars struggled to make it up the road intact. You may want to call the Zigzag Ranger Station and inquire about the condition of the road before coming here.

Why June: Burnt Lake is immensely popular, and with good reason. While Burnt Lake is great any time you can make it there, perhaps the best time to visit is in June. The rhododendrons are in bloom, lining the trail with pink flowers; though crowded, the trail isn't even remotely as busy as others in the area. This is as good as it gets near Mount Hood.

Hike: Begin with a gentle trail that cuts a wide path through the forest. While you are always gaining elevation, the ascent feels mild at best as you follow a fork of Lost Creek through second-growth forest. At 2.7 miles, reach a junction with a trail heading downhill on your left. Follow this short spur down to the top of Lost Creek Falls; to see more of the falls, you will have to cross the creek and bushwhack down to the base of this 40-foot falls. Photographers will want to spend some time practicing long exposure shots at this photogenic double cascade.

Return to the main trail and begin your final ascent to Burnt Lake. The trail continues at a mostly mellow uphill, cutting across the north slope of Zigzag Ridge. The trail mellows out at 3.7 miles and enters the basin containing the lake. Burnt Lake is a popular backpacking destination- expect stiff competition for the best sites near the lake. If you've come for the Mount Hood view, continue around the lake to the far end and make your way to the lakeshore, where at last Mount Hood comes into view. What a magnificent view! If you've managed to come here on a calm day the reflection of the mountain in the lake is unforgettable. Return the way you came.

If you have more energy and wish to continue towards outstanding views on the summit of East Zigzag Mountain, you can follow the Burnt Lake Trail uphill 0.8 mile to a junction with the Zigzag Mountain Trail. Turn right and hike 0.5 mile uphill to the summit of East Zigzag Mountain. Timing this hike can be difficult; while there are excellent displays of beargrass up here in June, snowdrifts can make the way up punishing. If you wish to hike up to East Zigzag, it's better to wait until the end of the month or perhaps early July. From the Burnt Lake TH, this hike is 10 miles round-trip with 2,300 feet of elevation gain.

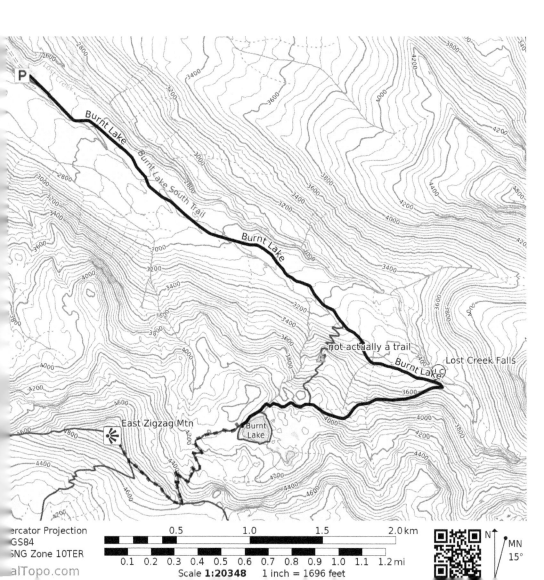

58. Fifteenmile Creek

Distance: 10.3 mile loop
Elevation Gain: 1,900 feet
Trailhead elevation: 2,476 feet
Trail high point: 2,867 feet
Other seasons: June – November
Map: Flag Point (Green Trails #463)
Pass: None needed.
Drivetime from Portland: 110 minutes

Directions:
- From Portland drive US 26 east to a junction with OR 35 on the side of Mt. Hood.
- Turn onto OR 35 and continue for 13.5 miles to a junction with FR 44 (Dufur Mill Rd.) between mileposts 70 and 71.
- If you are driving south from Hood River, this junction is approximately 25 miles south on OR 35.
- Turn right and continue on FR 44 for 5.2 miles.
- At a junction, turn right and continue on FR 44 for 3.1 miles.
- Turn right on unsigned but paved FR 4420 and continue for 2.2 miles to a junction.
- Drive straight, now on paved FR 2730 for 2.1 miles to rustic but charming Fifteenmile Campground. The trail departs from a sign on the left side of the campground, near the outhouse.

Why June: Let me be frank in saying that I love central and Eastern Oregon. I love the ponderosa pines, the drier climate and open skies. But I can't always make the long drive out to the eastern side of the state. This is when I make the trip out to Fifteenmile Creek, at the crossroads of western and eastern Oregon. June is the best time to visit before the area bakes in the heat of summer. Here you'll find tall ponderosa pines, curious and numerous rock gardens, diverse and unique flowers that peak every year in June, and the solitude you seek in a hike. There is only one problem with this hike: you descend first, meaning your elevation gain comes on the return trip. It's worth it. As the song goes, you can't always get what you want- but sometimes you get what you need.

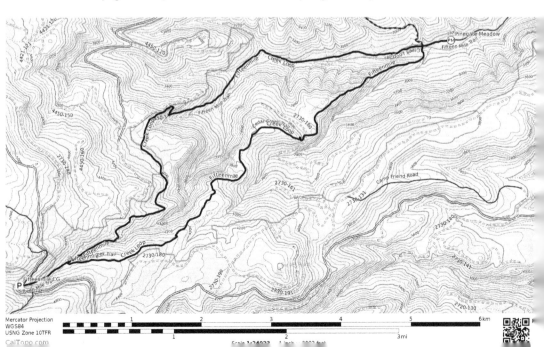

Hike: Head out from the delightful Fifteenmile Campground into the pine forests above rushing Fifteenmile Creek. After half a mile reach a junction with the Cedar Creek Trail and turn right to begin the loop, crossing the creek and ascending slightly up to the ridge. From here it's all downhill until your reunion with the Fifteenmile Trail. After 1.5 miles of descent you will reach Onion Flat, a park-like meadow dominated by tall ponderosa pines. From here on down you can feel the transition into Central Oregon high desert as the terrain changes with each step. Look over the ridgeline across the canyon for views of Mount Adams and at one spot, the tip of Mount Hood. Cross a decommissioned road at 3.5 miles and begin a steep descent down into the canyon, finally crossing Fifteenmile Creek and reaching a reunion with the Fifteenmile trail exactly 5 miles from the campground. A beautiful cedar grove here along the glassy, crystal-clear creek immediately before the junction provides an excellent resting spot. If one were so inclined, it is possible to hike in to this spot by driving FR 4421 down into the canyon and hiking the Fifteenmile trail 3.25 miles to this junction – an endeavor that would allow you to hike uphill first but also force you to drive for a very long time on rough roads. After lunch it is well worth it to continue downstream (to the right) on the Fifteenmile Trail another 0.3 mile to Pinegate Meadow, a grassy flat surrounded by a cluster of tall, arching ponderosa pines. Return then to the junction with the Cedar Creek Trail and continue straight to continue the loop.

Now on the Fifteenmile Trail, the climb out of the canyon begins with a relatively level stretch through flower gardens along Fifteenmile Creek. In late June look for whitish-pink Cascade lilies, a showy flower that grows profusely down in this canyon. Above you ancient ponderosas reign supreme. Before you begin your ascent in earnest, pass an enormous black Cottonwood tree in a cedar grove along Fifteenmile Creek. Shortly after, begin your ascent. You may have competition for the trail from a few descending mountain bikers but they are few and far between. The climb uphill is mostly gradual with a few switchbacks and a relatively easy grade. 2.5 miles from the junction at the bottom of the

canyon, reach an open meadow where you can look across the canyon while ponderosas beg to be photographed. Keen eyes may spot the Cedar Creek Trail on the ridge across the canyon. From this point on the climbing becomes even more gradual while the many wildflowers make you grab for your camera; look for red skyrocket and paintbrush, yellow balsamroot, stonecrop and many, many more. Pass by a road to your right but keep on the trail; you will reenter the forest. From here you'll eventually reach the remains of an old road. Turn left here and continue uphill, always climbing gradually. At about 3.8 miles from the trail junction (or about 1.5 miles down the Fifteenmile Trail from the campground) reach a scenic rock outcrop known as Pat's Point with a view across Fifteenmile Creek's canyon. Here you can hear the roar of the creek below as it tumbles through a dark and hidden canyon. The many and varied rock formations here invite exploration. Once past Pat's Point, the Fifteenmile trail then reenters the forest and climbs another 1.5 gradual miles to the campground and trailhead.

Ponderosa pines tower over the trail.

59. Rooster Rock

Distance: 10.8 miles out and back
Elevation Gain: 3,700 feet
Trailhead elevation: 1,261 feet
Trail high point: 4,559 feet
Other seasons: May- November
Map: Opal Creek Wilderness (Imus)
Pass: None needed.
Drivetime from Portland: 80 minutes

Directions to Old Bridge TH:
* From Portland, drive south on OR 213 to the town of Molalla.
* From the junction of OR 213 and OR 211 on the western edge of Molalla, drive 2.1 miles through town to a junction with South Mathias Road.
* Veer right on South Mathias Road.
* Drive this road for 1 mile south to a junction with S Feyrer Park Road, and veer left.
* Continue on this road for 1.6 miles until you cross the Molalla River and meet South Dickey Prairie Road.
* Turn right on Dickey Prairie Road and drive 5.4 miles to a sign on your right marking the Molalla River Recreation area. Turn right and cross the Molalla River. Here the road curves to the left immediately and becomes the Molalla River Road.
* Continue 11 miles to a junction with the Horse Creek Road on your right.
* Continue straight (ignoring the road veering downhill to the right) and drive another 1.7 miles to a junction with the road to Table Rock.
* Ignore the fork to the left signed for Table Rock, and turn right on Rooster Rock Road.
* Cross a bridge and immediately turn into the Old Bridge Trailhead on the left.

Why June: It's a long way up to Rooster Rock, but when you get there you won't regret making the trek. The pinnacle stands above fields of wildflowers, while you have outstanding views out to Mount Jefferson and the rest of the central Cascades. Even on a hot day, a gentle breeze cools you off while you relax for lunch up on this scenic ridgetop. Though there are other, easier hikes in the Table Rock Wilderness, this one is the closest to Portland, the easiest to find and perhaps the least crowded.

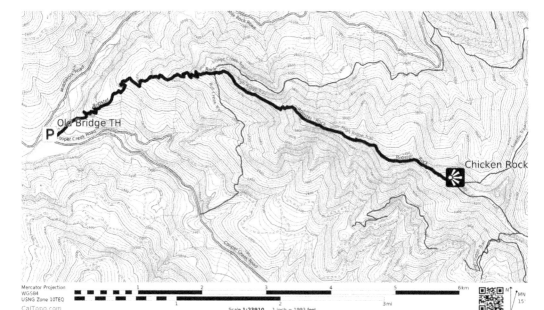

Fields of wildflowers line the slopes of Rooster Rock, in the Table Rock Wilderness.

Hike: Begin on the High Ridge Trail, a well-maintained path that climbs uphill above the Table Rock Fork of the Molalla River. Bright orange Tiger lilies and pink rhododendrons add color to this lower section of the trail throughout June. Continue uphill on a long series of switchbacks in second-growth forest until the trail opens up in a series of south-facing meadows with spectacular wildflower displays. The flower show here is fascinating, with an unusual mix of flowers that generally tend to grow in far drier climates. Look for little yellow sunflowers, blue-eyed Mary, red paintbrush and rosy plectritis, a pinkish poofball flower that grows in great profusion here. Re-enter the forest and soon reach a crossing of a wide trail that was once a road. Continue straight on the High Ridge Trail.

You will steeply switchback uphill from here until you reach the bottom of a long series of rock outcrops, which you parallel as the trail begins to level out. The High Ridge Trail follows this ridgecrest through a forest of second-growth lodgepole pine. Along the way, you'll pass a series of gigantic anthills in the woods. At a little less than 5 miles from the Old Bridge Trailhead, the trail emerges into the huge summit meadows below Rooster Rock. In June, these meadows feature one of the most impressive wildflower displays in this part of the Cascades. Look for masses of yellow Oregon sunshine, red paintbrush, blue and purple larkspur, lupine, fuzzy cat's ears, and in favorable years, huge white stalks of beargrass. The High Cascades spread out to the south, with views out to the peaks of the Bull of the Woods Wilderness and south to the Three Sisters.

Reach a junction with the Saddle Trail and turn left. Head up to the top of the ridge below Rooster Rock, where you reach another junction. Turn left and hike this short trail up to a rocky viewpoint known as Chicken Rock. Here the view is considerably better than the meadow below, with views north to Mounts Hood, Saint Helens, Adams and Rainier and views south to the Three Sisters. A better lunch spot would be hard to find in this area. When you are done, return the way you came or arrange a car shuttle to one of the other trailheads in the area.

60. Dome Rock

Distance: 10.2 miles out and back
Elevation Gain: 3,600 feet
Trailhead elevation: 1,590 feet
Trail high point: 4,791 feet
Other seasons: May- November
Map: Opal Creek Wilderness (Imus)
Pass: None needed.
Drivetime from Portland: 120 minutes

Directions:
- From Portland, drive south on Interstate 5 to exit 253 on the east side of Salem.
- Leave the freeway here at a sign for Detroit Lake and turn left on OR 22.
- Drive east on OR 22 for 41.2 miles to the dam over Detroit Lake.
- Continue straight on the highway for 5 miles to the Tumble Trailhead, on the left side of the highway.
- The trailhead is approximately 1 mile before the Detroit Ranger Station. If you reach this point, you have driven too far.

Why June: Like the Green Point Mountain Loop (Hike 56), this hike presents the classic choice of an easier hike with bad road access, or a harder hike with easy road access. You absolutely should opt for the more difficult hike, as the trail up is a delight. You'll pass through woods brightened in June by blooming rhododendrons, and you will have views down to Detroit Lake and out to Mount Jefferson. Best of all, the trail finally leads you to Dome Rock, one of the best viewpoints in this part of the Cascades. Extremely fit hikers can continue on a steep trail down to Tumble Lake, an intriguing lake in a dark bowl backed by rock pinnacles- but this is better for backpackers than it is day hikers.

Looking down at Tumble Lake from near the summit of Dome Rock.

Hike: The trail begins on an old roadbed that follows cascading Tumble Creek for 0.4 mile to a trail junction on your right. Turn right here and begin switchbacking steeply up through second-growth forest. Openings in the forest provide occasional views down to Detroit Lake and out to Mount Jefferson but for the most part you remain in the forest for several miles. In June thousands of pink rhododendrons line the trail, while stalks of white beargrass line the trail in some years.

As you climb, you'll have more and more views out to the mountains around you, and eventually down to Tumble Lake. The trail crosses an old clearcut and hidden spring at 3.5 miles known as Margie Dunham, where the trail passes into a small section of Santiam State Forest. From here you'll continue climbing through open woods until you meet the Dome Rock spur trail at 4.7 miles. Fork to the right and switchback up the rocky trail to the summit, where the views are magnificent. Dome Rock was once the site of a lookout tower and today the 360-degree panorama is intact. Mount Jefferson is the star attraction here but the view stretches from Mount Hood to the Three Sisters. Just as interesting are the dozens of other less-noteworthy summits visible everywhere. You could spend hours up here just trying to identify them all. Tumble Lake shimmers down in the valley below you, looking inviting. When you're ready, return the way you came.

If you're feeling energetic you can continue down to Tumble Lake but beware: the way is steep, and once you reach the lake, you probably will not want to leave. It's another 1.8 miles and 1,300 feet of elevation loss down to the lake- an easy descent but a very difficult return trip. This is best saved for backpackers.

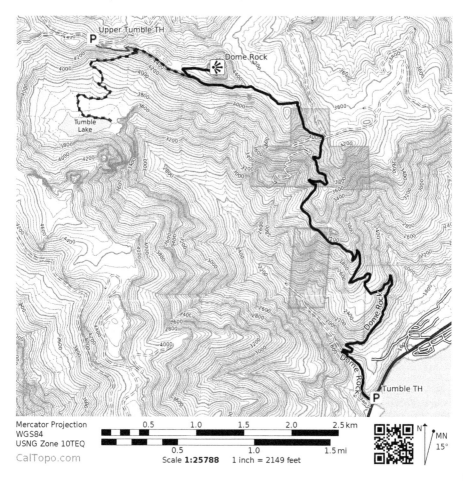

Mercator Projection
WGS84
USNG Zone 10TEQ

CalTopo.com

Scale **1:25788**   1 inch = 2149 feet

JULY

		Distance	EV Gain	Drive
61.	**Coldwater Peak**	13 mi	2,300 ft	120 min
62.	**Ape Canyon**	11 mi	1,700 ft	100 min
63.	**Lava Canyon**	2 mi	500 ft	100 min
64.	**Silver Star Mountain**	10.2 mi	2,900 ft	75 min
65.	**Bald Mountain and Muddy Fork**	6.8 mi	1,100 ft	85 min
66.	**McNeil Point**	11 mi	2,300 ft	85 min
67A.	**Heather Canyon**	10.2 mi	2,000 ft	80 min
67B.	**Elk Meadows and Gnarl Ridge**	11 mi	2,500 ft	80 min
68A.	**Lookout Mountain via High Prairie**	3 mi	600 ft	110 min
68B.	**Lookout Mountain via Fret Creek**	7.6 mi	2,100 ft	110 min
69.	**Bull of the Woods**	7.4 mi	2,000 ft	130 min
70.	**Bear Point**	7.8 mi	3,000 ft	125 min

July is my favorite month of the year. At long last, the mountains are snow-free and it's high time to go high up in the mountains. You won't find any lowland hikes here - every single hike featured in this section (save for one very notable exception) starts in the mountains and climbs even higher in the mountains. Here you'll find everything you dreamed about all winter and spring: expansive views, fields of wildflowers and mile after mile of trail that invites backpacking. And best of all - the weather is finally, after many months of rain and cold, just right.

Planning the perfect July hike isn't always easy. The longer drives to the mountains and warm, even hot days necessitate getting up earlier than some hikers would prefer. This isn't a problem for me as a morning person but for some people this can be a chore. With hot weather in the forecast, it is important to hit the trail before the heat of the day. In spite of the heat of summer, snowdrifts can still block trails earlier in the month. I've hit snow on almost all of these hikes in July ; for example, I remember that we hit large snowdrifts on my first visit to McNeil Point, which took place in late July 2012. This is always a possibility, especially after heavy snow years, and you should be prepared to turn around if you lose a trail under continuous snow. It seems hard to believe that this would be possible, but it is.

Speaking of preparation, you should always be prepared for inclement weather even in the middle of summer. While summer snowstorms are extremely rare, summer thunderstorms are not. You do not want to be high on a ridge top when the clouds roll in, as you are very much at risk of being struck by lightning. If you're out in the mountains and hear thunder, or see black clouds rolling in, get under tree cover and away from water and ride out the storm as best you can. After the clouds have parted, you may also want to keep an eye out for any fires the lightning may have caused.

Last but not least, July is also the height of alpine wildflower season. Almost all of these hikes feature excellent blooms throughout July. You should bring a wildflower identification guide and a camera (or your phone) for help identifying the many flowers found all over our region in July.

Photo on right: the arch on Ed's Trail, Silver Star Mountain (Hike 64)

61. Coldwater Peak

Distance: 13 miles out and back
Elevation Gain: 2,300 feet
Trailhead elevation: 4,189 feet
Trail high point: 5,726 feet
Other seasons: August- October
Map: Mount Saint Helens (Green Trails #364 and 332)
Pass: $8 pass per person at trailhead; a NW Forest Pass equals one individual pass
Drivetime from Portland: 120 minutes

Directions:
- From Portland, drive north on Interstate 5 approximately 60 miles to Castle Rock.
- At Exit 49, leave the freeway and turn right onto WA 504.
- Drive WA 504 for 52 miles to its end at the Johnson Ridge Observatory.
- Before you begin the hike, be sure to get your $8 volcanic monument pass inside the observatory. Every member of your party must get one. A NW Forest Pass is good for one individual pass.
- As this is a long hike, save your visit of the observatory for after the hike.

Why July: One of the best hikes in the Pacific Northwest, the long trek through Mount Saint Helens' flower-spangled blast zone to the view-packed summit of Coldwater Peak is something every Portland-area hiker should do at least once. But come prepared, as it's not easy. The trail passes the heart of the devastation wrought by the volcano's 1980 eruption, offering big views but absolutely no shade. Bring lots of water (at least 3 liters), sunscreen, a windbreaker and enough to stamina to make it there and back. But what an experience!

Hiking towards Mount Saint Helens on the way to Coldwater Peak.

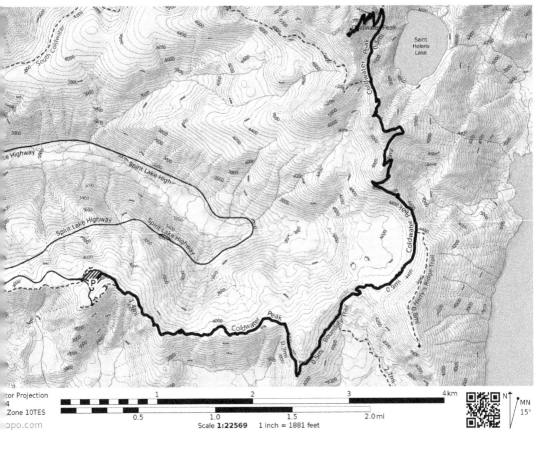

Note: Dogs are not allowed on this and other trails inside the blast zone at Mount Saint Helens National Volcanic Monument. This prohibition is to protect the fragile, recovering environment. Hiking off-trail is banned as well.

Hike: The hike begins at the Johnston Ridge Observatory. Take a moment of silence for the observatory's namesake, volcanologist David Johnston, whose camp was not far from this site and who passed away during the eruption. Then set out on the Boundary Trail, departing from the observatory. The trail descends somewhat along a view-packed ridge, immediately opposite Mount Saint Helens' devastated and malignant cone. The volcano will always be in view on this hike, offering many perspectives along the way. There is no shade, as mentioned; while flowers have come back to the devastation zone in full force, trees have yet to establish a foothold in the ashy wastelands north of the volcano. One thing that has come back, however, is huckleberries- and in fact, the bushes along the trail offer some of the finest berry picking in the area. At 2.7 miles, the trail reaches a junction with the Truman Trail, named for Harry Truman, the curmudgeonly octogenarian who perished in his lodge on Spirit Lake during the eruption. Keep left here.

Soon you will begin gradually climbing along Harry's Ridge, reaching a junction with a spur to the summit of Harry's Ridge at 3.7 miles. Keep left again, after which point the trail begins to seriously climb towards Coldwater Peak at last. This stretch can be punishing on hot days. The trail soon passes through a natural rock arch with views out to Mount Adams before reaching a junction with the Coldwater Trail at 5.4 miles. Keep right and hike along the steep slope above deep blue St. Helens Lake. In another half-mile you will at last reach the junction with the spur trail to Coldwater Peak. Turn left and hike 0.6 miles to the summit, where the view stretches across the blast zone to Mount Saint Helens, north to Mount Rainier, east to Mount Adams...and seemingly the infinite beyond. Return the way you came.

62. Ape Canyon

Distance: 11 miles out and back
Elevation Gain: 1,700 feet
Trailhead elevation: 2,871 feet
Trail high point: 4,367 feet
Other seasons: August- October
Map: Mount Saint Helens (Green Trails #364S)
Pass: NW Forest Pass
Drivetime from Portland: 100 minutes

Directions:
- From Portland drive north on I-5 for 28 miles.
- Following signs for WA 503 and Cougar, leave the interstate at exit 21 and turn right at the stop light.
- Follow WA 503 for 28 winding miles to Cougar.
- Continue beyond Cougar on the same road; WA 503 becomes FR 90 along the way.
- Approximately 7 miles past Cougar, turn left on FR 83 at signs for Lava Canyon.
- Follow this paved road 11 miles to the Ape Canyon Trailhead on the left, just before the Lava Canyon Trailhead at road's end.

Why July: Mount Saint Helens is a fascinating, achingly beautiful place. The 1980 eruption transformed the surrounding landscape: the volcano's glaciers were replaced with dust and boulders, while the surrounding forest was leveled by the eruption's pyroclastic cloud. This fantastic hike up and into Ape Canyon takes you from the edge of a lahar into a dark and majestic old-growth forest spared from the mountain's wrath, and into a huge volcanic plain where wildflowers grow in great abundance in July. This hike is absolutely at its best in July, before the wildflower meadows dry up, and while streaks of snow still descend from the heights of the volcano.

Hike: The first part of the trail follows the Muddy River's wide lahar, a visible and obvious remnant of the 1980 eruption. Although the trail stays in the woods for the most part, there are several opportunities to follow short user trails out to views of Mount Saint Helens and the vast plain created by the eruption. Soon enough, however, you will begin climbing into a most welcome old-growth forest. If it seems odd that there is an old-growth forest this close to Mount Saint Helens, it shouldn't; the mountain's 1980 eruption devastated the north flanks of the mountain, with its pyroclastic cloud eviscerating everything within 10 miles of the volcano's north face. But this is the south side of the mountain, where the devastation was mostly limited to mudflows. This forest will cool you off as you climb on the inevitable hot July day.

As you ascend, you'll no doubt encounter mountain bikers heading in either direction, uphill or downhill. Give them a wide berth and wait until they pass- they are generally courteous, and as excited to visit this place as you are. Less interesting and far more irritating are the black flies occasionally found in this forest. There aren't too many places in our region that provide a home to this scourge of the forest but this is one of them. They aren't always there, but when they are- you'll be hiking fast, or wishing you were riding a bike. The last time I visited they were nowhere to be found, but the first time we were nearly forced to run, so irritating were the flies. Hopefully they won't be out when you visit.

At 3 miles from the trailhead you'll begin to lose a little elevation as the trail drops a bit after reaching the crest of the ridge above Ape Canyon. Keep an eye out for occasional glimpses north towards Mount Rainier. Soon the glimpses get better, as the trail once again skirts the Muddy River's mudflow for a second time. Bright orange tiger lilies grow along the trail here in great abundance, adding color to the scene. From here, things get better with every step. The view of Mount Saint Helens gets better the closer you get. At 4.6 miles, meet the Loowit Trail at a pass. Turn right onto the Loowit and hike around the lip of Ape Canyon's narrow crevice. This spot may hold snow into July, so be careful. At this same spot, make sure you turn around and look east. Here, Mount Adams looms in the distance, directly above Ape Canyon's narrow crack in the ground. This is one of the iconic spots in the area around Mount Saint Helens, and you will want to spend some time here taking pictures.

From here, the Loowit Trail drops slightly into the Plains of Abraham, a huge flat on the eastern slope of Mount Saint Helens. How far you go from this point on is entirely up to you. The most logical stopping point is at a spring that flows across the trail at 5.5 miles from the trailhead, but you can realistically go as far as you want, or can handle. It's hot and dusty here in the summer but the scenery is uniformly great, and the views fantastic at every step. When you can bear it, return the way you came.

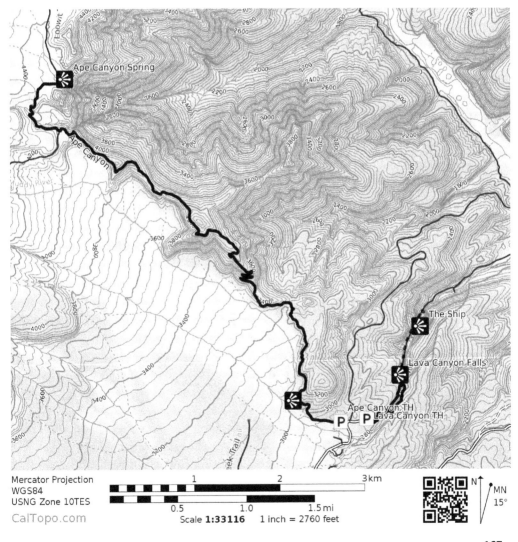

Mercator Projection
WGS84
USNG Zone 10TES
CalTopo.com

Scale **1:33116**   1 inch = 2760 feet

63. Lava Canyon

Distance: 2 miles out and back
Elevation Gain: 500 feet
Trailhead elevation: 2,843 feet
Trail high point: 2,843 feet
Other seasons: August- October
Map: Mount Saint Helens (Green Trails #364S)
Pass: NW Forest Pass
Drivetime from Portland: 100 minutes

Directions:
- From Portland drive north on I-5 for 28 miles.
- Following signs for WA 503 and Cougar, leave the interstate at exit 21 and turn right at the stop light.
- Follow WA 503 for 28 winding miles to Cougar.
- Continue beyond Cougar on the same road; WA 503 becomes FR 90 along the way.
- Approximately 7 miles past Cougar, turn left on FR 83 at signs for Lava Canyon.
- Follow this paved road 11 miles to road's end at the Lava Canyon Trailhead, just after you pass the Ape Canyon Trailhead on the left.

Why July: Most of our low-elevation hikes along rivers are best in the rainy season, when the higher mountains are snowed under and these canyons the best places to visit. Lava Canyon is the rare canyon that is better in the summer. The waterfalls and lava formations are spectacular in any season, but the trail is exposed and dangerous in any season other than summer. Come in July before it gets too hot for the best experience. With several scenic waterfalls, a thrilling suspension bridge and many fascinating lava formations, this is worth the longer drive it takes to get here. This is an excellent stop after hiking nearby Ape Canyon (see the previous two pages) but it's also wonderful as an easier day trip to this corner of the Mount Saint Helens region.

Warning: This is absolutely not a trail anybody afraid of heights should attempt. The trail follows narrow cliff edges without benefit of a guardrail. For these reasons it is not an appropriate trail for children or dogs.

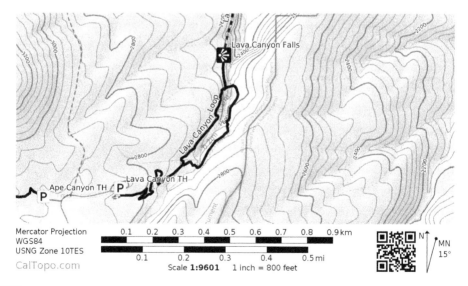

Hike: Begin at the information board, where you should turn left (right leads to a series of secluded picnic sites). The paved trail drops to a junction at a bridge over the Muddy River. This is the start of your loop. Either direction is fine, but let's say you should go straight. From here, the pavement fades away and the trail begins a traverse along the canyon wall. The trail passes above a waterfall before reaching a junction at a suspension bridge just 0.7 mile from the trailhead. Here is where things get real, as they say. The suspension bridge is the continuation of the loop, but for an exhilarating look at the canyon's most impressive waterfall, keep straight here.

The trail drops steeply downhill about 0.1 mile to a small, rocky flat next to the canyon's major waterfall, a 130-foot plunge known as Lava Canyon Falls. The flat next to the river here makes for a convenient spot to take a break but **DO NOT** go anywhere near the water or the cliff edges here- people have been swept away and died after trying to get closer to the numerous falls along the canyon. Hikers desiring a better look at the big falls can follow the Lava Canyon Trail and then turn around when a clear view of the falls presents itself (roughly 150 feet down the trail from the flats). But this stretch of trail is dangerously exposed and so narrow that it's impossible to safely pass anyone going in the opposite direction- and there are no guardrails. Keep that in mind and be mindful of anyone continuing their hike in either direction before you stop to take a picture. The trail does continue downstream but very soon enters the forest, eventually arriving at a ladder in the canyon. Instead I suggest you turn around and hike back uphill to the suspension bridge, where you can turn left and cross the bridge to complete your loop.

Cross the suspension bridge now. The bridge dangles more than 100 feet over Lava Canyon, offering views of this remarkable place. Here you at least get a good view of the canyon. Take a moment to consider that Lava Canyon was unknown until after the 1980 eruption. Lahars triggered by the eruption scoured the canyon clean, revealing the waterfalls and lava formations you can see today. Nowhere will you get a better view than from the bridge. But beware: the bridge shakes, and will frighten some people. So make your way across at your own leisure and follow the trail upriver. Here and there you will have views of the river, but stay on the trail- the terrain is steep and unforgiving. When you arrive at the metal bridge over the river, cross it and turn left to return to the trailhead.

64. Silver Star Mountain

	Grouse Vista Trail	Grouse Vista + Ed's Trail
Distance:	6.8 miles out and back	10.2 miles out and back
Elevation Gain:	2,100 feet	2,900 feet
Trailhead Elevation:	2,420 feet	2,420 feet
Trail High Point:	4,392 feet	4,589 feet
Other Seasons:	mid-June- mid-November	mid-June- mid-November
Map:	download map online	download map online
Pass:	Washington Discover Pass	Washington Discover Pass
Drivetime from PDX:	75 minutes	75 minutes

Directions:
- From Portland, drive Interstate 5 north of Portland to exit 11. Turn right here onto WA 502 at signs for Battle Ground.
- Drive WA 502 for 5.8 miles to a junction with WA 503 in the center of Battle Ground. Turn left and continue north on WA 503 for exactly 5.6 miles to a junction with Rock Creek Road, marked by a sign for Lucia Falls and Moulton Falls. Turn right here.
- Follow this road for 8.3 miles to a junction with Sunset Falls Road. Turn right here.
- Drive on Sunset Falls Road for 2 miles to a junction with Dole Valley Road. Turn right.
- Drive on Dole Valley Road, which becomes Road L1000, for exactly 5.1 miles to a junction with road L1200 on your left, where pavement ends on Road L1000. Turn left here.
- Drive this gravel road, which as of summer 2017 was in good shape, for exactly 5 miles to the Grouse Vista Trailhead on your right. From here, the Grouse Vista Trail departs on the left side of the road while the Larch Mtn Trail departs on the right.

Why July: Silver Star Mountain rises above Portland and Vancouver, appearing tantalizingly close. The mountain is an even better destination than it appears from afar, with fields of wildflowers, far-reaching views and many different trails to offer hikers variety. Visiting Silver Star, however, is not as easy as one would assume for a mountain so close to the metro area. Many of the roads that lead to the mountain are rocky and rough, and many of the trails leading to the summit require a tremendous amount of elevation gain. Combining the Grouse Vista Trail, which has the easiest and best road access, with Ed's Trail, the most spectacular of all the Silver Star trails, is absolutely the way to do this hike. Early to mid-July is the best time to visit Silver Star, when the tremendous wildflower displays along the mountain's ridges are at peak and the skies open and blue. While the area is beautiful in any weather, you want blue skies to fully take in the far-reaching views.

Hike: Begin by following the Grouse Vista Trail uphill to a junction with the Tarbell Trail just 0.1 mile from the trailhead. The Tarbell Trail offers a longer approach for the fit hiker but the trail is brushy, occasionally steep and was the site of a logging operation in summer 2017, so this should only be an option for more adventurous hikers. Instead keep right on the Grouse Vista Trail as it climbs in fits and starts, sometimes gradually and sometimes intensely. Things get better at 1 mile from the trailhead, as the trail rounds Pyramid Rock and enters the glorious wildflower meadows for which Silver Star Mountain is known. Although the way up remains steep, the meadows will lift your spirits. From here, the Grouse Vista Trail alternates meadow and forest until it reaches a junction with the road that marks the northside route at 3 miles from the trailhead. Turning right will lead you to the summit- and if you're only looking for a moderate hike, you should just head on to the summit right now. Hikers looking for a more satisfying day through some of the best scenery in the region should turn left to hike the Ed's Trail Loop.

There are two ways to do this, but as with all things it's probably better to save the best for last. So head down the old road that now serves as the Silver Star northside trail. You'll meet a junction with Ed's Trail in just 0.1 mile, but stay on the old road. Views open up to the north towards a trio of Washington volcanoes: Mount Saint Helens, Mount Rainier and Mount Adams. The old road passes through fields of wildflowers, more than you can even count. At 1.6 miles, meet Ed's Trail. Turn right and walk this spectacular trail that heads north on a return trip towards the summit of Silver Star. The trail is a bit rough in some spots but the scenery is hard to beat. You'll pass through an arch at 1 mile from the last junction, a scenic highpoint of an already gorgeous trail. And to think: you are able to hike this trail without having to drive the absolutely horrendous road that leads to the northern Silver Star Trailhead. From the arch, continue 0.6 mile to a reunion with the northside trail. Turn left, and this time continue on the road to the summit for the hike's scenic climax. Once you've basked in the flowers and views, return to the junction with the Grouse Vista Trail, and follow the Grouse Vista Trail downhill to the trailhead.

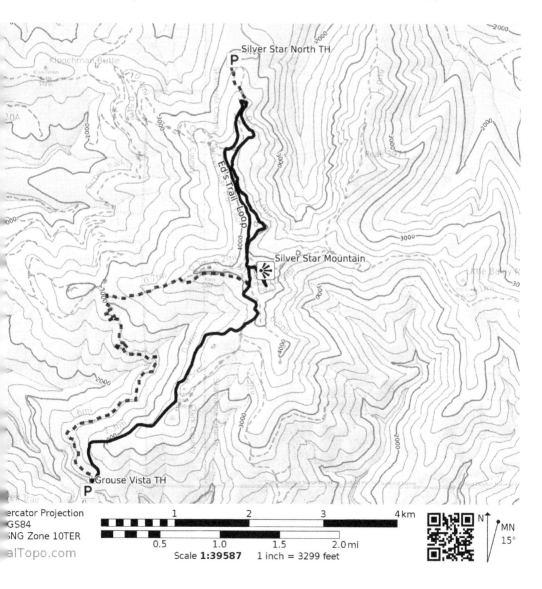

Scale **1:39587**   1 inch = 3299 feet

5. Bald Mountain and Muddy Fork

	Bald Mountain	Muddy Fork
Distance:	2.5 miles out and back	6.8 miles out and back
Elevation Gain:	700 feet	1,100 feet
Trailhead Elevation:	3,918 feet	3,918 feet
Trail High Point:	4,589 feet	4,589 feet
Other Seasons:	mid-June- mid-November	mid-June- mid-November
Map:	Mount Hood (Geo-Graphics)	Mount Hood (Geo-Graphics)
Pass:	NW Forest Pass	NW Forest Pass
Drivetime from PDX:	85 minutes	85 minutes

Directions:
- Drive to the junction of US 26 and Lolo Pass Road.
- Drive Lolo Pass Road 4.2 miles to a junction on your right with FR 1825.
- Turn right and drive 0.6 mile to a junction at a bridge.
- Keep straight (do not cross the bridge) on what is now FR 1828.
- Follow this paved road for 5.5 miles of rough pavement to a junction with FR 118 on your right. Turn right here.
- Drive 1.6 gravel miles to the overcrowded Top Spur Trailhead. Parking is limited in spite of the trailhead's popularity; come early if you want a good parking spot.
- You can drive to this trailhead via Lolo Pass as well; from Lolo Pass, follow FR 1828 downhill to the southwest 3 miles of warped, winding pavement to the junction with FR 118 described above. FR 118 will be on your left.

Why July: The short hike to Bald Mountain's famed wildflower meadows and superb view of Mount Hood is almost too easy. It shouldn't be this easy to get such rewards. For a longer hike, you can follow the Timberline Trail gradually downhill to one of the most imposing spots in our region: the Muddy Fork canyon. Here the Muddy Fork of the Sandy River rages down the steep flanks of Mount Hood, offering gaping views of the northwest face of Mount Hood. It doesn't get any better than this in July.

Hike: The Top Spur Trail climbs gradually through the woods 0.5 mile to a junction with the Pacific Crest Trail. Delicate white avalanche lilies grow in profuse quantities in this forest in early July. At the junction with the PCT, turn right and just 300 feet later, arrive at a confusing junction with the Timberline Trail. Here the Timberline Trail and Pacific Crest Trail meet at a 4-way junction- the Timberline Trail turns left and straight, while the Pacific Crest Trail turns right. Keep straight, now on the Timberline Trail, for just 400 feet to an unmarked junction with the spur trail to the summit of Bald Mountain on your left.

The Bald Mountain Spur Trail cuts between two large trees and climbs steeply for 0.3 mile to

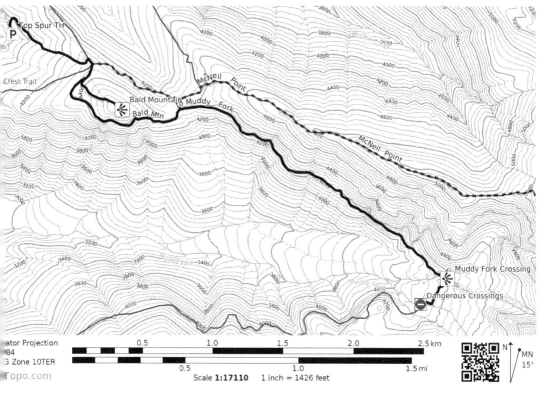

ator Projection
84
5 Zone 10TER
Fopo.com

Scale **1:17110**   1 inch = 1426 feet

Bald Mountain's forested summit. All that remains of the lookout tower that once stood here are the concrete foundations. From the summit, follow the trail through the brush about 40 feet until it emerges at steep hanging meadows with a view out to Mount Hood, 200 feet above the Timberline Trail. What a view it is! Here the mountain looks almost close enough to touch, towering over the terminal canyon of the Muddy Fork of the Sandy River. Below you is the Timberline Trail- and this is where you should go next. Return the 0.3 mile to the Timberline and turn left. You will follow the Timberline for 0.3 mile into the hanging meadows you saw from above, where the view of Mount Hood is just as good. Even better are the flowers- in July look for a cornucopia of blooms, from red paintbrush to purple and blue larkspur to yellow Oregon sunshine, and so many more. This is one of the finest photography spots in northwest Oregon, and is worthy of a long rest. If this is all you want to see, then return to the Timberline-PCT junction, continue straight on the PCT another 200 feet, and then turn left on the Top Spur Trail for 0.5 mile to the Top Spur Trailhead.

If you're interested in hiking to the Muddy Fork crossing, continue straight on the Timberline Trail towards Mount Hood. The trail continues through Bald Mountain's meadows for a bit before re-entering the forest. You will pass a junction with a short connector trail to the Timberline Trail that takes you to McNeil Point (see the next hike) before settling into a gradual downhill traverse on the Timberline. The trail opens up dramatically at 1.9 miles from the Bald Mountain meadows into the devastation of Muddy Fork's canyon. Here a 2001 flash flood decimated the canyon, knocking trees down in a manner reminiscent of the eruption of Mount Saint Helens. The view is incredible- look up the craggy, broken, eroded face of Mount Hood 7,500 feet to its distant summit. Waterfalls pour off Yocum Ridge, adding to the scene. The Timberline continues across both forks of the Muddy Fork but both crossings are quite difficult, and are best saved for folks hiking the entire Timberline Trail around Mount Hood. Instead, return the way you came.

66. McNeil Point

Distance: 11 miles out and back
Elevation Gain: 2,300 feet
Trailhead elevation: 3,921 feet
Trail high point: 6,162 feet
Other seasons: July – October
Map: Mount Hood Wilderness (Geo-Graphics)
Pass: NW Forest Pass
Drivetime from Portland: 85 minutes

Directions:
- Drive to the junction of US 26 and Lolo Pass Road.
- Drive Lolo Pass Road 4.2 miles to a junction on your right with FR 1825.
- Turn right and drive 0.6 mile to a junction at a bridge.
- Keep straight (do not cross the bridge) on what is now FR 1828.
- Follow this paved road for 5.5 miles of rough pavement to a junction with FR 118 on your right. Turn right here.
- Drive 1.6 gravel miles to the overcrowded Top Spur Trailhead. Parking is limited in spite of the trailhead's popularity; come early if you want a good parking spot.
- You can drive to this trailhead via Lolo Pass as well; from Lolo Pass, follow FR 1828 downhill to the southwest 3 miles of warped, winding pavement to the junction with FR 118 described above. FR 118 will be on your left.

Why July: McNeil Point's stone shelter has always been one of the iconic spots on Mount Hood, and its popularity in recent years is ascendant. This is a great destination any time you can actually make it there but it's never better in late July. The flower show along the trail typically peaks throughout the month, and McNeil Point itself is usually snow-free

Mount Hood from the McNeil Point Shelter.

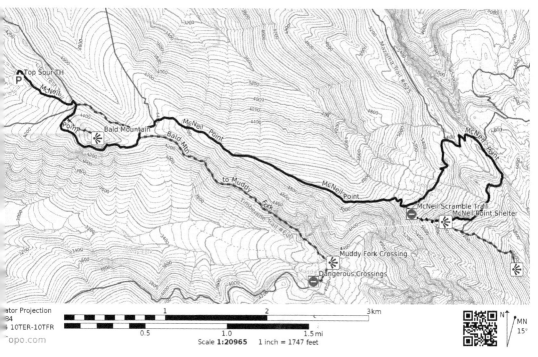

ator Projection
34
10TER-10TFR
opo.com

Scale **1:20965**   1 inch = 1747 feet

by the middle of the month. Most hikers begin their hike to this famed destination at the overcrowded Top Spur Trailhead. This is the shortest way to McNeil Point as well as the closest trailhead to Portland; expect to see a lot of people, and arrive early in the day if you want more solitude or a better parking spot.

Hike: Begin by hiking up a rooted, rocky trail 0.6 mile to a junction with the Pacific Crest Trail. Turn right and arrive at another junction in just 100 yards. Here the PCT and Timberline Trail meet in curious fashion, each curving around the slopes of Bald Mountain opposite one another. Continue straight on what is now the Timberline Trail. You will pass the open slopes of Bald Mountain, where the view of Mount Hood is perhaps the best view of the northwest face of the mountain. At a little over 1.3 miles from the trailhead, reach a junction with a connector trail to the Timberline Trail. Turn left and hike over a ridgecrest to the Timberline Trail in just 500 feet. Turn right, pass the McGee Creek Trail and continue uphill on the Timberline Trail.

The trail mostly stays in the forest, passing an outstanding viewpoint of Mount Hood on the way up before entering meadows below McNeil Point. Follow the Timberline Trail past a couple of ponds to a junction with the Mazama Trail at 4.2 miles. Continue another 0.3 mile to a junction with the McNeil Point Trail on your right. This spur trail climbs along a fork of McGee Creek before angling right, cutting back towards McNeil Point. Reach the stone shelter at McNeil Point at 5.4 miles. The view of Mount Hood here is astounding. Expect crowds, though. You can continue uphill towards Mount Hood a ways further if you so desire. Return the way you came.

There are other ways to reach McNeil Point. While the Top Spur Trail provides the easiest and closest approach to Portland, there are two other ways to get there that also quite enjoyable. The first starts at the obscure McGee Creek Trailhead and climbs to the Timberline Trail not far past the Bald Mountain Junction; the other starts at the Mazama Trailhead and climbs Cathedral Ridge to the meadows below McNeil Point. If you want to try these other approaches, bring a map of the Mount Hood area and explore to your heart's desire. While both trailheads are a little further away from Portland than the Top Spur approach, both are wonderful and offer far more solitude than the approach described here.

67A. Heather Canyon

Distance: 10.2 miles out and back
Elevation Gain: 2,000 feet
Trailhead elevation: 4,457 feet
Trail high point: 5,936 feet
Other seasons: July – October
Map: Mount Hood Wilderness (Geo-Graphics)
Map Note: See the map on the following two pages for a detailed map of this area.
Pass: NW Forest Pass
Drivetime from Portland: 80 minutes

Directions:
- From Portland drive US 26 east to a junction with OR 35 on the side of Mt. Hood.
- Turn onto OR 35 and continue for 7.7 miles to a junction on your left signed for the Elk Meadows Trailhead
- Turn left here, and keep left at an immediate junction with an ODOT facility.
- Continue down this road 0.3 mile to the Elk Meadows Trailhead on the right side of the road.
- The Heather Canyon Loop begins on the left side of the road.
- If you're headed to Elk Meadows and Gnarl Ridge instead, follow the trail to the right.

Why July: Umbrella Falls, Heather Canyon, Elk Meadows and Gnarl Ridge are four outstanding destinations accessible from the same trailhead on the east side of Mount Hood. This area is renowned for its fantastic views, tumbling waterfalls and fields of July wildflowers. Extremely fit hikers should take the opportunity to combine all of these destinations into a wonderful 17-mile day hike. Mere mortals will be content to split these two destinations into separate, extremely rewarding dayhikes. When trying to decide which of these hikes to include I could not come to a final decision- they are both so great, and present such an interesting contrast, that I decided to include both hikes here.

Hike: The Heather Canyon loop begins on the left side of the road, across from the Elk Meadows Trailhead. Locate the trail and follow it through open woods 0.2 mile to a crossing of the trailhead road. Find the trail on the opposite side of the road and continue hiking uphill, soon arriving just above the East Fork Hood River's narrow canyon. If you are so inclined, you can add a short side trip to Sahalie Falls at a side trail. Continue up the canyon until the trail begins to level out. You will reach a junction with the Umbrella Falls Trail, part of a loop that connects to the Elk Meadows Trail. Turn left here and reach the base of Umbrella Falls at 2.1 miles. This cascading cataract is among the most photogenic waterfalls in the Mount Hood area, and you'll likely have to share it with a few other admirers. When you're ready to continue, cross the bridge at the base of the falls and continue along the Umbrella Falls Trail.

From here, the trail momentarily turns left and quickly climbs to a crossing of Mount Hood Meadows' access road at 2.4 miles. Cross the road and locate the trail a short distance uphill. It is here that you will leave the crowds behind. The Umbrella Falls Trail then climbs gradually through increasingly open woods for 1.4 miles to a junction with the Timberline Trail at 3.8 miles. Turn right here and head north on the Timberline Trail. The Timberline now passes through meadow after meadow, all of them overflowing with flowers of all varieties, from paintbrush to monkeyflower to some of the most stunning displays of lupine found on Mount Hood. Along the way you'll pass under several of Mount Hood Meadows' ski lifts, a reminder that this area is more well-known to skiers than it is to hikers. The way is mostly easy, offering tumbling creeks, wildflowers and views of Mount Hood until the trail drops into Clark Creek's canyon at 5.8 miles. Here you will cross the verdant south fork of Clark Creek. Masses of wildflowers line the cascading south fork of Clark Creek, which is known as Heather Canyon. The Timberline Trail crosses the south

Mount Hood and Heather Canyon.

fork just above Pencil Falls. Once across the creek, the trail follows the south fork for a bit before dropping into the north fork's more impressive canyon. This fork presents a fascinating contrast- unlike the south fork's flowers and cascades, the north fork flows through a deep, sandy glacial canyon. Crossing this fork of Clark Creek is usually not difficult, but you may need to get your feet wet- rockhopping is difficult, and it's probably easier to take your shoes off and find the shallowest place to simply ford the creek.

Once across, the Timberline climbs up the north side of Clark Creek's sandy moraine to a junction with the Newton Creek Trail at 7.2 miles. If your objective is combining this hike with the hike to Gnarl Ridge, you will continue straight on the Timberline Trail to a difficult crossing of Newton Creek. Here the creek rages through a rocky glacial canyon similar to that found at Clark Creek, but Newton Creek is deeper and faster than its southern neighbor, and the crossing is routinely rated among the most difficult on the Timberline Trail. Once across, continue a little under a mile to the junction with the Gnarl Ridge Trail, where you turn left. Continue then 2.4 more miles uphill to the sweeping view on the flanks of Gnarl Ridge (see the following two pages). Most hikers will opt to simply turn right on the Newton Creek Trail and save Gnarl Ridge for another day.

From the junction of the Timberline and Newton Creek Trails, turn right to follow Newton Creek downhill. The trail follows Newton Creek's canyon downhill to a junction with the Elk Meadows Trail at 9.1 miles. Turn right on the Elk Meadows Trail and hike 1.1 mostly level miles back to the Elk Meadows Trailhead.

177

67B. Elk Meadows and Gnarl Ridge

	Elk Meadows	Gnarl Ridge
Distance:	5.8 mile semi-loop	11 miles out and back
Elevation Gain:	800 feet	2,500 feet
Trailhead Elevation:	4,457 feet	4,457 feet
Trail High Point:	5,159 feet	6,718 feet
Other Seasons:	June- October	August - October
Map:	Mount Hood (Geo-graphics)	Mount Hood (Geo-graphics)
Pass:	NW Forest Pass	NW Forest Pass
Drivetime from PDX:	80 minutes	80 minutes

Directions:
- See directions on pages 176-177.

Why July: Umbrella Falls, Heather Canyon, Elk Meadows and Gnarl Ridge are four outstanding destinations accessible from the same trailhead on the east side of Mount Hood. This area is renowned for its fantastic views, tumbling waterfalls and fields of July wildflowers. Extremely fit hikers should take the opportunity to combine all of these destinations into one long but rewarding day hike. Mere mortals will be content to split these destinations into two different, extremely rewarding dayhikes. When trying to de-cide which of these hikes to include I could not come to a final decision- they are both so great, and present such an interesting contrast, that I decided to include both hikes here.

Hike: From the Elk Meadows Trailhead, follow the Elk Meadows Trail on the right side of the road. The trail is mostly level for the first mile, crossing Clark Creek on a bridge before arriving at an unbridged crossing of Newton Creek at 1.2 miles from the trailhead. The crossing is not terribly difficult, but as with all crossings of streams originating in glaciers, it will be more difficult on your return trip as the stream volume increases later in the day due to snowmelt. Even later in the day it isn't terribly difficult. Once past the crossing, the Elk Meadows Trail gains 600 feet in just 0.8 mile, passing by some enormous Douglas-firs along the way. At exactly 2 miles from the trailhead, you reach your first trail junction, this time with the Gnarl Ridge Trail on your left and the Bluegrass Ridge Trail on your right. If you have no interest in visiting Elk Meadows, turn left here to start the climb towards Gnarl Ridge. Otherwise, continue straight towards Elk Meadows.

Past the Gnarl Ridge-Bluegrass Ridge junction, you will meet several trail junctions as you hike around Elk Meadows. First of all, follow the Elk Meadows Trail to a T-junction with the Elk Meadows Perimeter Loop at 2.2 miles. Turn right here. Keep left at another junc-tion with the Bluegrass Ridge Trail at 2.6 miles, and continue to another junction with the Elk Meadows Trail in just 0.2 mile. Turn left here. Cross Cold Spring Creek and reach an unmarked junction with the spur trail to the Elk Meadows Shelter. Turn left here and hike this short trail to the historic shelter in the heart of Elk Meadows. The view across the meadows to Mount Hood is impressive, and the meadows support a tremendous variety of wetland flowers such as shooting stars and elephantshead. If you've only planned for a moderate hike, make this your destination.

When you're done visiting the shelter, return to the Elk Meadows perimeter loop. Con-tinue around the meadows another 0.4 mile to a junction with a tie trail that takes you to the Gnarl Ridge Trail. If you're heading to Gnarl Ridge, turn right here. If you just wanted to hike to Elk Meadows, keep left and continue 0.4 mile to the end of the loop. Following signs for Hood River Meadows, turn right here and continue 2.4 miles back to the Elk Meadows Trail.

If you've opted instead to hike up to Gnarl Ridge, however, you should turn right at the junction with the Gnarl Ridge Tie Trail. The tie trail departs from the Elk Meadows perimeter loop and climbs briskly for 0.6 mile to a junction with the Gnarl Ridge Trail at 4 miles from the trailhead. Continue now 0.3 mile to a junction with the Timberline Trail just above its crossing of Newton Creek. From here, the Timberline climbs through increasingly open woods until you break out, all of a sudden, onto the side of Gnarl Ridge just beside Lamberson Butte. You are almost immediately greeted with one of the finest views of Mount Hood, towering over Newton Creek's deep, sandy canyon. At an elevation of over 6,700 feet, you will feel like you've climbed high into the sky. On your way back, ignore the Timberline Trail and keep straight on the Gnarl Ridge Trail until you hit the Elk Meadows Trail. Turn right here and hike the last 2 miles back to the trailhead.

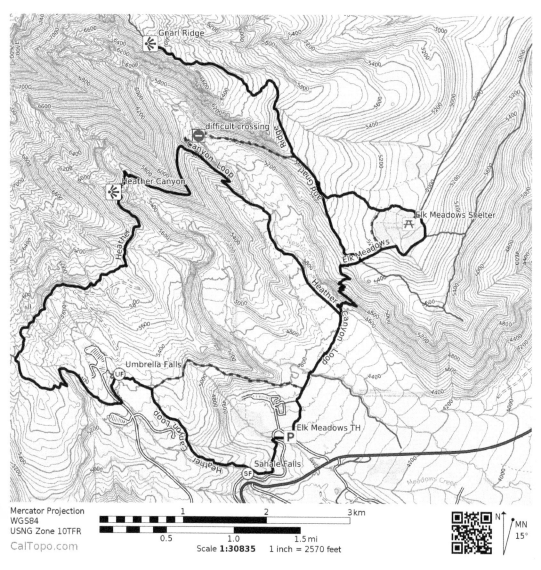

68A. Lookout Mountain via High Prairie

Distance: 3 mile loop
Elevation Gain: 600 feet
Trailhead Elevation: 5,953 feet
Trail High Point: 6,533 feet
Other seasons: August- October
Map: Mount Hood (Green Trails #462)
Pass: NW Forest Pass
Drivetime from Portland: 110 minutes

Directions:
* From Portland drive US 26 east to a junction with OR 35 on the side of Mt. Hood.
* Turn onto OR 35 and continue for 13.3 miles to a junction with FR 44 (Dufur Mill Rd.) just after Little John Sno-Park.
* Turn right and continue on FR 44 for exactly 3.8 miles to a poorly-marked junction with FR 4410. Turn right here.
* Drive this washboarded and dusty gravel road uphill 4.5 miles to its end at a junction with the Bennett Pass Road.
* Turn left and drive 100 yards to the trailhead on the left side of the road.

Why July: Of the four ways to reach the panoramic summit of Lookout Mountain, the approach via the High Prairie TH is by far the easiest, and offers the best experience for less-conditioned hikers. The view from the top stretches from Mount Rainier to the Three Sisters and out across the dry expanse of central Oregon, offering much for such a small package. The only downside of this hike is that it's almost too easy, and for many it will be too short to justify the long drive to the trailhead. For a more difficult hike, see the hike on the next page.

Mount Hood from Lookout Mountain.

Hike: From the High Prairie TH, locate the trail on the opposite side of the Bennett Pass Road. After just a dozen yards or so, turn right to begin your loop. The trail passes through the wildflower meadows of High Prairie before entering the woods. You may be out of breath right from the beginning of the hike- at more than 5,900 feet of elevation, High Prairie is taller than most of the surrounding peaks in the Cascades. You'll only get higher from here. Continue on this trail through the woods until views begin to open up all around. The trail wraps around a scenic rock pinnacle with a fantastic view of Mount Hood. From here, you'll climb uphill to a junction with the Divide Trail at a switchback at 1.2 miles. Keep left here.

The trail then wraps around the southwest side of Lookout Mountain's wide summit plateau, passing many and varied July wildflowers, . Here the trail braids bit, offering scenic views in every direction. Choose your own adventure along the rock pinnacles (but watch your step) and soon you will arrive at a junction with the return trail, a former road, at 1.4 miles. Continue straight, pass another junction with the Divide Trail and keep left here to continue to the summit. The view is otherworldly. To the north, look for the trio of Washington volcanoes, hovering above the peaks of the Gifford Pinchot National Forest. The view stretches south to Mount Jefferson and the Three Sisters. To the east, the view stretches from a sliver of the Columbia River south to the rolling wheat fields and rugged canyons of central Oregon. The star of the show, of course, is Mount Hood, just six miles to the west. The remains of the erstwhile lookout tower provide a spot to stop and rest, and take in the view.

If you've got some extra time, Senecal Spring is a worthwhile detour. The spring, located just below the summit of Lookout Mountain, is the source of Fifteenmile Creek. To locate the spring, follow the Divide Trail downhill from the summit of Lookout Mountain for about 500 feet until you locate the side trail on the left leading to the spring. Follow the trail downhill 0.2 mile to the spring. This is a peaceful place! Then return to the summit.

To return to the trailhead, you could return the way you came but it's more fun to make a loop. Return to the saddle just west of the summit and turn right on what was once a road servicing the lookout tower on the summit. You will hike downhill through the woods for 1.4 miles on this old road to the High Prairie Trailhead.

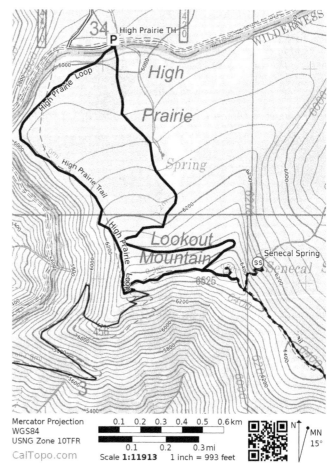

Mercator Projection
WGS84
USNG Zone 10TFR
CalTopo.com

0.1 0.2 0.3 0.4 0.5 0.6 km

0.1   0.2   0.3 mi
Scale **1:11913**   1 inch = 993 feet

MN
15°

68B. Lookout Mountain via Fret Creek

Distance via Fret Creek TH: 7.6 miles out and back
Elevation Gain: 2,100 feet
Trailhead Elevation: 4,594 feet
Trail High Point: 6,533 feet
Other seasons: August- October
Map: Flag Point (Green Trails #463) and Mount Hood (Green Trails #462)
Pass: None needed
Drivetime from Portland: 110 minutes

Directions:
- From Portland drive US 26 east to a junction with OR 35 on the side of Mt. Hood.
- Turn onto OR 35 and continue for 13.3 miles to a junction with FR 44 (Dufur Mill Rd.) just after Little John Sno-Park.
- Turn right and continue on FR 44 for 5.2 miles.
- At a junction with FR 17, turn right to continue on FR 44 for 3.1 miles.
- Turn right on unsigned but paved FR 4420 and continue for 2.2 miles to a junction.
- Drive straight, now on paved FR 2730 for 2.1 miles to rustic but charming Fifteenmile Campground.
- Continue another 200 yards to the trailhead at a pullout on the left (but the trail departs to the right, uphill) just before the road crosses Fret Creek.

Why July: Of the four ways to reach the panoramic summit of Lookout Mountain, this is the moderate option and perhaps the most rewarding. The hike to the summit passes a peaceful lake on its way to a view-packed ridge where the views seem to stretch out forever. Flowers grow profusely along this ridge in July, adding color to an already-beautiful scene. Make this hike a July tradition.

Looking west to Mount Hood from the slopes of Lookout Mountain.

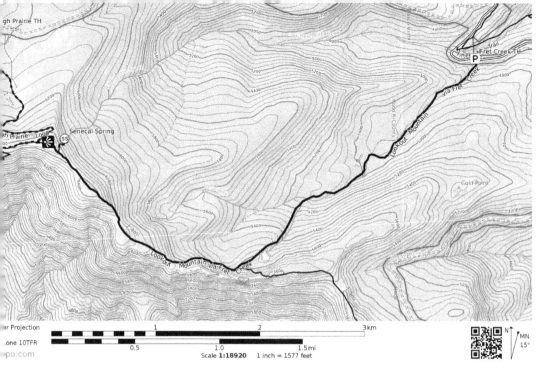

Hike: Begin at the Fret Creek TH. You will climb steeply as you parallel Fret Creek in a forest consisting of scattered larch and Douglas fir. On the way up you cross Fret Creek twice on bridges before reaching shallow Oval Lake at about 2.1 miles from the trailhead. Take a minute to visit this shallow but scenic lake, tucked under rock pinnacles known as the Palisades. The trail continues another 700 feet to a junction with the Divide Trail at a little over 2.2 miles.

Turn right on the Divide Trail and begin hiking uphill through the woods. Eventually the trail begins to open up as it climbs steeply up Lookout Mountain's southeast face. The trail here can be rocky and the way steep, but the climbing doesn't last too long. You will soon emerge at a saddle below the summit of Lookout Mountain. Explorers and hikers who love secret spots can follow the unsigned spur trail in this saddle down to Senecal Springs (the source of Fifteenmile Creek, Hike 58), which served as the water source for the erstwhile lookout tower that once stood on the summer.

Back at the saddle again, continue on the Divide Trail towards the summit of Lookout Mountain, which you reach via an old road at 3.8 miles. The view here is incredible: you can see every Cascade high point from Mount Rainier to the Three Sisters and Broken Top, and everything in between. Look east to the long, dry sweep of central Oregon, and look north to the Gorge and to Hood River. The star attraction, of course, is Mount Hood just seven miles to the west. You could spend hours up here trying to identify every feature you can see (some do). It is possible to camp on the summit, and backpackers can gather water from Senecal Springs. Sunsets and sunrises up here are amazing, but very cold even in summer. Return the way you came.

Hikers desiring a longer day have many options, but perhaps the best is to follow the Divide Trail southeast from the junction just above Oval Lake. In just 0.3 mile the trail climbs to a high, precarious ridge crest beside a collection of rock pinnacles known as the Palisades. This is an exceedingly fun place to explore, but watch your step- there are cliffs all around here. From the Palisades the trail descends 1.3 miles to trail's end at Flag Point's access road. Here several different trails come together, offering more options than I can even print here. Flag Point's lookout tower is 0.6 mile uphill (to the right) on the road.

69. Bull of the Woods

Distance: 7.4 mile loop
Elevation Gain: 2,000 feet
Trailhead elevation: 3,609 feet
Trail high point: 5,509 feet
Other seasons: June- October
Map: Opal Creek Wilderness (Imus)
Pass: none needed
Drivetime from Portland: 130 minutes

Directions:
- From Portland, drive southeast on OR 224 to Estacada.
- Stay on OR 224 past Estacada and continue approximately 25 miles to Ripplebrook.
- Just past Ripplebrook OR 224 becomes FR 46. Continue straight on FR 46 for 4.2 miles from Ripplebrook to a junction with FR 63, where you turn right, following signs for Bagby Hot Springs.
- Drive this 2-lane paved road for 3.5 miles to a junction with FR 70, signed for Bagby Hot Springs.
- Continue straight on FR 63 for 2.1 miles to a junction with FR 6340.
- Turn right and drive 7.8 gravel miles uphill to the junction of FR 6340 with FR 6341.
- Fork to the right and drive 3.5 miles of rough pavement to the well-signed trailhead.
- Parking is on the right side of the road while the trail departs on your left.

Why July: Once July finally rolls around, you have the world at your feet. You can go hiking almost anywhere. The best hikes this time of year have much to offer, and this wildly scenic loop up and over the summit of Bull of the Woods is no exception. The trail passes through impressive displays of ancient forest, wildflower-spangled ridges, and culminates at a summit with an impressive 360-degree view, complete with lookout tower. This is as good as it gets, and this is why this is the best individual dayhike in the Bull of the Woods Wilderness.

Hike: The trail begins with a gradual climb through ancient forest. As you hike away from the road, you'll have views through the trees of the rugged mountains that surround Pan-

sy Lake and Pansy Basin. The trail climbs at a very gradual rate, and is never steep. After about 0.8 mile, reach a junction with an abandoned trail down into rugged Pansy Basin. Continue straight on the main trail. At 1.2 miles, reach a junction with the Dickey Lake Trail (549). As with all trail junctions in the Bull of the Woods, the junction is marked with only a number. For the time being, continue straight to a profusion of trails that encircle Pansy Lake. The main trail heads left around the lake, but you may want to investigate the lake. There are a number of excellent campsites around the lake, making the lake an outstanding destination for a family-friendly backpacking trip.

To continue the loop, return to the main trail and switchback up 0.8 mile to a saddle, where you meet the Mother Lode Trail (558), which descends down into the burned forest on your right. Keep left and begin climbing, at times steeply, through ancient forest on the south slopes of Bull of the Woods. Occasional views through the trees open up to Mount Jefferson to the southeast. At 1.2 miles from the junction at the saddle, meet the Welcome Lakes Trail (554) at another saddle. Turn sharply to the left and hike 0.5 mile through dense forest until the trail opens up into alpine splendor just below the summit of the mountain. The trail switchbacks steeply up to the open summit, with an abandoned lookout tower and panoramic views stretching from Mount Rainier to the Three Sisters. In July, the flower display here is outstanding, with red paintbrush and white cat's ears dominating. What a fantastic spot! Sadly, you cannot enter the lookout tower, as it is locked and closed to public visits. Explorations around the summit reveal more stupendous views, gardens of July wildflowers, and much more. If you look hard enough, you can even find the lookout tower's outhouse, most of which is still standing just a short distance below the summit.

When you decide it's time to leave, follow the trail that heads north from the summit (550) as it descends along a scenic ridgecrest of rocky viewpoints and flower gardens. One mile below the summit of Bull of the Woods, reach a junction with the Dickey Lake Trail (549) on your left. Turn here and begin descending through scenic forest with an incredible amount of rhododendrons. Blowdown can be a problem on this trail but the way is never in doubt. The trail reaches shallow Dickey Lake in about a mile. A trail leads to the lake, but it isn't really worth your time. Soon after that, you'll meet the Pansy Lake Trail. Turn right here and hike 1 mile back to the trailhead.

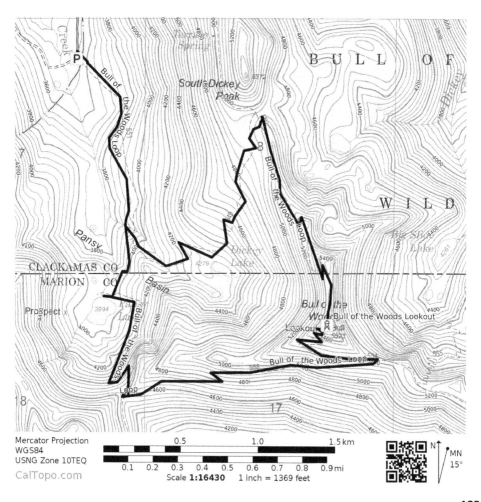

Mercator Projection
WGS84
USNG Zone 10TEQ
CalTopo.com

Scale **1:16430**   1 inch = 1369 feet

70. Bear Point

Distance: 7.8 miles
Elevation Gain: 3,000 feet
Trailhead elevation: 3,029 feet
Trail high point: 6,034 feet
Other seasons: August – October
Map: Mount Jefferson Wilderness (Geo-Graphics)
Pass: None needed
Drivetime from Portland: 125 minutes

Directions:

- Drive south from Portland on Interstate 5 to Salem.
- At Exit 253 outside Salem, leave the freeway and reach a junction with OR 22.
- From Salem, drive OR 22 east for 49.2 miles to Detroit.
- Turn left at a sign for Breitenbush, Elk Lake and Olallie Lake onto FR 46.
- Drive 11.6 miles to a junction with FR 4685 on your right. Turn right.
- This road is paved at first as it crosses the North Fork Breitenbush River but then transitions to a good gravel road.
- Drive 4.6 miles to a large parking lot on your right, located in a large open flat.
- You can also reach the trailhead by driving to Estacada on OR 224 and continuing on this road 25 miles to Ripplebrook, and then another 34 miles on FR 46 to the junction with FR 4685 described above. This approach is a bit longer but far more scenic.

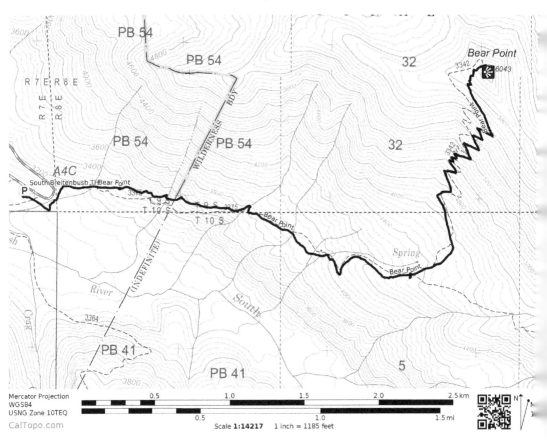

Mercator Projection
WGS84
USNG Zone 10TEQ
CalTopo.com

Scale **1:14217**   1 inch = 1185 feet

Mount Jefferson and Park Ridge from Bear Point.

Why July: While the rugged terrain north of Mount Jefferson hides many great views of the glaciated giant, none surpass the panorama found at Bear Point. At this rocky and exposed location, just four miles northwest of Mount Jefferson, you'll find a view almost unparalleled in the region. You'd better get in shape though, as the trail is hot, steep and dusty. July is the best time to do this hike, as the hike typically melts out by early in the month. Once the snow melts, you'll find the flowers and views just to your liking.

Hike: The trail leaves from the large parking lot and almost immediately meets a junction with the Crag Trail, an abandoned route that heads into the heart of the 2017 Whitewater Fire. Keep straight and follow the South Breitenbush Trail uphill into the verdant forest above the South Breitenbush River. As you ascend, the forest begins to change character, passing from lowland forest to the dry forest more associated with the high Cascades. The trail passes several small creeks, cascading down from the slopes of Bear Point. At 1.5 miles you will pass the flattened ruins of a seedling shed, a remnant from another large fire in the 1960s. At 2.2 miles from the trailhead, you will meet the Bear Point Trail on your left at a large cairn. There may or may not be a sign so keep your eyes peeled.

Turn left at the cairn and follow the Bear Point Trail through the brush as the trail follows a creekbed for a short ways. The trail does not receive much maintenance so it may be necessary to fight through the brush a little. As the trail begins to climb, you will leave the darkness behind and enter a long uphill traverse in open woods. Mount Jefferson soon appears, towering above the headwall of the South Breitenbush canyon just a few miles to the south. The Bear Point Trail continues switchbacking up increasingly open slopes until it reaches Bear Point's panoramic summit at 3.9 miles. The view is jaw-dropping: Mount Jefferson rises above the rugged ridge south of Bear Point, while peaks all the way to Mount Rainier line the horizon to the north. Bear Lake shimmers in the basin below. With a view like this, you won't be surprised to discover that this was once the site of a lookout tower. The tower was dismantled in 1968, and all that remains today is some rebar and broken glass. When you can bear it, return the way you came.

AUGUST

		Distance	EV Gain	Drivetime
71A.	Foggy Flat	13.6 mi	2,000 ft	160 min
71B.	Killen Creek and High Camp	8.4 mi	2,400 ft	160 min
72.	Bird Creek Meadows	10.8 mi	1,800 ft	120 min
73.	Paradise Park	13 mi	2,900 ft	65 min
74.	Yocum Ridge	17.4 mi	3,700 ft	75 min
75.	Cairn Basin and Elk Cove	11.4 mi	2,400 ft	150 min
76.	Cooper Spur	7.8 mi	3,100 ft	130 min
77.	Serene Lake Loop	12.6 mi	3,000 ft	100 min
78.	Big Slide Lake	12 mi	2,500 ft	90 min
79.	Park Ridge	7 mi	1,400 ft	150 min
80.	Jefferson Park via South Breitenbush	13 mi	3,500 ft	125 min

At last we've reached the cream of the crop of hiking in our area. It doesn't get any better than this- and there's no excuse to go hiking anywhere else at this time of year. In August, look for hikes that take you high up into the mountains. Sometimes this involves longer drives than many hikers would like - while up until this point I've made every effort to keep hikes under 2 hours drive from Portland, some of the hikes listed are well more than that. There is reason to this! To me, August is the time to expand your horizons, to travel far and wide to hike the best there is to offer in the area. What follows here are my ten favorite August hikes in the region, at least within a reasonable 3 hours or so of Portland. All ten of these hikes are backpackable, with many excellent campsites and secluded spots (some more than others, of course).

All of these hikes involve traveling high on mountain peaks, passing meadows or volcanic highlands, to spectacular vistas of the Cascades. Many of these hikes are very popular, some more than others. Expect crowds on weekends, even on weekdays. Please respect these fragile environments by staying on the main trail, packing out all garbage, using responsible wilderness bathroom protocols, and by camping only in designated spots and not on fragile wilderness meadows. In other words, Leave No Trace ethics are of vital importance here. As the saying goes: take only pictures and leave only footprints.

August weather is perhaps the most predictable of the year. Up in the high country expect warm, sunny days but cool, crisp nights. Thunderstorms are common in the Cascades this time of year and you should always be prepared for them. Avoid high ridges (at least half of these hikes) during thunderstorms, and be prepared to turn around quickly when you hear thunder or see lightning. This is fire season too- keep an eye out for fires when hiking. DO NOT build campfires- they are unnecessary, and risk getting out of control quickly. It doesn't take much. Regardless, you should always be prepared for any kind of weather when traveling in the mountains in August. Cold nights are very common. As always, practice vigilance by bringing the Ten Essentials and by leaving a plan of your travels with a friend or family member.

Photo on opposite page: Mount Hood from the end of Yocum Ridge (Hike 74)

71A. Foggy Flat

Distance: 13.6 miles out and back
Elevation Gain: 2,000 feet
Trailhead elevation: 4,587 feet
Trail High Point: 6,103 feet
Other Seasons: September
Map: Mount Adams Wilderness (USFS)
Pass: None needed
Drivetime from Portland: 160 minutes

Directions:

- From Portland, drive east on Interstate 84 to Hood River.
- At Exit 64 on I-84, leave the freeway and reach a junction at the end of the off-ramp.
- Turn left and drive to the toll bridge over the Columbia River. Pay the $1 toll and cross the river.
- At the far end of the bridge on the Washington side, turn left on WA 14.
- Drive 1.5 miles west on WA 14 to a junction with WA 141 ALT, just before a bridge over the White Salmon River. Turn right here.
- Drive 2.2 miles to a junction with WA 141. Turn left here.
- Drive 18.9 miles to the small town of Trout Lake.
- Continue straight on what is now Mt Adams Road (FR 23) for 1.5 miles to a junction.
- Keep left (right leads to the south and east sides of Mount Adams) to stay on FR 23.
- Drive 23 miles, ignoring all side roads along the way, to a junction with FR 2329 near Taklakh Lake. The last several miles of this road are gravel.
- Turn right on FR 2329, following signs for Taklakh Lake.
- Drive 1.5 miles to Taklakh Lake, ignoring signs for Olallie Lake along the way.
- Continue past Taklakh Lake, where FR 2329 worsens into a rough, rutted, potholed road that requires patience.
- Drive 1.9 miles beyond Taklakh Lake to the Divide Camp Trail on your right.
- Continue 2.4 increasingly rough miles to the Killen Creek Trailhead on your right.

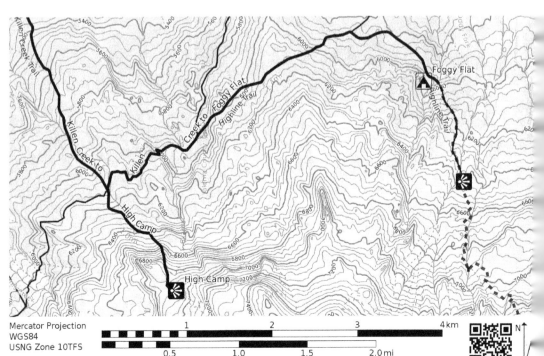

Why August: It's a long drive to the north side of Mount Adams but it is absolutely worth it. This side of the glaciated giant is renowned for its spectacular meadows of August wildflowers, cascading creeks and tumbling glaciers. This trek to Foggy Flat features the best of what Mount Adams has to offer, and yet its length and obscurity keeps most hikers away. The length of both the drive and hike make this more of a backpacking destination but it can be done as a hike in one day if you're willing to make it a LONG day.

Hike: Begin at the Killen Creek Trailhead. You'll hike up the Killen Creek Trail through the forest, at times gaining elevation steeply via a series of steps cut into the trail. The Killen Creek Trail receives heavy equestrian use and the trail is quite dusty due to the pounding of horse hooves. Eventually the way begins to open up, revealing fantastic wildflower meadows and excellent views south to heavily glaciated Mount Adams. The trail levels out, passes through meadow after meadow and then reaches the Pacific Crest Trail at 3.2 miles. Turn left to continue on your way to Foggy Flat.

The Pacific Crest Trail traverses the wondrous alpine meadows on the north side of Mount Adams. In 0.9 mile you'll cross Killen Creek directly above a waterfall; so beautiful is this spot that you may be tempted to stop here. Beyond this point, you will reach a junction with the Highline Trail in just 0.2 mile. The PCT turns left to continue north, but you turn right to continue hiking around Mount Adams. The next 1.7 miles follow the Highline Trail up and down through the woods, at times steeply, to a junction with the Muddy Meadows Trail. Once you reach this trail at 6.2 miles, the trail levels out somewhat. Continue 1 more mile at a slight uphill grade to Foggy Flat's meadow. At first, the meadow doesn't look like much, and the view of Mount Adams is slightly obstructed. But explorations reveal hidden ponds, tumbling creeks and secret campsites. This is an excellent place to spend the night, on the northeast side of Mount Adams, far removed from the hustle and bustle of the modern world. Few people make it over here. The Highline Trail continues beyond Foggy Flat towards Devils Garden and Avalanche Valley. While the views are incredible, you will be faced with difficult creek crossings, faint trail and a lot of elevation gain. It's worth it, but is best left to adventurous backpackers. Return the way you came.

Mount Adams from the rugged terrain southeast of Foggy Flat.

71B. Killen Creek and High Camp

Distance: 8.4 miles out and back
Elevation Gain: 2,400 feet
Trailhead elevation: 4,587 feet
Trail High Point: 6,103 feet
Other Seasons: September
Map: Mount Adams Wilderness (USFS)
Pass: None needed
Drivetime from Portland: 160 minutes

Directions:
- See directions for Hike 71A.

Why August: Similar to Foggy Flat (see the previous two pages) and starting from the same trailhead, the trip to High Camp on the north side of Mount Adams is worthy of the long drive and steep, dusty trail. With a name like High Camp, you should expect large snow patches here even into August. But August is absolutely the time to visit, as this area dazzles with alpine wildflowers and stupendous views of the icy northwest face of Mount Adams. Backpacking up here, either as a standalone trek or as an add-on after visiting Foggy Flat (Hike 71A), rewards visitors with fantastic sunsets and extremely cold, windy nights. Don't bother with the long drive here unless you are certain to have warm, sunny weather.

Hike: Begin at the Killen Creek Trailhead. You'll hike up the Killen Creek Trail through the forest, at times gaining elevation steeply via a series of steps cut into the trail. The Killen Creek Trail receives heavy equestrian use and the trail is quite dusty due to the pounding of horse hooves. Eventually the way begins to open up, revealing fantastic wildflower

Mount Adams at High Camp.

meadows and excellent views south to heavily glaciated Mount Adams. The trail levels out, passes through meadow after meadow and then reaches the Pacific Crest Trail at 3.2 miles. For High Camp, turn right on the Pacific Crest Trail locate the the trail about fifty feet to your right from the end of the Killen Creek Trail, and turn left.

Follow the High Camp Trail uphill through increasingly open terrain. At times the trail is faint, but it is very difficult to lose. You will weave around talus slopes, pass through gaps between huge rocks and gain a lot of elevation in a short amount of time on your way up to High Camp. The High Camp Trail eventually rounds a corner and traverses a slope, delicately passing above a snowfield. Hikers with a fear of heights may have trouble here. This is also your clue that you are almost there, as High Camp is located at the top of this traverse. Once you reach High Camp, an alpine plateau located at the base of the massive Adams Glacier, the high country is yours to explore! Good campsites abound, but expect very cold nights even in the summer. Great views also abound on clear days: west to Mount Saint Helens, north to Mount Rainier and Goat Rocks, and of course, south to the icy northwest face of Mount Adams. Return the way you came.

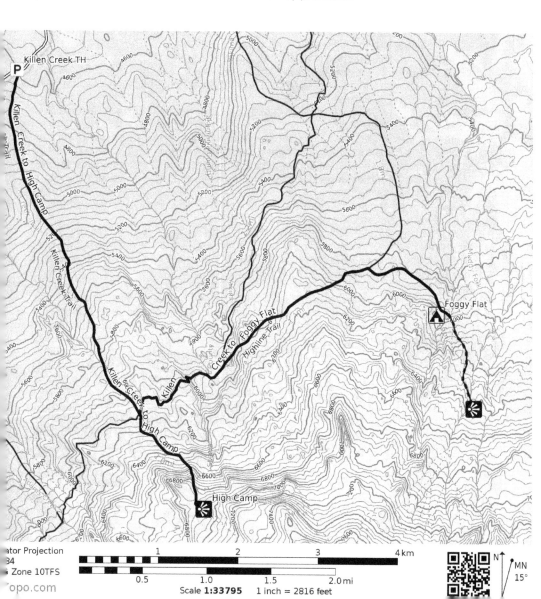

72. Bird Creek Meadows

Distance: 10.8 miles out and back
Elevation Gain: 1,800 feet
Trailhead elevation: 5,561 feet
Trail High Point: 6,506 feet
Other Seasons: September
Map: Mount Adams, WA #367S (Green Trails)
Pass: NW Forest Pass
Drivetime from Portland: 130 minutes

Directions:
- From Portland, drive east on Interstate 84 to Hood River.
- At Exit 64 on I-84, leave the freeway and reach a junction at the end of the off-ramp.
- Turn left and drive to the toll bridge over the Columbia River. Pay the $1 toll and cross the river. At the far end of the bridge on the Washington side, turn left on WA 14.
- Drive 1.5 miles west on WA 14 to a junction with WA 141 ALT, just before a bridge over the White Salmon River. Turn right here.
- Drive 2.2 miles to a junction with WA 141. Turn left here.
- Drive 18.9 miles to the small town of Trout Lake.
- At a gas station at the edge of Trout Lake, keep right on what becomes the Mount Adams Recreation Highway.
- Drive 1.2 miles to a Y-junction. Bear right at a sign for the South Climb Trailhead, Sno-Parks and Bird Creek Meadows.
- Drive 0.7 miles to another Y-junction. Keep left at a sign for the South Climb Trailhead, your destination. Ignore the right turn, signed for Bird Creek Meadows. This would take you to the Yakima Reservation Trailhead for Bird Creek Meadows, but this trailhead has been closed since the Cougar Creek Fire in 2015 and it is not known when the road will reopen.
- Follow signs for the South Climb Trailhead for 9 miles, the first half paved and the second half gravel, to Morrison Creek Forest Camp.
- Turn right onto FR 500, which quickly becomes narrow and rutted. Continue 2.6 miles to the South Climb Trailhead at road's end. While low-clearance vehicles can make it to the trailhead, the constant dips, ruts and potholes make this last stretch of road much easier in a higher-clearance vehicle.

Why August: The fabled meadows of Bird Creek Meadows on the southeast side of Mount Adams are among the most scenic destinations in the Pacific Northwest. Rumors of terrible roads and endless burned forests have kept the crowds away, but you can make the trek if you plan on a long day and don't mind driving a few miles of bad road. Once you get there, you will find fields of August wildflowers, stunning views up the sprawling glaciers on Mount Adams' southeast flank and the kind of solitude one normally doesn't find in such a beautiful destination. Please note that camping is prohibited on the Yakima Reservation side of this hike, so you can only visit for the day.

Hike: Begin your hike on the wide, well-travelled South Climb Trail. You will hike uphill on this popular trail alongside climbers of all abilities, all hoping to make the 12,276 foot summit of Mount Adams. The trail climbs through forest burned in the Cougar Creek Fire of 2015. At 1.4 miles and 700 feet of elevation from the trailhead, you will reach a junction with the Round the Mountain Trail. Here you turn right and leave the climbers behind.

The Round the Mountain Trail leaves the burn and climbs gently along the southern slopes of Mount Adams. Before long, the trail passes through the Aiken Lava Bed. The lava issued forth from Mount Adams between 4,500 and 6,000 years ago, perhaps the most geologically recent display of volcanism on the mountain. The trail weaves through the huge boulders the lava flow left behind before descending a bit into meadows on the east side of the lava flow. At 3.5 miles, the trail leaves the lava behind and enters glorious Bird Creek Meadows at the boundary of the Yakima Reservation. At the boundary the Round the Mountain Trail meets the Snipes Mountain Trail; continue straight. The trail now passes through some of the finest alpine wildflower meadows in the entire region. As always, stay on the trail and do not pick flowers or trample fragile meadows. You will meet the Crooked Creek Trail at 4 miles, where you once again have the option to explore. For this hike, you should stay on the main trail, continuing straight.

The trail network in Bird Creek Meadows is well-signed, but the area is still in the process of being rehabilitated after the 2015 fire that burned directly to the edge of Bird Creek Meadows. Continue straight for 0.6 mile more to a junction marked by a sign for the picnic area. Turn left and hike uphill, passing a sign for the Trail of the Flowers, to another junction. Keep left at a sign for the Hellroaring Viewpoint and continue another 0.5 mile of increasingly open terrain to the aforementioned Hellroaring Viewpoint. There is no mistaking the spot- you will know it when you see it. Here Mount Adams appears larger than life, towering over the deep canyon of Hellroaring Creek. Glaciers and waterfalls dot the eastern face of the mountain. Stop here, at one of the finest viewpoints in the region. Return the way you came.

If you'd rather have a shorter hike but a longer drive, you can also access this area from the Yakima Reservation side. The roads and trails have mostly been closed since the 2015 fire but may reopen in time for the summer hiking season. The Hellroaring Viewpoint is only a little over 3 miles from the Bird Creek Meadows Trailhead, leaving you with more than enough time and energy to explore more of this area. For more information and to see if the Bird Creek Meadows Trailhead has reopened, check online.

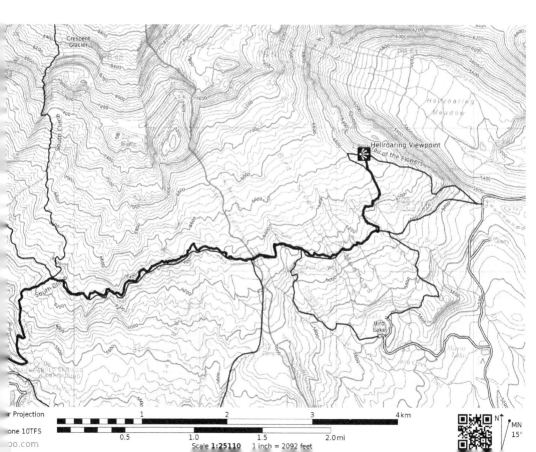

73. Paradise Park

Distance: 12.8 miles out and back
Elevation Gain: 2,800 feet
Trailhead Elevation: 5,874 feet
Trail High Point: 6,092 feet
Other seasons: mid-July, September-October
Map: Mount Hood Wilderness (Geo-Graphics)
Pass: NW Forest Pass
Drivetime from Portland: 90 minutes

Directions:
- From Portland, drive US 26 east to Sandy.
- From Sandy, continue approximately 28 miles to Government Camp.
- At a sign for Timberline Lodge, turn left onto the Timberline Lodge Road.
- Drive 5.5 miles uphill to the lodge and its large parking lot. The trail leaves from behind the lodge.

Why August: Paradise Park is near the top of any list of best hikes on Mount Hood. The mountain towers over fields of wildflowers, revealing scenes that overwhelm the senses. It is truly a place worthy of its name. Get in shape first, though; this is perhaps the most deceptively difficult hike in the region. Getting there is in some ways the easy part- but the way back features 1,300 feet of elevation gain, uphill that can drag you down at the end of a long hike. Save some energy for the return trip, or better yet, backpack here and save your return for another day. However you do it, this is a trip you will want to make again and again. Because you gain so much elevation on the return, avoid this hike on hot days.

Hike: Begin by following the paved trail beside Timberline Lodge uphill. After 0.2 mile, you will intersect the Pacific Crest Trail. Turn left here. You will pass under a pair of ski lifts on your way out of the complex around Timberline Lodge. Views stretch south to Mount Jefferson and the Three Sisters. Closer at your feet, lupine blooms profusely along this stretch of the trail in August, and at peak bloom the scent of its perfume is overwhelming. All the while the trail is slowly losing elevation, a descent that is not noticeable- until the return trip. At 1.3 miles the trail dips into Little Zigzag Canyon, the often-dry source of the Little Zigzag River. Continue another 1.2 miles of gradual downhill to the Zigzag Overlook, a view of the Zigzag River's impressive canyon. You need to go down there next. The trail descends through the woods 600 feet in 1 mile to a crossing of the Zigzag River at 3.6 miles from Timberline Lodge. The PCT crosses the river just downstream of an impressive waterfall. The crossing is not usually terribly difficult, but you may need to locate rocks or a downed log to cross with dry feet. As with any other crossing of a stream that originates in a glacier, earlier in the day is better. The crossing will be more difficult on the return trip.

From the crossing, the PCT climbs 0.4 mile to a junction with the Paradise Park Loop Trail on your right. This short stretch of the Timberline was plagued with blowdown in the summer of 2017. Turn right to hike into Paradise Park. As with the Timberline here, this trail was also plagued with blowdown in the summer of 2017- hopefully the trails in this little corner of the wilderness have been fixed by the time you visit. The Paradise Park Loop Trail exits the woods and follows a low-flowing tributary of the Zigzag River through fields of wildflowers uphill into Paradise Park, which you reach at 5.1 miles. Here you will reach a junction with the Paradise Park Trail #778, a long, forested route that arrives at the park via a trailhead near Rhododendron. A right turn here will lead you to one of the iconic views of Paradise Park, as seen above. The displays of beargrass for which this area are famed only occur once every few years, so you'll need to be patient and visit many times to experience this. Back on the loop trail, the way continues through the meadows and forested islands of Paradise Park another 0.8 to Split Rock, a large, broken boulder that resembles a giant, cracked egg. This is a popular rest spot, and if you're not interested in a loop, this is where you should turn around. Skipping the loop will save you approximately 1.2 miles. If you're continuing, follow the loop trail back into the woods, where you will meet the PCT at 6.5 miles. Turn left.

The PCT traverses the cliffs and slopes below Paradise Park, revealing waterfalls tumbling down from the park. Pass a junction with the aforementioned Paradise Park Trail at 8.5 miles, and just 0.4 mile later, reach the end of the Paradise Park Loop. Continue downhill to the crossing of the Zigzag River, and once across, steel yourself for the 3.6 miles of uphill trail back to Timberline Lodge.

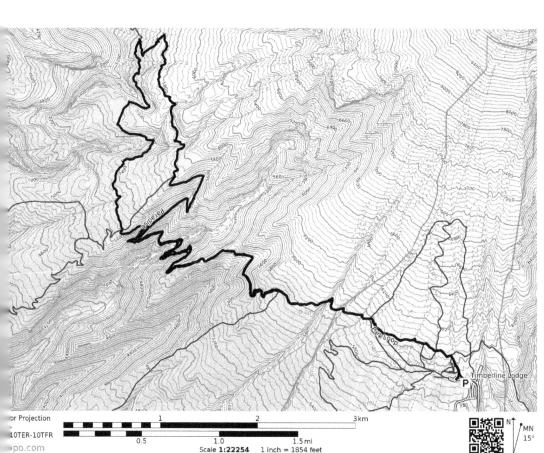

74. Yocum Ridge

Distance: 17.4 miles out and back
Elevation Gain: 3,700 feet
Trailhead elevation: 2,459 feet
Trail high point: 6,150 feet
Other seasons: July – October
Map: Mount Hood Wilderness (Geo-Graphics)
Pass: NW Forest Pass
Drivetime from Portland: 75 minutes

Directions:

- From Portland drive east on US 26 to Zigzag and Rhododendron.
- Just after a stop light with a sign for East Lolo Pass Road (FR 18), turn left on Lolo Pass Road and follow the Sandy River north.
- Stay on Lolo Pass Road for 4 paved miles.
- Immediately after a large sign for Mount Hood National Forest, turn right at a junction with FR 1825 that is labeled "campgrounds trailheads".
- Drive 0.6 mile of paved road to a junction with FR 1825 at a bridge.
- Turn right to stay on FR 1825. Continue on FR 1825 another 1.3 miles, staying left at every junction, until you reach a junction with FR 100.
- Turn left and drive 0.5 mile of rough pavement to the large Ramona Falls parking lot.
- Leave nothing of value in your car as break-ins and clouting is an occasional problem.

Why August: Yocum Ridge might be the best hike in this book. It has everything hikers dream about- huge views, lacy waterfalls, fields of wildflowers and less people than you would expect. You have to work for it, though- at more than 17 miles round-trip, it is out of reach for most day hikers. The easy grade and huge scenery makes it easier than it sounds but it still makes for an extremely long hike- a better plan is to haul a backpack up here and experience the best of what our region has to offer.

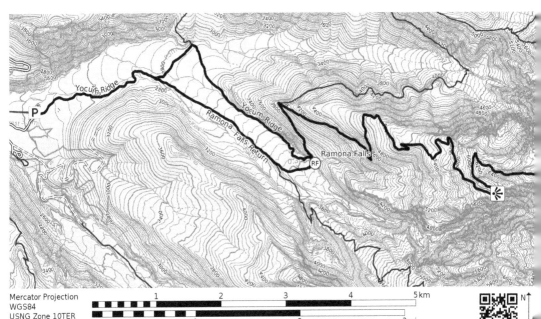

Mercator Projection
WGS84
USNG Zone 10TER
CalTopo.com

Scale **1:37002**   1 inch = 3084 feet

Hike: Begin at the signboard and follow a wide, easy trail along the Sandy River. The trail follows the river at a respectable distance; every few years the river floods, carving out new channels. A previous flood took out the road to an old trailhead in the 1990s, and successive floods have forced the trail further and further away from the river and into the forest. At a little over a mile, reach a ford of the river as Mount Hood looms above the river's canyon. In the past the Forest Service would place a seasonal bridge over the river here, but the bridge washed out in a thunderstorm in 2014, killing a hiker in the process. As a result, the Forest Service decided to eliminate the seasonal bridge altogether. These days it is necessary to locate a log to cross the river, something that is usually fairly easy. Once across the river, follow the trail a short ways to a junction. Although it is shorter to just turn right and follow signs to the PCT, you should instead keep straight and continue 0.5 mile to a junction with the Ramona Falls Trail. Turn right here.

This lovely trail, which follows tumbling, mossy Ramona Creek for 2 miles, is the perfect appetizer for your trek up Yocum Ridge. The trail follows the glassy creek through verdant woods at the foot of Yocum Ridge. The scenic ramparts of the ridge tower above this valley, creating shadows and keeping the forest cool even on hot days. The trail reaches lacy Ramona Falls at 3.7 miles. Take a moment to rest here before setting off to Yocum Ridge.

To hike Yocum Ridge, turn left and hike 0.6 mile steeply to a junction with the spur trail to Yocum Ridge. Turn right here and follow this trail gradually uphill under huge old-growth hemlock trees. The Yocum Ridge Trail stays in the forest, slowly climbing for nearly 4 miles. Finally the trail trades forest for meadows, at which point Mount Hood appears before you, larger than life. Continue straight to one of Oregon's greatest viewpoints: here the Sandy River pours out of Reid Glacier in a series of waterfalls. This extraordinary view may be the best lunch spot in the state of Oregon.

The trail does continue from here if you have the energy to manage it. The trail turns away from Mount Hood and climbs 0.7 mile to the ridgecrest. You are now on the rocky, open flanks of Mount Hood. If you're backpacking, there are campsites hidden discretely all around.

Return the way you came to Ramona Falls. From there, rather than turn right to follow Ramona Creek, keep straight until you reach a junction with the Pacific Crest Trail. Turn right and follow the PCT back to the river crossing, and then continue straight to the trailhead.

75. Cairn Basin and Elk Cove

	Cairn Basin	Elk Cove
Distance:	8.1 mile semi-loop	11.4 miles out and back
Elevation Gain:	1,900 feet	2,500 feet
Trailhead Elevation:	4,457 feet	4,460 feet
Trail High Point:	5,906 feet	5,913 feet
Other Seasons:	July- October	July - October
Map:	Mount Hood (Geo-graphics)	Mount Hood (Geo-graphics)
Pass:	NW Forest Pass	NW Forest Pass
Drivetime from PDX:	150 minutes	150 minutes

Directions:
- Drive to the junction of US 26 and Lolo Pass Road. Turn left here onto Lolo Pass Rd.
- Drive this road 10.6 miles to Lolo Pass. Reset your odometer here.
- Fork downhill to the right on what is now FR 1810. The road transitions to gravel immediately after Lolo Pass.
- Drive 1.3 miles to a junction with FR 640. This is the road to the McGee Creek TH.
- Continue another 4.4 miles to a junction with FR 1811, the road to the Mazama TH.
- Continue straight on what is now paved road for 5.2 miles to a junction with FR 16. If you were to continue straight, you would eventually reach Lost Lake and Hood River.
- Turn sharply to the right onto FR 16 and drive 5.6 miles of narrow pavement to another junction at a sharp curve, this time with FR 1650.
- Turn a sharp right onto FR 1650 and drive 2.9 miles of rocky gravel road to a fork.
- Keep left and drive 0.9 mile to road's end at the Vista Ridge TH.

Why August: It seems like it takes an eternity to drive to the Vista Ridge TH. I know this because I am always beyond relieved to arrive at the trailhead after spending more time driving backroads than even I can tolerate. But the virtues of starting here far outweigh the pain of getting here; this is perhaps the nicest corner of the Mount Hood area, and its scenic beauty reveals itself again and again in hikes along Vista Ridge.

Hike: Begin at the trailhead by hiking uphill on a wide, dusty trail. In just 0.4 mile, reach an unsigned junction at a signboard. Left takes you to Owl Point's spectacular vista, but we want to turn right. The Vista Ridge Trail soon enters forest burned during the 2011 Dollar Lake Fire, and climbs 2.1 miles through this terrain, gaining 1,200 feet along the way, to a junction on your right with the Eden Park Trail. The most direct way to Elk Cove is to continue straight but if you have the time and energy for a longer trip through wildly scenic terrain, turn right. You will switchback downhill into lush woods spared by the fire to a crossing of Ladd Creek. Try to cross the creek on the rocks, much easier during the morning before snowmelt begins in earnest. Soon after the crossing you'll reach lovely Eden Park, a meadow set in a narrow basin with a view of the top half of Mount Hood. Turn right at a sign to hike around the basin. The Eden Park Trail then begins switchbacking up through hanging gardens to meet the Timberline Trail at Cairn Basin, 4.1 miles from the trailhead. Cairn Basin marked the fireline during the Dollar Lake Fire, and parts of it burned. Thankfully the stone shelter here is intact, and the wildflowers are as great as ever. From Cairn Basin, turn left to follow the Timberline Trail around the north side of

Mount Hood. You need to cross Ladd Creek again (there was a log here as of August 2016) before climbing a bit to reach the Vista Ridge Trail at the edge of Wyeast Basin. If you're feeling bushed, you can turn left here and return to the trailhead, making a 8.1 mile loop. Hikers with more energy should continue to Elk Cove, perhaps the most idyllic alpine basin on Mount Hood.

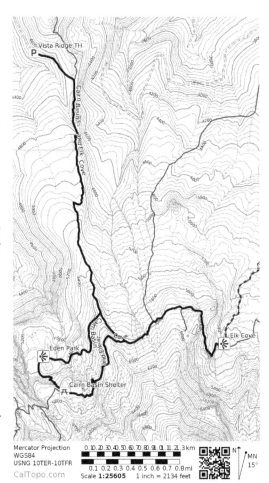

Keep straight to continue hiking east around Mount Hood. You'll pass the Pinnacle Ridge Trail in another 0.4 mile and begin curving around the side of rugged Barrett Spur. The Timberline Trail then descends around the north side of Barrett Spur to Elk Cove's narrow basin, reaching the cove at 1.3 miles from Wyeast Basin. The cove is a magnificent place that lends itself to wandering; take the time to follow the Timberline through the basin to the junction with the Elk Cove Trail, to meander along the wildflower-spangled creek, and go wherever else your heart desires. On the return, hike the Timberline Trail back 1.3 miles to Wyeast Basin and this time turn right. The Vista Ridge Trail descends a third of a mile to the Eden Park Junction described above, and then 2.1 miles to Owl Point Junction near the trailhead. Turn left here to hike 0.4 mile to the trailhead.

76. Cooper Spur

Distance: 7.8 miles out and back
Elevation Gain: 3,100 feet
Trailhead elevation: 5,853 feet
Trail high point: 8,911 feet
Other seasons: September
Map: Mount Hood Wilderness (Geo-Graphics)
Pass: NW Forest Pass
Drivetime from Portland: 130 minutes

Directions:

- From Portland, drive east on Interstate 84 to Hood River.
- Leave the freeway at Exit 64, signed for Mount Hood. Drive downhill to a T-junction and turn right on OR 35.
- Follow this highway 22 miles south to a junction with Cooper Spur Road on the right, just before the Polallie Trailhead. Turn right here.
- Drive 2.4 miles uphill to a junction near the Cooper Spur Mountain Resort.
- Turn left onto Cloud Cap Road and continue 1 mile to the winter snow gate.
- Continue on what is now a rocky, tedious and bumpy gravel road for 9.2 slow miles to road's end at Cloud Cap Saddle. The trail leaves from the well-signed trailhead near Cloud Cap Saddle Campground.
- **Note:** The last 6 miles of gravel road have more than 20 waterbars, large bumps constructed in the road to prevent erosion. You will need to drive slowly to prevent your car from bottoming out on the waterbars. Any vehicle can make it to Cloud Cap but you may want a higher-clearance vehicle just in case.

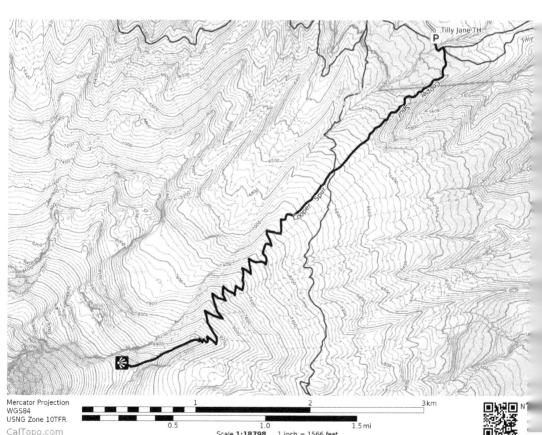

Hiking towards Cooper Spur.

Why August: The trek up Cooper Spur delivers hikers to the highest point on Mount Hood reachable by trail. The trail is so high that you may find yourself gasping for breath. The season for this hike is reasonably short, only from late July until the first snowstorm of the fall, whenever that is. August is thus the best time to do this hike. In addition to the incredible views of Mount Hood, hikers are also treated to far-ranging views of the Cascades, good displays of lupine along the trail and the satisfaction of climbing halfway up Oregon's highest peak.

Hike: Begin on the Timberline Trail, climbing among huge high-altitude mountain hemlock. You will climb higher and higher, but always at a steady but never too steep grade, until it leaves the forest at around 1 mile from the trailhead. Continue to a junction with the Tilly Jane Trail, where you will find the historic stone shelter located near the trail. Once upon a time there were six shelters located along the Timberline Trail, but today this is one of three still standing (the others are located at McNeil Point and Cairn Basin, both found in this book). The Timberline Trail forks to the left as it continues its southern trajectory around Mount Hood, but you will continue straight, now on the Cooper Spur Trail.

The trail begins a steady, inexorable climb up Cooper Spur's sandy ridge. The views are eye-popping, as you make your way up the narrow ridge between two glaciers on Mount Hood. Although the way is never terribly steep, the increasingly high elevation takes a toll on your lungs, forcing you to slow down. As you climb, you may also smell sulfur issuing from vents on the side of Mount Hood- a rare reminder that you're hiking on volcano that is still considered active. After more than 2 miles of climbing, the trail tops out momentarily at Tie-In Rock, a large boulder on the top of the ridge. This is where climbers traditionally roped up to continue their ascent of Mount Hood; today the trail is often snow-free for another half-mile beyond this point. When the trail disappears into the snow and ice, STOP! Do not continue onto the dangerously steep icefields beyond. Instead return the way you came.

77. Serene Lake Loop

Distance: 12.6 mile loop (including all side trips)
Elevation Gain: 3,000 feet
Trailhead Elevation: 4,079 feet
Trail High Point: 5,054 feet
Other Seasons: July- October
Map: High Rock (Green Trails #493)
Pass: None needed
Drivetime from Portland: 100 minutes

Directions:
- From Portland, drive OR 224 to Estacada. Continue straight on OR 224 as it follows the Clackamas River 25 miles to Ripplebrook Camp Store.
- Continue straight on OR 224 another 0.5 mile to a bridge over the Oak Grove Fork and a junction with FR 57.
- Following a sign for Timothy Lake, turn left on FR 57.
- Drive this paved road 6.9 miles to a junction with FR 58 on your left.
- Turn left and drive FR 58 for 3.4 miles of one-lane paved road to a junction with FR 5810 signed for Hideaway Lake.
- Turn left and follow FR 5810 for 5.3 miles of good gravel road to a junction on the left with Hideaway Lake Campground.
- Continue straight on FR 5810 another 0.3 mile to the Shellrock Lake TH on your right.

Why August: Serene Lake might be the nicest backcountry lake between Mount Hood and Mount Jefferson. Set between the Roaring and Clackamas Rivers, this deep lake is an inviting destination for hikers and backpackers in August. If you've come all this way, plan on making the full loop around this area to experience the best of what Clackamas country has to offer.

Hike: Begin at the Shellrock Lake TH. The trail climbs through the woods before descending a bit to reach Shellrock Lake at 0.6 mile. The trail curves around the lake, passing several excellent campsites. Continue around the lake and then begin climbing steadily uphill towards Frazier Turnaround. At 1.8 miles, reach a junction with the Grouse Point Trail - this is the start of your loop. Turn right and hike downhill on what is clearly an old road just 0.15 mile to Frazier Turnaround. From Frazier Turnaround, turn left on the Serene Lake Trail and hike downhill through a mixed forest. As elsewhere on this loop, look for huckleberries here. At 0.8 mile from Frazier Turnaround, reach a junction with the trail to Middle and Upper Rock Lakes. This trail climbs gradually up to Middle Rock Lake, and then follows the right side of the lake; from here, the trail gets faint, curves around the head of the middle lake and turns, climbing steeply to Upper Rock Lake. There is one nice campsite at the Upper Lake.

Back at the Rock Lakes Junction, continue

west towards Serene Lake. Shortly after the Middle Lake junction, pass a junction with the trail to Lower Rock Lake. Take a few minutes to hike the short trail down to this lake, then continue towards Serene Lake. The trail now loses elevation as it works its way around the rocky slopes separating the Rock Lakes Basin from Serene Lake. After some downhill and then some steep uphill, reach Serene Lake at 5 miles. If you're backpacking, the best campsites are on the far end of the lake. Upon leaving Serene Lake, the trail climbs the far end of the lake's basin. Reach a junction with the Grouse Point Trail a little under a mile from Serene Lake. Turn left and hike 0.5 mile, passing over the ridgecrest to a junction on your left. Turn left here and hike 100 yards to a viewpoint north, overlooking Serene Lake and out to Mount Hood and Mounts Saint Helens, Rainier and Adams. This is one of the best views in all of Clackamas country!

Continue from here as the Grouse Point Trail tumbles down a steep slope, angling towards Cache Meadow. Reach the meadow at 7.6 miles, where you will find nice flower displays even in August. This is a peaceful and quiet place; take a few minutes to enjoy it. At the far end of the meadow, reach a pair of confusing junctions: first, turn left just before you reach a pond. You will soon reach a four-way junction at the site of the old Cache Meadow shelter. There will be a sign for the Cripple Creek Trail. Keep left to stay on the Grouse Point Trail. The trail then leaves the meadow, passes a trail sign that reads only "517" (the trail's number) and then begins climbing furiously one final time on its way out of Cache Meadow's basin. At a little over 9 miles, finally crest the ridge holding Frazier Mountain and reach a junction on the remains of an old road. Turn right and begin working your way downhill. The next 0.9 mile is a feast of the senses, as you pass fields of huckleberries and excellent views south to Mount Jefferson. Finally, at 10 miles, reach a reunion with the Shellrock Trail on your right. Turn right here and hike 1.8 miles back to the trailhead.

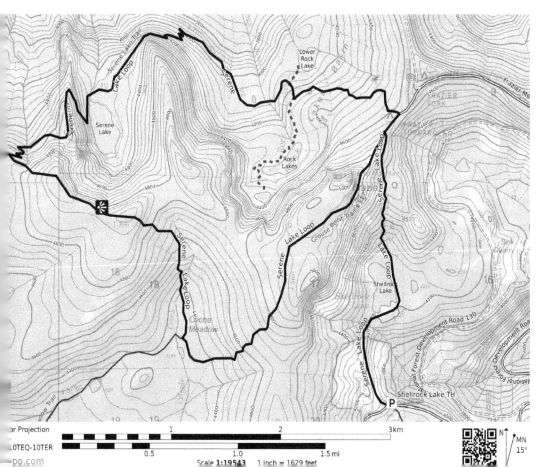

or Projection

.OTEQ-10TER

po.com

1   2   3km

0.5   1.0   1.5 mi

Scale 1:19543   1 inch = 1629 feet

N
MN
15°

78. Big Slide Lake

Distance: 12.2 miles out and back
Elevation Gain: 2,200 feet
Trailhead elevation: 2,892 feet
Trail high point: 4,359 feet
Other seasons: July- November
Map: Opal Creek Wilderness (Imus)
Pass: None needed
Drivetime from Portland: 90 minutes

Directions:
- From Portland, drive southeast on OR 224 approximately 20 miles to Estacada.
- From Estacada, drive southeast on OR 224 for approximately 25 miles to the old guard station at Ripplebrook.
- Just past Ripplebrook OR 224 becomes FR 46. Continue straight on FR 46 for 4.2 miles from Ripplebrook to a junction with FR 63.
- Turn right onto FR 63, following signs for Bagby Hot Springs.
- Drive this 2-lane paved road for 3.5 miles to a junction with FR 70, signed for Bagby
- Hot Springs. Ignore this turnoff and continue straight on FR 63.
- Drive another 2.1 miles on FR 63 to a junction with FR 6340 on your right.
- Turn right on this gravel road and drive 0.6 mile to a junction, where you keep straight.
- Continue on FR 6340 another 2.1 miles to a junction with FR 140 with a sigh for the Dickey Creek Trail. Turn left here.
- Drive this narrow, rocky road for 1 mile to a T-junction. The trailhead is on the right, but the best parking is on the left. There is also room for a couple of cars on the shoulder FR 140 about twenty yards before the junction.

Big Slide Lake and its charming little island.

Why August: You could spend every weekend in August hiking high up in the mountains but sometimes you just need a change of pace. This long but rewarding trek to Big Slide Lake, tucked away in a small basin in the remote Bull of the Woods Wilderness, is just what the doctor ordered. The trail seesaws up and down through stupendous ancient forest on the way to the scenic lake, a place that is ideal for backpacking. This hike is great whenever you can get here but you might appreciate it the most in August.

Hike: The only downside of this hike is that the beginning is somewhat protracted. Begin on decommissioned road FR 140. Follow this road for a half-mile to the remains of a bridge. Cross the bridge and abruptly begin a descent into the bottom of Dickey Creek's deep canyon. Trail crews have installed stairs to help mitigate some of the worst of the descent but it's still rough and steep- and of course, this is elevation you have to gain on the way out. At a little over a mile from the trailhead, you will finally arrive at the bottom of the canyon, where the trail immediately enters a grove of massive Douglas firs. This is an awesome and welcome place. From here, the trail passes through several outstanding groves of ancient forest, a swamp and several nice views down to Dickey Creek. At 3.5 miles, you will cross Dickey Creek. Earlier in the season this can be a tricky crossing, but

in August it is at worst a rock hop. For an easier hike you can turn around here, but what's the fun in that?

Once across the creek, the trail switchbacks up the walls of the canyon at a steady grade, leveling out after a little over a mile from the crossing. From here, traverse a series of rock slopes far above Dickey Creek until you reach an unmarked junction with the spur to Big Slide Lake at 6 miles from the trailhead. Turn right and descend steeply to the lake. User trails lead to campsites around this scenic lake, which features a small but charming island. This is a great destination for a day, and an even better one for a full weekend. Return the way you came.

Backpackers should consult a topographic map or guidebook to learn more about the vast and varied network of trails in the Bull of the Woods Wilderness Area.

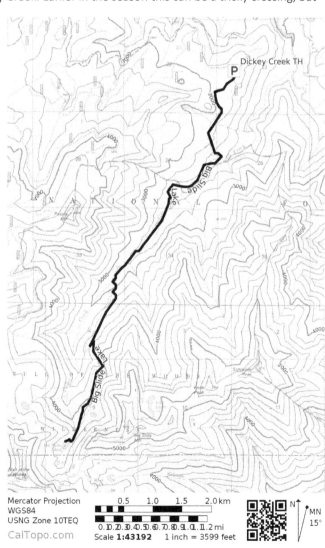

Mercator Projection
WGS84
USNG Zone 10TEQ
CalTopo.com

0.5   1.0   1.5   2.0 km
0.1.2.3.4.5.6.7.8.9.0.1.2 mi
Scale **1:43192**   1 inch = 3599 feet

N
MN
15°

79. Park Ridge

Distance: 7 miles out and back
Elevation Gain: 1,400 feet
Trailhead elevation: 5,510 feet
Trail high point: 6,910 feet
Other seasons: late July, September- early October
Map: Mount Jefferson Wilderness (Geo-Graphics)
Pass: NW Forest Pass
Drivetime from Portland: 150 minutes

Directions:
- From Portland, drive approximately 18 miles to Estacada on OR 224.
- Continue straight through Estacada and drive another 24.7 miles to the Ripplebrook Guard Station.
- A short distance after Ripplebrook, OR 224 becomes FR 46 at a junction with FR 57. Continue straight (right) on FR 46.
- Drive another 22.3 miles on FR 46 to a junction with the Olallie Lake Road (FR 4690). You will notice that "Olallie" is painted on the road to mark the direction.
- Continue past this junction 6.6 miles to a junction with the Skyline Road (FR 4220) on your left at Breitenbush Pass.
- Turn left here and drive 1 mile of gravel road to a large gate.
- Past the gate, the Skyline Road becomes a rocky, rutted, narrow track. It is 5.8 miles of slow, monotonous agony from the gate to the PCT Trailhead on your right, just before Breitenbush Lake. The trailhead is in a large lot made of bright red cinders.
- Be aware of your car's ability to handle the Skyline Road. While passenger cars can handle the road, a high-clearance vehicle is better. This is a bad, bad, bad road.

The view of Mount Jefferson from Park Ridge is unforgettable.

Why August: Park Ridge is great at any time, but never more so than in August. You follow a stretch of the PCT through some of the highest, most beautiful terrain in the state. Snow lingers here into August, seemingly at the top of the world. Just make sure you plan your visit for a clear day as the view of Mount Jefferson from Park Ridge is unforgettable.

Hike: The trail begins at a signboard at the trailhead. Hike a hundred yards to a junction where you meet up with the main trail. Turn left and hike through alpine forest with small meadows as you ascend gently out of the basin that holds Breitenbush Lake. Pass by a couple of talus slopes where pikas meep as you pass and enter forest burned in the Pyramid Butte Fire in 2010. Look out to your right to rocky Pyramid Butte, badly scorched in the fire bearing its name. Once you leave the fire zone behind you will begin a moderate ascent through unburned forest until you reach a crest at about 6,100 feet. Descend for a bit before beginning another moderate climb; soon the trail levels out and passes through a series of rocky meadows that are covered in snow until late in July most years.

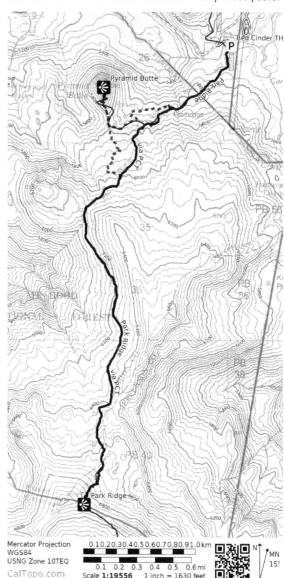

The tip of Mount Jefferson peeks out behind Park Ridge, reminding you of your destination ahead.

At approximately 2.5 miles from the trailhead, leave the forest behind and enter a moonscape of rockslides, snow patches and scattered ponds fed only by snowmelt. The trail braids here in many places as it passes by ponds and through scattered clumps of weather-beaten trees. Follow cairns across the tundra until you reach Park Ridge's snowy, boulder-strewn headwall. Soon you will arrive at a permanent snowfield; follow footsteps here up to the summit of Park Ridge, where the view will knock your socks off. Mount Jefferson towers over the meadows and lakes that make up Jefferson Park. A more amazing view is hard to imagine. Most hikers will want to make this their final destination. Return the way you came.

Though wildly beautiful, Jefferson Park is 2 miles and 1,000 feet of elevation below the summit of Park Ridge, miles and elevation you will need to regain on the way back to your car. If you are backpacking, there are few if any good sites on Park Ridge, and you should absolutely continue into Jefferson Park. For more information, see the next hike.

Mercator Projection
WGS84
USNG Zone 10TEQ
CalTopo.com

0.1 0.2 0.3 0.4 0.5 0.6 0.7 0.8 0.9 1.0 km
0.1   0.2   0.3   0.4   0.5   0.6 mi
Scale **1:19556**   1 inch = 1630 feet

N
MN
15°

80. Jefferson Park via South Breitenbush

Distance: 12.8 miles out and back
Elevation Gain: 3,300 feet
Trailhead elevation: 3,032 feet
Trail high point: 5,967 feet
Other seasons: late July, September- early October
Map: Mount Jefferson Wilderness (Geo-Graphics)
Pass: None needed
Drivetime from Portland: 125 minutes

Directions:

- Drive south from Portland on Interstate 5 to Salem.
- At Exit 253 outside Salem, leave the freeway and reach a junction with OR 22.
- From Salem, drive OR 22 east for 49.2 miles to Detroit.
- Turn left at a sign for Breitenbush, Elk Lake and Olallie Lake onto FR 46.
- Drive 11.6 miles to a junction with FR 4685 on your right. Turn right.
- This road is paved at first as it crosses the North Fork Breitenbush River but then transitions to a good gravel road.
- Drive 4.6 miles to a large parking lot on your right, located in a large open flat.
- You can also reach the trailhead by driving to Estacada on OR 224 and continuing on this road 25 miles to Ripplebrook, and then another 34 miles on FR 46 to the junction with FR 4685 described above. This approach is a bit longer but far more scenic.

Why August: Jefferson Park is the place that dreams are made of. Its swimmable lakes, fields of August wildflowers and huge views of Mount Jefferson have long made it one of Oregon's cherished backcountry destinations; it is the rare place that not only lives

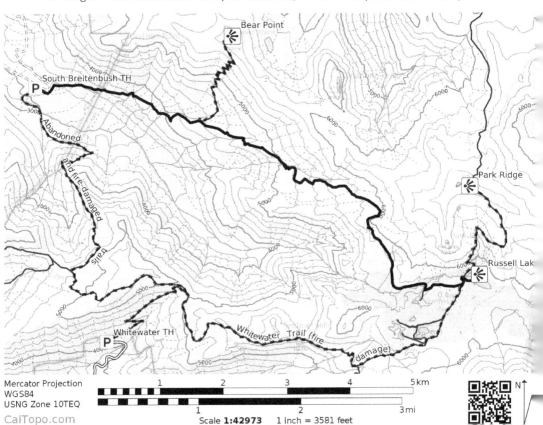

up to the hype but exceeds it. Such beauty draws enormous crowds, and in recent years the Jefferson Park area has shown many signs of overuse. Complicating matters is the Whitewater Fire of summer 2017. The blaze burned its way to the edge of Jefferson Park, consuming much of the forest south and west of the park- including the entirety of the Whitewater Trail, which for many years has been the most popular route into the park. Presented here is an approach via the South Breitenbush River that is longer, quieter and untouched by fire in recent years. It is certainly more difficult, and the trail is rocky and rough in spots, but it is a trek worthy of such a beautiful destination.

Hike: From the signboard, the South Breitenbush Trail enters a dark forest near the banks of the South Breitenbush River. Immediately reach a junction with the Crag Trail, an abandoned path that enters the heart of the burn. Keep left instead to follow the South Breitenbush Trail. The trail then begins a long traverse away from the South Breitenbush River, climbing at a moderate grade through a dark and lush forest. The trail crosses several small creeks, passes the remains of a shed and meets the Bear Point Trail at 2.1 miles. Bear Point features one of the best views of Mount Jefferson (see Hike 70) but is a detour best saved for a separate trip. Continue straight instead.

The next two miles of the South Breitenbush Trail are rocky and rough. Thankfully the grade is never steep, but the numerous rocks and ruts on the trail force hikers to slow down just when many want to speed up. On hot days this stretch of trail can be punishing. Once upon a time the views on this stretch of trail were enough to spur hikers on but over time the trees have grown up, and what were once great views are now mere glances. The good times return once the trail passes an outstanding view ahead to Mount Jefferson. At exactly 4 miles the trail passes a small tarn with a view of the top half of the mountain. The rest of the way is gorgeous, as the trail passes through a series of lush, kaleidoscopic wildflower meadows, a taste of what's to come. From here the South Breitenbush Trail is a feast of the senses. Views of Mount Jefferson spur hikers along. Here you will likely get your first sense of the extent of Whitewater Fire, as the trail looks out to the ridges and rocky points northwest of Mount Jefferson, the heart of the blaze. Reach the trail's high point of nearly 6,000 feet at 4.6 miles.

Looking ahead to Mount Jefferson.

From here the trail curves to the right and drops down through a rocky gulch into Jefferson Park. The trail enters the quiet northwestern corner of Jefferson Park at 5 miles. From here you will follow the trail through meadows and then along the South Breitenbush River, now just a mere creek. The river banks are absolutely lined with wildflowers in August. The trail follows the river 1.4 miles to trail's end at a junction near Russell Lake. Where you go from here is up to you. A visit to Jefferson Park is not complete without a lot of time for exploration. If you're backpacking, remember to stay only in designated sites. DO NOT camp on fragile wildflower meadows. Campfires are banned.

Return the way you came.

SEPTEMBER

		Distance	EV Gain	Drive
81.	Ecola State Park: Crescent Beach	4 mi	600 ft	95 min
82.	Cape Falcon	5 mi	300 ft	100 min
83.	Mount Saint Helens	8.2 mi	4,600 ft	100 min
84.	Lewis River Falls	6.4 mi	400 ft	120 min
85.	Indian Racetrack and Red Mountain	7.4 mi	1,500 ft	90 min
86.	Takhlakh Lake and Council Bluff	4.7 mi	1,000 ft	140 min
87.	Lost Lake	7.3 mi	1,300 ft	100 min
88.	Tumala Mountain and Plaza Lake	10.8 mi	2,400 ft	60 min
89.	Olallie Backcountry Loop	7 mi	1,300 ft	125 min
90.	Olallie Lake and Ruddy Hill	10.3 mi	1,300 ft	125 min

September is all about huckleberries, high mountain lakes and crystal-clear skies. All of the destinations above are accessible months before September, but all are also known for early-summer mosquitoes and mid-summer crowds. Better to save them all for after Labor Day in September, when both crowds and mosquitoes are gone. The nights are cold but the skies are often clear, and if you time it right, the huckleberries are ripe and ready for picking. There are, of course, many places you can go in September. The hikes described here run the gamut from the aforementioned high mountain lakes to road trips to the Oregon Coast to a hike to the summit of an active volcano. Just as with July and August, you can go anywhere and do anything.

September has some of the year's most reliable weather. In most years, you can expect sunny days with highs in the 50s and 60s in the mountains. You can likewise expect very cold nights. Plan ahead and bring lots of warm clothing- it's worth it. While the weather is often reliable, you should always check the forecast ahead of time. September rainstorms are a regular occurrence, particularly later in the month, and the days shorter and nights colder. Snowstorms in the mountains are rare but possible, especially on Mount Saint Helens. Always plan ahead when planning a visit to the mountains.

Speaking of planning ahead: hunting season in the Pacific Northwest begins in September. Always respect hunters and wear bright clothing (or better yet, BLAZE ORANGE) when you venture out into the woods in September. The danger of hunting accidents is overstated, but it is still a good idea to know when hunting season begins if you're headed out to the Cascades.

One other thing that is good to know is when area campgrounds close- many close after Labor Day weekend, but others stay open until the third or fourth weekend of the month. If you're planning on a weekend camping trip, check ahead and make reservations when you can. If you're headed up to the Olallie Lake area (Hikes 89 and 90), consider staying at the Olallie Lake Resort. The resort offers rustic cabins and yurts that offer a delightful place to stay. There's no electricity or plumbing- just kerosene lamps and outhouses. You would be hard-pressed to find a better place to stay on a cold, crisp September night.

Photo on opposite page: Takhlakh Lake and Mount Adams (Hike 86)

81. Ecola State Park: Crescent Beach

Distance: 4 miles out and back
Elevation Gain: 600 feet
Trailhead elevation: 196 feet
Trail high point: 304 feet
Other seasons: all year
Map: pick up a map of the park at the fee booth when you enter
Pass: State Park day use fee ($5) or yearly pass
Drivetime from Portland: 95 minutes

Directions:
- From Portland, drive west on US 26 to road's end at a junction with US 101 just north of Cannon Beach.
- Follow signs for Cannon Beach and head south on US 101 until you reach the first junction on your right for Cannon Beach.
- Turn right for Cannon Beach, and keep right, following signs for Ecola State Park.
- Drive 1.6 miles to a fee booth, where you pay the $5 day use fee to enter the park.
- Just after the booth, arrive at a junction. Left leads immediately to the Ecola Point Trailhead (the start of the longer hike) while right leads you to Indian Beach.

Why September: By the time September rolls around, I'm often ready to do something besides go hiking every weekend. Sometimes it just feels great to go to the beach. The cool air of the Oregon Coast feels refreshing, even vital after a long, hot summer. This short but rugged hike down to Crescent Beach in Ecola State Park is great in any season, but is never better than after Labor Day, when the crowds are mostly gone and the seastacks, tidepools and explorable caves are a welcome refuge from Valley heat. You can also combine this with the hike north to Tillamook Head, an adventure described in the first hike of this book.

Lookout out to Crescent Beach from inside a sea cave.

Note: As with most beach hikes, this hike is significantly easier and more fun during low tides. While you can reach the beach and enjoy it during high tide, you can only explore the tide pools and sea caves during low tide. Check a tide table for Cannon Beach before you leave the house and try to time this hike for low tide if possible.

Hike: The hike begins at Ecola State Park's main trailhead. If this scene looks familiar, it should- this spot has featured in several movies, among them *Point Break* and *The Goonies*. Views lead south to Crescent Beach, your destination. Locate the trail on the south side of the parking lot by the bathroom, marked for Crescent Beach. A sign warns of the trail being for experienced hikers only. Follow this trail up a bit until it meets the park's access road. Follow the road for a short distance and then turn right to follow the trail down into the forest. You will lose elevation into a small gully, then gain it back to reach the trail's high point of 304 feet. All of the small ups and downs contribute to making this hike more difficult than it would appear- but not as difficult as the folks at the state park would have you believe. Along the way you'll at least be compensated with views down to Crescent Beach and the cool breeze blowing in from the ocean.

At about 1 mile from the trailhead, the Crescent Beach Trail meets the Oregon Coast Trail, continuing south. Keep right for Crescent Beach. You will descend, at times steeply, via a series of switchbacks and stairs to the beach, which you reach at 1.2 miles. Once you're there, it will be very difficult to leave. Crescent Beach is about 2/3 of a mile long, but offers so much to see and spending less than an hour here will make the trip feel much too short. The trail drops you into the middle of the beach, so it's entirely up to you which way you should go first. Walking left (south) along the beach will take you to the huge rock walls of Chapman Point. During very low tides you can walk around the point to Chapman Beach (and the north end of Cannon Beach) but time your passage carefully. Waves crash over the point much of the time, making for an intimidating passage. Less intimidating is the walk to the north end of the beach. Here you will find tidepools, small sea caves and dramatic views south along Crescent Beach. Or you could just sit down, open up a book and take in the beautiful scenery.

When you decide it's time, return the way you came.

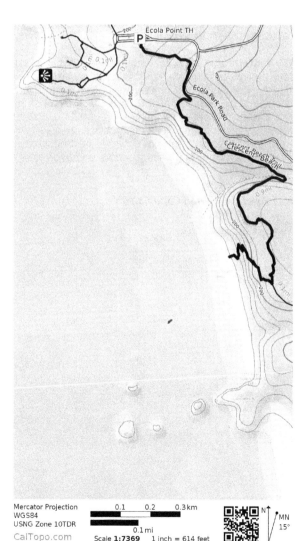

Mercator Projection
WGS84
USNG Zone 10TDR
CalTopo.com

0.1 0.2 0.3 km

0.1 mi
Scale **1:7369** 1 inch = 614 feet

MN
15°

82. Cape Falcon

Distance: 5 miles out and back
Elevation Gain: 300 feet
Trailhead elevation: 99 feet
Trail high point: 238 feet
Other seasons: all year but extremely muddy in most seasons
Map: pick a trail map at the trailhead
Pass: None needed
Drivetime from Portland: 100 minutes

Directions:
* From Portland, drive US 26 approximately 74 miles northwest to its end at a junction with US 101 just north of Cannon Beach.
* Merge onto US 101 and drive south past Cannon Beach for 14 miles to Oswald West State Park.
* Pull into the day use parking lot on your left for Short Sand Beach, where US 101 crosses Short Sand Creek. There is no day use fee as of this writing.

Why September: People love to visit the coast in the summer but in truth there are too many tourists to make it an enjoyable hiking experience most of the time. After Labor Day, on the other hand, is an outstanding time to visit the Coast, as the crowds are mostly gone and the weather cool and refreshing, rain or shine. This hike out to the tip of Cape Falcon is best in September, as this is almost the only time of the year this hike isn't a muddy, squelching mess. The rewards are many- a trail through a rare coastal old-growth forest, a chance to visit one of Oregon's best beaches, a waterfall that tumbles directly onto the beach, and spectacular views of Oregon's rugged coastline. It doesn't get any better than this.

Short Sand Beach and Cape Falcon.

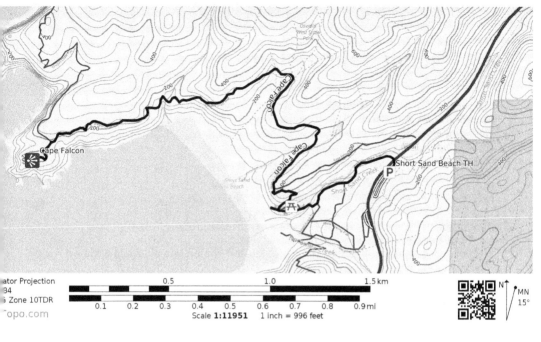

ator Projection
34
5 Zone 10TDR
opo.com

Scale **1:11951**   1 inch = 996 feet

Hike: Start by following the paved trail under US 101 and into a forest of huge Coastal Sitka spruce trees along Short Sand Creek. Keep right at both junctions and soon reach a bridge over Short Sand Creek. Cross the bridge and reach a picnic area just above Short Sand Beach at 0.6 mile from the trailhead. Short Sand Beach is perhaps my favorite in Oregon- rugged cliffs frame the beach on both ends, a waterfall tumbles down onto the beach at its north end and the rocks along the beach are fun to explore. If the tide is low, take the time to explore the beach before you continue the rest of your hike. If the tide is high, save your beach time for later. From a signboard at the picnic area, locate the Cape Falcon Trail. Turn right here.

The Cape Falcon Trail climbs gently to the Kramer Memorial, named for a writer who helped lead a citizen campaign to preserve Oregon's beaches. From here the trail enters the deep, dark forest above Short Sand Beach. The trail passes by and under some huge Coastal Sitka spruce trees along the way. You'll notice that some spots of the trail are still a bit muddy even in the dry conditions of September; in the winter, this is the muddiest trail I have ever had the misfortune to hike. A friend of mine once had to buy a new pair of pants in Cannon Beach after doing this hike because he was so muddy he couldn't go out to eat in his hiking clothes. You won't have this experience in September.

At 1.9 miles the trail passes above Blumenthal Falls, the waterfall that tumbles onto the north end of Short Sand Beach. The beach looks surprisingly close but cannot be reached from this part of the trail. From here the trail becomes more rugged, climbing a bit before leveling out on Cape Falcon's headland. The trail reaches an unsigned junction at 2.4 miles. Continuing straight will take you further north on the Oregon Coast Trail towards Arch Cape and Cannon Beach but we want to turn left to hike out to the end of Cape Falcon. So turn left and hike through a path cut into the salal to a series of viewpoints that lead out to the Pacific and south towards Short Sand Beach and Neahkahnie Mountain. Every side trail here is worth exploring but watch your step- some of these side trails lead to points that are exposed and even dangerous. The views are tremendous, of course.

Return the way you came.

83. Mount Saint Helens

Distance: 8.2 miles out and back
Elevation Gain: 4,600 feet
Trailhead elevation: 3,744 feet
Trail high point: 8,281 feet
Other seasons: July – October
Map: Mount Saint Helens (Green Trails #364S)
Pass: NW Forest Pass + Mt St Helens Climbing Permit
Drivetime from Portland: 100 minutes

Directions:
- From Portland drive north on I-5 for 28 miles.
- Following signs for WA 503 and Cougar, leave the interstate at exit 21 and turn right at the stop light.
- Follow WA 503 for 28 more winding miles to Cougar.
- Continue straight on WA 503 for 3 miles to a junction with FR 25. Continue straight, now on FR 90.
- Drive 3.2 miles on FR 90 to a junction with FR 83 and signs for the Climbers Bivouac, Lava Canyon and Ape Caves. Turn left here.
- Drive 3 miles on FR 83 to a junction with FR 81. Turn left here.
- Drive 1.7 miles to a junction with the spur road to the Climbers Bivouac, FR 830.
- Turn right and drive 2.6 gravel miles to the Climbers Bivouac Trailhead.

Why September: Mount Saint Helens erupted on May 18, 1980, eviscerating much of the surrounding terrain and killing 57 people. Today the volcano is still active, and signs of its fiery, catastrophic capabilities are everywhere. And yet, it is possible to hike to the top of the volcano in good weather for much of the year. The best time to climb the mountain is definitely in May, when the road to the trailhead is mostly melted out and the mountain is covered in snow, offering few impediments to summiting the mountain other than a need for climbing gear. This book, however, is a hiking guide – and thus the best time to hike to the summit is usually in September. The route is clear of snow, the weather not so hot and the skies clearer than the hazy days of July and August.

Note about permits: You need a climbing permit to do this hike. Permits are available for purchase starting in January or February – meaning you need to plan for this hike months in advance. Only 100 permits are issued per day, so permits sell out quickly! Every individual in your group needs a permit. As of September 2017 permits cost $22 per person. Because you need to buy the permit in advance, you are locked in to your summit date; there are no refunds, so if weather forces you to cancel your hike, you won't be able to get your money back. For more information about purchasing a permit, see this link: http://www.mshinstitute.org/explore/climbing-permits/purchasing-your-permits.html

Note about preparation: This is a hike, but also a climb. Most people start very early in the morning (typically sometime between 3-6AM) in order to get a head start on the heat of the day. The later you start, the hotter you will be climbing through the boulders in the middle part of this hike. You also need to pack water – a lot of water. There is none to be found on the hike, and this is an extremely difficult, exposed hike. Packing at least 4 liters is a good idea – and maybe more. Finally – this is a mountain, and mountains create their own weather. Packing gear for any weather from heat to rain to snow is essential, and you should absolutely turn around if the weather is anything less than pleasant.

Note: Dogs are not allowed on this and other trails inside the blast zone at Mount Saint Helens National Volcanic Monument. This prohibition is to protect the fragile, recovering environment. Hiking off-trail is banned as well.

Hike: The hike begins as a moderate climb through the forest. You follow the Monitor Ridge Trailhead through the forest for 1.8 miles, gaining 1,000 feet, to a junction with the Loowit Trail at treeline. From here the real climb begins and the good times are over. The Monitor Ridge Trail proceeds to begin a steep climb through a long boulder field. The climb through the boulders is tremendous fun on the way up – and tremendously irritating on the way down. As there isn't a dedicated trail for much of this part of the climb, you will need to follow trail markers (and perhaps other hikers) to find your way through the boulders. It sounds more difficult than it actually is – as there are no trees anywhere here, you cannot possibly get lost – only frustrated. If you're hiking with friends or with a group, it's a good idea to stick together here so you can give advice on the easiest and safest passage. This is also why you need an early start- it gets hot here later in the day.

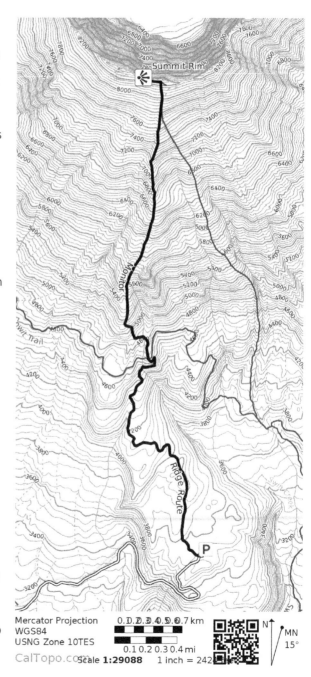

Once you've passed through the boulder field, you will be back on trail, passing remnants of the mountain's glaciers. The last ¾ of a mile is extremely steep but much easier going than the boulder field, as the trail rockets up the volcano's dusty, ashy south face towards the summit. The views here are exceptional to the south towards Mount Hood and to the east towards Mount Adams. The best view of all, of course, awaits you at the summit, which you reach at 4.1 miles from the trailhead. Here you can look down into the smoky, steamy crater of the volcano, and out across the blast zone to Spirit Lake, and beyond to Mount Rainier and points north. It is one of the most awe-inspiring views a hiker can ever see, and worth the trudge it took to get here. There is room at the summit rim for a decent number of people, but watch your step and absolutely stay away from the edge of the rim – a fall would be fatal.

Return the way you came, remembering to watch your step as you make your way down through the boulder field.

Mercator Projection
WGS84
USNG Zone 10TES

0.0 0.1 0.2 0.3 0.4 0.5 0.6 0.7 km

0.1 0.2 0.3 0.4 mi

CalTopo.com Scale **1:29088**   1 inch = 242

N

MN
15°

84. Lewis River Falls

Distance: 6.4 miles out and back
Elevation Gain: 400 feet
Trailhead elevation: 1,521 feet
Trail high point: 1,802 feet
Other seasons: all year but can be very cold and snowy in winter
Map: pick a trail map at the trailhead
Pass: NW Forest Pass
Drivetime from Portland: 110 minutes

Directions:
* From Portland, drive east on Interstate 84 to Cascade Locks.
* Leave the freeway at exit 44 and follow the off-ramp to the Bridge of the Gods.
* Pay the $2 toll and cross the river.
* On the far side, turn right at a junction with WA 14.
* Drive 5.9 miles, passing through Stevenson along the way, to a junction signed for Carson and the Wind River Road. Turn left here.
* Drive the Wind River Road north for 14.2 miles to a T-Junction. Turn right here to stay on the Wind River Road.
* Continue 12.9 miles of winding road to a junction with the Curly Creek Road on your left, just after the Wind River Road crosses over Old Man Pass.
* Turn left and drive the Curly Creek Road downhill for 5.1 miles to its end at a junction with FR 90, the Lewis River Road. Turn right.
* Drive FR 90 for 9.9 miles to a sign for Lower Lewis River Falls. Turn right here and drive into the trailhead at the day-use lot.
* **Note 1:** FR 90 near Lewis River Falls has washed out several times in the past. The entire drive is paved except for a short stretch of gravel road that is a bit rough.
* **Note 2:** You can also drive here via Cougar and around Swift Lake. This approach will take you at least 20 minutes longer, and is much more winding and curvy than the approach described above. Nevertheless, if you're visiting this area in the winter, this is a safer approach as it stays at a much lower elevation.

Why September: As a rule most waterfall hikes are better in winter and spring, when creeks and rivers flow at their highest and the higher mountains are snowed in. The waterfalls on the Lewis River are the exception to the rule. Although this area is accessible for most of the year, and although the falls are indeed very impressive during winter and spring's high flows, they are even more graceful during summer's low flows. September is a fantastic time to visit this area, as the summer crowds are mostly gone (expect to see a decent number of people just the same). As mentioned above, the hike is accessible for much of the year; however, hikers should be **very** careful when visiting in the winter, as snowstorms are common in spite of its low elevation, and road washouts are a very real possibility during rainy periods (which in this area, is pretty much all winter).

Hike: Begin at the Lower Falls Trailhead. Follow a trail from the signboard by the bathroom and walk the short distance down to an overlook of Lower Falls. What an impressive sight! The Lewis River here falls gracefully 43 feet over a wide ledge into an extremely deep pool. It is tempting to stop here and spend a long time taking in the falls, this viewpoint is not even 200 feet from the trailhead; so after taking a good long glance, mosey on up the trail to your right, heading upriver. The trail parallels the Lewis River from above, offering the occasional staircase down to the river. There are a number of trails here, but just keep hiking along the river to stay on your way.

At 1.4 miles, the trail reaches a junction. The stretch of trail straight ahead is washed out, so turn left and briefly detour up to a trailhead by the road. The trail then drops back down to a riverside view of Middle Falls. Though not as impressive as the lower or upper falls, this wide slide is exceptionally scenic and worth a long stop. Later in September the vine maple here will begin to turn red, enhancing the scene even more. When you can finally pull yourself away from the Middle Falls, continue hiking upstream.

Beyond Middle Lewis River Falls, the trail enters an impressive grove of ancient forest. It can be easy to get waterfall fever as you near the upper falls, but take a moment to appreciate the giants here along the trail- this small grove is only a taste of the fantastic old growth found all throughout this area. The trail then leaves the old growth and reaches a beach with a view ahead, at last, to Upper Lewis River Falls at 2.9 miles from the lower falls. This wide and rocky beach is a great place to stop for lunch. Beyond this beach, the trail switchbacks steeply uphill 0.2 mile to a junction with a spur trail down to a viewpoint above the lip of Upper Lewis River Falls. Turn right and walk the short distance down to the ledge, where you can look down at the top of the falls from the safety of this fenced-off viewpoint. Turn around here and return the way you came.

Hikers desiring a longer hike can continue 0.7 mile upstream past the Upper Falls to the upper Lewis River Trailhead. While there are no waterfalls, this stretch of trail is peaceful and features some huge trees. From the upper trailhead, the Quartz Creek Trail begins on the opposite side of the road. This beautiful rollercoaster of a trail follows Quartz Creek through old-growth for miles as it enters the mysterious Dark Divide.

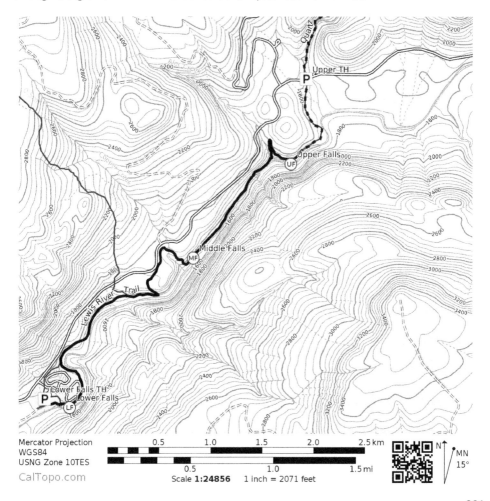

85. Indian Racetrack and Red Mountain

Distance: 7.4 miles out and back
Elevation Gain: 1,500 feet
Trailhead elevation: 3,494 feet
Trail high point: 4,971 feet
Other seasons: October
Map: Indian Heaven (Green Trails #365S)
Pass: None needed
Drivetime from Portland: 90 minutes

Directions:
- From Portland, drive east 44 miles on Interstate 84 to Cascade Locks.
- Leave the freeway at exit 44 and follow signs for the Bridge of the Gods.
- Pay $2 to cross the Columbia River. Cross the bridge and turn right on WA 14.
- Drive this highway through Stevenson and arrive at a junction with the Wind River Road 5.9 miles later.
- Turn left, following signs for Carson and continue on the Wind River Road 5.8 miles to the second junction with Old State Road on your right. T
- urn right here, and only 0.1 mile later, turn left on Panther Creek Road (FR 65).
- Stay on FR 65 and ignore all less major roads for 16 miles to the Falls Creek Horse Camp. You can park here or at the trailhead on the side of the road a couple hundred yards up FR 65. The trail departs to your right.

Why September: Situated between Mount Saint Helens and Mount Adams, the Indian Heaven Wilderness does not charm and amaze with glaciated peaks and volcanic destruction but rather with tranquil ponds, vast meadows and views out to its volcanic neighbors. September is the time to visit Indian Heaven Wilderness. The days are crisp, the area's huckleberry leaves turn a brilliant shade of red and the mosquitoes are long gone. This wonderful hike will take you to a meadow where local tribes raced horses for generations, and from there, you can follow trails up to Red Mountain's lookout tower, the area's best view. Just make sure you come here in September; this hike is inaccessible in winter, and earlier in the summer the Indian Heaven Wilderness is also frequently known as the "Mosquito Heaven Wilderness". It does live up to its name.

Hike: Begin by hiking on the mostly level Indian Racetrack trail. Reach a signboard after 0.1 mile and fill out your permit. Continue straight towards Indian Racetrack. The trail crosses Falls Creek on a bridge and begins climbing through a mostly-open forest of pine, with an understory of bright-red huckleberry bushes. The trail soon tops out into Indian Heaven's plateau and reaches a pond at the edge of Indian Racetrack at about 2 miles from the trailhead. Follow the trail through the meadow to a trail junction. Area tribes raced horses in these meadows for generations. This historic spot makes for an excellent rest stop.

To continue on to the summit of Red Mountain, turn right at the junction and walk 100 feet. Look to your left for a trail with a signpost headed off into the forest to your left. When you find the trail, follow it steeply uphill 0.8 miles to its end on rough gravel road 6048 just below the summit lookout. Turn right and continue walking uphill on the road. You will pass a wooden garage to its end at the lookout atop the 4,977 foot summit. The lookout tower is no longer staffed and is showing signs of disrepair but the view is as good as ever. Stretching out below you is the entirety of the Indian Heaven Wilderness, with the racetrack at your feet. To your left is the broken-bottle top of Mount Saint Helens. To your right is Mount Adams, looming huge above its surroundings. Behind you, to the south, is Mount Hood. Access inside the lookout is prohibited. When you are ready to leave at last, return the way you came.

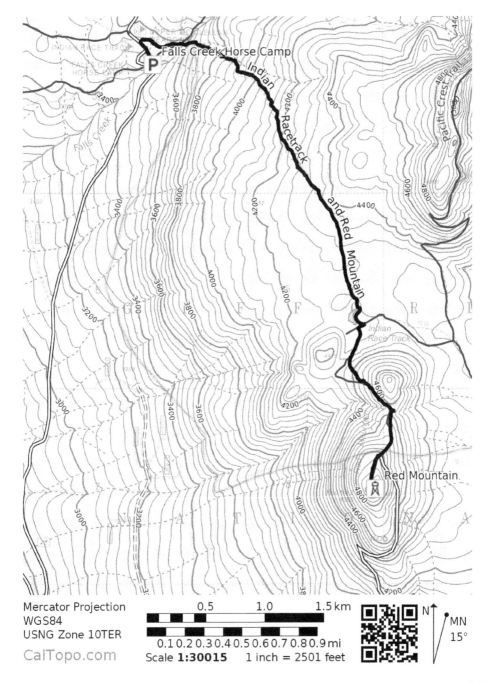

Mercator Projection
WGS84
USNG Zone 10TER

CalTopo.com

0.5   1.0   1.5 km

0.1 0.2 0.3 0.4 0.5 0.6 0.7 0.8 0.9 mi
Scale **1:30015**   1 inch = 2501 feet

N
MN
15°

86. Takhlakh Lake and Council Bluff

	Takhlakh Lake	Council Bluff
Distance:	1.3 mile loop	3.4 miles out and back
Elevation Gain:	100 feet	900 feet
Trailhead Elevation:	4,401 feet	4,293 feet
Trail High Point:	4,500 feet	5,116 feet
Other Seasons:	July- October	July- October
Map:	Mt Adams (Green Trails #367S)	Mt Adams (Green Trails #367S)
Pass:	day use fee ($5)	none needed
Drivetime from PDX:	140 minutes	140 minutes

Directions:
- From Portland drive Interstate 84 approximately 60 miles east to Hood River.
- At Exit 64, leave the freeway and turn left at the bottom of the exit ramp.
- You will quickly arrive at a toll bridge over the Columbia River. Pay the $1 toll, cross the narrow bridge and arrive at a T-junction with WA 14 on the far side of the bridge.
- Turn left and drive 1.5 miles west to a junction with WA 141 ALT, just before WA 14 crosses the White Salmon River. Turn right here.
- Turn right on WA 141 ALT and drive 2.2 miles north to a junction with WA 141, just north of the town of White Salmon (the alternate route avoids the slow uphill drive through town).
- Turn left on WA 141 and drive 19 miles north to the small town of Trout Lake.
- At a Y-junction in Trout Lake, keep right to continue driving towards Mount Adams.
- Drive 1.2 miles to another junction, where you keep left.
- Drive 18.9 miles north on what is now FR 23 to a junction with FR 90, signed for the Lewis River and Cougar.
- Fork to the right. The road changes to gravel and continues 2.8 winding miles to a T-junction: left goes to Council Lake and right leads to Takhlakh Lake.
- For Council Lake, turn left and drive 1.2 miles to road's end at Council Lake CG.
- For Takhlakh Lake, turn right and drive 2.2 miles of paved road to a junction with the road to Olallie Lake's small campground.
- Keep straight and drive 0.3 mile more to Takhlakh Lake's Campground.
- Turn right and drive into the campground. Park in the small day-use lot on your left.

Why September: It's a long drive from Portland, but once you arrive at the gorgeous mountain lakes north of Mount Adams you won't want to leave. Luckily most of these lakes feature campgrounds, making it possible for hikers to stay the night (or many nights). The best of these lakes are Takhlakh Lake and Council Lake. You've definitely seen photos of Takhlakh Lake (including one on page 213)- the lake's picture-perfect view of Mount Adams has graced many postcards and calendars over the years. Council Lake is more obscure, but just as beautiful, and features a dark blue-green shade only found in the deepest of mountain lakes. September is the best time to visit, as the crowds are gone, the huckleberry leaves turn orange and red and the elk are bugling. When visiting the area during this time it is a good idea to wear blaze orange, as September marks the beginning of hunting season.

Hike: It doesn't matter where you start, but this writeup begins at Takhlakh Lake. From the day use area, walk down to the lakeshore and locate the trail that circles Takhlakh Lake. The view of Mount Adams here is superb- you will no doubt find yourself snapping pictures by the dozen, before you've ever started your hike. Once you feel like starting your hike, turn left to hike around Takhlakh Lake in a clockwise direction. The trail is mostly level and stays near the lakeshore. On the far end of the lake, you will reach a junction with the Takh Takh Meadows Trail. If 1.3 miles around the lake isn't long enough, you can add on this loop through meadows on the south side of the lake. Otherwise, continue around the lakeshore until you reach the day use area again, at which point it's time to move on. I usually like to do this loop as part of a camping trip to Takhlakh Lake- to stay at the campground, check online to reserve a campsite and be sure to note when the campground closes for the season, usually sometime in late September.

Not even 2 miles to the west, Council Lake has a very different feel. The campground is free, and quite rustic. Unlike Takhlakh Lake, however, Council Lake does not feature a view of Mount Adams. For the view you seek, you will need to hike up to the summit of Council Bluff. Locate the Boundary Trailhead at the edge of Council Lake Campground and follow this trail, actually an abandoned road, uphill through the woods. Motorcycles and dirt bikes are allowed on this trail, and you should expect to encounter at least a few bikers on this section of your hike. At 1.3 miles, you will see a trail that leaves the road: turn right here and follow this spur out an excellent view across to Mount Adams. For an even better view, return to the road and reach an unmarked junction at 1.4 miles. Turn right here and follow this short trail 0.3 mile to the summit of Council Bluff, where the view is stunning! Mount Adams towers over Council Lake to the east, while the view stretches from Mount Rainier in the north to Mount Hood in the south. When you can bear it, return the way you came.

If you've still got time for more exploration, consider following a rough but very distinct trail halfway around the west side of Council Lake. The trail follows this deep lake for a half-mile around its western shore until petering out near a rockslide. It's worth your time.

87. Lost Lake

	Lost Lake	Lost Lake Butte
Distance:	3.3 mile loop	4 miles out and back
Elevation Gain:	100 feet	1,200 feet
Trailhead Elevation:	3,185 feet	3,264 feet
Trail High Point:	3,185 feet	4,470 feet
Other Seasons:	May- October	June- October
Map:	Government Camp (GT# 461)	Government Camp (GT# 461)
Pass:	$8 day-use fee	$8 day-use fee
Drivetime from PDX:	110 minutes	110 minutes

Directions:
- From Portland, drive east on Interstate 84 to Hood River.
- Leave the freeway at Exit 62, immediately after arriving in Hood River.
- Just after you exit the freeway, turn right onto Mount Adams Avenue opposite a gas station. This road becomes Country Club Road.
- Drive 3.2 miles to a T-junction with Barrett Drive. Turn left.
- In just 0.2 mile, keep straight at a stop sign. Continue 1 more mile to a junction with OR 281. Turn right.
- Drive 2 miles to a junction on your right, immediately after passing the Apple Valley Country Store, signed "Dee Parkdale Next Right". Turn right here (do not continue straight uphill).
- Drive 2.2 miles on this highway, passing Tucker Park along the way, to another junction on your right, signed for Lost Lake. Veer right here.
- Drive 4 miles on this road to a junction with Lost Lake Road. Turn right.
- Cross the West Fork of the Hood River and reach a junction with Rainy Lake Road in just 0.3 mile. Keep left to continue towards Lost Lake.
- Drive 13.3 miles on this paved road to Lost Lake's entrance booth.
- Pay the $7 fee and drive through the resort complex to the picnic area at the lakeshore, 0.4 mile from the booth. This is the trailhead.

Why September: Lost Lake has what may be the iconic view of Mount Hood – so iconic, in fact, that it is featured on one of the state's quarters. The lake is located so deep in the mountains that early settlers in the Hood River Valley decided the lake was in fact lost, while local tribes called the lake E-e-kwahl-a-mat-yam-lshkt – or "heart of the mountains". The fame has brought many visitors over the years, and in spite of its location it is among the most popular destinations near Mount Hood. September is an ideal time to visit; the crowds have diminished (somewhat) and the weather is as good as it gets. If you come later in the month the vine maple around the lake is turning red, offering a beautiful contrast to the old-growth forest and views for which the lake is famous.

Hike: As the trail around the lake is a loop, you can start from anywhere. I like to start it at the picnic area where the views are best, as this way you can begin and end the hike with Mount Hood in your face. Follow the short trail down to the lakeshore loop and turn right. This trail follows the lakeshore, passing through several fantastic groves of ancient Western red cedar. There are several boardwalks that offer hikers a chance to keep their feet dry through the boggy sections of the trail.

At a little over 2 miles from the trailhead, reach a junction with the Huckleberry Mountain

Trail. This connector leads uphill to the Pacific Crest Trail on the ridge to the west of Lost Lake. Stay on the Lakeshore loop. The next mile back to the trailhead along Lost Lake's eastern shore passes directly below campgrounds, offering hikers a plethora of options to extend their trip. One worthwhile option is to ditch the lakeshore loop in order to explore the aptly-named Old-Growth Trail. This trail cuts through several outstanding groves of ancient cedar trees, but also requires you to pass through parts of Lost Lake's enormous campground. When you reach the resort, follow the lakeshore trail or roads back to the picnic area and your vehicle. Hikers looking for a longer day have the option of hiking to the summit of Lost Lake Butte, a volcanic cone east of Lost Lake.

If you wish to hike to the summit of Lost Lake Butte, return to the trailhead and walk around the lake into the campground. Locate the Lost Lake Butte Trailhead at the edge of the campground and head uphill. Cross a junction with the Skyline Trail (a precursor to the PCT) and continue straight. The Lost Lake Butte Trail climbs at a gentle grade uphill on this volcanic butte towards a former lookout site. At 2 miles from Lost Lake, you will reach the summit. Here the view of Mount Hood is outstanding to the south, but alas you cannot also see Lost Lake. A lookout structure stood here until 1962, when it was destroyed during the legendary Columbus Day Storm. Return the way you came.

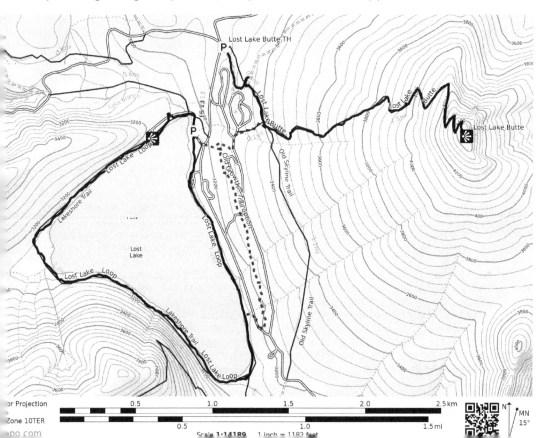

Scale 1:14189   1 inch = 1182 feet

88. Tumala Mountain and Plaza Lake

	Tumala Mountain	Plaza Lake
Distance:	3.2 miles out and back	10.8 miles out and back
Elevation Gain:	1,100 feet	2,400 feet
Trailhead Elevation:	3,993 feet	3,993 feet
Trail High Point:	4,779 feet	4,779 feet
Other Seasons:	June- October	June- October
Map:	Green Trails #492	Green Trails #492, 493
Pass:	None needed.	None needed.
Drivetime from PDX:	60 minutes	60 minutes

Directions:
- From Portland, drive southeast on OR 224 to Estacada.
- From the junction of OR 224 and OR 211, continue 2.9 miles to a junction with Fall Creek Road on your left.
- Turn left and drive 0.3 mile to a T-junction. Turn left to stay on Fall Creek Road.
- Drive 0.2 mile to a junction with Tumala Mountain Road. Turn right here.
- Drive 12.9 paved miles to the trailhead on the right side of the road at several large boulders, which are spraypainted "Trailhead- No Shooting".
- The road is bermed and decommissioned 1.2 miles further up the road.

Why September: It is utterly baffling why the area around Tumala Mountain east of Estacada is unknown to most Portland hikers. Just an hour from Portland via paved roads, Tumala Mountain is the gateway for longer and even wilder hikes into the Salmon-Huckleberry Wilderness, one of the wildest places in western Oregon. This hike is a perfect gateway to this wilderness retreat; the shorter version climbs to Tumala Mountain's former lookout site, where the views stretch from downtown Portland to Mount Rainier and south to Mount Jefferson; the longer version drops downhill through scenic terrain to a quiet lake surrounded by huge, majestic Douglas-firs. In September expect to see mushrooms, fall color on the hillsides and far-ranging views on clear days- and few people. What could be better?

Hike : There are three trails that depart from this trailhead. Locate the Old Baldy Trail, heading uphill from the trailhead into the Salmon-Huckleberry Wilderness. The trail charges steeply uphill before leveling out somewhat. At 0.7 mile you'll reach a junction with the Fanton Trail, another way to do this hike (the Fanton Trailhead, though slightly closer, is more difficult to find and features less parking). Continue straight and keep climbing until you reach the junction with the spur trail to the summit of Tumala Mountai at 1.3 miles from the trailhead. For an easy hike with a huge payoff, turn right here.

The spur trail to Tumala Mountain climbs gradually for 0.3 mile to an unsigned junction with a gravel road just below the summit. Turn left here and walk the road to the summit, where the view north to Mount Hood is impressive. A set of concrete stairs are all that remains of the lookout tower that once stood here. Take the time to explore the summit; following trails to the north end will reveal views north to Washington's volcanoes and northwest to downtown Portland. It does not take long to realize that this is one of the peaks you can see from the horizon in Portland. Keen eyes or binoculars can pick out buildings and bridges downtown. For an easy hike, return the way you came.

If you're keen on continuing the hike, return to the spur trail junction and turn right. The trail quickly begins to lose elevation, dropping nearly 600 feet in just under a mile from the Tumala Mountain junction. After leveling out somewhat, the trail passes a rocky slope above Tumala Meadow, where you will have views down into this marshy meadow. The trail reaches a junction at 3.3 miles. Continuing straight will take you further north into the Salmon-Huckleberry Wilderness, but we want to go to Plaza Lake. Turn right and immediately reach a trailhead along Abbot Road. You could also drive to this spot but the road is many miles of rutted, narrow, potholed misery- it's better hiking than it is driving.

For Plaza Lake, walk along the Abbot Road for 0.9 mile until you locate the Plaza Lake Trailhead on the left side of the road. Leave the road here and hike downhill into Plaza Lake's small basin. The trail passes some truly huge trees, mostly Douglas fir. Later in the month the vine maple in the rock slides turns bright red, offering some early fall color. The trail finally reaches Plaza Lake at 0.6 miles from Abbot Road and 4.9 miles from the trailhead. The lake is surrounded by huge trees but forget backpacking- the single campsite along the lake was consumed in a spot fire in September 2017, and is now an ugly mess of burned timber. A trail once continued all the way to the Salmon River (Hike 118) but is now lost in downed trees and thick rhododendrons. Return the way you came. On the way back, when you reach the Fanton junction, keep right to return to the trailhead and your vehicle.

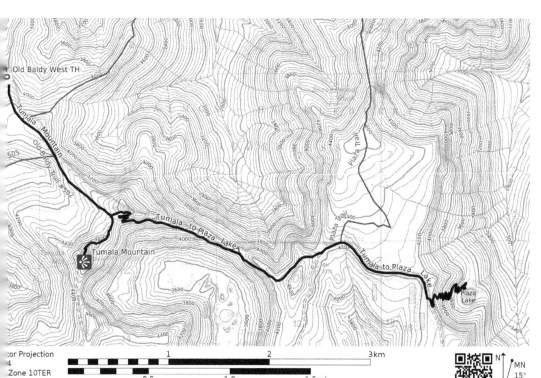

89. Olallie Backcountry Loop

Distance: 8.1 mile loop
Elevation Gain: 1,000 feet
Trailhead elevation: 4,956 feet
Trail high point: 5,355 feet
Other seasons: July- August
Map: Breitenbush (Green Trails #525)
Pass: None needed
Drivetime from Portland: 125 minutes

Directions:
- From Portland, drive south on OR 224 to Estacada.
- From Estacada, drive southeast on OR 224 approximately 25 miles to the Ripplebrook Guard Station.
- A short distance after Ripplebrook, OR 224 becomes FR 46 at a junction with FR 57. Continue straight (right) on FR 46.
- Drive another 22.3 miles on FR 46 to a junction with the Olallie Lake Road (FR 4690) – you will notice that "Olallie" is painted on the road with an arrow to mark the direction.
- Turn left here onto FR 4690 and drive 6.1 miles of narrow pavement and another 1.9 miles of rocky gravel to a junction with the Skyline Road, FR 4220.
- Turn right here and drive 5.1 gravel miles to the Olallie Lake Resort.
- Drive past the resort entrance and 100 feet later, turn right into the signed parking area for the Pacific Crest Trail.

Why September: Most people who make the long drive up to Olallie Lake don't venture far from the lake itself. Their loss. The backcountry of the Olallie Scenic Area features some of the finest mountain lakes in the entire region. September is absolutely the time to visit this area- both the mosquitoes and summer crowds are gone, the weather crisp and golden and the ubiquitous huckleberry bushes turn a deep shade of red. This excellent loop combines the Lower Lake and Red Lake Trails, with side trips to Timber Lake and a viewpoint of Fish Lake.

Hike: Begin at the Pacific Crest Trail's inconspicuous trailhead. Although you parked at the lot for the Pacific Crest Trail, this loop does not feature the PCT at all (see the next hike for this stretch of the PCT). Instead return to the Skyline Road and turn left to walk back down the road. Pass the turnoff for the Olallie Lake Resort and continue down the road 0.7 mile to a junction on your left for Lower Lake Campground. Leave the Skyline Road here and walk into the campground, where you will find the Fish Lake Trail. Start on the trail here. Soon you will reach Lower Lake. The trail skirts the edge of the lake, soon arriving at a junction with the Lodgepole Trail at 1.5 miles. Your loop turns left, but for the moment you should keep straight to check out a viewpoint of Fish Lake. Continue 0.3 mile on the Fish Lake Trail until it reaches a cliff edge with a view down to deep, green Fish Lake. The trail does continue down to the lake but this adds 1.6 miles and 400 more feet of elevation gain to your day's hike. Instead, return to the Lodgepole Trail Junction and turn right to continue on the loop.

The Lodgepole Trail climbs through the woods 0.3 mile to an unmarked junction on your left with the unofficial spur trail to Gifford Lake. Just as with Fish Lake, this spur trail; is absolutely worth your time. Though unmaintained, this short trail is easy to follow and takes you 0.2 mile to gorgeous Gifford Lake, one of the jewels of the Olallie backcountry. Despite lacking an official trail to the lake there are plenty of campsites, should you wish to backpack here. Then return to the Lodgepole Trail and turn left to continue your loop. In a little under a mile you'll arrive at a junction with the Red Lake Trail. Turn left here.

The Red Lake Trail climbs through the woods south of the wonderfully-named Twin Peaks. The path is as rocky and rough as they come- decades of water running down the trail have sculped a path more like a creekbed than a trail, and you'll soon be wishing the trail would just get there already. In a little over a mile, meet the PCT at a junction near Top Lake. Continue straight and drop down a bit to a junction just north of Top Lake. Turn left and skirt the northern end of the lake, where views open to the east towards conical Olallie Butte. Continue east on the Red Lake Trail another 0.4 mile to a junction with the Timber Lake Trail on your right. As with the other lake-related detours on this hike, the 0.7 mile spur to Timber Lake is well worth your time. The trail cuts a mostly-level path through open woods to Timber Lake, where you will find several excellent campsites. Take some time to look around for views of both the lake and Mount Jefferson, looming above the lake from some vantages. Return to the trail and turn right. You'll reach the Skyline Road in another 0.7 mile. Turn left and walk up the road 0.3 mile to the PCT Trailhead at hike's end.

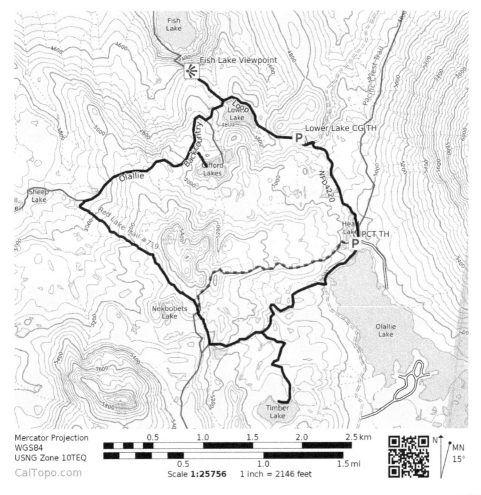

Mercator Projection
WGS84
USNG Zone 10TEQ

CalTopo.com

0.5   1.0   1.5   2.0   2.5 km

0.5   1.0   1.5 mi
Scale **1:25756**   1 inch = 2146 feet

N
MN
15°

90. Olallie Lake and Ruddy Hill

Distance: 10.3 mile loop
Elevation Gain: 1,300 feet
Trailhead elevation: 4,949 feet
Trail high point: 5,928 feet
Other seasons: July- August, October
Map: Green Trails #525 (Breitenbush)
Pass: None needed
Drivetime from Portland: 125 minutes

Directions:
- From Portland, drive south on OR 224 to Estacada. From Estacada, continue on OR 224 approximately 25 miles to the Ripplebrook Guard Station.
- A short distance after Ripplebrook, OR 224 becomes FR 46 at a junction with FR 57. Continue straight (right) on FR 46.
- Drive another 22.3 miles on FR 46 to a junction with the Olallie Lake Road (FR 4690) – you will notice that "Olallie" is painted on the road with an arrow to mark the direction.
- Turn left here onto FR 4690 and drive 6.1 miles of narrow pavement and another 1.9 miles of rocky gravel to a junction with the Skyline Road, FR 4220.
- Turn right here and drive 5.1 gravel miles to the Olallie Lake Resort.
- Drive past the resort entrance and 100 feet later, turn right into the signed parking area for the Pacific Crest Trail.

Why September: There is no finer place in all the Oregon Cascades than Olallie Country in September. The huckleberry leaves turn red, the skies are clear and the crowds gone for the season, just in time for the area's scenic apex. There are lots of trails up here, but many of them will leave you wanting more- more lakes, more views and more miles. Presented here is a loop that combines the area's three largest lakes, the area's best view-point and so much more. You won't find a better September hike anywhere in the region.

Hike: From the trailhead, follow the Pacific Crest Trail as it climbs lightly above Olallie Lake. At a little under a mile, the trail passes a series of bluffs with excellent views south to Mount Jefferson, just 10 miles to the south. Continue another 0.5 mile to a junction with the Red Lake Trail. Keep straight and soon reach Cigar Lake, where you will meet a junction with the steep spur trail to the summit of Double Peaks. Energetic hikers will enjoy this side trip, but our hike stays on the PCT.

Stay on the PCT as it passes Upper Lake at 2.4 miles. There are several good campsites here, and this makes a good spot to take a break. Beyond Upper Lake, the PCT passes through a long meadow with a view ahead to Mount Jefferson, then commences climbing gradually, reaching a rocky point known as the Many Lakes Viewpoint. Here you have a view down to many of the area's lakes, backed by Olallie Butte. Continue south on the PCT until you reach a junction with the Ruddy Hill Trail at 4.4 miles. Turn right here and climb this steep trail a little under 0.4 mile to the summit of Ruddy Hill, where the view is stunning. Look south to Mount Jefferson, towering over Park Ridge and Pyramid Butte. At the summit are the remains of a wooden phone box, propped against a tree. The origins of this box are unknown, but it dates to the 1920s or 1930s. When you've finished with Ruddy Hill, hike back down the trail to the PCT and turn right. In just 0.1 mile, reach a junction with the Horseshoe Saddle Trail on your left. Turn left here and hike this scenic trail 0.9 mile downhill to Horseshoe Lake's car campground, reachable only for vehicles with high clearance. Meet the Skyline Road here. Turn left to walk down the road.

Walk this rough but historic road, constructed in the 1920s, downhill 1.1 miles to Monon Lake. As you reach the lake, look for the Monon Lake Trail on your right. Turn here to resume hiking on trail. The Monon Lake Trail follows the southern edge of the large lake, offering excellent views north to Olallie Butte. Puncheon bridges offer passage across the marshy sections of trail. At 1.3 miles from the Skyline Road, reach an unsigned junction with the Monollie Trail at a cairn. Turn right here, walk across the narrow band of rock separating Monon and Olallie Lakes, and turn right on the Olallie Lake Trail. It is 1.5 miles along the lakeshore. You will be treated to stunning views across the lake and south to Mount Jefferson. At the north end of the lake you will reach the Olallie Lake Resort. At the resort you can purchase beverages and snacks. Overnight stays require a reservation. To find your car, walk out the resort's short access road and turn left on the Skyline Road. Walk a few steps to the PCT trailhead on your right.

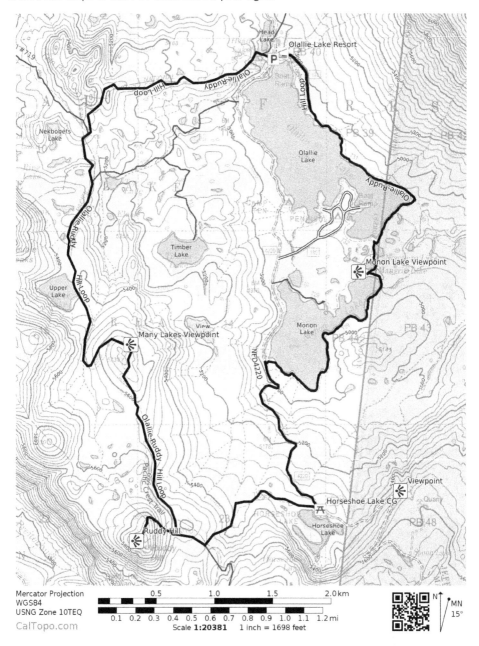

Mercator Projection
WGS84
USNG Zone 10TEQ
CalTopo.com

Scale **1:20381**   1 inch = 1698 feet

OCTOBER

		Distance	EV Gain	Drive
91.	Hoyt Arboretum	4.2 mi	500 ft	10 min
92.	Coldwater Lake	6.8 mi	500 ft	120 min
93.	June Lake	2.8 mi	400 ft	100 min
94.	Ramona Falls	6.9 mi	1,100 ft	75 min
95.	Ponderosa Point	6.2 mi	1,300 ft	80 min
96.	Tamanawas Falls and Lamberson Spur	10 mi	2,200 ft	80 min
97.	Boulder Lake	10 mi	1,800 ft	110 min
98.	South Breitenbush River	4 mi	500 ft	120 min
99.	Bagby Hot Springs	3.2 mi	300 ft	90 min
100.	Opal Creek	10.8 mi	1,500 ft	120 min

It's October, and all you want to do is go find some fall color, somewhere. The Pacific Northwest has a reputation for lacking in fall color compared to other parts of the United States. This reputation is somewhat deserved. As we do not have large tracts of deciduous forest, there aren't all that many places where you can go hiking and experience the height of fall color that you can in, for example, New England. But this does not mean that we do not have glorious fall color out here. The hikes presented here offer a wide variety of the best fall has to offer, from the kaleidoscope of color found at Hoyt Arboretum to the glorious vine maple of Ramona Falls to the changing larch trees found on Lamberson Spur on the east side of Mount Hood. While none of this can truly compare to the displays of fall color found east of the Rockies, they don't have our mountains, waterfalls and ancient forest. As always, it's a great privilege to live in the Pacific Northwest.

October is also the month when the weather truly begins to change, to transform into the long winter ahead. There are as many rainy days in October as there are sunny days, and this is the month when you should start obsessively checking the weather in the days before your hike. Always make sure you check the snow levels before venturing out into the mountains- mountain snow is increasingly common in October, and some places become increasingly difficult to access. It is for this reason that there are no hikes presented here above 6,000 feet in elevation- that high elevation is often snowed in by early October. With any luck though, you'll get a sunny, crisp day for your October adventure.

With all of this talk about the weather, it should go without saying that you need to be prepared before you head for the hills. Always take the Ten Essentials and always let somebody know where you are going and when you plan on returning. Any number of things can happen to you out there, and it's a good idea to make sure somebody knows what to do in case you get lost, your car breaks down, a tree falls on a forest road and blocks you in, and so on and so forth. You should always be prepared in case you need to spend a few days outside. Bring blankets, extra clothes and extra food in your car, and enough warm layers in your bag to make any unintended stay outside as safe as you can make it. October is a great time to be outside- if you are prepared for anything.

Photo on opposite page: unnamed falls on Opal Creek (Hike 100)

91. Hoyt Arboretum

Distance: 4.2 mile loop
Elevation Gain: 500 feet
Trailhead elevation: 713 feet
Trail high point: 861 feet
Other seasons: all year
Map: Forest Park (Green Trails 426S)
Pass: None needed
Drivetime from Portland: 10 minutes

Directions:
- Drive west from downtown Portland on US 26 to Exit 72, signed for Washington Park and the Oregon Zoo.
- Exit the highway here and follow signs uphill to the Zoo parking lot. You can also park by the Forestry Center, which is closer to the actual trailhead of the hike.
- Likewise, this is perhaps the easiest hike in this book to reach via public transportation. Take either the MAX Blue or Red line trains to the Washington Park stop. Get off the train, take the elevator up to ground level and follow signs to walk to the Vietnam Memorial, the beginning of this hike.

Why October: The Pacific Northwest has a reputation for not having great displays of fall color. This is only partially true. To be sure, our forests are primarily coniferous, and many of our native deciduous trees do not change color as dramatically as those east of the Rockies. But there are great displays of fall color to be found if you know where to look – and the easiest such place near Portland is Hoyt Arboretum in Washington Park, just a 10-minute drive or train ride from downtown. By definition an arboretum is a tree garden – and here you will find many different trees from all over the world, many of which turn a million shades of yellow, orange and red throughout October. The many trails that crisscross the arboretum offer hikers myriad options – too many to list here; a good map of will help you navigate the park. Make this an annual fall color pilgrimage in October.

Hike: The easiest way to navigate the arboretum is to use the Wildwood Trail through Washington Park and then pick and choose which trails you want to hike to make a loop on your return. Locate the Veterans Memorial in Washington Park, which is by the official beginning of the Wildwood Trail. Find the Hoyt Arboretum sign at the entrance to the memorial and follow the spiraling trail uphill, pausing for reflection at each stop on the way up. When you reach the top of the memorial, follow signs for the Wildwood Trail to begin your hike. You will follow the Wildwood Trail as it meanders through Washington Park, passing side trail after side trail on the way. All of these trails are worth a detour, but none are included in this featured hike. The Wildwood Trail then passes a viewpoint north to Mount Saint Helens, and then drops into the forest, eventually reaching Washington Park's archery range at 1.2 miles. Continue hiking along the Wildwood as it passes above the Japanese Garden and under a few homes at the edge of the park, until you reach a Fairview Boulevard at 2.5 miles. Cross the road to continue on the Wildwood Trail.

Up until now the trail has mostly stayed in the monocultural Douglas fir woods so commonly found in Portland's West Hills. Once across Fairview Boulevard, the Wildwood enters the heart of the arboretum and the nicest and most interesting forest in this hike. The Wildwood passes a small grove of Ponderosa pines and drops into the Redwood grove that is as surprising as it is beautiful. Yellow and orange vine maple add to the red bark of these coastal beauties here. The Wildwood Trail drops to a viewing deck built around the largest specimens of Coast redwood and Giant Sequoia found in the park. The benches here offer a fantastic place to stop, sheltered by the forest canopy.

From the Redwood grove, follow the Wildwood downhill to a series of junctions that mark the continuation of this loop. This is where this loop opens up to offer hikers all sorts of options. You can choose either the Redwood Trail or the Creek Trail to begin hiking south towards the trailhead. Both of these trails arrive at the same location, a small trailhead on SW Fischer Lane. Whichever of the two you choose, once you reach the Fischer Lane trailhead you are faced with more options.. If you choose to follow the Redwood Trail left from here, you'll pass a small grove of orange-needled Japanese Larch trees on your way to Hoyt Arboretum's interpretive center – from here, locate the Overlook Trail and follow it back to the Wildwood by the first large water tank. If you chose to follow the White Pine Trail from Fischer Lane, you can follow this short and lovely trail to a junction with the Hemlock Trail, which takes you to a junction with the Wildwood Trail just above the Vietnam Veterans Memorial. Or you can choose your own adventure and spend a full day exploring the trails here. Whatever you do, you can follow signs back to the Wildwood Trail and eventually you will arrive at the trailhead by the zoo, and the end of your loop.

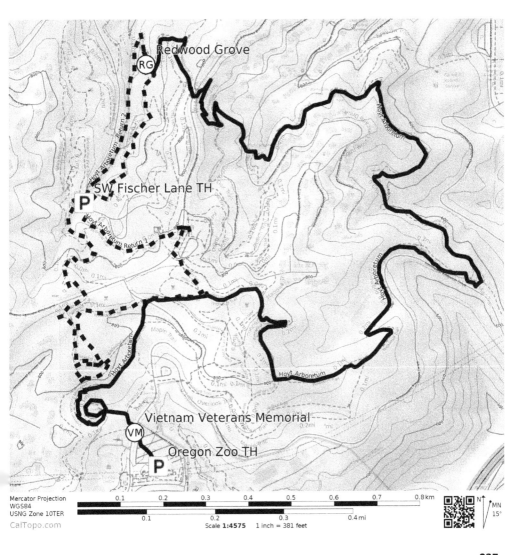

92. Coldwater Lake

Distance: 6.8 miles out and back
Elevation Gain: 500 feet
Trailhead elevation: 2,512 feet
Trail high point: 2,600 feet
Other seasons: May- October
Map: Spirit Lake (Green Trails #332)
Pass: NW Forest Pass
Drivetime from Portland: 120 minutes

Directions:
- From Portland, drive north on Interstate 5 into Washington, to Exit 49 in Castle Rock.
- Leave the freeway at Exit 49 and turn right onto WA 504.
- Follow this winding road for 41 miles to a junction at a sign for Coldwater Lake and Johnston Ridge.
  Turn right and drive 2 miles to a junction on the left signed for Coldwater Lake. Turn left and drive into the boat ramp parking lot, which is also the trailhead for this hike.

Why October: The north side of Mount Saint Helens is the place to go in southwest Washington for fall color, and few destinations feature displays as spectacular as beautiful Coldwater Lake during the first half of October. Vine maple lines the lake and much of the slopes above the lake, offering a million minute variations of red and orange, and even purple. This hike is ideal in less than ideal weather as well, as there's no view of Mount Saint Helens on this hike other than at the trailhead. Like most hikes though, this one is better on a sunny day.

Note: Dogs are not allowed on this and other trails inside the blast zone at Mount Saint Helens National Volcanic Monument. This prohibition is to protect the fragile, recovering environment. Hiking off-trail is banned as well.

Hike: From the boat ramp, locate the trail departing to the left. The trail sets out following the north shore of Coldwater Lake. As you walk along, take the time to reflect on the creation of Coldwater Lake. The colossal debris flows triggered by the 1980 eruption of Mount Saint Helens dammed Coldwater Creek, creating this huge lake. Today, the lake is 200 feet deep and occupies most of the flat space in this narrow valley. The trail follows the lake, following one ledge above the lake to another, for nearly its entire length. For much of the way the trail climbs slightly and then drops, winding in and out of young groves of young alders and cottonwoods. Breaks in the forest offer views to the far end of the lake, towards Minnie Peak's spires on your left and Coldwater Peak's imposing summit on the right, towering above each side of the lake. Snow often accents the summits above the lake in October, a reminder that winter is coming.

As the trail mostly follows the lake, keep your eyes trained on your surroundings. Red vine maple grows profusely around the lake and up the slopes of the peaks along the lake. All throughout October, the slopes above the lake are a million shades of green, yellow, orange and red- with the highest slopes fully red by the beginning of October. More surprising are the few straggler flowers that grow along the trail into October, among them a surviving few paintbrush and pearly everlasting. Frogs and crickets are commonly seen near side creeks. If you're lucky, you may even spot the herd of elk that live along the lake.

At 3.4 miles the trail reaches a huge landslide, where views open up at last to the far end of the lake, which has been out of sight up until this point. Continue to the end of the slide, where the view is at its best. Boulders strewn all over here offer hikers a place to sit, with the best view on the hike right in front of you. While the trail does continue from here, the view is so great and the boulders so tempting that you won't find a better destination than this. On rainy days you may be forced to retreat into the forest, but on sunny days this spot is hard to beat. This is the recommended turnaround spot for this hike. Return the way you came.

If you're looking for a longer hike, the trail continues around the lake 1.3 miles to its upper end. At a junction, turn right and hike down a switchback to a bridge over Coldwater Creek. This makes for a 9.4 mile hike round-trip. From here, the trail switchbacks 1.8 miles up the hill and up onto South Coldwater Ridge, where it meets a trail headed to Coldwater Peak (see Hike 61). Up here you will at last have the views many crave. But once on the ridge, you're kind of stuck- back down is a long hike, while the trail along the ridge is exposed, not always the most fun in cold, windy October. The ridge trail continues 3.4 miles west to a trailhead along WA 504, located about 1.5 miles uphill from the Coldwater Lake Trailhead. From here, it's a cold, windy and exposed road walk along the highway shoulder for 1.7 miles to complete this long loop. If you're up for this longer hike, a car shuttle between the South Coldwater Trail and Coldwater Lake Trailhead is probably the best strategy.

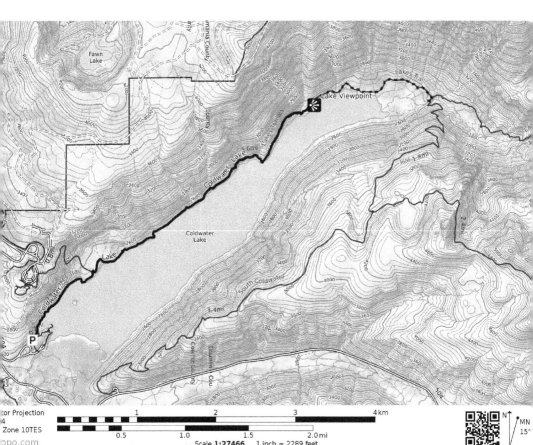

93. June Lake

Distance : 2.8 miles out and back
Elevation Gain: 400 feet
Trailhead Elevation: 2,732 feet
Trail High Point: 3,146 feet
Other seasons: October
Map: Mount Saint Helens #364 (Green Trails)
Pass: NW Forest Pass
Drivetime from Portland: 100 minutes

Directions:
- From Portland drive Interstate 5 or 205 north approximately 20 miles to the town of Woodland, WA.
- Leave the freeway at Exit 21 and immediately reach a junction with WA 503. Turn right.
- Follow WA 503 east for 22.5 miles to a junction with another spur of WA 503 arriving from Battle Ground and Amboy; this alternate route is just as winding and will only save you time if you live in the area.
- Continue straight and drive 11.7 miles, passing through the town of Cougar, to a junction with FR 83, signed for Ape Cave, the Climbers Bivouac and Lava Canyon.
- Turn left and drive 3 miles to a junction with FR 81, signed for the Climbers Bivouac.
- Keep right at this junction to continue towards June Lake.
- Continue 3.9 miles on FR 83 to the June Lake Trailhead on your left, just after Marble Mountain Sno-Park.
- Turn left and drive 100 yards into the trailhead parking lot.

June Lake on a windy, rainy and cold early fall day.

Why October: The short trail to June Lake is among the easiest hikes near Mount Saint Helens. While you can hike to the lake at almost any time (many make the trek on snow-shoes during the winter months), it is never better than in October, when the vine maples around the lake blaze orange and red. It is beautiful in any weather, but if you're lucky, you may catch the mountain, freshly coated in white after some early fall snows. Save this hike for an October weekend when you want to get outside but do not have the time or energy to go for a longer hike.

Hike: From the trailhead, follow the wide trail along June Lake's outlet creek. On the way up, you'll pass a few views of Mount Saint Helens but will mostly stay in the forest. Unlike many hikes in this area, this is equally great on cloudy and rainy days (which are so common here, especially in October): while you won't have views of the great volcano, the gloom enhances the mood of the forest here and makes for better photographic conditions. The trail climbs gradually through these gloomy woods, passing red and orange vine maple along the way, to a bridge below a small grove of huge ancient hemlock. You're

almost there. Soon you'll enter the lake's outwash plain, where the trail braids a bit. Cut to your right, following the trail towards the lake. At the far end of the lake is a 74-foot falls that seems to tumble from nowhere; it is, in fact, fed by springs above the lake. This is a peaceful spot, particularly on weekdays when you'll likely see nobody at the lake. Return the way you came.

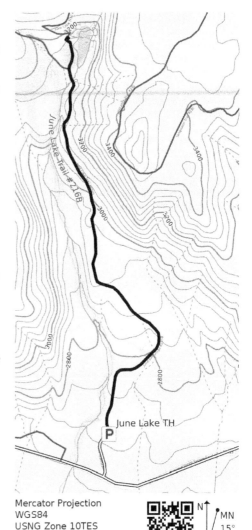

From the lake, the trail switchbacks up to a junction with the Loowit Trail, passing the spring-fed falls along the way. Once you reach the Loowit Trail, where you go is up to you. Left leads you through lava fields known as the Worm Flows and over Chocolate Falls (which rarely flows, and is not nearly as exciting as its name would suggest) to Monitor Ridge, where climbers attempt to summit the great volcano. Right, on the other hand, leads you to Ape Canyon and eventually the north side of the volcano. Unless you have the time to explore, it's better to turn around at June Lake.

Unlike most destinations in this book, June Lake is accessible in winter. As such, this is a popular destination for winter travel, either on snowshoes or cross-country skis. I'm not much of a fan of either, but if you're up for visiting in winter you'd be hard-pressed to find a better and easier trip with such a large payoff. For more information about visiting in winter, contact the Gifford Pinchot National Forest or Mount Saint Helens National Volcanic Monument. A winter Sno-Park pass is required.

Mercator Projection
WGS84
USNG Zone 10TES

CalTopo.com

N
MN
15°

94. Ramona Falls

Distance: 6.9 miles out and back
Elevation Gain: 1,100 feet
Trailhead elevation: 2,468 feet
Trail high point: 3,478 feet
Other seasons: July – October
Map: Mount Hood Wilderness (Geo-Graphics)
Pass: NW Forest Pass
Drivetime from Portland: 75 minutes

Directions:
- From Portland drive east on US 26 to Zigzag and Rhododendron.
- Just after a stop light with a sign for East Lolo Pass Road (FR 18), turn left on Lolo Pass Road and follow the Sandy River north.
- Stay on Lolo Pass Road for 4 paved miles.
- Immediately after a large sign for Mount Hood National Forest, turn right at a junction with FR 1825 that is labeled "campgrounds trailheads".
- Drive 0.6 mile of paved road to a junction with FR 1825 at a bridge.
- Turn right to stay on FR 1825. Continue on FR 1825 another 1.3 miles, staying left at every junction, until you reach a junction with FR 100.
- Turn left and drive 0.5 mile of rough pavement to the large Ramona Falls parking lot.
- Leave nothing of value in your car as break-ins and clouting is an occasional problem.

Why October: Ramona Falls is beautiful in any season, any time you can make it to the falls. My favorite time to visit is in the fall, when fantastic displays of orange and red vine maple line the banks of Ramona Creek. The hike is equally great on both sunny and rainy days, making this the ideal October hike. A visit on a sunny day reveals views ahead to Mount Hood at the Sandy River crossing and rainbows across Ramona Falls, while rainy days make the fall color and verdant moss absolutely pop. It is almost the ideal fall hike.

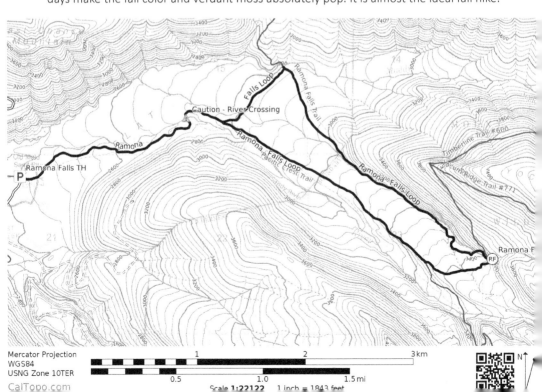

Ramona Falls, always beautiful and always peaceful.

Hike: Begin by following the wide trail from the trailhead along the lip of the Sandy River's canyon. The forest here is scraggly, with few large trees. As a result, you'll have many views down to the rampaging river. At 1.2 miles, the trail curves to the left to cross the Sandy River. Ahead, Mount Hood looms over the end of the canyon, just a few miles to the southeast. In the past the Forest Service placed a seasonal bridge over the river here, but discontinued the practice after the bridge washed out in a flood, killing a hiker in the process. Instead look upstream and down for logs across the river. If you cannot find a log on which to cross, turn around- **DO NOT ATTEMPT TO FORD THE RIVER**. It is too swift and cold to ford safely. Once across the river, follow the trail upstream until you reach a junction with the PCT. This is the start of your loop. Turn left here.

Follow the Ramona Falls Trail through the woods for 0.5 mile to a junction on your right with...the Ramona Falls Trail. Turn right here and follow the trail into deeper forest along cascading Ramona Creek. The creek flows over downed trees, through glassy pools and small riffles; a carpet of moss blankets the forest along the creek. This is one of the most photogenic streams near Mount Hood. Above you to the left are the lowest ramparts of Yocum Ridge, stained brilliant shades of orange and yellow in the rain. After 1.9 miles the trail reaches a junction with the Timberline Trail at the base of lacy Ramona Falls, where you will almost certainly encounter crowds. It is possible to backpack here, but look for sites far away from the falls and closer to the PCT's crossing of the Sandy River. If you're looking for a longer hike, you've got lots of options, the best of which is the long journey up Yocum Ridge (see Hike 74). This is a difficult trip in October given the lack of daylight, but if you love backpacking and can handle extremely cold nights, it might be for you.

Beyond Ramona Falls, follow the Timberline Trail a short distance to a junction with the Pacific Crest Trail and turn right. The trail follows the Sandy River a little under 2 miles to the junction near the river crossing. Turn left, cross the Sandy on downed logs and hike a little over 1 mile back to the trailhead.

95. Ponderosa Point

Distance: 6.2 miles out and back
Elevation Gain: 1,300 feet
Trailhead elevation: 2,925 feet
Trail High Point: 4,021 feet
Other seasons: April- November
Map: Mount Hood (Green Trails #462)
Pass: None needed.
Drivetime from Portland: 80 minutes

Directions:
* From Portland drive Interstate 84 approximately 60 miles east to Hood River.
* At Exit 64, leave the freeway and drive to a T-junction at the bottom of the exit ramp.
* Turn right on OR 35 and drive 23.1 miles south towards Mount Hood.
* Immediately after crossing the East Fork of the Hood River, look for the trailhead on your left at a small lot with a signboard.

Why October: Merely good during the summer months, the moderate hike up to Ponderosa Point above the Hood River Valley is truly spectacular in October, when the display of fall color along the trail is absolutely stupendous. Tree lovers will love this hike: the trail follows a ridge at the western edge of the rain shadow, and is one of the few places you can see Western red cedars and Mountain hemlocks co-mingling with ponderosa pines, larch and even a few aspen trees. While you can appreciate this in any weather, come here on a clear day to best experience the outstanding view of Mount Hood at Ponderosa Point. Expect to encounter mountain bikers on this hike, and give them space.

Mount Hood from Ponderosa Point.

Hike: The hike begins at the obscure Zigzag Trailhead, deep in the Hood River canyon (not to be confused with Zigzag Mountain, southwest of Mount Hood). The trail follows OR 35 a short ways before settling into a long series of switchbacks through the woods. In October expect to see copious amounts of vine maple in various shades of yellow, orange and red. While never steep, the Zigzag Trail gains 850 feet in just 1.2 miles – or just enough to get your blood flowing on a cold October morning. At 1.2 miles the trail reaches a four-way junction: to your left is the Dog River Trail at its southern terminus; straight is a fragment of the Surveyor Ridge Trail; and to your right is a spur trail to a viewpoint of Mount Hood. While Ponderosa Point is to your left, take a minute to investigate the viewpoint on the right. Follow this short spurt trail as it descends around a corner in the ridge to obstructed views to the north and east to Mount Hood; better views can be had but require effort. Return then to the four-way junction and continue on the Dog River Trail, heading uphill into the woods.

The trail follows the gentle crest or a ridge, weaving in and out of dark dells where Western Red Cedars grow large over watery seeps in the hillside. The variety of trees is a delight, and hikers will enjoy identifying the many species that grow along the ridge. The easiest to identify are Western Red Cedar, whose shaggy, peeling bark is an instant identifier; the ponderosa pine, with its orange bark and tall trunks; and larch, a deciduous conifer whose needles turn a striking shade of yellow-orange in late October before dropping to the ground. After a mile or so from the trail junction, the Dog River Trail begins to descend. The Dog River Trail is far more popular with mountain bikers than it is with hikers, and you will almost certainly encounter bikers – on this stretch of trail, be sure to step out of the way as they descend the trail at speeds faster than you. At 1.7 miles from the trail junction, the trail seems to end at a road. Follow the road 100 yards, then locate the unsigned trail on the left side of the road. Just after you leave the road, look for a spur trail to your left out to a viewpoint. Turn here and walk out to Ponderosa Point, a rockpile between huge ponderosa pines where at last you are greeted with an excellent view of Mount Hood, just across the valley. On a clear day this spot is hard to beat! The rocks are ideal for a picnic but watch your step – it would be easy to fall down onto the rocks below. On a cold, clear day, bring a thermos of coffee or soup and soak in the view! Return the way you came.

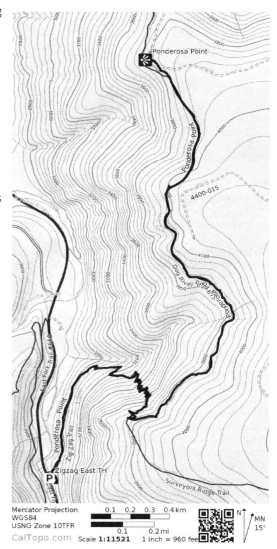

Mercator Projection
WGS84
USNG Zone 10TFR

CalTopo.com Scale **1:11521**

0.1 0.2 0.3 0.4 km

0.1   0.2 mi

1 inch = 960 feet

N

MN
15°

96. Tamanawas Falls and Lamberson Spur

	Tamanawas Falls	Lamberson Spur
Distance:	4 miles out and back	10 miles out and back
Elevation Gain:	500 feet	2,200 feet
Trailhead Elevation:	3,065 feet	3,065 feet
Trail High Point:	3,452 feet	5,182 feet
Other Seasons:	May- September	July- September
Map:	Mount Hood Wilderness	(Geo-graphics)
Pass:	NW Forest Pass	NW Forest Pass
Drivetime from PDX:	80 minutes (either direction)	80 minutes (either direction)

Directions:
- From Portland, drive east on Interstate 84 to Hood River.
- Leave the freeway at Exit 64, signed for Mount Hood. Drive downhill to a T-junction and turn right on OR 35.
- Follow this highway 23.8 miles south to the Tamanawas Falls Trailhead on your right.
- You can also drive here via US 26 and Government Camp, and this drive takes almost the same amount of time as the route described above. The problem with this approach is that you have to drive over Mount Hood, where the weather is less reliable and sometimes problematic in October. If you'd like to take this route, drive to Government Camp on US 26 and then continue to the junction with OR 35. Turn onto OR 35 and drive 14.8 miles to the Tamanawas Falls Trailhead on your left.

Why October: There are good fall color hikes and there are great fall color hikes – and then there is Tamanawas Falls. Located on the east side of Mount Hood, this easy ramble to a spectacular falls boasts a kaleidoscopic display of color throughout October that bests almost every other hike in the area. Come here in early October and the vine maple that lines Cold Spring Creek blazes a million shades of yellow, orange and red; later in the month, the canyon's cottonwood and larch trees turn orange and yellow, towering over this frigid gorge. Just make sure you come early in the day – this is an extremely popular hike, and as the day goes on it gets crowded here. Adventurous hikers can follow an obscure trail above Tamanawas Falls to a viewpoint of Mount Hood, looming over an impressive collection of golden larch trees.

Hike: From the trailhead, follow the trail to a bridge over the East Fork of the Hood River. Cross the bridge and immediately reach a junction with the East Fork Trail. Turn right. This trail follows the raging East Fork from a wide bench above the river. Soon you will cross a bridge over Cold Spring Creek and reaches a junction. Turn left here to hike to Tamanawas Falls. The Tamanawas Falls Trail follows Cold Spring Creek at a close distance through its narrow canyon. As elsewhere on this hike, the colorful displays of vine maple found here are breathtaking (the first weekend of October seems to be the sweet spot here). At 1.5 miles the trail reaches a junction just before a rockslide; right heads uphill towards the obscure Lamberson Spur Trail, while straight leads you to Tamanawas Falls. Whether you want a longer hike or not, head straight for the time being. The trail immediately reaches the aforementioned rockslide; in October 2016, a huge rockslide here buried the trail in boulders and rubble; navigating through the boulders can be difficult. Hopefully the trail has been fixed by the time you read this. Just beyond the slide, the falls comes into view. Follow the trail to the 109-foot falls, tumbling into a rocky splash pool. If you just came for a short hike, return the way you came.

For those looking to continue their day, the hike up Lamberson Spur is interesting but features only one decent view – at the end of the hike. It is the most obscure, least-hiked trail on Mount Hood, and maintenance is sporadic at best. I love this trail, but many will not. To find the trail, return to the junction and head uphill. The Tamanawas Tie Trail heads uphill and intersects the Elk Meadows Trail after just 0.4 mile. Turn left and follow the Elk Meadows Trail as it follows the canyon rim a total of 0.9 mile to a junction with the Lamberson Spur Trail, just after you pass above Tamanawas Falls (which can be heard but not seen). Turn right to hike up Lamberson Spur. This path cuts though the woods north of Cold Spring Creek, climbing southwest towards Mount Hood. Blowdown can be a problem here, but the way is never in doubt. Along the way you will pass many larch tree, whose orange needles add color to an otherwise dark forest. Late in October these deciduous evergreens change color from green to gold and finally a deep orange, brightening the woods with blazing bursts of color. The Lamberson Spur Trail climbs 1,300 feet in 1.9 miles to a meadow, where Mount Hood at last comes into view, towering above the upper

reaches of Cold Spring Creek's canyon. The viewpoint is not as satisfying as you want it to be, as some trees block a full view of Mount Hood. Nevertheless, the meadow- previously used as a staging area in firefighting operations- is a fascinating and beautiful spot just the same. The trail does continue beyond Lamberson Spur but quickly becomes lost in the woods. It's better to return the way you came.

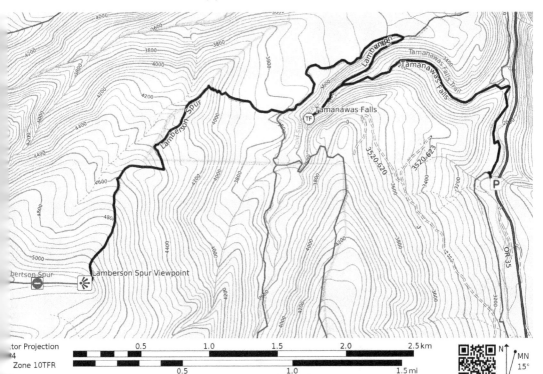

97. Boulder Lake

Distance: 10 mile loop
Elevation Gain: 1,800 feet
Trailhead elevation: 4,367 feet
Trail high point: 5,605 feet
Other seasons: June- September
Map: Mount Hood (Green Trails #462)
Pass: None needed
Drivetime from Portland: 110 minutes

Directions:
- From Portland, drive east on US 26 for 49 miles to a junction with OR 35.
- Turn right and drive around Mount Hood 4.7 miles to a poorly-marked intersection with FR 48 just after crossing the White River.
- Turn right and drive down FR 48 for exactly 6.9 miles to a poorly-marked turnoff on FR 4890 on your left.
- Drive this paved road for 3.7 miles to a junction and continue straight, now on FR 4881 for 2.5 paved but brushy miles.
- Reach a junction with FR 4880 and turn left for 4 narrow, washboarded gravel miles to the well-marked trailhead on your left.

Why October: At Boulder Lake east meets west, where Douglas fir and Western red cedar mix with larch, cottonwood and even a few aspens. This delightful loop is never better than in October, when the fall colors are at their peak and the weather crisp. The greatest reward awaits hikers at the summit of Bonney Butte: a chance to spend some time with Hawkwatch, an organization that tracks the fall migration of these majestic birds. With some luck, you might get to hold one, even if only briefly.

Boulder Lake is an oasis of fall color.

Hike: The trail leaves from the trailhead and pushes uphill, passing small Spinning Lake en route to Boulder Lake. Reach deep, aquamarine Boulder Lake at 0.3 mile from the trailhead. Your loop begins here. Before you leave the lake, take the time to hike the loop trail around Boulder Lake. This trail passes several outstanding campsites, cuts through the talus slopes on the far end of the lake and treats hikers to some of the finest displays of fall color in the Mount Hood National Forest. Maples, cottonwoods and aspens compete for the attention of hikers and slow the progress of photographers to a crawl. Once you return to the junction at the head of the lake, turn right to hike to Little Boulder Lake.

The trail leads over some small ups and downs to Little Boulder Lake in 0.6 mile. Take a moment to check out this large but shallow lake, backed by Echo Point's cliffs. Then turn left to follow a trail that leads to a gravel road, just east of the lake. The loop follows this road uphill for 1 mile to a junction with the Forest Creek Trail. Turn right. From here you will follow this trail through deep forest along the ridge above both Boulder Lakes. Along the way you will pass a few good viewpoints down to the lakes below but for the most part you will stay in the forest. The trail passes over Echo Point at 2.2 miles from the road junction and quickly descends to Bonney Meadows, a huge prairie situated between Echo Point and Bonney Butte. Keep straight at a junction and follow the edge of Bonney Meadows for 0.3 mile

to another junction, this time with the Boulder Lake Trail. Turning right here leads you downhill through deep old-growth 1.8 miles to Boulder Lake, but if you've got the time and energy, turn left instead. You will quickly reach Bonney Meadows Campground, accessible from the north via a terrible road.

To find Bonney Butte, walk out the campground access road and turn right on FR 4891. Walk the road 0.25 mile to the unmarked junction with Bonney Butte's unsigned access road on your left. Walk up the road 0.5 mile to the summit, where you'll find Hawkwatch and huge views of Mount Hood. When you're ready to leave, return to the campground. Locate the Boulder Lake Trail and then hike 2 miles downhill to Boulder Lake. Turn left here and walk the short trail back to the trailhead.

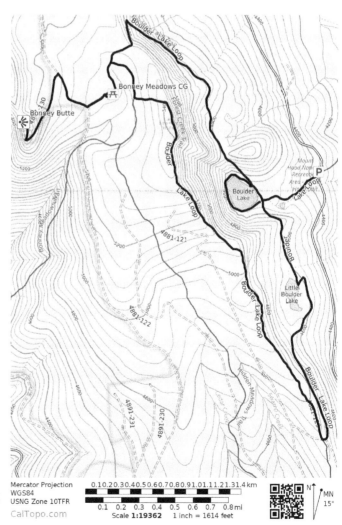

Mercator Projection
WGS84
USNG Zone 10TFR
CalTopo.com

0.1 0.2 0.3 0.4 0.5 0.6 0.7 0.8 0.9 1.0 1.1 1.2 1.3 1.4 km

0.1   0.2   0.3   0.4   0.5   0.6   0.7   0.8 mi
Scale **1:19362**   1 inch = 1614 feet

N
MN
15°

98. South Breitenbush River

Distance: 4 miles out and back
Elevation Gain: 500 feet
Trailhead Elevation: 2,300 feet
Trail High Point: 2,794 feet
Other Seasons: April- October
Map: Breitenbush (Green Trails #525)
Pass: None needed
Drivetime from Portland: 120 minutes

Directions:
- From Portland, drive south on Interstate 5 to Salem.
- At Exit 253, leave the freeway at a sign for Detroit Lake and Bend.
- Turn left on OR 22 and drive east 49 miles to Detroit.
- Turn left at a sign for Breitenbush, Elk Lake and Olallie Lake onto FR 46.
- Drive 11.6 miles to a junction on your right with FR 4685.
- Turn right, drive across the bridge over the North Breitenbush River and continue 0.6 mile to the trailhead on your right.

Why October: October features as many rainy days as sunny days, and sometimes you want to get out of town and far away before the days flip to November and the gloom of winter arrives. This is a great time to go hike along the South Breitenbush River. The forest floor is verdant and mossy, mushrooms push through the duff, growing in great number along the trail, and fall color is found in flourishes along the trail. Sure, driving 2 hours to hike 4 miles seems like overkill but consider this: there are lots of other trails around here, and if you're up for a much longer hike, you have lots of options.

Hike : From the trailhead, walk a short distance to a trail junction above the South Breitenbush Trail. This trail begins 1 mile to the northwest at a trailhead just outside of Breitenbush Hot Springs; if you want a longer hike you can start there but this lower section is not all that exciting. At the junction, turn left and begin hiking southeast on the South Breitenbush Trail. After just 0.4 mile, you'll reach a junction on your right with the Emerald Forest Trail. A right turn here takes you into territory managed by the good folks at Breitenbush Hot Springs; if you have a little time, you can follow this trail just a short ways down to a bridge over the South Breitenbush River for a look at the river.

From this junction, continue straight and enter an incredibly lush forest. The moss is like a shag carpet on the forest floor, and seems almost too green to be true on rainy days. Soon the trail enters a forest that was absolutely pummeled in a 1990 windstorm. Some of the trees blown down were as much as 8 feet thick; the trail weaves around and sometimes over these fallen giants. It is in this tangle of blowdown that the trail reaches an unmarked junction with a short spur trail to a viewpoint of South Breitenbush Gorge. Once upon a time this was a popular hiking destination, and many hikers hiked this trail for a view of the gorge, a narrow slot canyon in the South Breitenbush River. Today the Gorge is difficult to locate, lost in a maze of blowdown. If you can find it, follow user trails down to the edge of the gorge. It is difficult to get a good photo, and don't try too hard- the canyon walls can be slippery.

Back on the trail, continue another 0.3 mile to the wooden bridge over Roaring Creek, a far more accessible scenic highlight. Here Roaring Creek cascades down a mossy slope in most photogenic fashion, passing under the bridge on its way to the South Breitenbush River. This is one of the most beautiful places you will ever see, and this marks the end of the recommended hike. There is a lot of space around the bridge for a stop, and it is equally easy to wander down to the South Breitenbush River if you wish.

If you're looking for a longer hike, you've got lots of options. The South Breitenbush River continues 3.1 miles through the woods by the river to its upper trailhead in a large flat that also marks the trailhead for Bear Point (Hike 70) and Jefferson Park (Hike 80). On a rainy day the section of trail along the river above Roaring Creek is a good addition; there aren't many highlights but this trail is peaceful and solitary. If you've got a lot of energy, you could continue all the way to Bear Point, making for a 18 mile hike with 3,900 feet of elevation gain- but one of the best hikes you will ever do. The great thing about this area is that there are no wrong answers when it comes to hiking.

Finally, this hike is an excellent addition to a stay at Breitenbush Hot Springs. This beloved resort is the place to go in October for a hot soak on a cold day or weekend. The resort has a new-age vibe, all vegetarian food and is quite spendy, but worth it. For more information, see www.breitenbush.com. You must make a reservation to stay at the resort. If you're staying at Breitenbush, you can find the lowest trailhead for this hike by crossing the bridge over the river inside the resort and continuing on a lane until you reach the South Breitenbush Trailhead on your right.

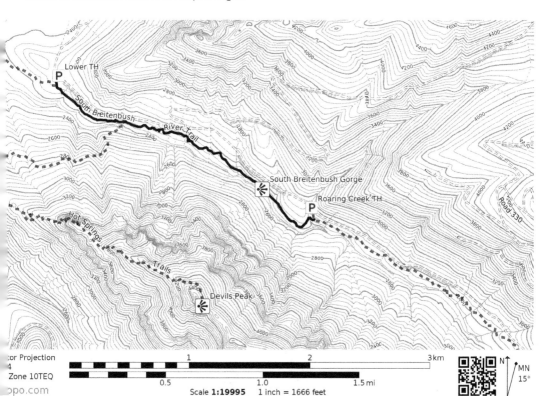

99. Bagby Hot Springs

Distance: 3.2 miles out and back
Elevation Gain: 300 feet
Trailhead elevation: 2,081 feet
Trail high point: 2,399 feet
Other seasons: March- November
Map: Bull of the Woods Wilderness (Geo-graphics)
Pass: NW Forest Pass + special soaking pass
Drivetime from Portland: 90 minutes

Directions:
- From Portland, drive 18 miles southeast on OR 224 to Estacada.
- Continue on OR 224 approximately 25 miles to the old guard station at Ripplebrook.
- Just past Ripplebrook OR 224 becomes FR 46. Continue straight on FR 46 for 4.2 miles beyond Ripplebrook to a junction with FR 63. Turn right here, following a sign for Bagby Hot Springs.
- Drive this 2-lane paved road for 3.5 miles to a junction with FR 70, once again signed for Bagby Hot Springs. Turn right.
- Drive FR 70 and drive 6.8 miles to the hectic, well-signed trailhead on your left.
- **Note 1:** Leave nothing of value at this trailhead – due to its extreme popularity, the Bagby Trailhead has been the site of break-ins and theft in the past. The situation has improved in recent years but is still very much a possibility.
- **Note 2:** A special pass is also required for this trail, which you can buy either at the Ripplebrook Country Store or at the trailhead. The extra $5 is intended to help maintain the aging but very popular buildings at the hot springs.
- **Note 3:** Do NOT use your GPS or Google to find the trailhead. Both will tell you either that the roads to Bagby are closed, and will direct you onto steep, rough and potentially dangerous gravel roads high in the mountains. The roads to the trailhead never close; they just aren't maintained from November to April. Be very, very careful if

you're planning on coming here after October- getting stuck in the snow up here would be a very unpleasant if not dangerous experience.

Why October: Bagby Hot Springs is among the most famous hikes in the entire state of Oregon. And with good reason, too- there aren't many hikes that follow a cascading stream through a tremendous old-growth forest to a historic and highly satisfying hot springs. Throughout the year crowds overwhelm the tubs and stalls at the hot springs, forcing people to wait a long time to soak. The crowds thin (somewhat) as fall draws near, but the hot springs are as envigorating as ever. I've always felt that a soak feels better on a cold, rainy autumn day. Red and orange vine maple add color to the scene, making for a perfect fall hike!

Hike: The trail sets out from the parking lot and almost immediately crosses the Hot Springs fork of the Collawash River on a large bridge. Soon you will enter a magnificent forest of ancient Douglas firs, some as many as eight feet thick. The trail is nearly level here, and you may find yourself rushing to get to the hot springs. At 1.5 miles, cross another bridge and enter the area around the hot springs. The rustic bath structures and tubs are charming. You may need to wait in line for one of the private rooms but it's well worth it! Once you get to soak, you'll need buckets of cold water to regulate the hot water temperatures to your liking. People have been coming here for centuries- and to ensure people can come here for centuries to come, please respect the rules. Do not enter the guard station or any other locked buildings. Clothing is optional at the restored bathhouses. Liquor and other controlled substances are prohibited.

The trail continues past the Hot Springs another 6 miles to beautiful Silver King Lake. This is a fantastic hike but isn't recommended on rainy days, as the trail becomes very brushy and is plagued with downed trees. Hikers must ford the Hot Springs Fork as well, no easy task after heavy fall rains. Later in the month there isn't enough daylight to complete the hike unless you're out for a trail run. It's better to return the way you came.

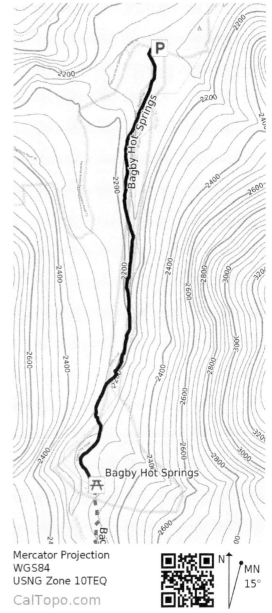

Mercator Projection
WGS84
USNG Zone 10TEQ

CalTopo.com

N
MN
15°

100. Opal Creek

Distance: 10.8 miles out and back (semi-loop)
Elevation Gain: 1,500 feet (expect lots of minor ups and downs)
Trailhead elevation: 1,952 feet
Trail high point: 2,372 feet
Other seasons: March- November
Map: Opal Creek Wilderness (Imus)
Pass: NW Forest Pass
Drivetime from Portland: 120 minutes

Directions:
- From Portland, drive south on Interstate 5 approximately 47 miles to Salem.
- Leave the freeway at exit 253 in Salem, signed for Detroit Lake and Bend. At the end of the exit ramp, turn left onto OR 22.
- Drive OR 22 east for 23 miles to the second flashing light in Mehama.
- At a sign for the Little North Fork Recreation Area (and directly across from the North
- Fork Crossing restaurant), turn left.
- Follow the paved two-lane road up the Little North Fork for 15 miles to the end of pavement at the entrance to the Willamette National Forest.
- Continue another 1.5 miles of gravel road to a junction with FR 2207.
- Following signs for Opal Creek, keep straight (left) on FR2209 and continue 4.2 miles to the trailhead at a large metal gate on the road. There is room for several dozen cars to park – and yet the trailhead will be full on nice weekends even in October.
- **Note:** Do not block the gate.

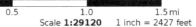

Why October: Famed for its ancient forests and emerald pools, Opal Creek was the site of one of Oregon's fiercest timber battles in the 1980s. Today the area is extremely popular and is showing signs of abuse and overuse. This is particularly the case in the summer, when thousands of area hikers trek up here to swim and play in the deep pools along Opal Creek. I much prefer the fall up here, when the undergrowth turns orange and red and the crowds thin out. Any time to visit is great, but this is my favorite time of year up here. In spite of its low elevation this is not a good destination in the winter, as it snows a lot here- use caution when visiting between December and March. No matter when you visit, be sure to treat this beautiful place with the love and respect it deserves.

Hike: The hike begins by following the closed road that leads to Jawbone Flats. Walk along this road as it skirts along cliffs and through deep forest high above the Little North Santiam River. The road crosses cascading Gold Creek on a high bridge at 0.4 mile and reaches a junction with the Whetstone Mountain Trail shortly afterwards; hikers desiring a long and difficult but highly satisfying hike can follow this trail up to Whetstone Mountain's view-packed summit, returning via the Gold Creek and Battle Ax Creek Trails for a 16 mile loop with about 4,000 feet of elevation gain. But we're just going to Opal Creek. Continue on the Jawbone Flats Road. The trail soon enters a grove of massive Douglas firs that tower above the trail. Not to be outdone, the vine maple that grows long the road sports impressive displays of fall color. It is a beautiful place.

At 2.1 miles pass what remains of Mertin Mill and its collection of mining and logging relics. The building that stood here collapsed in 2016 and all that remains is a pile of boards. A short trail behind the boards leads to Sawmill Falls, also known as Cascadia de los Niños, a 20-foot plunge on the Little North Santiam River. Take a moment to check out this peaceful spot before continuing your hike.

Soon after Mertin Mill and the falls, you will come to a junction with the Kopetski Trail on your right. Save this for later and continue 1.2 miles to Jawbone Flats. This former mining village has been converted over the years to an educational retreat, complete with restored cabins that can be rented. Leave the residents in peace and continue through town, following signs for Opal Pool. Beyond Jawbone Flats, the old road re-enters the woods and passes under golden maple leaves, reaching a junction with the Kopetski Trail. Hikers desiring a moderate hike should turn right here to return to the trailhead via a short loop, but hikers looking for more adventure should continue up the road. You will soon meet the Kopetski Trail again, and this time you should turn right.

The trail passes high above Opal Creek for a ways, crossing Flume Creek in between tiers of its waterfall, until returning close to creek level. The way becomes rockier and steeper but the scenery is incredible, with the creek tumbling into emerald pool after emerald pool. The Kopetski Trail reaches Cedar Flats at 5.4 miles from the trailhead. This collection of ancient cedars and huge campsites marks the end of the trail - while a rough trail does continue upstream, it is brushy and goes nowhere useful.

Hike the trail back to the road and turn left, back towards Jawbone Flats. Turn left again and hike the short trail down to the bridge over Opal Pool. Take a moment to check out this gorgeous gem set inside Opal Creek's rocky gorge. From here, the Kopetski Trail continues 1.5 lovely miles along the Little North Santiam River's south bank to a bridge over the river. On the far end of the bridge, reach a reunion with the Jawbone Flats road. Turn left and hike 2.3 miles back up the road to the trailhead.

NOVEMBER

		Distance	EV Gain	Drive
101.	Warrior Rock on Sauvie Island	6.4 mi	3 ft	60 min
102.	Forest Park: Newberry Road Loop	5.7 mi	500 ft	20 min
103.	Forest Park: Ridge Trail Loop	4 mi	900 ft	20 min
104.	Forest Park: Firelane 1-3 Loop	5 mi	700 ft	20 min
105.	Milo McIver State Park	6 mi	500 ft	45 min
106.	Cape Horn	7 mi	1,200 ft	40 min
107.	Multnomah-Wahkeena Loop	5.8 mi	1,500 ft	35 min
108.	Benson Plateau via the PCT	14 mi	3,800 ft	50 min
109.	Dry Creek Falls	9.4 mi	1,000 ft	50 min
110.	Herman Creek	9 mi	1,800 ft	50 min

November is one of the busiest, rainiest, harshest months of the year. The rain seems to arrive for good every year around the first of November, bringing it with it darkness, wind, and heavy mountain snows. As you turn clocks back, you'll find increasingly little daylight under which to play. It is for this reason that all of the hikes presented here are within an hour drive of Portland. You don't have much time, much daylight and the weather stinks-it's best to stay close to come.

You will find several hikes here in Forest Park, Portland's urban wilderness. You can go to Forest Park any time you want, at any point in the year. I love to go on weekdays in the summer when I'm off work, for example. But November is my favorite time to visit the park, as the fall color peaks later here than it does in the mountains, and the trails are not yet inundated with the rain and mud they hold all winter and into spring. November is also the time I begin to return to the Gorge after several months of high-mountain hiking. As the mountains become increasingly snowed in, I begin to return to my fall and winter haunts. The Gorge hikes presented here are all known for excellent displays of fall color, and all of them are at their best on rainy days (save for Cape Horn, which you should save for the rare and welcome sunny day in November). The mist hangs in the Gorge, offering many scenic photo opportunities and accentuating the last of the fall color.

As you might expect, you should prepare for November hiking by bringing all your winter raingear and the Ten Essentials. All of these hikes are close to Portland and very easy to access, and other than the long trek up to the Benson Plateau, none of them have any threat of snow in November. The best piece of gear in November is a good raincoat, and the second best is a detailed forecast for wherever it is you are going. After all: sometimes it feels like the cold November rains will last forever. You might as well get out and enjoy the time you have.

Photo on opposite page: tall trees in the mist on Benson Plateau (Hike 108)

101. Warrior Rock on Sauvie Island

Distance: 6.4 miles out and back
Elevation Gain: 3 feet
Trailhead elevation: 23 feet
Trail high point: 26 feet
Other seasons: all year
Map: none available or needed
Pass: $10 day-use pass (must be purchased on Sauvie Island)
Drivetime from Portland: 60 minutes

Directions:
- From downtown Portland, drive north on US 30 to a junction with Bridge Avenue just before the St. Johns Bridge.
- Continue under the bridge and drive 4 miles further north to a junction on your right signed for Sauvie Island. Turn right here.
- Cross the bridge and soon arrive at the Cracker Barrel market (no relation to the restaurant chain) on the left. Stop here and purchase the $10 Sauvie Island day-pass.
- Once you've purchased the pass, continue 1.8 miles to a junction with Reeder Road.
- Turn right and drive 4.4 miles to a junction at a stop sign. Continue straight and drive 6.2 miles to the end of pavement.
- Continue straight 2.3 miles to the end of Reeder Road at the trailhead.

Why November: Sauvie Island, situated between the mouth of the Willamette River and the gentle northern turn of the Columbia River is where Portlanders go when they want a quick getaway. Throughout the year people visit the island to pick berries, trample through corn mazes and experience hidden nude beaches. Whatever you happen to be into, you're likely to find it on the island. It shouldn't be surprising that you'll find hikes here, too. The best of these hikes is a walk through the woods or along Columbia

River beaches to Warrior Rock's still-active lighthouse. In November you'll hike under huge bigleaf maple trees whose bright yellow leaves dot the trail. On sunny days you'll have occasional views out to Mount Saint Helens, towering over the foothills on the opposite side of the Columbia River. Adventurous hikers can make a loop by following the beach to the lighthouse but this is easier said than done.

Hike: The easiest way to do this hike is to follow the road through the woods all the way to the lighthouse. Locate the trail at the signboard and follow it around a small field. You may see cows grazing in this field - possibly right up to the fence at the edge of the trail. Continue on the trail, which soon meets up with an old road. You will follow this road through the woods for the rest of the way. As you hike, take a moment to appreciate the peacefulness of the setting; the deciduous forest here is more reminiscent of the forest and trails you can find east of the Rocky Mountains. Every time I come here I am struck by the resemblance to the forests found in Illinois, my other home state. Birds are frequently seen along the trail and in the woods, and a visit early in the day gives you a greater chance of seeing deer. Less exciting is the large number of deep puddles on the road, some of which will force hikers to retreat to the side of the road. After periods of heavy rain nearly the entire way is muddy. Expect your visit to be no different. The road curves to the right at a little over 3 miles from the trailhead and reaches a beach along the Columbia River. Turn right here and you'll see the lighthouse, sitting atop Warrior Rock's basalt outcrop. The lighthouse is still operational, and is used to help guide traffic along the river. Take the time to hang out by the lighthouse before returning to the road. Once you reach the road again, turn back and hike back to the trailhead.

If you'd like to try a somewhat more adventurous approach to the lighthouse, you can hike along the beach as far as you can. To find the beach from the trailhead, simply turn right and follow the short trail to the beach. You'll

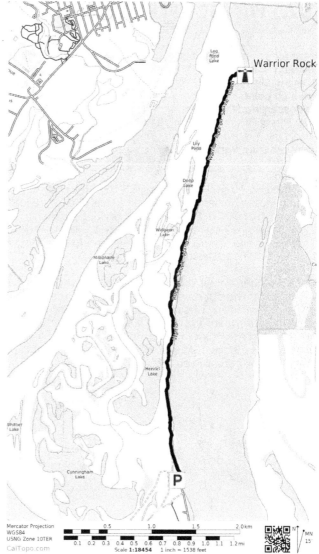

then follow the Columbia River north towards the lighthouse. The way is easy going for the first mile, as the beach is wide and sandy. You'll see people hanging out here on the beach, and you'll likely also see at least one huge ship making its way along the river. The way gets more difficult as you continue north, as the beach contracts in some spots into a narrow, muddy strip along the river. Hikers unprepared for this may find the experience unpleasant. Equally unpleasant is the brush that lines the beach; expect lots of blackberry, thorny and almost impossible to penetrate. If you need to leave the beach for the safety of the old road, there are only a few trails that connect the beach to the road- otherwise you're looking at a short but very unpleasant bushwhack. Continue as far as you can on the beach until you reach either the lighthouse or a connection to the road, and then follow the road to and from the lighthouse.

102. Forest Park: Newberry Road Loop

Distance: 5.7 mile semi-loop
Elevation Gain: 500 feet
Trailhead elevation: 700 feet
Trail high point: 920 feet
Other seasons: all year
Map: Forest Park (Green Trails #426S)
Pass: None needed
Drivetime from Portland: 20 minutes

Directions:
- Drive north from Portland on US 30, St. Helens Road to the Linnton neighborhood.
- Continue 2.7 miles beyond the St. Johns Bridge to a junction with NW Newberry Rd.
- Turn left and drive 1.5 miles to an obvious pullout on the left side of the road. There is room for 6-7 cars but you might want to come early to get a parking spot.
- **Note:** Winter storms damaged Newberry Road in early 2017, closing it for the year. Check online to see if it has reopened before you visit.

Why November: Forest Park is great for hikers who want to get their miles in during the fall and winter without driving very far. Although the trails are muddy, the far northern section of Forest Park is less crowded than the southern end of the park and offers much to charm water-weary hikers. This fantastic loop starts at the far northern end of Forest Park and passes through some of the least-crowded parts of the park before ending up back where you started. As with all other hikes in Forest Park, there are many options to extend your hike should you feel like it.

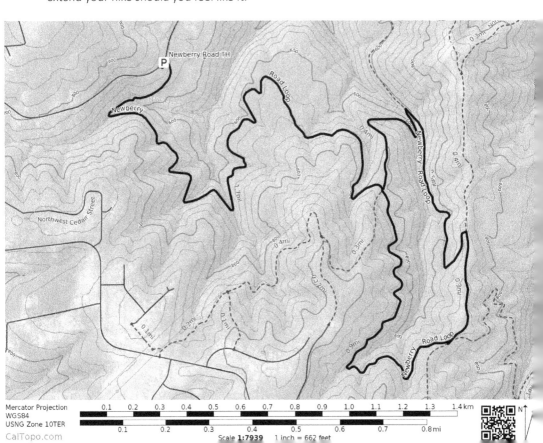

Mercator Projection
WGS84
USNG Zone 10TER
CalTopo.com

Scale 1:7939   1 inch = 662 feet

The Wildwood Trail winds through dark, verdant forests at the northern end of Forest Park.

Hike: Begin on the Wildwood Trail, which cuts slightly downhill before leveling out in deep forest. As it winds in and out of gullies through the woods, you'll wonder if the entire hike looks exactly like this (it does not). The forest is among the most impressive in all of Forest Park, with a few ancient trees that somehow escaped being cut standing tall right along the trail. Ferns of all kinds seem to line the trail and moss is everywhere. While much of the Wildwood looks just like identical to what you see here, this section is somewhat more wild and less-crowded than the trail is south of Germantown Road, closer to the heart of Portland.

At 1.8 miles, reach a junction with Firelane 15. This marks the start of your loop, but for now you should continue straight on the Wildwood Trail. If you're interested in a side trip, turning right on Firelane 15 offers a few views of the farmland west of Forest Park before reaching a remote upper trailhead. Continuing straight on the Wildwood, you will reach a junction in 0.9 mile with the BPA Road. Here you should turn left and walk this wide road under powerlines for a quarter mile to a junction with Firelane 12 at an intersection known as Hole-in-the-Park. This spot earned this name because of an inholding inside Forest Park that was slated for development – through a collaborative effort of Metro, the Portland Parks Bureau and the Friends of Forest Park, this spot was saved and added to the park.

If you've got more time, continue straight on the BPA Road another 0.25 mile to a picnic table underneath BPA's high-tension wires, where you'll find a view north to Mount Saint Helens (albeit, obstructed by powerlines). But if you're pressed for time, turn left on Firelane 12 at the Hole-in-the-Park Junction. Firelane 12 drops gradually down into the canyon, where it meets a junction with Firelane 15 at about 3.5 miles into your loop. Turn left now onto Firelane 15 and climb steeply out of the canyon for 0.4 mile until you reach a reunion with the Wildwood Trail. From here, you're back on familiar ground, as your loop is now complete. Turn right and hike 1.8 miles back to the northern terminus of the Wildwood on NW Newberry Road.

103. Forest Park: Ridge Trail Loop

	Ridge Trail Loop	Ridge Trail-Wildwood Loop
Distance:	4 mile loop	8.1 mile loop
Elevation Gain:	900 feet	1,000 feet
Trailhead Elevation:	186 feet	186 feet
Trail High Point:	1,076 feet	1,076 feet
Other Seasons:	all year	all year
Map:	Forest Park (Green Trails #426S)	Forest Park (Green Trails #426S)
Pass:	None needed.	None needed.
Drivetime from PDX:	20 minutes	20 minutes

Directions:
- From downtown Portland, drive north on US 30 to a junction with Bridge Avenue just before the St. Johns Bridge.
- Turn left here and drive up this road 0.4 mile to a small lot on your left. There is room at this lot for only a few cars (no more than 5) and no parking elsewhere near here.
- While parking along Bridge Avenue offers the easiest hike, I prefer to start this hike at Cathedral Park in St. Johns. This will add nearly 2 miles to your hike but the walk across the St. Johns Bridge is exhilarating and offers great views of Mount Hood and downtown Portland. To locate Cathedral Park, drive across the St. Johns Bridge into St. Johns and turn left at the light just after you cross the bridge. Drive north on N Ivanhoe Street for two blocks to a junction with N Baltimore Street. Drive downhill on N Baltimore Street into Cathedral Park, located under the St. Johns Bridge. Park in the large lot there. From there, walk back to the bridge on city streets and cross the bridge on foot. The Ridge Trail is located about 100 feet south of the bridge junction on Bridge Avenue.
- It is easy to take public transit on weekdays (buses run infrequently on weekends). Bus 16 runs along Bridge Avenue and over the St. Johns Bridge, while buses 4, 44 and 75 run to St. Johns. Unfortunately, the bus will not let you off on the west side of the St. Johns Bridge, so you'll have to get off in downtown St. Johns and walk across the bridge. It's not all bad- downtown St. Johns is a nice place to hang out, and there are a number of fantastic shops and restaurants should you find yourself waiting for a spell for a bus to return to your part of Portland.

Why November: When the calendar flips to November and the weather turns cold and rainy, it's time to focus your attention to hikes much closer to home. This lovely slice of Forest Park is ideal on both sunny and rainy days, offers some late fall foliage (at least early in November), cascading streams and occasional views out to the Cascades. Best of all: it is long enough to make for a full day, but close enough to get you home after just a few hours in the woods. While the loop described here is only 4 miles, hikers with a lot more time and energy can hike a much longer loop that gives an even more complete tour of this part of Forest Park.

Hike: Start at the trailhead for the Ridge Trail on the west side of Bridge Avenue. Walk up the stairs and into Forest Park on the Ridge Trail. This path leads uphill to a fantastic view across the St. Johns Bridge to Mount Saint Helens and Mount Adams. From here, the trail climbs gradually under tall Douglas firs and arching boughs of yellow and orange maple (at least, early in the month) to a junction with Leif Erikson Drive at 0.6 miles. Turn right.

This closed road connects to nearly all of Forest Park Trails while maintaining a nearly-level grade, and as such is wildly popular with bicycles and trail runners. You'll walk this road 0.9 mile to a wide and well-signed junction with NW Springville Road. Turn left here.

You'll hike up this steep stretch of road that cuts through the northern end of Forest Park. I love hiking along Springville Road, as this trail is a road with a long and interesting history. The road is one of the oldest in the state of Oregon, having been built in the 1850s to connect the farms of the Tualatin Valley with the Willamette River. You will hike the road nearly to its current terminus. Just before you reach its remote northern trailhead, turn left on Firelane 7 and almost immediately begin descending. Continue to a junction with the Ridge Trail on your left at 2.6 miles. Turn left and descend 0.8 mile to Leif Erikson. Cross Leif Erikson and continue 0.6 mile to the trailhead on Bridge Avenue.

Hikers desiring a longer hike have many options. My favorite is to descend from Firelane 7 to the Wildwood Trail via the short and slippery Trillium Trail. Locate the Trillium Trail and hike 0.2 mile downhill to the Wildwood Trail. Turn right and hike the Wildwood 1.9 miles to a junction with Firelane 5. Turn left and hike 0.3 mile downhill to a junction with Leif Erikson Road. Turn left to begin hiking north, back towards the St. Johns Bridge. Follow Leif Erikson north 2 miles, passing numerous trail junctions along the way, to a junction with the Ridge Trail on your right. Turn right and drop back down the Ridge Trail to the St. Johns Bridge.

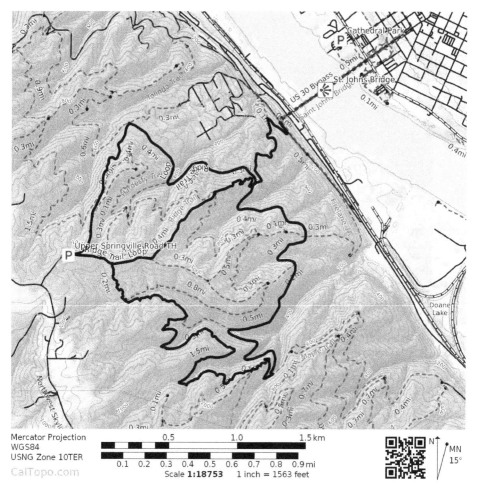

Mercator Projection
WGS84
USNG Zone 10TER
CalTopo.com

0.5   1.0   1.5 km

0.1 0.2 0.3 0.4 0.5 0.6 0.7 0.8 0.9 mi

Scale **1:18753**   1 inch = 1563 feet

N   MN
15°

104. Forest Park: Firelane 1-3 Loop

Distance: 5 mile loop
Elevation Gain: 700 feet
Trailhead elevation: 982 feet
Trail high point: 982 feet
Other seasons: all year
Map: Forest Park (Green Trails #426S)
Pass: None needed.
Drivetime from Portland: 20 minutes

Directions:
- From downtown Portland, drive north to NW Lovejoy Street and turn left to drive through the Pearl District and into NW Portland.
- Continue on NW Lovejoy beyond the junction with NW 23rd Avenue until it becomes NW Cornell Road.
- Follow NW Cornell Road through the West Hills and beyond the Audobon Society TH.
- At 2.7 miles from the corner of NW 23rd and NW Lovejoy, turn right onto NW Thompson Road.
- Follow NW Thompson Road for 1 mile to a junction on your right with NW 53rd Avenue. Turn right here.
- In just 0.1 mile, turn left at a sign for Firelane 1 and continue to a gate and small parking area that serves as the trailhead. Park on the side of the road and don't block the gate.
- **NOTE**: If you'd rather take public transportation, you can access this hike from Firelane 1's lower trailhead near the junction of NW St. Helens Road and US 30. Take Trimet's 16 bus northwest to the corner of NW Yeon Avenue and NW 44th Avenue (Stop ID 13637) and get off the bus here. Walk to the corner of NW St. Helens Road and NW Yeon Avenue (US 30) and cross NW St. Helens Road here. Turn left to walk down NW St. Helens Road. Walk about 400 feet to the poorly-marked lower Firelane 1 Trailhead. You'll walk on this brushy and occasionally steep section of Firelane 1 a total of 1.4 miles to the junction of Firelane 1 and Leif Erikson Drive. Continue hiking uphill on Firelane 1 another 0.5 mile to the junction of Firelane 1 and the Wildwood Trail, where you turn right to begin the loop described below. Overall this loop is about 1 mile longer than the loop described here but is equally satisfying.

Why November: This excellent loop passes through a somewhat-forgotten corner of Forest Park. Situated between the busy southern end of the park and the well-traveled trails branching off Saltzman Road, you'll find the peace and quiet you're seeking here. Expect trail runners as always on the Wildwood Trail and mountain bikes on the fire lanes. This is a great hike in the woods any time of year, but as with most other Forest Park hikes, it is best in the fall. In November, the trails are not as muddy as they will be in winter and spring, and you have the added bonus of seeing the last of fall's color.

Hike: Begin at the Firelane 1 gate just off NW 53rd Avenue. Walk downhill 0.4 mile to a 4-way junction with the Wildwood Trail at the start of your loop. Turn left here. If you've ever hiked along the Wildwood Trail before, this stretch is just like every other stretch of the trail- mostly level, winding in and out of gullies in deep forest. As you hike along, passing junctions with the Nature Trail and then the Chestnut Trail, you will begin to notice a number of large trees along the Wildwood. In fact, this stretch of the Wildwood contains the largest collection of old-growth trees left in Forest Park. Large maple leaves dot the forest floor but your eyes will likely be trained up at the scattered giants that tower over the trail. As with all other parts of Forest Park, you will pass many trails that offer passage down to Leif Erikson Drive, the old road that parallels the Wildwood Trail. Ignore all of these trails until you arrive at a junction with Firelane 3 at 2.5 miles. Turn right here to continue on the loop.

Firelane 3 is one of the most scenic of the firelanes- wide trails that were built as roads to allow firefighters access to the park. You'll hike downhill under arching bows of cottonwood and maple, reaching a junction with Leif Erikson Drive at just over 0.3 mile from the Wildwood Trail. Turn right to follow Leif Erikson. This stretch of Leif Erikson is my favorite in the park, as the wide trail follows a large rock wall under tall trees. Occasional openings in the trail offer views across north Portland. If you come here on the rare sunny day in November you'll marvel at how the sun filters through the forest canopy, offering bright spots in the gloom of the forest. At a little over 4 miles into the loop, reach a junction with Firelane 1 on your left- your return trail if you arrived via public transit. Continue a short ways to a junction with Firelane 1 on the right. Turn right here to hike steeply up to the Wildwood Trail, and continue on more gradual trail to the trailhead at 5 miles.

As this is Forest Park, you can extend this hike in any manner you choose- by hiking further north on the Wildwood and then dropping down to Leif Erikson on one of the many side trails in the park, or by continuing south on Leif Erikson and then returning to the Wildwood by way of the Alder or Dogwood Trails.

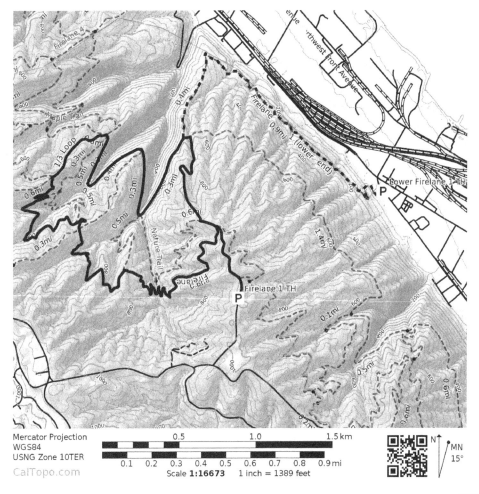

105. Milo McIver State Park

Distance: 6 mile loop
Elevation Gain: 500 feet
Trailhead elevation: 598 feet
Trail high point: 598 feet
Other seasons: all year
Map: Pick up a map of the trail system in the park
Pass: State Park day-use fee ($5) or annual pass ($30)
Drivetime from Portland: 45 minutes

Directions:
- From Portland, drive south on McLoughlin Boulevard to a junction with OR 224, and continue 5 miles to where OR 224 crosses over Interstate 205. You can also reach this point by driving I-205 south to exit 13, signed for OR 224.
- Continue on 224 for 1 mile to a junction with OR 212. Turn left here.
- Drive 1.6 miles on what is now both OR 212 and OR 224 to another junction, where you turn right to stay on OR 224.
- Drive 1.1 miles south on OR 224 to a junction signed for Carver, and McIver State Park. Fork to the right here.
- Drive 0.2 mile, crossing the Clackamas River along the way, to a junction with Spring-water Road. Turn left here at a sign for McIver State Park.
- Drive this country road 9 miles to a junction on your left signed for McIver State Park.
- Turn left and drive 0.4 mile to a fee booth. Pay the day use fee here unless you've got a State Parks pass.
- Continue a short distance to a junction on your left. Keep straight and drive a few hundred feet to another junction, where you turn left for the Milo McIver Viewpoint. This is the trailhead for this hike.

Why November: Milo McIver State Park is perfect for those November days when you want to get outside for a hike, but don't want to drive very far. The park has the feel of being further in the country than it actually is, and offers hikers miles of trails to explore just 45 minutes from downtown Portland. In November the bigleaf maple trees add color to the bucolic splendor of the park, and the various shelters and bathrooms along the loop give hikers many chances to escape the worst of November's wet, windy weather.

Hike: Follow the paved trail to Milo McIver Viewpoint, the start of the hike. The viewpoint offers a scenic vantage down to the Clackamas River as it bends around the bluffs and farmland typical of this part of the Willamette Valley. On a clear day you can see out to Mount Hood and other Cascade high points- but seeing as how you came here in November, the chances of a clear day are not very high. From the viewpoint, walk back towards the trailhead a short distance and locate the gravel trail that departs to your right. This brand-new trail, constructed in 2017, descends very gradually to the bottom of the bluff, arriving at Vortex Meadow at 0.7 mile. Now, about Vortex Meadow: In 1970, this meadow was the site of Oregon's first and only state-sponsored rock festival. President Nixon was due to visit Portland, so state officials decided to distract potential protesters by offering a music festival at then-new McIver State Park. The ruse worked, and the festival drew up to 100,000 participants in spite of a lineup that lacked national headliners. In the end, President Nixon ended up not visiting Portland. Consider this as you walk through this large meadow. Once across the meadow, you will reach a road. Cross the road, turn right and follow this trail to another junction at a little over a mile. Turn left here onto the Riverbend Trail.

The Riverbend Trail follows the base of bluffs to a junction with the Maple Ridge Trail at 1.5 miles. Along this trail you will have a few opportunities to shorten your hike but the recommended option follows the Maple Ridge Trail for its entirety, all the way around the bend in the Clackamas River. The trail here passes through dark, gloomy forest typical of the Willamette Valley's forest preserves, with lots of graceful deciduous trees and mossy Douglas firs towering over the trail. At 3.1 miles, the Maple Ridge Trail reaches a paved road by the Clackamas River. Here you will need to locate the Riverbend Trail on the opposite side of the road, but you may first be tempted to turn right on the road and locate the bathrooms and picnic shelter just a couple hundred yards up the road. This makes the hike's most convenient rest stop.

From the picnic area or from the end of the Maple Ridge Trail, locate the Riverbend Trail as it follows the Clackamas River around its wide bend. You'll also be following Milo McIver State Park's famed disc golf course, but you're doubtful to see too many people out playing in November. You will follow the Riverbend Trail for approximately 1.5 level miles along the river to a road crossing just after the trail leaves the river. Cross the road and reach the same trail junction you passed earlier just after you crossed Vortex Meadow. Here the signs encourage you to hike the Vortex Loop through the meadow, but it's even easier to turn continue straight, now on familiar trail through the meadow. If you decide to loop around the meadow, the trail becomes vague and you may be required to backtrack or hike off trail through the meadow until you reach the trail descending down from the bluffs. From the edge of the meadow, follow the gravel trail back up to the viewpoint, at which point you turn right to return to the trail.

106. Cape Horn

Distance: 7 mile loop
Elevation Gain: 1,200 feet
Trailhead elevation: 491 feet
Trail high point: 1,311 feet
Other seasons: August- January (lower portion closed Feb-July for habitat protection)
Map: none needed
Pass: none needed
Drivetime from Portland: 40 minutes

Directions:
* From Portland drive north on Interstate 205 across the river into Washington.
* At exit 27, just across the Columbia River, leave the freeway and exit onto WA 14.
* Drive 19.5 miles east on WA 14 to a sign for the Cape Horn Trailhead. Turn left onto Salmon Falls Road.
* Immediate turn right onto Canyon Creek Road and turn into the trailhead here.

Why November: The Cape Horn Loop is one of the most famous in all the Columbia River Gorge. The views up and down the Columbia River and convenient access make for an enticing experience, especially for novice hikers. The best time to do this hike is in the fall, when the huge bigleaf maples along the trail feature great displays of fall color. Like many other Gorge hikes, this is a great destination on rainy days but an even better destination on the rare November sunny day. Another good time to come here is in April when the forest floor is filled with blooming blue camas, but the lower portion of this loop is closed for protect nesting falcons, so you can only do part of the hike.

Hike: Begin by crossing the road from the signboards at the trailhead, where you will locate a new sign and immediately reach a junction. Turn right to hike the loop in a counterclockwise direction. The trail switchbacks uphill amongst large bigleaf maples, whose fall color typically peaks sometime between the last week of October and the first two weeks of November. The wide and well-graded trail eventually tops out at 1.3 miles from the trailhead at the trail's high point of just over 1,300 feet. From here, you'll eventually reach an old road-bed that takes you to a road crossing at 2.1 miles. Cross the road and locate the trail on the other side. From here you'll follow an old road through prairies with views out to the Oregon side of the Gorge until the trail drops back into the woods, reaching the main Cape Horn viewpoint at 2.6 miles. When I first hiked this loop, it was a combination of official trail and unofficial scramble trails. Over the past 5 years, the Friends of the Gorge and Forest Service have constructed an outstanding loop trail and a series of excellent viewpoints.

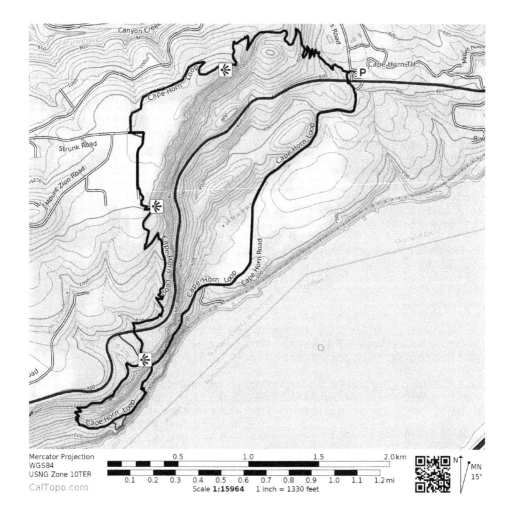

Scale **1:15964** 1 inch = 1330 feet

While it can be tempting to just turn around here and declare victory, I suggest continuing as the best viewpoints and the hike's waterfall are still ahead. Follow the trail as it drops downhill through the woods to a tunnel underneath WA 14 at 3.6 miles. From here, the trail passes a few excellent viewpoints out to the Columbia River before settling into a long traverse downhill to almost river level.

One of the advantages of this hike is that unlike many other Gorge hikes, you actually get fairly close to the Columbia River. The trail finally bottoms out at 4.7 miles, and soon passes the hike's wispy waterfall.

The falls runs fairly low even in November but this is a scenic spot just the same. From here the trail passes through a talus slope, first climbing and then dropping steeply to trail's end at 5.5 miles. From here, follow Cape Horn Road 1.5 miles back uphill to a trail on your left. Turn left, walk through a tunnel under WA 14, and then turn right to return to the trailhead.

107. Multnomah-Wahkeena Loop

Distance: 5.8 mile loop
Elevation Gain: 1,500 feet
Trailhead elevation: 50 feet
Trail high point: 1,546 feet
Other seasons: all year
Map: Bridal Veil (Green Trails #428)
Pass: None needed
Drivetime from Portland: 35 minutes

Directions:
- Drive east from Portland on Interstate 84 to Multnomah Falls, exit 31. Beware that this is a left-lane exit.

Why November: Among the most famous hikes in the Gorge, the loop connecting Wahkeena Falls and Multnomah Falls is great at any time. Maybe the best time to visit is in November, when you can take in the fall colors and graceful waterfalls for which this area is known. Just make sure to bring a rain coat, rain pants and boots, because you're probably going to get wet.

Note: Like most other hikes in the western Gorge, this area was burned during the Eagle Creek Fire in September 2017. The extent of the damage is unknown as of press time; expect these trails to be closed until at least Spring 2018.

Hike: While many people begin at Multnomah Falls and hike the loop in a clockwise direction, I like to hike up Wahkeena Falls and save the paved trail above Multnomah for the end, followed up by a cup of coffee or lunch at the Multnomah Falls Lodge. From

the huge parking lot at Multnomah Falls, walk through the tunnel under the freeway and cross the Historic Highway to the lodge. Turn right and look for the Gorge Trail heading west from the far lodge parking lot. This trail parallels the Historic Highway at a tasteful distance for 0.3 mile to Wahkeena Falls. Once at Wahkeena, follow the paved trail uphill to the base of the falls. Wahkeena means "most beautiful", and once you've seen it, you will agree with this assessment. This is my favorite waterfall in the Gorge.

Beyond Wahkeena, the paved trail begins ascending the canyon walls via a series of tight switchbacks. Once you reach the top of the canyon, the pavement ends at a junction with the short trail to Lemmon's Viewpoint. Take a minute to check out the view and then turn uphill to continue the hike. The trail follows Wahkeena Creek upstream, crossing it on a stone bridge and paralleling this rushing torrent through a narrow slot canyon. This is one of the nicest stretches of trail in the Gorge. Cross the creek again on

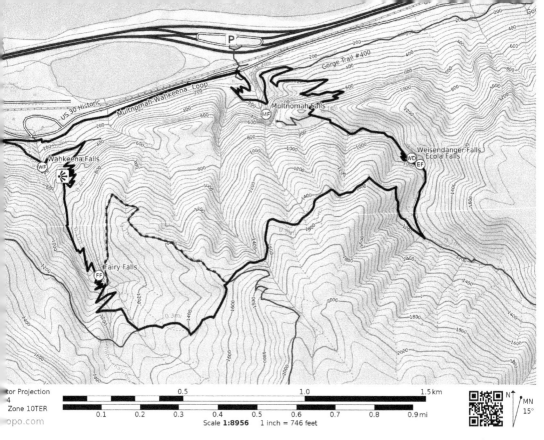

tor Projection
4
Zone 10TER
opo.com

Scale **1:8956**   1 inch = 746 feet

another stone bridge and begin an uphill traverse beside the cascading creek, which stair-steps down a mossy rockslide in a most photogenic fashion. Continue uphill some more until you at last leave Wahkeena Creek. Shortly after this point, reach Fairy Falls. If you've ever seen a photo of this famous falls you may be surprised to discover that at 20 feet tall, it is quite small. The beauty of Fairy Falls is in the micro, not the macro. Shortly thereafter, reach a junction with the Vista Point Trail. This trail goes to the same place you're going, but for now stay on the Wahkeena Trail. Switchback uphill some more and at last reach the top of the canyon at a junction with the trail to Angels Rest. Turn left.

From here, you'll hike through deep forest on a wide trail lined with ferns. Meet the Vista Point Trail again in 0.3 mile and continue hiking east. The trail begins to lose elevation, dropping in huge switchbacks towards Multnomah Creek. Reach a junction with the Larch Mountain Trail just above Multnomah Creek in 0.7 mile from the past trail junction. Turn left. You will descend on a trail that follows tumbling Multnomah Creek downstream. Pass above Ecola Falls on your right (the falls remains mostly out of sight) and switchback on muddy trail down to the base of Weisendanger Falls. The trail then passes through a cavern that overhangs the trail; turn around and look upstream to a most pleasing sight: the curve of Multnomah Creek through this narrow canyon, ending with Weisendanger Falls. This spot gets me every single time.

From here, follow Multnomah Creek downstream to the top of Multnomah Falls, where the trail becomes paved again. You will start to see tourists here. Continue downhill on the paved trail for eleven switchbacks to the base of the falls (expect to get soaked in any weather), and then to the lodge.

108. Benson Plateau via the PCT

Distance: 14 miles out and back
Elevation Gain: 3,800 feet
Trailhead elevation: 221 feet
Trail high point: 3,975 feet
Other seasons: May- October
Map: Bonneville Dam (Green Trails #429)
Pass: NW Forest Pass
Drivetime from Portland: 50 minutes

Directions to Herman Creek Trailhead:
- Drive Interstate 84 East from Portland to exit 44 for Cascade Locks.
- Drive through town, east, and then pass under the freeway at the far end of town.
- Continue straight and east on Frontage Road.
- After 2 miles you will come to a sign for Herman Creek Campground.
- In the winter you may need to park here as the road is gated; otherwise, drive up the campground road to the trailhead.

Why November: The Pacific Crest Trail is among the most famous trails in the country, if not the world, and so it stands to reason that it would be uniformly popular everywhere- especially in the Columbia River Gorge. And yet, this convenient stretch of the PCT south of Cascade Locks is almost deserted; through-hikers avoid it, opting to hike down Eagle Creek instead, and area hikers avoid it due to rumors of its tedium. In truth, this is not among the best hikes in the Gorge. But come November, when fog hangs at tree level in the Gorge, the leaves are dropping and the days turn cold, this is a lovely hike that offers big elevation gain without ever feeling too challenging. Of course, the later in November you do this hike, the more likely you are to encounter snow. You need to be prepared for this possibility and be prepared to turn around if you lose the trail in the snow.

Hiking along the Benson Plateau on a snowy, windy, cold day.

Note: Like most other hikes in the western Gorge, this area was burned during the Eagle Creek Fire in September 2017. The extent of the damage is unknown as of press time; expect these trails to be closed until at least Spring 2018.

Hike: Begin at the Herman Creek Trailhead. Follow the trail uphill to a crossing of the powerline corridor road. Locate the trail on the other side of the road, and commence climbing uphill on a wide trail. At 0.7 mile, reach a fork in the trail. Fork to the right on the Herman Bridge Trail and descend 0.4 mile to the metal bridge over raging Herman Creek. Once across the bridge, you will begin a gentle climb out of the canyon. The trail gains 450 feet of elevation over the next 0.9 mile, weaving through mossy, misty woods to a junction with the Pacific Crest Trail at 2 miles. Turn left here.

The Gorge is almost always dark and foggy in November, and this is an excellent trail for such days. The PCT winds uphill at an easy grade, gaining 2,800 feet over the next 5 miles on its way up the Benson Plateau. The mist hangs almost at tree level, accentuating the last of autumn's color. As you ascend, you'll pass one viewpoint down to Herman Creek and out to Cascade Locks. From here, you'll begin to notice the beargrass lining the trail, your clue that you're almost there. Reach the Benson Plateau at 6 miles into the hike. The plateau is an eerie place, especially in the fall. The trees are tall and thin and the trails straight as they cut across this strangely flat place high in the Gorge. Not long after the trail tops out, pass a trail junction on your right and reach a campsite. Most hikers will want to turn around here.

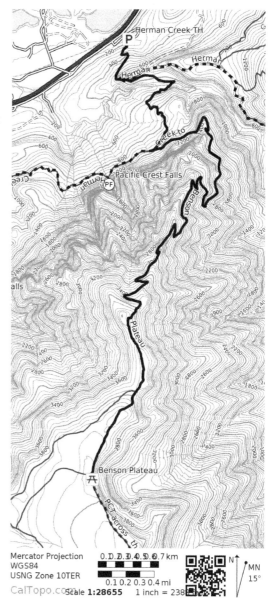

From here the Pacific Crest Trail cuts a straight line through the Benson, passing junctions with several marked connector trails. Later in November you are almost certain to encounter snow up here (if you haven't already). Here's one thing you need to know about navigating in the snow: if you aren't sure where the trail is, **TURN AROUND**. There's very little up here you haven't seen before, and as the forest looks strangely similar throughout the plateau, it would be very easy to get lost. This lesson is equally applicable if you hit snow before you reach the top of the plateau, too.

Return the way you came.

Mercator Projection
WGS84
USNG Zone 10TER

CalTopo.com

0.1 0.2 0.3 0.4 0.5 0.6 0.7 km
0.1 0.2 0.3 0.4 mi
Scale **1:28655**   1 inch = 238

MN
15°

109. Dry Creek Falls

	via PCT	via Herman Creek	Shuttle
Distance:	5.2 miles out / back	9.4 miles out / back	7.3 miles one way
Elevation Gain:	800 feet	1,000 feet	1,600 feet
Trailhead Elevation:	141 feet	221 feet	221 feet
Trail High Point:	846 feet	956 feet	956 feet
Other Seasons:	all year	all year	all year
Map:	Bonneville Dam (Green Trails #429)	Bonneville Dam (Green Trails #429)	Bonneville Dam (Green Trails #429)
Pass:	NW Forest Pass	NW Forest Pass	NW Forest Pass
Drivetime from PDX:	45 minutes	50 minutes	50 minutes

Directions to PCT Trailhead in Cascade Locks:
- Drive Interstate 84 east from Portland to Cascade Locks.
- At exit 44, leave the freeway and drive downhill into Cascade Locks.
- At a sign for Bridge of the Gods, turn right and drive uphill towards the bridge.
- Turn right into the PCT parking lot on the right.

Directions to Herman Creek Trailhead:
- Drive Interstate 84 East from Portland to exit 44 for Cascade Locks.
- Drive through town, east, and then pass under the freeway at the far end of town. Continue straight and east on Frontage Road.
- After 2 miles you will come to a sign for Herman Creek Campground.
- Turn right and drive uphill into the campground and trailhead.

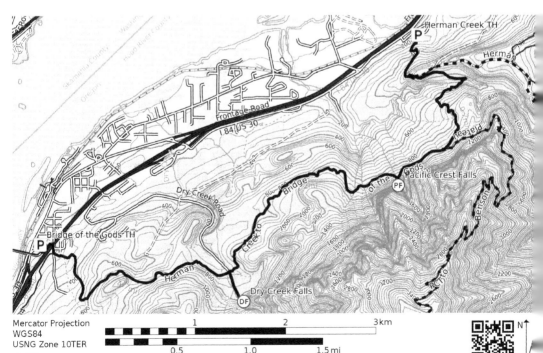

Mercator Projection
WGS84
USNG Zone 10TER
CalTopo.com

Scale **1:29697**   1 inch = 2475 feet

Why November: Dry Creek Falls is tucked away in a quiet side canyon south of Cascade Locks, yet still manages to be a popular hiking destination even in the fall and winter. The last of the yellow and orange maple leaves hang in the trees, the creeks run high and everything seems misty and mysterious. Most people visit the falls via a boring but perfectly cromulent section of the Pacific Crest Trail departing from the heart of Cascade Locks. With more time and energy, you can hike here from Herman Creek for a longer, more satisfying hike. The best plan is to establish a car shuttle and do this entire hike one way.

Note: Like most other hikes in the western Gorge, this area was burned during the Eagle Creek Fire in September 2017. The extent of the damage is unknown as of press time; expect these trails to be closed until at least Spring 2018.

Hike: Whether you are doing this hike as an out and back or a car shuttle, I recommend starting at the Herman Creek Trailhead. If you'd rather start at the trailhead in Cascade Locks, skip to the end of this entry. From the trailhead set off on a muddy trail that climbs steeply uphill to a powerline crossing. Locate the trail on the far end of the clearing and continue hiking uphill. At 0.6 mile, reach a fork in the trail. Turn right on the Herman Bridge Trail (406E) and quickly descend to a large metal bridge over Herman Creek. In January the creek will be a raging torrent, and you will appreciate the existence of the bridge. Cross the bridge and begin a steady climb through a peaceful forest. At 1.9 miles from the trailhead, reach a junction with the Pacific Crest Trail. Turn right here.

The PCT immediately traverses a huge talus slope, offering views out to Table Mountain and down to Cascade Locks. Not far from here, you will cross a creek in a gully just below cascading Pacific Crest Falls. Agile hikers can scramble closer to the base of the falls but it is not easy! Not far past the falls, the trail passes a series of rock pinnacles. Take a few minutes to investigate this fascinating spot. Beyond the pinnacles, the trail passes another huge talus slope and enters a lovely woods of older Douglas fir and huge ferns. The trail passes by a fern-covered depression and then drops to a bridge over Dry Creek at 4.4 miles. Cross the bridge and come to a crossing of a closed road. Turn left here and walk this road 0.3 mile to the base of the 75 foot falls. The falls and creek were at one time Cascade Locks' water source; you will note the concrete water works at the base of the falls. In spite of man's hand this is a wildly scenic place, and you will wish to spend some time relaxing at the base, even in winter. Unless you managed to set up a car shuttle (which requires at least two vehicles and some advance planning), return the way you came.

Dry Creek Falls

If you set up a car shuttle, return to the PCT and turn left to continue hiking towards Cascade Locks. The next 2.6 miles to Cascade Locks are muddy and not all that interesting, but because the hike is shorter and the access easier, you will meet many more people here. The trail passes through second-growth forest as the freeway noise becomes more and more noticeable, ending seemingly at a dirt street near the freeway at 7.2 miles from the Herman Creek Trailhead. From here continue another 0.1 mile to the trailhead at Bridge of the Gods.

110. Herman Creek

	Nick Eaton Falls	Forks of Herman Creek
Distance:	4.4 miles out and back	9 miles out and back
Elevation Gain:	600 feet	1,800 feet
Trailhead Elevation:	240 feet	240 feet
Trail High Point:	812 feet	1,522 feet
Other Seasons:	all year	all year
Map:	Bonneville Dam (Green Trails #429)	Bonneville Dam (Green Trails #429)
Pass:	NW Forest Pass	NW Forest Pass
Drivetime from PDX:	50 minutes	50 minutes

Directions to Herman Creek Trailhead:
- Drive Interstate 84 East from Portland to exit 44 for Cascade Locks.
- Drive through town, east, and then pass under the freeway at the far end of town. Continue straight and east on Frontage Road.
- After 2 miles you will come to a sign for Herman Creek Campground.
- In the winter you may need to park here as the road is gated; otherwise, drive up the campground road to the trailhead.

Why November: Herman Creek is under-appreciated compared to other trails in the Gorge. There are no dazzling waterfalls, no huge views and no obvious destinations to draw the crowds. Many use the trail to make connections to other places in the Gorge, such as Indian Point, Green Point Mountain and the Benson Plateau (all of which are in this book). Yet, in November, the trail reaches its scenic apex as the rains return. Fog often shrouds the Gorge as the winter rains return, while the leaves retain their fall colors into the middle of November. Plan on a trip here for the first part of November, and prepare to get wet – you're almost certain to get rained on most days.

Note: Like most other hikes in the western Gorge, this area was burned during the Eagle Creek Fire in September 2017. The extent of the damage is unknown as of press time; expect these trails to be closed until at least Spring 2018.

Hike: From the Herman Creek Trailhead, follow the trail as it climbs steeply uphill to a junction at the powerline corridor. Continue straight and climb some more, reaching a junction with the Herman Bridge Trailhead at 0.7 mile. Keep left and continue hiking uphill at a steady pace to a four-way trail junction at Herman Camp, 1.4 miles from the trailhead. Keep straight and begin hiking into Herman Creek's canyon. In spite of its name the Herman Creek Trail rarely approaches the creek, staying a few hundred feet above creek level in the canyon. Mist hangs in the forest here on most November days, sometimes almost down to ground level. The effect can be comforting, or spooky depending on your point of view.

At 2.2 miles from the trailhead, the trail crosses an unnamed creek at the base of a tall, wispy waterfall known as Nick Eaton Falls. Though wildly scenic, this is a difficult waterfall to photograph. For hikers looking for a shorter, easier day, this is a good place to turn around. If you're planning on a longer hike, continue. The trail curves into Camp Creek's canyon, finally crossing the creek at 2.8 miles. This crossing can pose a challenge – if it has rained a lot recently, expect a creative rock hop to cross with dry feet. From here, the trail curves around the south side of Camp Creek's canyon, regaining its position in the woods a few hundred feet above the creek.

At 4 miles, reach a junction on your left with the Casey Creek Way Trail, a steep connector to the top of Nick Eaton Ridge to the east. Look for a campsite by the right side of the trail just a short distance after this junction – if you're planning to hike down to the forks of Herman Creek, look for an unsigned trail on your right at this campsite that leaves the Herman Creek Trail. This trail, a snippet of the abandoned West Fork Herman Creek Trail, dives steeply downhill to the confluence of both forks of Herman Creek; a short bush-whack will lead you to a view of a pair of waterfalls on the east fork. This is a dramatic spot, easily the best goal for a reasonable hike in the Herman Creek canyon.

Return the way you came. Hikers desiring an even longer day can continue further up Herman Creek's canyon, passing Slide Creek Falls and eventually emerging at Cedar Swamp Camp at a little over 7 miles from the trailhead. Expect to encounter snow beyond this point in November. The Herman Creek Trail ends at Wahtum Lake, a little over 10 miles from the trailhead.

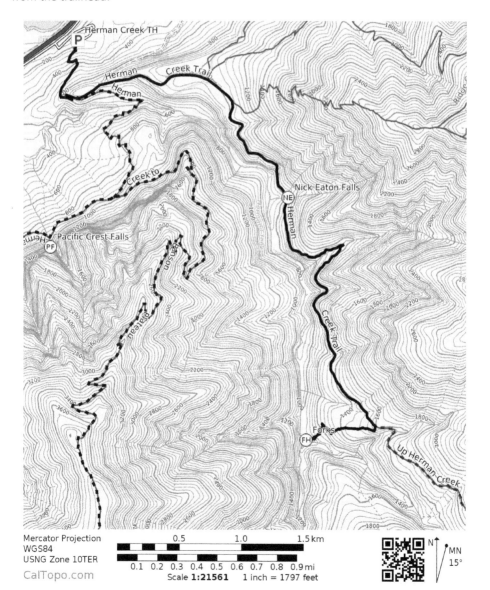

DECEMBER

		Distance	EV Gain	Drive
111.	Cape Disappointment	3.5 mi	1,000 ft	150 min
112.	Fort Stevens State Park	7.4 mi	100 ft	120 min
113.	Gnat Creek	7.6 mi	900 ft	100 ft
114.	Triple C Loop	2.2 mi	300 ft	60 min
115.	Powell Butte	5.6 mi	800 ft	25 min
116.	Mount Talbert	2.6 mi	700 ft	25 min
117.	Scouters Mountain	1.2 mi	200 ft	30 min
118.	Salmon River Trail	9.2 mi	400 ft	70 min
119.	Shellburg Falls	5.7 mi	700 ft	85 min
120.	Silver Falls State Park	7.9 mi	1,000 ft	75 min

December is always a chaotic time. The holidays are approaching, and with it holiday shopping, travel plans and even finals. Sometimes it's hard to find the time to get outside. That's why so many of the hikes presented here are located close to Portland. The three hikes in the Metro area presented here are fantastic escapes from the holiday rush, and are great when you only have a couple hours to get outside. I cherish these quick get-aways, and you will too.

Speaking of escapes, there are also two hikes along the Coast near Astoria. They are here for three reasons very specific to December: First of all, US 30 to Astoria stays lower than every other highway to the Coast, and snow and ice are rare on the highway; second of all, I love visiting Astoria in December, when all the tourists are gone and I just need to get away from it all; and last but not least, December was when Lewis and Clark arrived in this area back in 1805. Both hikes near Astoria presented here have connections to the journey and winter of Lewis and Clark, and history buffs will appreciate walking in the footsteps of the Corps of Discovery. Plan a weekend trip out here around the holidays; for the best experience, reserve one of the yurts available at both Cape Disappointment and Fort Stevens State Parks.

December also features some of the worst weather of the year, and some of the shortest days. Snow is a threat almost everywhere outside the Portland metro area, and the long nights and cold mornings make it hard to get out of bed and go hiking. While you can set your watch by the predictability of the rain, we are sometimes blessed with seven to ten days of cold, crisp and clear weather in December- these are some of my favorite times to get out and go hiking. I love packing a thermos of coffee, my camera and my down jacket, and just getting outside. It's the best!

When traveling in December, you should always remember to keep your car packed with extra blankets, extra food and anything else you might need in case of snow, ice or car trouble. While all of the hikes offered here stay close to well-maintained highways, you should always assume nobody will come to your rescue. And if the weather outside is truly frightful, well you should stay inside and dream of where to go hiking when the weather warms up.

Photo on opposite page: Behind South Falls on a day after it snowed (Hike 120)

111. Cape Disappointment

	Cape Disappointment	McKenzie Head
Distance:	3 miles out and back	0.5 mile out and back
Elevation Gain:	800 feet	200 feet
TH Elevation:	21 feet	19 feet
Trail High Point:	226 feet	210 feet
Other Seasons:	all year	all year
Map:	None needed.	None needed.
Pass:	WA Discovery Pass ($10/day)	WA Discovery Pass ($10/day)
Drivetime from PDX:	150 minutes	150 minutes

Directions:
- From Portland, drive US 30 north and west approximately 90 miles to Astoria.
- At a junction at the west end of downtown Astoria, turn right onto US 101 to follow the Astoria-Megler Bridge over the Columbia River. This bridge is 4.3 miles long, much of it not high above the river, and may unnerve some drivers.
- On the far end of the bridge, turn left to stay on US 101.
- Follow US 101 north for 11 miles to the town of Ilwaco.
- At the second light in downtown Ilwaco, turn left at a sign for Cape Disappointment State Park to follow 2nd Avenue. Follow this road 2 miles to the state park.

Why December: Cape Disappointment is just that much of the year; there are better hikes along the Coast, and it's a long drive from Portland. But plan on a trip here in December, when high winds and heavy rain batter the Coast; the short hikes here are ideal for a rainy day. Furthermore, Cape Disappointment is historically significant; Lewis and Clark camped here on their journey before crossing the river to the Oregon side of the Columbia. If the weather is truly nasty, you can spend the day at the Lewis and Clark Museum here, a museum worth the long drive from Portland.

Cape Disappointment Hike: Although the short hike to Cape Disappointment from Waikiki Beach intersects several parking areas, you will appreciate the longer hike, which passes though groves of Sitka Spruce, offers several lovely views and visits one of the most scenic spots on the Washington Coast. Plan on a workout, though; this hike offers constant ups and downs that make it more difficult than you might imagine.

Begin at the Waikiki Beach Trailhead and walk the paved walkway directly away from the trailhead towards the forest. When you reach the forest, look for a wide trail that climbs and descends a rollercoaster of hills above the Pacific Ocean. Side trails offer occasional views, but nothing spectacular. At about 0.7 mile, reach the Lewis and Clark Museum. I strongly recommend stopping at the museum, but you might want to wait until after the hike, lest you enter with muddy boots and leave impatient to finish your hike. Follow the trail around the museum / interpretive center and commence another steep and muddy descent to a small parking area next to a Coast Guard station. From here, the trail passes above Dead Man's Cove, a small but spectacular beach tucked underneath Cape Disappointment's cliffs. A rough trail leads down to the cove, but be very careful – it is steep, muddy and the cove is dangerous at high tide. From the cove, follow the trail as it picks up a paved road coming up from the Coast Guard station and follows it to Cape Disappointment's lighthouse. The lighthouse, built in 1856, is the oldest functioning lighthouse on the West Coast. A building next to the lighthouse allows Coast Guard employees to

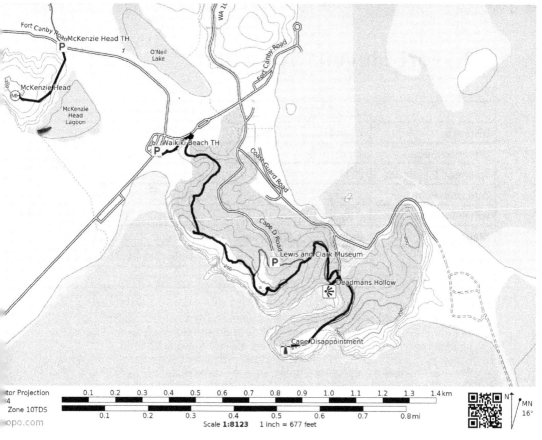

tor Projection
4
Zone 10TDS
opo.com

| 0.1 | 0.2 | 0.3 | 0.4 | 0.5 | 0.6 | 0.7 | 0.8 | 0.9 | 1.0 | 1.1 | 1.2 | 1.3 | 1.4 km |

| 0.1 | 0.2 | 0.3 | 0.4 | 0.5 | 0.6 | 0.7 | 0.8 mi |

Scale **1:8123**   1 inch = 677 feet

N MN 16°

watch ships entering the Columbia from the ocean. This is the most dangerous stretch of water in the world for ships for a multitude of reasons, among them weather, the current of the Columbia River and shallow waters at points. If you see a ship coming into Astoria's harbor, take a few minutes to watch it come into harbor – it's a fascinating and even thrilling experience. Return the way you came.

McKenzie Head Hike: This short trail takes you up a handful of switchbacks to the top of McKenzie Head, where you will find battlements leftover from World War II. Lewis and Clark also made the trip up to the top of McKenzie Head during their stay in the Cape Disappointment area in November and December 1805. From the trailhead, follow the wide trail uphill to the top of the head, where you will find views south to the Columbia River and out to Tillamook Head. Keen eyes can spot the Tillamook Head Lighthouse, known locally as "Terrible Tilly". Most interesting up here is the concrete bunker underneath the summit's head. A remnant of World War II fortifications, the bunker is fun to explore; just bring a light. Return the way you came.

Lewis and Clark Interpretive Center: The museum you passed on your hike is worth the stop, either during your hike or after it. You will be able to walk through the journey of Lewis and Clark from the Mississippi to the Pacific, including their stop at Cape Disappointment in November and December 1805. The exhibits go a long way in explaining the difficulty of the journey. History buffs will love this place, but almost anybody will enjoy it. There aren't many better places to warm up after a hike on a cold, wet December day. As of this writing the center is open Wednesday through Sunday from 10AM to 5PM.

112. Fort Stevens State Park

	Clatsop Spit	Coffenbury Lake
Distance:	4.8 miles out and back	2.6 mile loop
Elevation Gain:	0 feet	100 feet
Trailhead Elevation:	19 feet	28 feet
Trail High Point:	22 feet	79 feet
Other Seasons:	all year	all year
Map:	get map at park entrance	get map at park entrance
Pass:	State Park Pass / entrance fee	State Park Pass / entrance fee
Drivetime from PDX:	120 minutes	110 minutes

Directions:
- From Portland, drive US 26 west 73 miles to its end at a junction south of Seaside.
- Exit onto US 101 north and drive through Seaside and Gearhart for 13.3 miles to a junction with Columbia Beach Lane, signed for Fort Stevens State Park.
- Follow signs north and west for 3.9 miles to Fort Stevens State Park. Along the way the road changes names several times, so make sure you follow signs where possible.
- Turn left into Fort Stevens State Park. Make sure you get a map at the park entrance!
- Coffenbury Lake is located near the campground; follow signs to the lake, and then turn left into the parking lot at the lake.
- From Coffenbury Lake, keep straight on the park road and follow signs for "Shipwreck". Reach the parking lot at road's end, just 0.6 mile from Coffenbury Lake.
- To locate Clatsop Spit, drive back to the first junction you meet and turn left. Drive 1.2 miles north to a junction with Jetty Road, and turn left. Drive 3.4 miles to road's end at Area D, a large parking lot that offers access to Clatsop Spit.
- During icy periods in the winter, you may wish to avoid driving over the Coast Range and instead take US 30 to Astoria. This route is 30 minutes longer but much lower in elevation. From Portland, drive US 30 north and then west approximately 90 miles to Astoria. At a junction with US 101 under the Megler Bridge, continue south on US 101 over Youngs Bay and into Warrenton. At the first junction in Warrenton, turn right at a sign for Fort Stevens State Park and follow signs 6 miles to the park.

Why December: The northwestern tip of Oregon has a rich history. Lewis and Clark spent the winter of 1805 at nearby Fort Clatsop; Fort Stevens was constructed during the Civil War and served as a bulwark against potential British attacks during the 19th Century; the ship the Peter Iredale wrecked along the beach near Fort Stevens in 1906; and the fort came under attack from a Japanese submarine during World War II. With all this in mind, history buffs will want to visit, and hikers will enjoy the park too. I like coming here in December to commemorate the Lewis and Clark expedition, but also to experience the park at its quietest time of the year. These two hikes offer a full day of easy wandering with many rewards; plan on capping off your day with a visit to the wreck of the Peter Iredale to complete your journey.

Clatsop Spit Hike: The hike to the edge of Clatsop Spit, the northwestern tip of Oregon and the point where the Columbia River meets the Pacific Ocean, is about as straightforward as hikes get: you just follow the beach until you can't anymore. You may want to consult a tide table before you visit, as the hike is easier during low tide. From the Area D parking lot, follow a trailhead downhill to the beach and turn left. Follow the beach as best you can (during high tide you may be forced into the dunes and forest at times to avoid the rising tide) north and west towards the obvious end at the South Jetty. You are in fact following the mouth of the Columbia River, a violent stretch of water that is nearly seven miles wide at this point. Hikers will have fun watching ships make their way out to sea through dangerously choppy waters. Keen eyes can pick out the Cape Disappointment lighthouse (see Hike 111) on the other side of the river. Driving on the beach is allowed at this time of year but you won't see too many vehicles here, and they are rarely as intrusive as they are on wider, longer beaches. You'll likely have little company at all, save for the birds, and the beach, and the wind. At 2.4 miles reach the jetty, at the northwestern tip of Oregon. It is a mesmerizing, violent and dangerous place: watch huge waves from the Pacific crash into and over the jetty from the relative safety of the dunes. Few places feel like the edge of the world more than this spot. **DO NOT UNDER ANY CIRCUMSTANCES ATTEMPT TO WALK ON THE JETTY.** To the south you will see the viewing blind of Area C (a lot you passed on the drive to the trailhead), but reaching this trailhead from the jetty requires crossing a shallow lake, water that is deposited by the huge waves crashing over the jetty. It's better to just return the way you came. On the way back you'll have views south to Astoria, the Megler Bridge and huge Saddle Mountain (Hike 51). If the tide is coming in you can easily head cross-country to intersect Jetty Road, but this isn't preferable other than in times of high water.

Coffenbury Lake Hike: If you've got more time and energy, consider hiking this 2.6 mile loop around a tranquil lake near Fort Stevens' huge campground. From the parking lot on the north side of the lake, locate the trail on the right side of the lake. In December it will be muddy in spots, but not overly so for the most part compared to most places along the Coast (it's still muddy). The trail passes near the shore of the lake, occasionally ducking into secluded groves of Sitka Spruce and Douglas fir. Along the way keep your eyes out for birds – we saw a heron here when we visited. At a trail junction at the far end of the lake, fork left to continue your loop. The south end of the lake is quite muddy but this stretch is mercifully short, and soon you'll be hiking north on your way back to the trailhead. Follow the trail through the park's picnic area, and finally around the north end of the lake and back to your car.

Wreck of the Peter Iredale: Before you leave the park, make sure to stop at the wreck of the Peter Iredale, a ship that crashed into the beach here in 1906. The rusting hull of the ship is buried in the beach here and is an exceptionally scenic (and exceptionally popular) destination. Follow signs from Coffenbury Lake that say "Shipwreck" to road's end at the beach. The ship is difficult to visit at high tide but is otherwise a short and easy walk.

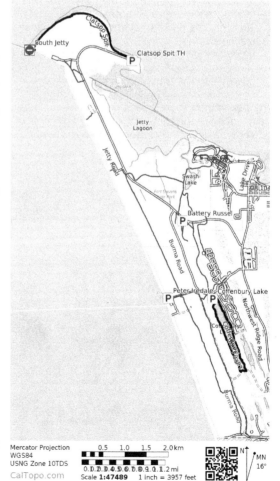

Mercator Projection
WGS84
USNG Zone 10TDS
CalTopo.com
0.5   1.0   1.5   2.0km
0.0.0.0.0.0.0.0.0.1.2 mi
Scale **1:47489**   1 inch = 3957 feet
N
MN
16°

113. Gnat Creek

	Gnat Creek from Fish Hatchery	Gnat Creek (from lower TH)
Distance:	5 miles out and back	7.6 miles out and back
Elevation Gain:	700 feet	900 feet
Trailhead Elevation:	283 feet	121 feet
Trail High Point:	797 feet	797 feet
Other Seasons:	all year	all year
Map:	None needed.	None needed.
Pass:	None needed.	None needed.
Drivetime from PDX:	100 minutes	100 minutes

Directions:
- From the St. Johns Bridge at the north end of Portland, drive US 30 north and west approximately 68.4 miles to a turnoff for Gnat Creek Fish Hatchery on your left. The fish hatchery is approximately 20 miles east of Astoria.
- Turn into the parking lot and park in the small lot near an information kiosk and trailhead.
- If you are opting for the longer hike, continue 1 mile west from the fish hatchery on US 30 to a turnoff signed for Gnat Creek Campground. Turn right and drive 0.1 mile downhill to the trailhead on your right.

Why December: There's something to be said about hiking in the woods, along a rushing stream, deep in the throes of winter. So many of our classic winter hikes fit this profile, and yet for a variety of reasons so few of these classics are located in the Coast Range.

While this lovely hike along Gnat Creek east of Astoria cannot compare to Salmon River, Silver Falls and other winter classics, it can hold its own in the scenery department and offers a considerable degree of solitude – something you will appreciate a great deal.

Hike: At the fish hatchery parking lot, you will see a trail sign with a gate marking the start of the Upper Gnat Creek Trailhead. This is the official trailhead, but it takes you into a labyrinth of interpretive trails that can be confusing – it is best to save this for the end of your hike. Instead walk along the fish hatchery road about 200 yards until you reach Barrier Falls, a 5-foot drop on Gnat Creek that is highly scenic. Take a moment to check out the falls. You will notice a trail below you, next to the falls; this is part of the interpretive trail that you should save until the end of your hike. For now, walk up the road a little more until you reach the Upper Gnat Creek Trail on your right. Turn right here and quickly reach an unmarked trail junction near a large metal sculpture of Sasquatch – this should be enough of a reason to do this hike! Fork to the left here to continue your hike.

The trail parallels Gnat Creek from a wide bench well above creek level for the first 1.6 miles of the hike. At first you will pass through some old clearcuts, and most of the time you will be far enough away from the creek to question why I would consider putting this hike into this book. But soon you will enter some lovely forest, and the trail drops down to creek level and all is forgiven. The last half-mile of this trail is a delight, as you follow Gnat Creek through a lovely and remote forest. Reach a fork in the trail, at which you keep right; this is a short loop at trail's end. Pass by Bigfoot Creek, and soon reach a picnic site at a wooden bench just above Gnat Creek. Just down from here is another wooden bench – both make for great lunch destinations. Plans call for an extension of the trail another 2 miles upstream to 100-foot Gnat Creek Falls, but as of this writing the falls is located on private property and visiting is highly discouraged. Return the way you came to Barrier Falls. If you've got some extra time, take a few minutes to hike the interpretive trails around Barrier Falls – they are confusing and require more time than you might expect. It is for this reason that I recommend checking them out after your main hike is finished.

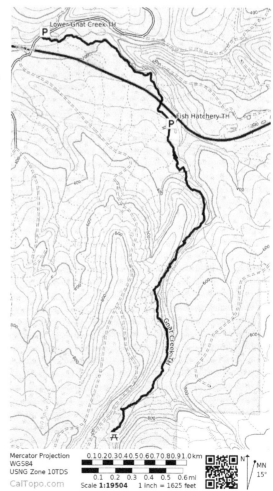

Hikers desiring a longer hike can start at a trailhead near Gnat Creek Campground, a mile downstream from the fish hatchery. From the trailhead described in the directions above, hike along rushing Gnat Creek 1.1 miles, passing through verdant forest until you reach a crossing of US 30. Carefully make your way across the highway and continue 0.2 mile to the fish hatchery, where you will locate the trail described above.

114. Triple C Loop

Distance: 2.2 mile loop
Elevation Gain: 300 feet
Trailhead elevation: 1,155 feet
Trail high point: 1,341 feet
Other seasons: all year
Map: None needed
Pass: None needed
Drivetime from Portland: 60 minutes

Directions:
- Drive west from Portland on US 26. Approximately 31 miles past the US 26 / OR 217 split in Beaverton, turn left at Timber Junction at a sign for Timber.
- Drive 2.9 miles south to the small town of Timber, and reach a junction with Cochran Road. Turn right here.
- Drive 0.6 mile to the end of pavement, and then continue 1.9 gravel miles to the Reehers Camp Trailhead, just past the campground here of the same name.
- Turn left and park in the large parking area here.

Why December: The Coast Range is full of trails, with more than enough variety to satisfy most hikers and enough solitude to make the trip worth it. Navigating the maze of logging roads, the recent clearcuts and winter's heavy rains provide significant impediments; it is imperative to choose a location that is easy to find, close enough and short enough to time for the few hours you may have between showers, and interesting enough to make you want to leave the house. The Triple C Loop, departing from the Reehers Camp area

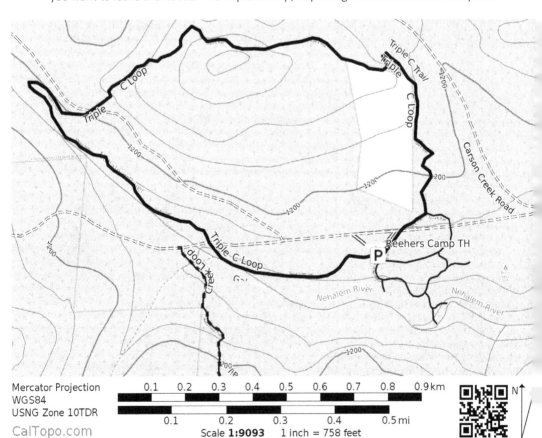

Mercator Projection
WGS84
USNG Zone 10TDR

0.1 0.2 0.3 0.4 0.5 0.6 0.7 0.8 0.9 km

0.1 0.2 0.3 0.4 0.5 mi

Scale **1:9093**   1 inch = 758 feet

Large cedars on the Triple C Loop.

just west of the small town of Timber, should satisfy all of these needs. The trail passes through verdant, moss-draped forest, weaves along a scenic stretch of the Nehalem River and offers enough variety to make the short drive worth it. Hikers who live on the west side of the Portland metro area will particularly enjoy this loop, as it is not even a 40-minute drive from the 185th Avenue exit heading westbound on US 26.

Hike: This loop can be hiked in either direction but I find it easier to follow in a counterclockwise direction. From the trailhead, follow the parking lot past the bathroom and cross the road, where you will find a trail sign on the opposite side. Follow this trail north, passing some large and mossy trees, to a junction. Right leads to Reehers Camp, but you want to turn left. If you've got the time, go check out Reehers Camp. From 1934 to 1941, this was the site of a Civilian Conservation Corps camp used to help replant Tillamook State Forest. Today the site serves as a convenient base camp for explorations of this part of the Coast Range.

So keep left at this junction. The Triple C Loop climbs gradually through second-growth woods, passing under vine maple, whose leaves cover the ground in winter. If you come here at the beginning of November instead, you'll find decent displays of fall color. In December, you'll find this trail rougher and wilder. The loop winds around a knoll and descends into even darker woods, eventually reaching another road crossing at 1.15 miles. Cross the road and follow the trail downhill as it begins to parallel the Nehalem River.

The trail then follows this most fascinating river for the rest of the loop. Now, about the river: originating in the rough and rocky mountains southeast of Astoria, the river flows in a meandering, crooked path through the Coast Range, eventually emptying into the Pacific Ocean at Nehalem Bay (see Hike 13). Here the river is narrow, and after the cold rains of November and December, it will be raging. The trail follows the river to another crossing of Cochran Road at 1.75 miles. Locate the trail on the opposite side of the rain and follow it past a small grove of large Western red-cedar a little over 0.4 mile back to the trailhead and the conclusion of the Triple C Loop.

115. Powell Butte

Distance: 5.6 mile loop
Elevation Gain: 800 feet
Trailhead elevation: 443 feet
Trail High Point: 631 feet
Other seasons: all year
Map: download map online
Pass: None needed
Drivetime from Portland: 25 minutes (50 minutes on the bus)

Directions:
- From downtown Portland drive southeast on Powell Blvd, also known as US 26.
- Continue on Powell Blvd. for about 5 miles past Interstate 205 to a junction with SE 162nd Drive. Turn right here.
- Drive uphill into the Powell Butte parking complex.
- If you're using public transit, take the #9 Bus to the corner of SE Powell Blvd. and SE 164th Avenue (stop ID 4608). Walk back to the junction with SE 162nd Avenue, cross Powell here and walk uphill on SE 162nd Avenue into Powell Butte Nature Park.

Why December: Almost every year in December there is a period when the clouds part, the temperatures drop and the views seem to stretch forever. With very short days and icy trails, hiking can be dangerous in spite of the beauteous conditions. This is the time to go to Powell Butte. With views of five Cascade volcanoes and much of the Portland metro area and only 25 minutes from downtown Portland, this park is ideal for that cold, clear week in December. And if you can't time it for a cold, clear period, the hike is nice on a rainy day as well – you just won't get the views. During very rainy periods trails may be closed – please do not hike here during these times.

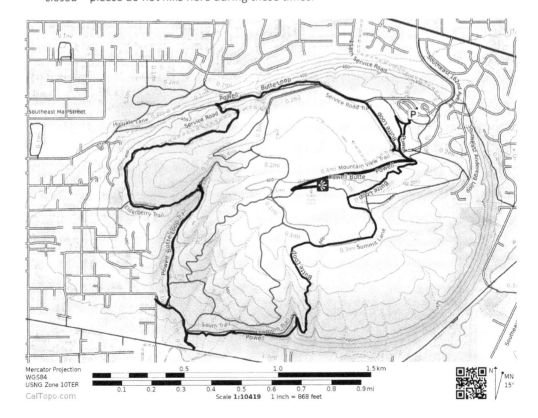

Mercator Projection
WGS84
USNG Zone 10TER
CalTopo.com

Scale **1:10419**   1 inch = 868 feet

Hike: Begin at the trailhead and follow the paved Mountain View Trail uphill towards Powell Butte's summit. On the way up you'll pass several side trails, but stay on the paved trail as it gradually winds uphill. At just 0.6 mile, reach the butte's wide summit at a rounded point. On December's clear days, you'll see Mounts Rainier, Adams and Saint Helens in Washington, while Mount Hood looms just 40 miles to the east. Mount Jefferson peeks out over ridges to the south, frozen and distant. It is fantastic that we have places like this in the metro area, accessible year-round. From the summit, continue straight on what is now Summit Lane, pass a junction with the Wildhorse Trail (a cutoff that avoids the butte's summit views) and follow this trail around the quiet east side of the butte's summit meadow. Reach a junction with South Trail in 0.4 mile. If you're short on time, you can keep straight on Summit Lane to return to the trailhead; but if you have the time, turn left to drop down into the forest on a longer loop.

South Trail cuts through the meadows into the forest and drops down to the south side of Powell Butte. You'll pass a few larger cedars en route to a junction with a trail that leads to the Springwater Corridor. Cyclists can instead start their hike here, provided they cycle in from some other more remote trailhead. Unless you cycled here, ignore the Springwater Trail and instead follow the Cedar Grove Trail through verdant forest to a junction with the Elderberry Trail. At every trail junction you are offered the possibility of returning to the top of the butte, but we're following the longest loop. Turn left on the Elderberry Trail and follow it around the west side of Powell Butte until it begins climbing again. You'll pass Pipeline Trail (following this trail will take you immediately back to the trailhead parking lot) and continue on the Elderberry Trail until you meet Pipeline Trail a second time. Cross the trail and head downhill to complete the Elderberry Trail. At the bottom of a set of steps, meet Holgate Lane – a continuation of SE Holgate Blvd.. Follow Holgate Lane uphill until you run into the Pipeline Trial, and then turn left and follow this wide gravel trail back to Mountain View Trail. Turn left and walk a few minutes back to the parking lot.

116. Mount Talbert

Distance via Sunnyside Road TH: 2.6 miles out and back
Elevation Gain: 700 feet
Trailhead Elevation: 296 feet
Trail High Point: 745 feet
Other seasons: all year
Map: use maps on signs in the park
Pass: None needed.
Drivetime from Portland: 25 minutes

Directions:
* From Portland drive Interstate 205 south to Exit 14, signed for Sunnyside Road.
* Exit the freeway and turn left onto Sunnyside Road.
* Follow Sunnyside Road for a little over a mile to a junction with SE 117th Ave.
* Turn right and drive into the parking lot for Mount Talbert Nature Park.
* Alternately, you can take Trimet Bus 155 from Clackamas Town Center if you don't have a car or don't want to drive. Go to www.trimet.org for more information. Get off the bus at the SE 117th Avenue stop (Stop ID 11296).

Why December: This short loop up and over the forested summit of Mount Talbert in Happy Valley is ideal for those short December days when you want to go for a hike but don't want to leave the city. In sunny weather it is a worthwhile excursion with limited views out to the Metro area (but not any of the volcanoes beyond), while in rainy weather it is just short enough to make it worth your while. There is a larger trail network here that gives you the option of a longer hike if you feel like making it a longer day. But you will appreciate this park even more before or after a day of stressful holiday shopping. This is a peaceful place, one that we are lucky to have so close to home.

Sun filters through the fog on a cold December day at Mount Talbert.

Hike: The hike begins at the Sunnyside Road Trailhead, on the north side of the park. Follow the gravel trail downhill to a metal bridge across Mount Scott Creek. From here the trail passes through a small meadow, soon reaching a junction with the Cedar Park Trail, another approach. Keep left and begin climbing through a lovely forest of surprisingly large Western Red Cedar and green sword ferns. In December this stretch of trail is a bit muddy, but never too muddy. At 0.4 mile from the trail, reach a junction with the Park Loop Trail, the beginning of the loop across the summit. You can turn either direction, but I recommend forking to the left to begin the loop. While you are here, use the maps at every trail junction to help you navigate, and perhaps extend your hike as needed.

The Park Loop Trail climbs at a gentle grade up the eastern face of Mount Talbert, offering views out to Happy Valley. At 0.8 mile you will reach a junction with the Summit Trail. Turn right here and climb to the forest summit of Mount Talbert. Although there are no views, the forest is quite peaceful. The trail reaches the summit at 1.1 miles from the trailhead. Take a minute or two to bask in this small accomplishment – only in Portland can you climb a mountain in December without barely breaking a sweat! From the summit, follow the Summit Trail downhill to a junction with the West Ridge Trail at 1.4 miles, where you turn right. You will follow this muddy but mostly level trail through the forest for 0.3 mile to a reunion with the Park Loop Trail at 1.7 miles. Turn right here and regain a bit of elevation as you make your way across the north side of Mount Talbert. At 2.2 miles, you will return to the first Park Loop junction. Turn left, hike 0.2 mile to the Cedar Park Junction and keep left 0.2 mile to the trailhead and the end of your hike.

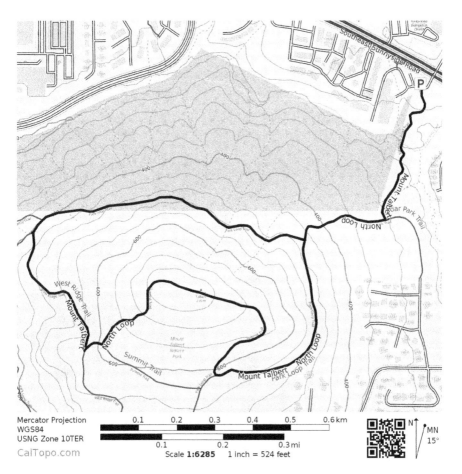

Mercator Projection
WGS84
USNG Zone 10TER
CalTopo.com

Scale **1:6285**   1 inch = 524 feet

117. Scouters Mountain

Distance: 1.2 mile loop
Elevation Gain: 200 feet
Trailhead elevation: 893 feet
Trail high point: 943 feet
Other seasons: all year except in winter storms
Map: See map on Metro website / follow maps on site
Pass: None needed.
Drivetime from Portland: 30 minutes

Directions:
- From Portland, drive Interstate 205 southeast to Exit 14, signed for Sunnyside Road.
- At the end of the exit ramp, turn left onto Sunnyside Road to drive into Happy Valley.
- Drive east on Sunnyside Road through Happy Valley for 3 miles to a junction with SE 152nd Drive. Turn left here.
- Drive north on 152nd Drive, which soon becomes 147th Avenue. A total of 1.3 miles from Sunnyside Road, turn left onto SE Boy Scout Lodge Road.
- Follow this road uphill into the parking lot for Scouters Mountain Nature Park.

Why December: This brand-new nature park offers much to love in a small size: lovely forest, a fantastic picnic shelter that's open year-round and a fantastic view of Mount Hood, a view that seems closer than any other in the Metro area. It is so very easy to be much too busy during the holiday season. Short, nearby hikes such as Mount Talbert (Hike 116) and Scouters Mountain are a welcome break from the chaos of this time of year. Come here on a clear, cold day in December when you only have the time to get out for a few hours. This particular hike is short enough that you can complete it while also being out for holiday shopping or a holiday meal- a welcome dessert indeed.

The picnic shelter at Scouters Mountain, looking out to Mount Hood.

Hike: As the hike is a loop you can start in either direction, but I like to save the good stuff for the end of the hike. From the signboard in the parking lot, turn left and cross the road to locate the Boomer Trail heading downhill. The Boomer Trail heads downhill a bit and turns right, paralleling the park entrance road at a distance. Unlike many hikes in the Portland metro area, there are no houses in sight here and car noise is at a minimum (albeit, still a low roar in some spots). The forest here is lovely, and the trail peaceful. At a little over 0.5 mile the trail crosses the park's entrance road and begins to bend around the southwest side of Scouters Mountain. Note here the signs about boomers- more commonly known as mountain beavers, a rodent that burrows underground and has been sighted on Scouters Mountain.

At 0.75 mile from the trailhead, reach a junction. Ahead of you the trail is gated, as it leads to the edge of the park's property. Instead turn right on the Boomer Trail and climb 0.25 mile to the summit of Scouters Mountain. A huge picnic shelter sits on the summit, and at last Mount Hood comes into view. The view is glorious, as the mountain appears closer than it does at almost any other point in the Metro area (with Powell Butte the only possible exception). At this point a brief history of Scouters Mountain is necessary. The mountain is one of the Boring volcanoes, along with other such Portland-area peaks as Mount Tabor, Powell Butte, Mount Talbert, Mount Sylvania, Mount Scott and Rocky Butte. The property here was Boy Scout Land and a lodge stood on the summit where the picnic shelter is now. When maintenance of the property became too cumbersome for the Boy Scouts, Metro was able to step in along with several other agencies in order to purchase the property. Scouters Mountain Nature Park opened in 2014 a result of these efforts. Once you've taken the time to bask in the view, follow the trail from the signboard on the summit downhill 0.2 mile to the trailhead and your vehicle. What a nice way to spend a couple of hours on a cold winter day!

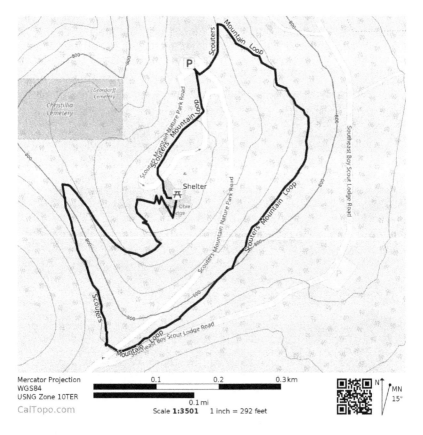

118. Salmon River Trail

	Old Salmon River Trail	TH to Rolling Riffle Camp
Distance:	5.2 miles out and back	9.2 miles out and back
Elevation Gain:	300 feet	400 feet
Trailhead Elevation:	1,524 feet	1,524 feet
Trail High Point:	1,599 feet	1,739 feet
Other Seasons:	all year	all year
Map:	Green Trails #461	Green Trails #461
Pass:	NW Forest Pass	NW Forest Pass
Drivetime from PDX:	70 minutes	70 minutes

Directions:
- From Portland southeast on US 26 for 35 miles to the small community of Welches.
- Approximately 1 mile past the stoplight and shopping center in Welches, turn right at the Subway in Zigzag onto E Salmon River Road.
- Drive 2.7 miles south passing several homes along the way to the Old Salmon River Trailhead on your right.
- There are several trailheads along this stretch of road, but the one you want is the first one you will see on the right.

Why December: The Salmon River Trail is one of the most beautiful hikes in the Mount Hood National Forest, and is one of the best winter hikes close to Portland. The low elevation of Salmon River's wide canyon allows hikers a chance to follow a raging river through an impressive forest of ancient Western Red Cedar and huge Douglas fir without having to

work much for it. Hikers desiring a longer trip can hike deeper into Salmon River's canyon to Rolling Riffle Camp, a flat beside the river near the mouth of Salmon River's foreboding gorge. Check the snow levels before you leave for the hike; on days when the snow level drops to 1,500 feet it will be snowing here, and conditions will be treacherous. If you can make it to the trailhead in the snow, this hike is a veritable winter wonderland.

Hike: Begin at the Old Salmon River Trailhead. The trail descends to the riverside and turns left. Within a few minutes of leaving the trailhead, you will be overwhelmed by the beauty of the scene. The trail winds through a grove of massive cedars beside the rampaging Salmon River. You will need to cross a few side streams on your way, likely necessitating rock hops in December. Also beware of downed trees and mud; the ravages of winter turn a mellow hike into a more demanding experience, your trade-off for being able to visit such a wild place in the middle of winter. At 1.4 miles, the trail seems to end at the road on a narrow spot along the river. Follow the road for 500 feet to locate the trail on your right. From here the old growth is a little less impressive, but the trail follows the river a little more closely. At a little over 2 miles the trail reaches the Green Canyon Campground, closed in December, on your left. Follow the trail to its upper trailhead at a bridge over the Salmon River at 2.6 miles. Hikers looking for an short day should turn around here.

If you're continuing on the longer hike, cross the road and locate the trail just across the road cutting into a narrow bank above the river. The trail follows the river for a while before the way levels out in another impressive grove of ancient forest. At 4.3 miles, the trail reaches Rolling Riffle Camp, a flat beside the Salmon River that serves as a campground. You should turn around here. Beyond Rolling Riffle Camp the trail begins to climb to avoid a narrow, impassible gorge in the river canyon. If you wish to continue it is 1.5 more miles to a bluff above the river with a view down to the narrow canyon below, but above Rolling Riffle Camp you are likely to encounter snow and ice in December. Return the way you came.

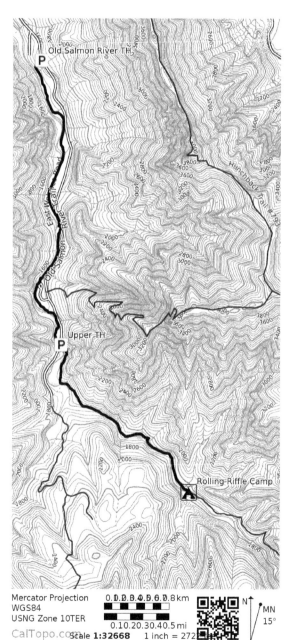

Mercator Projection
WGS84
USNG Zone 10TER

CalTopo.com

0.0 0.1 0.2 0.3 0.4 0.5 0.6 0.7 0.8 km
0.1 0.2 0.3 0.4 0.5 mi
Scale **1:32668**   1 inch = 2722

MN
15°

119. Shellburg Falls

Distance: 5.7 mile loop
Elevation Gain: 700 feet
Trailhead elevation: 918 feet
Trail high point: 1,627 feet
Other seasons: all year, but the falls run low in summer
Map: Pick up a copy of the trail system map at the trailhead
Pass: None needed
Drivetime from Portland: 85 minutes

Directions:
- From Portland, drive south on Interstate 5 for 47 miles to Salem.
- At a sign for Detroit Lake and Bend at Exit 253, leave the freeway and turn left (east) onto OR 22.
- Drive east 21 miles on OR 22 to the small town of Mehama.
- Turn left on Fern Ridge Road at a flashing yellow light opposite the Gingerbread House (a restaurant) and drive north 1.1 miles to the small trailhead, on your right.

Why December: Only a few miles from nearby Silver Falls State Park, this scenic and pastoral loop in the Santiam State Forest feels like the forgotten sibling of the area. This is no redheaded stepchild, however; with three waterfalls that run strong in December, lush forest and well-maintained trails, you will feel like you stayed in the park without dealing with the crowds. You even get to walk behind a waterfall. What could be better?

Hike: Begin by hiking uphill on a road through the woods. This stretch of trail passes through private property so please stay on the road. Soon the way opens up as the trail

passes through a farm, complete with grazing cows. Leave the cows be and give them a wide berth as you hike. Soon you'll enter the forest again; ignore a trail on your right that does not go anywhere and stay on the road. Before long you'll cross Shellburg Creek just above Lower Shellburg Falls. This is the start of your loop, as the Shellburg Falls Trail takes off uphill to your left. The loop continues along the road. Take a minute to check out the somewhat obstructed view of Lower Shellburg Falls just below the road, and then continue along the road.

About a quarter-mile up the road from Lower Shellburg Falls, reach an unmarked junction with a trail on your right. Turn right here and walk on this spur trail, often muddy, to a junction on your right. Turn right here and walk a short ways downhill to a view of the top of Stasel Falls. This is the largest and most impressive falls on this hike, but unfortunately this is the best view you will get. The base of the falls is on private property. Be careful here, too; it would be very easy to slip and fall. When you're done with Stasel Falls, return to the road and turn right. Almost immediately after the unmarked junction with the Stasel Falls Spur, arrive at a junction on the left side of the road with the August Mountain Trail. Turn left here.

The August Mountain Trail sets off uphill through a lovely second-growth forest. Before long you will arrive at an unmarked junction. Keep right (left leads to Shellburg Falls), cross the road again, and continue uphill. The trail passes through open woods, reaching a high point on the hike. During colder periods in December you may encounter a bit of snow here. You then cross an abandoned road, after which the trail descends through gorgeous, lush woods to a series of trail junctions.

The August Mountain Trail ends at this junction. The Shellburg Creek Trail (this trail does not lead to the falls) turns right. Continue straight and reach a 4-way junction just a few steps later. All routes at this junction lead to the campground that serves as the upper trailhead for this hike, but the prettiest approach is to turn left on the Vine Maple Trail. This side of the Vine Maple Loop follows Shellburg Creek for about 0.4 mile to Shellburg Falls' car campground, closed in December. Hike through the campground a bit until you reach the road that runs through this preserve (this is the same road on which you were hiking earlier). Cross the road and locate the small trailhead on the other side of the road. Here you will find the Shellburg Falls Trail. Turn right here.

The Shellburg Falls Trail descends along its namesake creek, passing above the top of the falls. A series of stairs leads you to Shellburg Falls, an impressive 100 foot plunge that strongly resembles South Falls in nearby Silver Falls State Park. Just as at South Falls, the trail leads behind the falls before delivering you to the east side of the creek. A short spur trail leads downhill to the base of the falls via a set of stairs, where spray from the falls is intense. Beyond the falls, the trail quickly descends to the road junction just above Lower Shellburg Falls. Turn right here and walk the road back 1.4 miles to the trailhead.

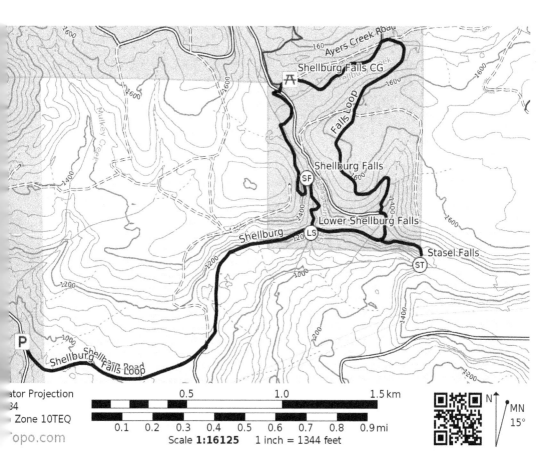

0.5   1.0   1.5 km

0.1   0.2   0.3   0.4   0.5   0.6   0.7   0.8   0.9 mi
Scale **1:16125**   1 inch = 1344 feet

120. Silver Falls State Park

Distance: 7.9 mile loop
Elevation Gain: 1,000 feet
Trailhead Elevation: 1,479 feet
Trail high point: 1,574 feet
Other seasons: all year
Map: None needed (if needed, pick up a trail map at the trailhead)
Pass: $5 park entrance fee (pay at the parking lot)
Drivetime from Portland: 75 minutes

Directions:
- From Portland, drive southeast on OR 213 for 30 miles towards Molalla and Silverton. Stay on OR 213, following signs for Silverton.
- In downtown Silverton, turn left on OR 214 and follow signs to Silver Falls State Park a total of 13.4 miles to a small parking lot beside the bridge over the North Fork of Silver Creek at a hairpin curve in the road.
- There are two main parking lots in the park, North Falls and South Falls. The latter is enormous and can hold unfathomable amounts of people (and yet it still fills in the summer), but I prefer to start at North Falls.
- If you wish to start at South Falls, continue on OR 214 another 2.3 miles to the huge lot at South Falls.

Why December: Were it almost anywhere else, Silver Falls State Park would be a national park and appear on postage stamps, posters and numerous travel brochures. As it is, it is one of Oregon's most-visited state parks and worth visiting at least once a year. The loop trail around the park passes ten waterfalls, four of which you can walk behind! Although the trails here are extremely well-traveled, they are rarely overcrowded anywhere but in the vicinity of South Falls, and the northern part of the park is fairly quiet. Furthermore, this is one of those trails that is great in any season. My favorite time to hike this loop is in December, when the falls are raging and the crowds significantly diminished. It's so nice to warm up by the fire in South Falls Lodge after a hike, and in December the lodge is decked out for Christmas. This loop is the perfect Christmas present, and is a wonderful stress reliever during the chaos of the holiday season. If it's been icy you might want to

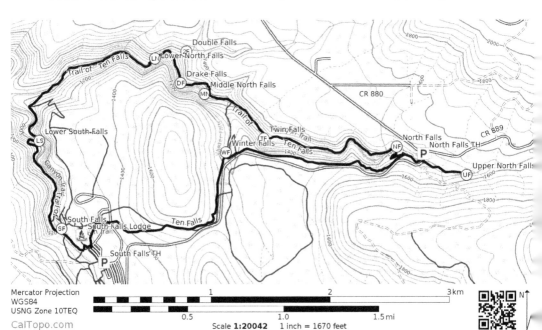

Behind North Falls on a rainy, nasty day in December.

check ahead and make sure the trails are open- during such times park rangers will on occasion close trails if there is too much ice to hike safely in the canyon.

Hike: I prefer to begin the hike at North Falls. This way, almost all of the waterfalls are in your face as you hike, and you can make a stop at the South Falls Lodge to warm up before you finish your hike. Hike downhill on the trail a short distance to a junction. Turn right and drop behind powerful North Falls, which splits into two tiers in the winter. The best views of the falls are found down the trail a ways. Continue downhill on a wide trail just above the roaring North Fork of Silver Creek another mile to Twin Falls, perhaps the least impressive falls in the park. The falls is difficult to see, but is worth a stop just the same. Continue downstream another 0.4 mile to a junction with the trail to Winter Falls. Given the short distance, you might want to take a few minutes to hike over to the apt-ly-named Winter Falls (it only flows in the winter), as you'll hike past the top of the falls on the last leg of your hike later in the day.

From the Winter Falls trail junction, continue straight another 0.3 mile to a junction with the spur trail to 106-foot Middle North Falls. Unlike Twin and Winter Falls, this is one the most impressive sights in the park. The spur trail ducks behind the falls without the benefit of a guardrail, passing frighteningly close to a raging torrent of water that may make you and others very uncomfortable. It is worth it! On the other side of the falls, you will reach a viewpoint of the falls where the short spur trail ends. Return then back to the main trail.

Just a short ways down the trail, pass small Drake Falls and arrive at a short spur trail to the base of Double Falls. Another falls that is aptly-named, this double-humped cascade is actually the tallest in the park at 184 feet. You will want to visit in the winter, though, as the volume of the falls fluctuates wildly and is reduced to a trickle by the summer.

Back on the main trail, a short walk around the corner reveals Lower North Falls. This is another short falls similar in size and shape to Twin and Drake Falls, but the views of Lower North are clear, revealing a beautiful slide that begs to be photographed. This spot is particularly beautiful in the fall, when it is framed by golden leaves on almost all sides.

From here, the North Fork of Silver Creek mellows out for almost a mile and the trail is almost level as it follows the creek, crossing it on a metal bridge in a scenic gorge about half a mile beyond Lower North Falls. At a little over 3 miles from North Falls, reach a junction with the Maple Ridge Trail on your left. Ignore this trail, which features no views of waterfalls and climbs steeply to the canyon rim in order to make a loop possible if you leave from South Falls. Continue straight on the Canyon Trail, cross and arrive at Lower Falls. This 93-foot curtain is one of the most beautiful in the park, and you get to hike behind it! The trail curves around a corner and passes behind the falls, where you will be treated to the rare experience of having a curtain of water pass directly over you. I like to stop here for a few minutes just to savor the experience.

Beyond Lower South Falls, the trail climbs to the top of the rim via a series of steps. You will follow a level trail along the south fork of Silver Creek for almost a mile until magnificent South Falls comes into view. Though it is technically not the tallest waterfall in the park, this 177-foot plunge is certainly the most powerful and perhaps the most striking. At a trail junction below the falls, you have the choice between a the left trail, which climbs directly to the South Falls Lodge, and the right trail, which passes behind the falls before curving up to the lodge. The choice is yours. Once you reach the top of the falls, follow the wide trails and signs to the South Falls Lodge. The lodge is a wonderful place to take a break, have lunch and warm up. In December the lodge is decorated for the holidays, with lights and a tree and everything. Sometimes even Santa Clause himself makes an appearance. Expect people here if the weather is even remotely decent. Of course, I like to come here on days when the weather is less than decent. I've spent countless hours here drying my boots and warming up by the fire after being drenched here on rainy days (when the park is almost deserted). The downside of stopping at the lodge on a rainy day is that you have to go back out into the rain to finish your hike. You may even need to purchase a cup of coffee from the small store to motivate you to get out the door. Or you could just start your hike here, ensuring that all you have left is the walk to your car.

Assuming you're heading back to North Falls, leave the lodge. Beyond the lodge, follow signs through parking lot A to the Rim Trail. This path cuts through the best old-growth forest in the park (some specimens are as large as six feet wide), occasionally passing over the paved bike trail that runs through this same general area, for a little over a mile until you reach a parking area at the top of Winter Falls. Continue along the Rim Trail for another mile, passing outstanding views first of the canyon reach the North Falls parking area.

But wait – you aren't done yet! Unless you are totally exhausted, you still have one more waterfall to see. Throw your stuff in the car and grab your camera and return to the Rim Trail. Duck under the highway and walk 0.3 mile along the North Fork of Silver Creek to gorgeous Upper North Falls, where you have opportunities galore to photograph this beautiful cascade. Then return the way you came to your car. The falls is absolutely worth the side trip!

APPENDIX 1: HIKES BY REGION

INDEX

Lower Macleay Park 53, 91, 92, 93
Lower South Falls 300
lupine 38, 84, 107, 110, 113, 127, 131, 132, 136, 137, 145, 159, 176, 196, 203
Lyle Cherry Orchard 86, 87, 107

North Falls 298, 299, 300

O

Oaks Bottom 54, 55
Oceanside 46, 47
Olallie Butte 231, 232, 233
Olallie Lake 123, 186, 190, 208, 210, 212, 224, 230, 232, 233, 250
Opal Creek 16, 58, 60, 61, 100, 158, 160, 184, 206, 235, 254, 255
Oswald West State Park 118, 216

P

Pacific Crest Trail 172, 175, 191, 193, 196, 199, 227, 230, 232, 243, 272, 273, 275
Paradise Park 196, 197
Park Ridge 14, 187, 188, 208, 209, 232
Pittock Mansion 53, 91, 92, 93
Plaza Lake 228, 229
poison oak 62, 86, 87, 94, 95, 99, 105, 129, 131, 149, 152
Ponderosa Point 244, 245
Powell Butte 278, 288, 289, 293
Punchbowl Falls 102

R

Ramona Falls 154, 198, 199, 235, 242, 243
Red Mountain 222
Ruddy Hill 232

S

Saddle Mountain 142, 143, 283
Salmon River 229, 285, 294, 295
Sandy River 17, 30, 172, 173, 198, 199, 242, 243
Sauvie Island 258
Scouters Mountain 292, 293
Shellburg Falls 296, 297
Short Sand Beach 118, 119, 216, 217
Silver Falls State Park 296, 297, 298, 303
Silver Star Mountain 8, 13–322, 162, 170, 303
Siouxon Creek 146, 147
Smith Rock 91, 114
Soapstone Lake 48, 49
South Breitenbush River 187, 211, 235, 250, 251
South Falls 298, 300
Stacker Butte 38, 39, 108, 111
Sullivan Creek Falls 61

T

Takhlakh Lake 212, 224, 225
Tamanawas Falls 246, 247
The Goonies 24, 215
Three Pools 59
Tillamook Head 24, 25, 214, 281
Timberline Trail 172, 173, 175, 176, 177, 179, 201, 203, 243
Triple C Loop 278, 286, 287
Tualatin Hills Nature Park 76

About the author:

Matt Reeder moved from Illinois to Oregon at age 7 with his family. He grew up hiking and camping all over the Pacific Northwest; he never felt more at home than on the trail. He moved back to Illinois at age 16 but returned 8 years later to settle in Portland. Since moving back to Oregon in 2005 he has logged more than 5,000 miles on the trail and has hiked the vast majority of the trails within a 2 hour drive of Portland. *PDX Hiking 365* is the end result of seven years of research and hiking, and is the first guidebook for the Portland area organized by season rather than by destination.

Matt is also the author of *Off the Beaten Trail: Fifty fantastic unknown hikes in NW Oregon and SW Washington* and *101 Hikes in the Majestic Mount Jefferson Region*. He lives in an old farmhouse in southeast Portland with his wife Wendy. When not on the trail or in the classroom, he spends his free time obsessing about music, following the Portland Trail Blazers and reading voraciously. You can usually identify Matt on the trail by his red St. Louis Cardinals hat, a visible sign of his lifelong love of the 2006 and 2011 World Series Champions

CPSIA information can be obtained
at www.ICGtesting.com
Printed in the USA
BVHW081518080820
585841BV00003B/16